WOMEN AND MIRACLE STORIES

NUMEN BOOK SERIES
STUDIES IN THE HISTORY OF RELIGIONS

EDITED BY

W.J. HANEGRAAFF

ADVISORY BOARD

P. Antes, M. Despland, RI.J. Hackett, M. Abumalham Mas, A.W. Geertz,
G. ter Haar, G.L. Lease, M.N. Getui, I.S. Gilhus, P. Morris, J.K. Olupona,
E. Thomassen, A. Tsukimoto, A.T. Wasim

VOLUME LXXXVIII

WOMEN AND MIRACLE STORIES

A MULTIDISCIPLINARY EXPLORATION

EDITED BY

ANNE-MARIE KORTE

BRILL
LEIDEN · BOSTON
2004

This book is printed on acid-free paper.

Library of Congress Cataloging-in-Publication Data

Women and miracle stories : a multidisciplinary exploration / edited by Anne-Marie Korte.
　p. cm. — (Studies in the history of religions, ISSN 0169-8834 ; v. 88)
Originally published: Leiden ; Boston : Brill, c2001.
Includes bibliographical references and index.
ISBN 90-04-13636-3 (pbk. : alk. paper)
　1. Miracles. 2. Women—Religious life. I. Korte, Anne-Marie, 1957- II. Studies in the history of religions ; 88.

BL487.W65 2003
202'.117—dc22

2003065312

ISSN　0169-8834
ISBN　90 04 13636 3

© *Copyright 2004 by Koninklijke Brill* NV, *Leiden, The Netherlands*

All rights reserved. No part of this publication may be reproduced, translated, stored in a retrieval system, or transmitted in any form or by any means, electronic, mechanical, photocopying, recording or otherwise, without prior written permission from the publisher.

*Authorization to photocopy items for internal or personal use is granted by Brill provided that the appropriate fees are paid directly to The Copyright Clearance Center, 222 Rosewood Drive, Suite 910 Danvers, MA 01923, USA.
Fees are subject to change.*

PRINTED IN THE NETHERLANDS

CONTENTS

Preface vii
List of Contributors ix

1. ANNE-MARIE KORTE
   Women and Miracle Stories: Introduction 1
2. MAGDA MISSET-VAN DE WEG
   Magic, Miracle and Miracle Workers in the
   Acts of Thecla 29
3. GISELLE DE NIE
   Fatherly and Motherly Curing in Sixth-Century Gaul:
   Saint Radegund's *Mysterium* 53
4. JACQUELINE BORSJE
   Women in Columba's Life, as Seen through the Eyes
   of his Biographer Adomnán 87
5. MARCEL POORTHUIS & CHANA SAFRAI
   Fresh Water for a Tired Soul: Pregnancy and Messianic
   Desire in a Medieval Jewish Document from Sicily 123
6. ANKE E. PASSENIER
   The Life of Christina Mirabilis: Miracles and the
   Construction of Marginality 145
7. MARIANNE ELSAKKERS
   In Pain You Shall Bear Children (Gen 3:16): Medieval
   Prayers for a Safe Delivery 179
8. WOUTER J. HANEGRAAFF
   A Woman Alone: The Beatification of Friederike
   Hauffe *née* Wanner (1801–1829) 211
9. ANNE VAN VOORTHUIZEN
   Māriyamma<u>n</u>'s *Śakti*: The Miraculous Power of a
   Smallpox Goddess 248
10. ILSE N. BULHOF
    Women and Miracles in the Stories of
    Ingeborg Bachmann 271

11. INEZ VAN DER SPEK
    Miracles of Desire: Transfigurations in Rhoda
    Lerman's *The Book of the Night* 299
12. ANNE-MARIE KORTE
    A Different Grace: Epilogue 325

Index of Authors 341
Index of Subjects 346

PREFACE

The remarkable presence and religious agency of women in miracles stories originating from diverging religious backgrounds and different historical periods are well known, but have not been subjected to multidisciplinary women's studies research up till now. This book aims to explore the gendered aspects of miracle stories, which are seen as a specific genre of religious discourse. Its primary focus is on women as characters in miracle stories, as writers and readers of miracle stories, and women's agency in religious practices that are considered 'miraculous'. By investigating what miracle stories can tell about women's religious aspirations and limitations, the book intends to contribute to the comprehensive project of restoring and reconstructing women's voices in religious discourse. At the same time, the book wants to contribute to the contemporary academic debates on the interpretation of miracle stories in a modern western context. For instance, if in some respects late modern culture can be characterized as a longing for re-enchantment, does this imply that assumptions concerning a gender-related opposition between faith and reason have been abandoned or rather reinstalled?

This book presents the results of a multidisciplinary research project in the fields of theology and religious studies, entitled 'Women and Miracle Stories'. The project was initiated by the Interdisciplinary Research Program Women's & Gender Studies in Religion of the Catholic Theological University of Utrecht and Utrecht University's Department of Theology. Scholars from the Catholic Theological University of Utrecht, from Utrecht University's Department of Theology and several other institutions have participated in the project, which set out to examine miracles with a special emphasis on gender and the position of women. The researchers came from many different fields, including religious studies, theology, philosophy, literature and history.

I would like to thank all the authors for their willingness to write and refine their contributions and for their patience and goodwill during the time-consuming process of rewriting and editing. For their input and their suggestions during earlier stages of this project I want to thank dr. Edien Bartels, prof. dr. Gerrie ter Haar, prof. dr. Ria

Kloppenborg and prof. dr. Martin Parmentier. Finally, I want to record my special gratitude to the following persons for their multifarious assistance and friendly support, indispensable for facilitating and finishing a project like this: dr. Angela Berlis, drs. Marianne Elsakkers, drs. Mischa Hoyinck, dr. Magda Misset-van de Weg and drs. Willien van Wieringen.

Utrecht, October 2000
Anne-Marie Korte

CONTRIBUTORS

Dr. Jacqueline Borsje is research scholar at the School of Celtic Studies of the Dublin Institute for Advanced Studies, Ireland. Her field is the Science of Religion, within which she wrote her dissertation entitled: *From Chaos to Enemy: Encounters with Monsters in Early Irish Texts. An investigation related to the process of Christianization and the concept of evil* (Turnhout 1997). Her current project is a study of Fate in early Irish literature.

Prof. dr. Ilse N. Bulhof was until 1998 associate professor of Philosophy at the Catholic Theological University in Utrecht, the Netherlands and professor of Philosophy of Religion at the University of Leiden, the Netherlands. She is author of i.a. *The Language of Science: A Study of the Relationship between Literature and Science in the Perspective of a Hermeneutical Ontology* (Leiden 1992) and co-editor of *Flight of the Gods: Philosophical Perspectives on Negative Theology* (New York 2000).

Drs. Marianne Elsakkers studied Old Germanic language and literature and is an independent scholar.

Prof. dr. Wouter J. Hanegraaff is professor in the History of Hermetic philosophy and related currents at the University of Amsterdam, the Netherlands. He specializes in the history of alternative and esoteric traditions in western culture from the Renaissance to the present. He is the author of *New Age Religion and Western Culture: Esotericism in the Mirror of Secular Thought* (Leiden 1996/Albany 1998), and co-editor of several volumes including *Female Stereotypes in Religious Traditions* (Leiden etc. 1995, with Ria Kloppenborg). His current research projects include an annotated translation of the Hermetic writings of the Renaissance poet Lodovico Lazzarelli, an analytic history of western conceptualizations of 'magic', and a study of Justinus Kerner and his female patients.

Prof. dr. Anne-Marie Korte teaches theological women's studies at the Catholic Theological University in Utrecht and at the Department of Theology at Utrecht University, the Netherlands. She is co-ordinator of the research project "Women and Miracles Stories". She has published i.a. a study on Mary Daly, *Een passie voor transcendentie* (Kampen

1992) and has co-edited several volumes of interdisciplinary research in theological women's studies, i.a. the series *Proeven van vrouwenstudies theologie* (Utrecht/Leiden 1989–1996).

Dr. Magda Misset-van de Weg studied theology at the Faculty of Theology Tilburg, the Netherlands. Her contribution to this volume is part of her dissertation *Sara & Thecla: Representations of Women in 1 Peter and the Acts of Thecla* (Utrecht 1998), which she wrote as assistant researcher at the Faculty of Theology at Utrecht University. She is currently working on a research project at the Department of New Testament Studies at the Catholic Theological University in Utrecht, the Netherlands.

Dr. Giselle de Nie was lecturer in medieval history at the Department of Historical Studies of Utrecht University, the Netherlands. Her research focuses upon the function of imagistic thought in early medieval religion. She published i.a. *Views From a Many-Windowed Tower: Studies of Imagination in the Works of Gregory of Tours* (Amsterdam 1987).

Drs. Anke E. Passenier studied theology at Utrecht University, the Netherlands, and is currently preparing a dissertation on Marguerite Porete and the role of women in medieval mysticism. Women's development of new forms of religious practices and theological concepts and the reception of these by ecclesiastical authorities are the main objects of her research.

Dr. Marcel Poorthuis is co-ordinator of the "Relation Judaism-Christianity" research program at the Catholic Theological University in Utrecht, the Netherlands and author of i.a. *Het gelaat van de Messias: Messiaanse Talmoedlezingen van Emmanuel Levinas* (Utrecht 1992) and co-editor of *The Centrality of Jerusalem: Historical Perspectives* (Kampen 1996), *Sanctity of Time and Space in Tradition and Modernity* (Leiden 1998) and *Purity and Holiness: The Heritage of Leviticus* (Leiden 1999).

Dr. Chana Safrai lectured Talmudic studies at the Catholic Theological University in Utrecht, the Netherlands and is author of i.a. *Women in the Temple: The Status and Role of Women in the Second Temple of Jerusalem* (Amsterdam 1991) and co-editor of *The Centrality of Jerusalem: Historical Perspectives* (Kampen 1996).

Dr. Inez van der Spek is NWO-researcher at the Faculty of Humanities at the University of Amsterdam, the Netherlands. She is author of i.a. *Alien Plots: Female Subjectivity and the Divine in the light of James Tiptree's 'A Momentary Taste of Being'* (Liverpool 2000).

Drs. Anne van Voorthuizen studied Religious Studies at the University of Utrecht and is freelance publicist and researcher.

1

WOMEN AND MIRACLE STORIES: INTRODUCTION

Anne-Marie Korte

> *Only that which is really different from the knower can trigger wonder; yet wonder will always be in a context and from a particular point of view.*
> Caroline Walker Bynum[1]

Women and Miracles: Key Questions

The articles in this anthology explore the relationship between women and miracles. What can we learn about 'miracles'—about their impact, their spell, their repellence—by focusing especially on women's (religious) positions, activities and aspirations? And conversely, what can be learned about the 'gendering' of religious texts and practices by studying miracles, and particularly miracle stories? By and large, these two questions constitute the point of departure of this book. They are the central issues in each of the individual studies, which range across a wide variety of specialisms within theology and religious studies.

There seems to be a growing interest in miracles in many different academic fields. The assumption that Western culture is headed down a path of irreversible secularization has come under repeated attack. This, in turn, has led scholars to consider anew the study of religious experience and phenomena. In past decades, most researchers in theology and religious studies eschewed miracles because of their non-rational, manipulative and sanctioning characteristics. However, this tendency has subsided. There is a growing curiosity about the significance of miracles and their function—in the establishment and spread of (new) religious movements, in popular faith and culture,

---

[1] Caroline Walker Bynum, "Wonder", *American Historical Review* 102 (1997), p. 3.

and in non-Western religions. Academics are showing a new inquisitiveness about the unique meaning of miracles as religious phenomena and as a means of religious expression and communication.²

In the study of miracles, an in-depth gender perspective is still seldom applied even though miracles contain intriguing gender aspects that are practically begging to be explored. In miracle stories, women often are more present and make themselves better heard than in other genres of religious writing, like doctrinal or liturgical texts. Famous examples from Western religious heritage immediately come to mind. Both the Hebrew Bible and the New Testament contain remarkable stories in which women, against all expectations, bear children, are miraculously healed, or obtain inexhaustible food supplies. Some biblical and apocryphal biblical texts suggest that women may have actively performed miracles. In miraculous healing incidents of classical and late antiquity—for instance the Epidaurus healings—sources such as Strabo explicitly refer to the healing of women. Many of the Christian saints who are known for their miracles are women. In medieval Dutch literature, there are some marvellous miracle tales featuring women such as Beatrijs and Mariken van Nimwegen. In the past 200 years, most apparitions of Mary and

---

² Recent contributions about the change in cultural and academic interest in miracles are: Walker Bynum, "Wonder", pp. 1–26; Jos Vranckx, *De terugkeer van het wonder: Het bovennatuurlijke op het einde van de eeuw* (Leuven/Kampen: Davidsfonds/Kok, 1997); Anne-Marie Korte, "Voorbij de verlegenheid: Nieuwe toe-eigeningen van het wonder", Anne-Marie Korte (red.), *Wonderen die de wereld nog niet uit zijn* (Kampen: Kok, 1998), pp. 89–106. Recent examples of this renewed interest can be found in Peter Brown, *Authority and the Sacred: Aspects of the Christianisation of the Roman World* (Cambridge: Cambridge University Press, 1995); Mart Bax, *Medjugorje: Religion, Politics and Violence in Rural Bosnia* (Amsterdam: VU Uitgeverij, 1995); Irmtraud Götz von Olenhusen (Hrsg.), *Wunderbare Erscheinungen: Frauen und katholischen Frömmigkeit im 19. und 20. Jahrhundert* (Paderborn: Ferdinand Schöningh, 1995); Michael E. Goodich, *Violence and Miracle in the Fourteenth Century: Private Grief and Public Salvation* (Chicago: University of Chicago Press, 1995); William A. Christian Jr., *Visionaries: The Spanish Republic and the Reign of Christ* (Berkeley: University of California Press, 1996); Torsten Fremer, "Wunder und Magie: Zur Funktion der Heiligen im frühmittelalterlichen Christianisierungsprozess", *Hagiographica* 3 (1996), pp. 15–88; Robert Bruce Mullin, *Miracles and the Modern Religious Imagination* (New Haven/London: Yale University Press, 1996); Ronald C. Finucane, *The Rescue of the Innocents: Endangered Children in Medieval Miracles* (Basingstoke: Macmillan 1997); Lorraine J. Daston, Katharine Park, *Wonders and the Order of Nature, 1150–1750* (New York: Zone Books, 1998); Richard H. Davis (ed.), *Images, Miracles, and Authority in Asian Religious Traditions* (Boulder/Oxford: Westview Press, 1998); Kathleen Ashley and Pamela Sheingorn, *Writing Faith: Text, Sign and History in the Miracles of Sainte Foy* (Chicago/London: The University of Chicago Press, 1999); Ruth Harris, *Lourdes: Body and Spirit in the Secular Age* (London: Allen Lane/The Penguin Press, 1999).

related miracles in the Western world have been witnessed by women and girls. In new and in non-Western miracle and faith healing, it is often women who act as a medium.

Miracles and miracle stories seem to provide us with a distinct opportunity to study women's subjectivity and agency. Women may play a very prominent role in miracle stories. Yet, women's presence in this genre has not received ample scholarly attention. This may result from the deeply rooted assumption that women have a 'natural' leaning towards the supernatural, a spiritual tendency either innate or learned, a special susceptibility to faith as well as to superstition and magic. These ideas were present in writings as early as Strabo's and have since been reaffirmed by many others, including St. Jerome in his *Contra Vigilantum*, David Hume in his *Natural History of Religion* and Simone de Beauvoir in *The Second Sex*.[3] Those who follow this line of thinking can easily link women's involvement in miracles with stereotypical ideas about faith versus rationality and femininity versus masculinity. To them, the issue needs no further explanation or inquiry.

In fact, women's involvement in miracles is not as self-evident as it seems. In mainstream Western culture, women's independent and public participation in religious affairs is controversial. Literary critic Elizabeth Alvilda Petroff pointed out how this disputatiousness influenced the representation of the 'female saint' in medieval Europe.[4] Noting that religious ideas about women were steeped in suspicion ('the good woman was the invisible woman, the silent woman'), Petroff observed that any woman prominently active in religion was open to accusations of transgression. For a woman "[t]o become a saint, one had to transgress somewhere, if only in order to become visible."[5] Her sin was her failure to adhere to conventional female behaviour, overstepping the boundaries of gender set by none other than God. According to Petroff, late medieval hagiographers faced

---

[3] See Peter Brown, *The Cult of the Saints: Its Rise and Function in Latin Christianity* (Chicago: University of Chicago Press, 1981), p. 20; p. 28; Simone de Beauvoir, *The Second Sex* (New York: Vintage Books, 1989), pp. 289–293; pp. 597–628; pp. 670–678.

[4] In Christianity, from the outset sanctity has been marked by the miraculous. See a.o. Brown, *The Cult of the Saints*; Donald Weinstein and Rudolph Bell, *Saints and Society: The Two Worlds of Western Christendom, 1000–1700* (Chicago: University of Chicago Press, 1982), p. 142.

[5] Elizabeth Alvida Petroff, *Medieval Women's Visionary Literature* (New York/Oxford: Oxford University Press, 1986), p. 166.

a complicated task when it came to depicting female saints. They had to stress how extraordinary and miraculous these women's deeds were by showing how they differed from the norm. Yet they also had to make clear that it was God, and not the saint herself, who willed the miracles to occur. They had to verify that a transgression by a saintly woman had been the will of God. If not, she would doubtlessly be branded a heretic, a witch or a whore. The fact that a woman could be empowered by God to independently and directly intervene in spiritual matters was sometimes considered even more miraculous than the very miracles this saintly woman performed.

However, historian Johan Huizinga argued that holiness itself transcends gender norms and conventions. While he acknowledged that our concepts of the hero, the genius and the 'great' historical figure are male models, this does not apply to our concept of the saint. He believed that holiness is the only concept capable of encapsulating the highest actualization of human potential and that, remarkably, gender plays no role in it: "Here, one is freed from the link between excellence and quantity; the holy is not measurable by worldly standards".[6]

The studies collected in this book are informed by Petroff's and Huizinga's approaches. Petroff's perspective impels us to ask 'what is so special about the *women* who are involved in miracles?', while Huizinga's moves us to enquire 'what is so special about *miracles* that so many women are actively involved in them?'. Connections between women and miracles cannot be taken for granted but must be traced and studied. As historian Caroline Ford put it: "The association of religion with the realm of the feminine must not be accepted as a given. It must be explained. To point to the feminization of devotion only reifies the category of the feminine without explaining what changes in forms of devotion meant to those concerned and how these changes relate to other kinds of historical change."[7]

---

[6] Johan Huizinga, "Historische grootheid: Een overpeinzing (30–3–1940)", Johan Huizinga, *Verzamelde Werken VII: Geschiedwetenschap hedendaagsche cultuur* (Haarlem: Tjeenk Willink, 1950), pp. 211–217, esp. p. 217.

[7] Caroline Ford, "Religion and Popular Culture in Modern Europe", *Journal of Modern History* 65 (1993), pp. 152–175, esp. p. 169.

Miracles: A Multidisciplinary Exploration

This book is the result of a multidisciplinary research project in the fields of theology and religious studies, entitled 'Women and Miracle Stories'. Scholars from the Catholic Theological University of Utrecht, from Utrecht University's Department of Theology and several other departments have participated in the research, which aimed at examining miracles with a special emphasis on gender and the position of women. The researchers are from many different fields, including religious studies, theology, philosophy, literature and history.[8]

The first step in this project was an attempt to create a shared frame of reference for the study of miracles. What approach to miracles could constitute a common point of departure? And what definition of miracles would be applicable in all of the different disciplines in the project? In response to the first question the researchers opted for a hermeneutical approach in which they would chiefly concern themselves with what miracles mean to the people involved, for example miracle-performers and witnesses, miracle story writers, readers and listeners. This approach was chosen over the apologetic and sceptical perspectives, in which miracles are studied either as a confirmation of religious truth and authority[9] or with such scepticism and suspicion as to disprove the existence of miracles and demonstrate the persistent human capacity to delude oneself and others.[10]

By opting for a hermeneutical approach, this research project falls into step with the trend of increasing scholarly interest in miracles as a religious phenomenon and as a means of religious expression

---

[8] See Anne-Marie Korte, "Schepping van het ongerijmde: Multidisciplinair onderzoeksproject 'Vrouwen verhalen wonderen' aan de KTU", Anne-Marie Korte (red.), *Proeven van vrouwenstudies theologie IV* (Utrecht: IIMO/IWFT, 1996), pp. 203–223.

[9] For example, see Colin Brown, *Miracles and the Critical Mind* (Grand Rapids: Eerdmans, 1984); René Laurentin, *Medjugorje: Récit et message des apparitions* (Paris: O.E.I.L., 1986); T.C. Williams, *The Idea of the Miraculous: The Challenge to Science and Religion* (Basingstoke: Macmillan, 1990); Joseph Houston, *Reported Miracles: A Critique of Hume* (Cambridge: Cambridge University Press, 1994).

[10] See, for instance, Joe Nickell, *Looking for a Miracle: Weeping Icons, Relics, Stigmata, Visions & Healing Cures* (Amherst: Prometheus Books, 1993); Rob Sijmons, *Occultisme in het Westen: Over kromme spijkers, verdunde medicijnen, katholieke wonderen, koude kernfusie en New Age; En over een enkel succes* (Amsterdam: Van Gennep, 1996); Ewald Vervaet, *Het verschijnsel Jomanda* (Amsterdam: Babylon-De Geus, 1997); Richard Dawkins, *Unweaving the Rainbow: Science, Delusion, and the Appetite for Wonder* (Boston: Houghton Mifflin, 1998).

and communication. The point is not to prove, explain (away), or disprove miracles, but to look for their concrete meanings for various groups of people. The advantage of this approach is that it enables the scholars to combine and compare research results from a variety of disciplines without the need to apply one and the same definition of miracles from the outset. After all, the focus of this project is the 'inner perspective', the words and the meanings attributed to miracles by those most directly involved.

The hermeneutical angle was also chosen because of the project's gender perspective and the type of reference material to be used. The research started by focusing on miracles as performed, experienced, described and (re)told by women. To this end, the researchers turned to (textual) sources such as oral and written accounts of miracles. As will become clear in the course of this book, most material of this kind consists of apocryphal texts, hagiography, novels and (excerpts from) letters and prayers. These sources usually do not explicitly mention dogmatic or philosophical debates about miracles—but at the same time, no discussion of the sources can ignore such debates. Admittedly, few dogmatic or philosophical debates about miracles have been conducted by women or have referred to women's lives. Nevertheless, it would be too simplistic to leave these debates aside. After all, the source texts are informed by ideas about miracles—ideas which came from the fields of theology, metaphysics and (natural) philosophy. Besides, the ideas themselves were not developed in isolation from gender-bound perspectives on (religious) reality. The studies in this book do not examine the individual theological and philosophical debates on miracles. These debates are dealt with only insofar as the hermeneutical approach requires miracles to be examined as told, as an integral part of the discourse in which they are recounted.

Although all of the researchers prefer a hermeneutical approach, they treat the main subject in quite different ways. The authors approach one of the key questions (What do miracles actually mean to people?) from widely divergent angles, ranging from existential psychology and social sciences to cultural anthropology and philosophy. This great diversity reflects the lack of consensus on the second question: How are we to define miracles? The question 'What is a miracle?' is intriguing in itself and has the potential to raise both established and new questions in the fields of theology, philosophy and religious studies. Miracles figure in the canons of most religious traditions. The interpretation of these miracles has a long and varied history. 'What is a miracle?' is a question which easily crosses the boundaries of various disciplines within theology and religious studies and is therefore a good point of departure for a multi-disciplinary research project. When one seeks a common definition of miracles, however, it is difficult to get beyond a comprehensive description of miracles which lists the greatest possible number of relevant phenomena and aspects. What follows below is a description which served as an initial definition of miracles for the purpose of this research project. It is based on an inventory of examples and case studies from various fields and different historical periods.

Many miracles are incidents of healing or salvation which defy all reasonable expectations. Such incidents may be experienced as an intervention from outside, by a higher power or by God. This type of miracle is characteristic of most classic religious miracle stories, but it also occurs in many spontaneously reported events experienced as 'miracles' in today's world. In the latter of these occurrences, most are not regarded as special or significant by all people but are miracle-like to those who experience them because of their profound, miraculous and life-changing effect. Such private miracles may be related to birth and death, separation and reconciliation, or other profound occurrences which are 'eye openers' and provide new insights into life. This aspect occurs especially often in everyday secular discourse about miracles, while miracles of more general significance are extremely rare in this discourse.

There are also miracles which do not directly answer to individual needs or wishes. For example, the corpse of a saint may appear not to have decomposed, the sun may spin on its axis, roses may suddenly bloom in December. This category of miracles also includes phenomena which underscore a particular individual's unique position, power or abilities. Examples of such abilities are precognitive dreams, prophecies, and the power to control animals or natural phenomena. These occurrences are amazing and unfathomable because they deviate from what is 'normal' or 'predictable'—in terms of the laws of physics, for instance. The events can be seen as a sign from an alternative or incomprehensible order or reality; the miracle is understood as an indication or proof that this other realm exists and 'makes a difference'.

In general, miracles have a positive effect. A miracle is an event that both meets and fails to meet expectations; what happens exceeds, but does not violate, the witnesses' 'expectations'. In some way a miracle brings salvation or changes things for the better. However, this does not exclude the possibility that a miracle will have a critical, disruptive or even destructive effect on those who are involved.

Actually, this comprehensive description is too general and too contemporary to do full justice to the various and evolving views on miracles discussed in this book. It is too general because it contains divergent and even contradictory ideas about miracles. For example, we find traces of Saint Augustine's well-known view that creation itself is the greatest miracle of all,[11] but we also find the very influential idea from the high Middle Ages that a miracle is *contra solitum cursum naturae*, contrary to the usual course of nature.[12] The description is too contemporary because it is heavily biased towards a Western, late Modern concept of miracles in which questions about the veracity and the evidential value of miracles are de-emphasized or even discarded altogether. Given the great difficulty of satisfactorily defining miracles, it seems of paramount importance that we confront the very dissimilarities and contradictions that exist in our concepts of miracles.

Historians Benedicta Ward and Caroline Walker Bynum, renowned for their studies of miracles and miracle stories of the Middle Ages, point out that European thought on miracles is characterized by a tremendous diversity and that it has undergone profound change through time. They believe that researchers cannot overemphasize the importance of this diversity in their work. Benedicta Ward argues that the current interest in miracles is hindered and probably even distorted by a fixation on the 'how', or the mechanics, of miracles. Do miracles breach the laws of physics? If so, then how? These questions have been central to the theological and philosophical debate on miracles since David Hume.[13] According to Ward, such enquiries have obscured a 'more varied, subtle and discreet' understanding of miracles which was particularly prevalent in the period before scholasticism. At that time, people were most interested in learning what, or whom, a miracle referred to, or what message it held for human-

---

[11] Augustine, *De trinitate*, W.J. Mountain, Fr. Glorie (eds.), *Corpus cristianorum: Series latina* 50 (Turnhout: Brepols, 1968), III. 4–10; V. 11–12.

[12] Caesarius of Heisterbach, *Dialogus miraculorum*, J. Strange (ed.), 2 vols. (Coloniae, Bonnae et Bruxellis: Heberle (Lempertz), 1851), Distinctio 10, c. 1, 2.

[13] David Hume, *An Enquiry Concerning Human Understanding*, Section X, "Of Miracles", *The English Philosophers from Bacon to Mill*, ed. and introd. by Edwin A. Burtt (New York: The Modern Library, 1939), pp. 652–667.

ity. These are questions which Ward believes we should reintroduce in current research into miracles and miracle stories.[14]

Caroline Walker Bynum points out the importance of recognizing not only how ideas about miracles have changed through time, but also the divergent schools of thought which have existed concurrently. There is a tendency to assume that at any given time, the prevalent understanding of miracles is the only one that exists. People often assume, for instance, that from the thirteenth to the eighteenth century there was a general and growing adherence to the philosophical view on miracles based on Aristotle's idea that wonderment exists by virtue of ignorance, and that the more we find out about the origin of the world, the less we will find astonishing.[15] According to Caroline Walker Bynum, however, the notion that knowledge and wonder are mutually exclusive was not characteristic of most medieval religious discourse—neither in the intellectual debate on miracles, nor in the hagiography or devotional practices of that age. She shows that these different forms of expression each had their own approaches to, and hypotheses about, miracles—and that each of these approaches and hypotheses was based on its own rationale. The miraculous was defined (in part) as the antithesis of that which could be investigated, imitated and generalized. "Wonder was a recognition of the singularity and significance of the thing encountered.... [It] was a response to something novel and bizarre that seemed both to exceed explanation and to indicate that there might be reason (significance—not necessarily cause) behind it."[16] Only an inquisitive approach which incorporates the very same attitude towards wonderment can lead us to what people in other ages and contexts have considered miraculous, according to Caroline Walker Bynum.

In line with Ward and Walker Bynum's recommendations, the researchers who contributed to this anthology were asked to choose and reason from a definition of miracles which satisfied two requirements. First of all, it should be applicable to their own field of study and to the reference material; and secondly, it should reflect an

---

[14] Benedicta Ward, "Signs and Wonders", Benedicta Ward, *Signs and Wonders: Saints, Miracles and Prayers from the 4th Century to the 14th* (Aldershot: Variorum, 1992), II, pp. 539–542, esp. p. 540; See also Benedicta Ward, *Miracles and the Medieval Mind: Theory, Record and Event, 1000–1215* (Philadelphia: University of Pennsylvania Press, 1982).

[15] *Aristotle's Metaphysics*, transl. with commentaries by Hippocrates G. Apostle (Bloomington: Indiana University Press, 1966), Book A, ch. I, 980a–983a, pp. 12–16.

[16] Walker Bynum, "Wonder", p. 3; p. 24.

acknowledgement of the unique and irreducible aspects of miracles, as pointed out by Ward and Walker Bynum.

Questions of Gender

I have already posited that links between women and miracles should not be taken for granted but in fact mapped out and studied. This research project began with an inventory of insights gained from what little relevant research had already been done. Textual material brought together from various periods and disciplines indicates that, through time, women in Western Europe have become more and more openly involved in rituals, cults, and activities surrounding miracles such as faith healing, pilgrimages, the veneration of saints, etc. While women in early medieval times performed practically no miracles,[17] this changed considerably in the high Middle Ages, when the number of female miracle-performing saints grew.[18] While most visitors to shrines and miracle sites were men until the late Middle Ages,[19] the balance subsequently tipped in favour of women.[20] The nineteenth and twentieth centuries are characterized by an ever stronger connection between women and miracles. In this period, women take centre stage as 'mediators', visionaries or go-betweens who liaise with another reality—and in this role they

---

[17] See Aline Rouselle, "La sage-femme et le thaumaturge dans la Gaule tardive: Les femmes ne font pas de miracles", André Pelletier (ed.), *La médecine en Gaule: Villes d'eaux, sanctuaires des eaux* (Paris: Picard, 1985), pp. 241–251; Elena Giannarelli, "Women and Miracles in Christian Biography (IVth–Vth centuries)", *Studia Patristica* 25 (1991), pp. 376–380; Benedicta Ward, "Apophtegmata Matrum", Ward, *Signs and Wonders*, I, pp. 63–66; H.-W. Goetz, "Heiligenkult und Geschlecht: Geschlechtsspezifisches Wunderwirken in frühmittelalterlichen Mirakelberichten?", *Das Mittelalter* 1 (1996), pp. 89–111.

[18] Peter Dinzelbacher, *Vision und Visionsliteratur im Mittelalter* (Stuttgart: Anton Hiersemann, 1981); Caroline Walker Bynum, *Holy Feast and Holy Fast: The Religious Significance of Food to Medieval Women* (Berkeley: University of California Press, 1987); Idem, *Fragmentation and Redemption: Essays on Gender and the Human Body in Medieval Religion* (New York: Zone Books, 1991); Idem, "Bodily Miracles and the Resurrection of the Body in the High Middle Ages", Thomas Kselman (ed.), *Belief in History* (Notre Dame: Notre Dame University Press, 1990), pp. 68–106.

[19] Rebekka Habermas, *Wallfart und Aufruhr: Zur Geschichte des Wunderglaubens in der frühen Neuzeit* (Frankfurt: Campus, 1991), pp. 45–66; Gerrit Verhoeven, *Devotie en negotie: Delft als bedevaartsplaats in de late middeleeuwen* (Amsterdam: VU Uitgeverij, 1992).

[20] See Irmtraud Götz von Olenhusen, "Vorwort", Götz von Olenhusen (Hrsg.), *Wunderbare Erscheinungen*, pp. 7–12; William A. Christian Jr., *Apparitions in Late Medieval and Renaissance Spain* (Princeton: Princeton University Press, 1981).

have practically no male counterparts.²¹ Quantitative research has shown that, in European history, women's involvement in miracles has grown. In this context, 'involvement' is loosely defined and also includes acting as a spectator, promoter or recipient of miracles.

Hardly any headway has been made towards interpreting this phenomenon, however. Only recently have there been any reflections on why women have been more involved than men, and these are based on assumptions about women's familial/social position and related psychological development and orientation. In historical, sociological and anthropological research, for instance, the focus is on women's (and children's) position as the least empowered sufferers. The use of authority or violence to resolve conflicts is an option less available to women (at home, within the family and locally). Involvement in miracles is seen as an appropriate way of contesting these restrictions. It provides an alternative in which women can actively promote their own well-being as well as that of their families or communities.²²

Psycholinguistic research has drawn attention to the empathic style of experiencing and speaking which is thought to be typical of many women. It may be related to specific problems women in Western societies have with separation during their psychological development—which are expressed in a taboo on aggression and in a negative view towards independence and autonomy. Women who develop in this way often have a subjective and emotional way of speaking about the events in their lives. Men, on the other hand, are socialized to

---

²¹ Thomas A. Kselman, *Miracles & Prophecies in Nineteenth-Century France* (New Brunswick: Rutgers University Press, 1983); Stéphane Michaud, *Muse et madone: Visages de la femme de la Revolution française aux apparitions de Lourdes* (Paris: Seuil, 1985); Alex Owen, *The Darkened Room: Women, Power and Spirituality in late Victorian England* (Philadelphia: The University of Pennsylvania Press, 1990); Sandra L. Zimdars-Swartz, *Encountering Mary: From La Salette to Medjugorje* (Princeton: Princeton University Press, 1991); David Blackbourn, *Marpingen: Apparitions of the Virgin Mary in Bismarckian Germany* (Oxford: Clarendon Press, 1993); Bax, *Medjugorje*; Götz von Olenhusen (Hrsg.), *Wunderbare Erscheinungen*; Christian Jr., *Visionaries: The Spanish Republic and the Reign of Christ*.

²² Zimdars-Swartz, *Encountering Mary*, passim; Bax, *Medjugorje*, pp. 53–66. For a similar view, see also Fatima Mernissi, "Women, Saints and Sanctuaries", Elizabeth Abel and Emily K. Abel (eds.), *The Signs Reader: Women, Gender & Scholarship* (Chicago/London: University of Chicago Press, 1983), pp. 57–68; Edien Bartels, *Een dochter is beter dan duizend zonen: Arabische vrouwen, symbolen en machtsverhoudingen tussen de sexen* (Utrecht: Van Arkel, 1993); Bartels' study of women in folk Islam shows that—despite the fact that in folk Islam holy women are outnumbered by holy men—it is predominantly women who 'deal with' and invoke these—usually local—saints.

objectify their own experiences and discuss them rationally.[23] According to this research, the result is that women tend to label profound events in their lives as 'miracles' or 'miraculous'. Moreover, women are presumed to be less concerned about (the conventions of) rationality and therefore to be more inclined—partly due to Romantic and Modern ideas about both piety and femininity[24]—to speak about their experiences in terms of miracles.

The explanations above are based on research into women's specific position and experiences—particularly modern European women. However, these explanations deal with neither religion nor miracles as such. They offer no specific links between women and miracles and no ways of identifying and confronting gender stereotypes concerning women and miracles. The studies mentioned above are more likely to confirm than question the classic, stereotypical image of women as less rational, less autonomous and therefore more susceptible to religion, magic and superstition. Moreover, to focus on women as the underprivileged or as outsiders "may obscure the role women have played in the actual creation of distinctive features of mainstream religious practice".[25]

The main intention of this book is not to explain women's involvement in miracles, but to bring their actual involvement—as evidenced in various kinds of texts—into view. The following questions are posed: What specific deeds or activities are attributed to women in miracle stories—and (how) do these activities reflect certain social, religious and cultural positions women occupy? What visions on women are reflected by particular types of miracle story? In cases where women perform miracles, what kind of miracles are attributed to them? How do women who (are said to) perform miracles

---

[23] Sara Mills (ed.), *Language and Gender: Interdisciplinary Perspectives* (London: Longman, 1995); Sally Johnson and Ulrike Hanna Meinhof (eds.), *Language and Masculinity* (Oxford: Blackwell, 1997); Gisela Schoenthal (Hrsg.), *Linguistik—linguistische Geschlechterforschung: Ergebnisse, Konsequenzen, Perspektiven* (Hildesheim: Olms, 1998).

[24] See Hugh McLeod, "Weibliche Frömmigkeit—männlicher Unglaube? Religion und Kirche im bürgerlichen 19. Jahrhundert," Ute Frevert (Hrsg.), *Bürgerinnen und Bürger: Geschlechterverhältnisse im 19. Jahrhundert* (Göttingen: VandenHoeck & Ruprecht, 1988), pp. 134–156; Heide Wunder, "Von der 'frumkeit' zur 'Frömmigkeit': Ein Beitrage zur Genese bürgerliche Weiblichkeit (15.–17. Jahrhundert)", Ursula Becher, Jörn Rüsen (Hrsg.), *Weiblichkeit in geschichtlicher Perspektive: Fallstudien und Reflexionen zu Grundproblemen der historischen Frauenforschung* (Frankfurt am Main: Suhrkamp, 1988), pp. 174–188.

[25] Walker Bynum, *Fragmentation and Redemption*, p. 57.

influence and affect the world around them? Which light does their actual involvement in miracles shed on their part in the shaping of religious traditions? What views have women developed with regard to miracles? What views on miracles come to light or are called into question when the actual involvement of women in miracles is examined? Questions like these are important because they help us to study women's subjectivity and agency in miracle stories. They also help us to resist the received ideas and many cliches on the subject of women and miracles.

From the very beginning, this research project has been aimed at the study of *miracle stories*, the assumption being that this material could provide most direct access to miracles as they have been experienced, articulated and passed down by women. Miracle stories also suit the hermeneutical approach mentioned earlier, which places a premium on the factual recounting of miracles. It is the act of telling which constructs the miracle as such. The miracle has an impact through its telling and interpreting. The effect of a miracle is closely related to the way in which it is understood. A miracle cannot be separated from the discourse in which it is told.[26]

However, texts about miracles as they are experienced and articulated by women happen to be extraordinarily rare. Even in our own time and culture we find but a handful of relevant sources. Nearly all we know about women and miracles we have learned indirectly; our knowledge has been told, described, passed down and commented on from an androcentric point of view. This research project would have been far too limited, if it had only dealt with material written by women, because this would have restricted the project to modern, contemporary literature. The opposite approach

---

[26] Different angles on this approach can be found in W.A. de Pater, "Wonder en wetenschap", W.A. de Pater, *Taalanalytische perspectieven op godsdienst en kunst* (Antwerpen: De Nederlandsche Boekhandel, 1970), pp. 58–112; J.-L. Derouet, "Les possibilités d'interpretation sémiologique des textes hagiographiques", *Revue d'histoire de l'Église de France* 62 (1976), pp. 153–162; Candace Slater, *Trail of Miracles: Stories from a Pilgrimage in Northeast Brazil* (Berkeley: University of California Press, 1986); Giselle de Nie, *Views from a Many-Windowed Tower: Studies of Imagination in the Works of Gregory of Tours* (Amsterdam: Rodopi, 1987); Eugen Drewermann, *Tiefenpsychologie und Exegese*, Bd. I: *Die Wahrheit der Formen: Traum, Mythos, Märchen, Sage und Legende*; Band II: *Die Wahrheit der Werke und der Worte: Wunder, Vision, Weissagung, Apokalypse, Geschichte, Gleichnis* (Olten: Walter Verlag, 1991); Jacqueline Borsje, "The Monster in the River Ness in 'Vita Sancti Columbae': A Study of Miracle", *Peritia* 8 (1994), pp. 27–34; Irena Backus, *Le miracle de Laon: Le déraisonnable, le raisonnable, l'apocalyptique et le politique dans les récits du miracle de Laon (1566–1578)* (Paris: Vrin, 1994).

promised to deliver better results. By putting the focus on miracle *narratives* the researchers tried to unveil women's voices, that is to say their perspectives or views, even though few of the stories were actually written by women. Through a carefully developed line of inquiry it is possible to elicit these voices without separating them from their narrative context: Is there any tension between the narrative point of view and the content, between the narrative rhetoric and the event recounted? Are there different or even contradictory versions of the miracle story? Does the miracle story contain ambiguities related to gender roles? Can echoes of women's voices be heard underneath a clearly androcentric narration?[27]

By asking these questions, the authors in this book are not trying to illustrate a world or culture that belongs exclusively to women. Women's lives and experiences are presumed to form a world, which is in some ways marginal and isolated, but in other ways not at all. Anthropologists Edwin and Shirley Ardener developed a model for studying the cultural expressions of marginalized groups in society. The model assumes that marginalized groups are for the most part included in the dominant culture—while recognizing that they are also excluded from it to some extent. When applied to women, this means that one should be aware of the possibility that their utterances and actions are 'double voiced'. Their expressions may contain irreconcilable tensions between a given women's culture and a dominant androcentric culture.[28] This has consequences for research into women and miracles. When women appeal for acknowledgement of their (involvement in) miracles, it is partly a way of seeking acknowledgement of themselves. They do this by presenting 'their' miracles in a way which is acceptable (to the dominant culture at least). At the same time, these women may also use the miracles to

---

[27] These questions have been applied to biblical texts by a.o. Elisabeth Schüssler Fiorenza, *In Memory of Her* (New York: Crossroad, 1984); Mieke Bal, *Lethal Love: Feminist Literary Readings of Biblical Love Stories* Bloomington: Indiana University Press, 1987); Ilana Pardes, *Countertraditions in the Bible: A Feminist Approach* (Cambridge: Harvard University Press, 1992); Regina M. Schwartz, *The Curse of Cain: The Violent Legacy of Monotheism* (Chicago: University of Chicago Press, 1997).

[28] Edwin Ardener, "Belief and the Problem of Women"; "The Problem Revisited", Shirley Ardener (ed.), *Perceiving Women* (New York: Halsted Press, 1978), pp. 1–27. For examples and an explanation of this type of interpretation of Old-Testament texts, see Fokkelien van Dijk-Hemmes, *Sporen van vrouwenteksten in de Hebreeuwse bijbel* (Utrecht: Faculteit der Godgeleerdheid Universiteit Utrecht, 1992); Idem, *De dubbele stem van haar verlangen*, teksten van Fokkelien van Dijk-Hemmes, verzameld en ingeleid door Jonneke Bekkenkamp en Freda Dröes (Zoetermeer: Meinema, 1995).

put their own problems, expectations and (religious) views on the public agenda. This duality may be present in texts both by women and about women. The interpretive model described here is applicable not only wherever there is a dominant androcentric culture versus a hidden, suppressed women's culture; it can also be used to study the relationship between various religious circles, such as the more official and established circles versus more informal and/or private circles—a distinction which is often quite relevant to the research of miracles and their interpretation.

Women and Miracle Stories

I. *Formative Christianity and the Early Middle Ages*

The first three articles in this book focus on texts with a similar background. The texts deal with the establishment and spread of Christianity. They are from second century Asia Minor, sixth century Gaul, and Ireland in the sixth and seventh centuries. In this period, miracles played an important part in establishing the credibility of the new religious beliefs and practices and of the religious authority of apostles, bishops, monks and saints. Against this background, the authors examine women's involvement in these miracle stories.

The first article, entitled "Magic, Miracle and Miracle Workers in the *Acts of Thecla*", is written by Magda Misset-van de Weg, researcher at the Catholic Theological University in Utrecht. The *Acts of Thecla*, a popular and widespread text in the early centuries of Christianity, probably dates from the middle of the second century C.E. It is one of the so-called Christian Apocryphal Acts, which are abundantly replete with magic and miracles. Miracles were an important feature of Christianity from its very inception and occur in profusion in both canonical and extracanonical traditions. In this context the miraculous events fulfil an instrumental role in what might be summarized as: convincing and converting prospective adherents and consolidating the faith of the communities represented in the narratives.

In view of the major role which is accorded to women in the *Acts of Thecla*, Misset-van de Weg seeks to visualize what the miraculous events as related in the *Acts of Thecla* reveal regarding the situation and status of women in (at least some, ascetic) Christian communities. What does the fact that women are cast as active agents in and during the miraculous events tell us about the validation, legitimacy and credence of their actions and position? By carefully unravelling the miraculous and magical features of this narrative in relation to women's position in the Christian community and society at large, Misset-van de Weg tries to answer these questions.

According to her, in and through the miracles recorded in the *Acts of Thecla*, an answer is provided to the problem of social tensions resulting from the conversion of women to an ascetic form of Christianity, which appears to be inextricably bound up with the problem of women's suffering as a result of asymmetry of power. The miraculous events told in this story sanction a woman's decision to detach herself from her family and the societal norms and values she is supposed to embody, and confirm the legitimacy of women's right to a certain form of autonomy, including the inviolability of women's bodies. Thecla/woman, 'unbound' both from the things of the world and in the end from the apostle Paul, is set free and commissioned to pursue her apostolic activities. As Misset-van de Weg shows, a chain of miracles in which women act as creative initiators and sensible participants leads in the *Acts of Thecla* to the validation of Thecla as a servant of God (*doulē tou theou*), and thereby of women's position of (apostolic) authority.

The second article in the first section deals with Western Christianity in the early Middle Ages, in the context of the origin of 'the cult of the saints' (Peter Brown). Do the miracle stories from this age indicate that women were able to shape religious traditions with a degree of autonomy and authority? Giselle de Nie, former lecturer in Medieval History at the University of Utrecht, examines this question in her study entitled "Fatherly and Motherly Curing in Sixth-Century Gaul: Saint Radegund's *mysterium*".

Up to the sixth century, sainthood and miraculous curing in the West had been attributed only to men, and their cures tended to resemble those of the fourth-century St. Martin, which in turn resembled biblical cures. Venantius Fortunatus and Gregory of Tours are the first to tell us about women's cures in Gaul, both during their lives and through their tombs after death. As far as we can tell from the reports, most of these do not differ significantly from men's cures, nor is it said that they healed only or especially women. And the two women saints whom we know most about, Monegund and the former queen Radegund, also associated themselves closely with the memory of St. Martin. Radegund, however, may have exercised the existing male curing tradition in a new, specifically gendered way.

According to De Nie a number of the miracles attributed to Radegund let us see what appear to be two new healing rituals. In the stories that survive, they are used only for women. In these rituals, the powerful Christian symbols—or *mysteria*—of Christ's death and resurrection and of treading upon a serpent as the embodiment of Evil are used in a way in which a woman plays the leading role; her independent worth and power are central. The first ritual symbolically images woman's reproductive capacity. The second appropriates a biblical action-model implicating woman which is, in this period, not mentioned as such anywhere else. Regarded as divine transformative images or power patterns that are immanent in contemporary visible reality, they are activated and made to produce visible results in a mimetic ritual.

Symbolic ritual and 'medical' curing are thus different aspects of the event that was perceived by contemporaries as 'a miracle'. Modern psychology and anthropology have rediscovered this principle: a patient's affective enacting, and thereby experiencing, of vital, religious metaphors and symbols can precipitate real emotional and physical transformation. With her two new healing rituals, De Nie states, Radegund developed what appears to be a first 'female' theology of a very practical kind.

The third article in the first section is about a text which—like nearly all early medieval miracle stories—chronicles the deeds of a male saint. At first glance this text offers little to our study. So what can it tell us about the relationship between women and miracles? Jacqueline Borsje, research scholar at the School of Celtic Studies of the Dublin Institute for Advanced Studies in Ireland tackles this question in her contribution entitled "Women in Columba's Life, as Seen through the Eyes of his biographer Adomnán".

Vita sancti Columbae (circa 700) is a thematic arrangement of the miracles performed by Columba, an Irish monk who is regarded as one of the major Irish saints. Columba left Ireland in 563 with twelve companions and founded a monastery on the Scottish island of Iona, which became an important centre of the Irish church. *Vita sancti Columbae* was composed by Adomnán (c. 628–704), a relative of Columba and his ninth successor as abbot of Iona. Adomnán collected stories about the miracles that Columba performed both during his life and after his death and presented them thematically: miracles of prophecy, of power, and miraculous angelic visions and apparitions of light and fire. As Borsje points out, a dualistic perception of 'miracle' and 'magic', of supernatural acts that do or do not have their source in the power of God, is constitutive to this genre of miracle telling.

The majority of the people playing a part in these anecdotes about miracles are male. Quantitatively seen, women play a marginal role in this *Life*. A possible reason for this—the fact that Columba lived in a male monastic community—is not totally satisfying since Columba's adventures among lay people in Ireland and Pictland are told as well. Borsje, however, does not attempt to answer the question about the quantitative role but instead seeks to analyze the qualitative role of women in this *Vita*. Adomnán apparently did not think women to be very important, but he describes women as people of flesh and blood, as examples and as symbols. Who are the women that are mentioned in the text? What is their social and ecclesiastical position? What function do they have in the stories? What is their relationship to Columba: do they co-operate with him or do they obstruct his work? Does he help or punish them?

On the basis of this first category of women (those who co-operate with Columba or are helped by him) being the largest, Borsje's conclusion regarding the pictured relationship between Columba and women is that they were usually on good terms. Women are not found among Columba's public opponents: neither the druids nor the perpetrators of violence. One woman is mentioned in connection with magic, but she is the victim of a false accusation. The only female opponent of Columba is a wife and mother, who bases her resistance upon care for her family. She obviously is a woman of flesh and blood, but she also is a symbol for the older order based upon compensation. With her 'foolish advice', she can be seen in contrast with two other wives who give their husbands 'sound advice'. These latter two women stand for the new religious order based upon trust in the saint and God. In this category we also can discover, according to Borsje, a woman who is herself part of a miracle and two women who are the subject of a miracle themselves.

II. *The High and Late Middle Ages*

The three articles in this section build upon the established theme by introducing a number of new questions and perspectives. Mainly, they ask what does coming into contact with miracles or being associated with miracles mean to women? The authors were able to deal with these questions, because they had access to more diverse sources, comprising not only hagiographies, but also letters and prayers.

The first article presents the now familiar quest for the rare occurrence—given the historical and religious context—of women's autonomy and authority in performing miracles. In this case, however, we explore a very different and lesser-known area of research: the position of women in Southern European Jewish communities in the Middle Ages. The article is called "Fresh Water for a Tired Soul: Pregnancy and Messianic Desire in a Medieval Jewish Document from Sicily". The authors are Marcel Poorthuis and Chana Safrai. Poorthuis co-ordinates a research program on the relationship between Judaism and Christianity at the Catholic Theological University in Utrecht. Safrai is a former lecturer of Talmudic studies at the same university.

Poorthuis and Safrai have studied a text from the *Genizah of Cairo* which is clearly relevant to the framework of 'Women and Miracle Stories': the so called 'messianic document'. It contains two narrators' accounts of a series of miraculous events in which a woman plays a major role. Historian Jacob Mann rescued this text from oblivion and published it in 1931. Since then, it has attracted a great deal of interest in scholarly circles and has been published several times. The text's date of origin is unknown. Scholars have suggested dates between the twelfth to the sixteenth centuries. It is probably (the fragments of) a letter, or a travelogue to be more precise, written in Sicily. Until now, too little attention has been paid to the fact that it tells of a pregnant woman, a rabbi's wife, receiving a messianic revelation.

Poorthuis and Safrai's study offers a translation of the text followed by a detailed analysis. They depart from the perspective of the text as a narrative in which miracles are a rhetorical device to convince readers of the messianic urgency of its content. They chart the roles of the different characters, their utterances, their staging and localization, and the overall gender patterns in this story.

The most prominent occurrence in this story is a pregnant woman's prophetic and miraculous act witnessed by two male visitors. In the seclusion of her own home, this woman receives a messianic revelation while making priestly gestures and being covered with a *talit*—religious deeds normally reserved for men. Her deeds and the miraculous events themselves clearly allude to being in labour and giving birth. The messianic metaphors in this delivery scene are obvious, but we also see that pregnancy and delivery are felt to have messianic significance *per se*. To Poorthuis and Safrai, this unique and complex story opens new perspectives concerning the position of women in Judaism regarding (messianic) prophecy and charismatic authority. This miracle story both confirms and challenges women's restricted position vis-à-vis the public rituals and institutional authority of Judaism.

I have already referred to the ambiguity of attributing miracles to women—does it establish or in fact restrict or even eliminate women's religious authority and influence? Anke E. Passenier, research scholar at the Department of Church History, Utrecht University, examines this question in depth in her work: "The Life of Christina Mirabilis: Miracles and the Construction of Marginality".

In the *Life* of Christina Mirabilis (Christina of St. Trond, 1150–1224) by the Dominican Thomas of Cantimpré the miraculous plays a central part. Whereas the other *Vitae* of women saints by this author—although not devoid of extraordinary events either—can be considered as spiritual biographies for religious women to model their lives after, Christina's *Vita* can hardly serve as such a model. It is too wrapped up in the miraculous that enfolds her life from the beginning to the end.

In this article Passenier tries to unravel the function of miracles and the miraculous in the specific context of the *Vita* of Christina. The analysis of specific miracles (death and resurrection, purgatorial torments, wonders of lactation and oil-exuding, miraculous somatic phenomena) serves here to address more general questions. According to Passenier, the function of the miraculous in the *Vita* of Christina Mirabilis is quite ambivalent. On the one hand, the miracles in the *Vita* authorize Christina's ministry, proving that she received her mission directly from God, without human intervention and even against the expectations and wishes of the most religious. On the other hand, we may observe that the miraculous restricts Christina's ministry by emphasizing her dramatic performance, bodily suffering and ecstatic abilities, thus stylizing a specifically female apostolate. Moreover, the miraculous episodes tend to override Christina's actual ministry and to marginalize her by stressing the uniqueness of her divine mission. The endowment with miraculous gifts appears to be an ambiguous privilege. Lacking religious authority through ordination women in particular seem to have benefited from the 'miraculous' as a source of religious power.

Since the *Vita* of Christina was conceived by Thomas of Cantimpré, who stylizes her life into a 'sermon on purgatory' to edify his public, the question must be asked, whether it is Christina of St. Trond or rather her hagiographer, who benefits from the miraculous. In a way the miraculous life of Christina functions as a divine authorization of his own preaching ministry, exhorting people to penance and conversion and of his own theological views on purgatory, religious life, the sacraments and, last but not least, female apostolate. Christina's is the specifically female task of embodiment of something other than herself. Is the wonder-woman Christina of Thomas's *Vita* more than a vivid illustration in the margin, more than a medium to his message, providing it with a divine halo? Such considerations, Passenier contends, might prevent a naive espousal of the 'miraculous' as a strategy for women to gain religious power. In the *Vita* of Christina it proves to be Janus-faced: its other side is the construction of female marginality, the elevation to an other-worldly realm at the cost of a place in 'real' history.

The third article in the second section focuses on a very different genre: popular medieval prayers and charms. This material provides a different view of women's involvement in miracles. What miracle stories were significant to women themselves? What role did miracles and miracle stories play in women's daily lives at that time? Marianne Elsakkers, who studied Old Germanic language and literature, attempts to answer these questions in her contribution: "In Pain You Shall Bear Children (Gen 3:16): Medieval Prayers for a Safe Delivery".

Throughout the Middle Ages, we hear women who are about to deliver praying for a miracle. Given the great risks to mother and child at childbirth, it is understandable that supernatural help, whether attributable to miracles or magic, was just as welcome as the help of midwives or physicians. A popular medieval childbirth charm—perhaps the most popular one—is the Latin *peperit* charm. According to Elsakkers, variant versions of this charm are found all over medieval Europe from the early Middle Ages until at least the beginning of the Renaissance. The large number of extant versions suggests that the text was well-known and probably widely used. It is quite remarkable that the 'core' text of the charm does not significantly change, although there are many textual variants—differing in time and place. Why was this prayer so popular in medieval Europe?

Formal analysis of the medieval *peperit* charm and its variant versions from all over Europe shows that the charm must have been part of an oral tradition: there is variation and formulaic repetition on every level (e.g. word, line, phrase), mnemonic devices are used, and instructions requiring active participation in word and deed of all present explain the practical function of the charm. Prayer and instructions make us aware of the somatic component of the charm and its (christianized) magic: the reciting and writing, the amulets, the measuring, and the binding and loosing rituals. The Latin of the prayer stresses its ritualistic power, at the same time, by contrast, explaining why the vernacular was so frequently used for the instructions. These verbal and performative rituals with their focussing on the parturient woman help to set the scene for the miracle the woman in labour so fervently desires. But the charm was also practical; evidence in literary texts corroborates this. The prayer could have offered real practical help to the soon-to-be mother because, as Elsakkers shows, the two rhythmically different sections of the prayer may represent a mnemonic device to help the woman with her breathing techniques: medieval Lamaze.

Medieval medicine consisted of empirical healing combined with different forms of supernatural healing. All of these forms of healing are represented in the *peperit* charm, but the prayer with its religious metaphors seems to be the frame within which medical and magical healing function. The prayer with its ritualistic language, analogous miracle stories, and its plea for a miracle is accompanied by magic and practical breathing techniques which are embedded in the rhythm of the prayer. It is the prayer which might actually help the woman in labour through her birth pains, and thus, God willing, effectuate a miraculously safe delivery.

III. *The 19th and 20th Centuries*

The last section of this book contains four articles which are characterized by their profound interest in the narrative structures of miracle stories. These articles are primarily based on recent sources, which allowed the authors to more thoroughly study the actual origin and function of the miracle stories. The main focus is the part women play in the actual construction of miracle stories.

The section opens with "The Beatification of Friederike Hauffe *née* Wanner (1801–1829)" by Wouter J. Hanegraaff, professor of the History of Hermetic Philosophy and related currents of thought, University of Amsterdam. When the popular Victorian novelist Catherine Crowe published her abridged translation of Justinus Kerner's *The*

Seeress of Prevorst in 1845, she made it possible for an English-speaking audience to become familiar with a 'miracle story' which had quickly achieved notoriety in Germany after its first publication in 1829. *Persona dramatis* of this miracle story is Friederike Wanner, born as a forester's daughter in the small Souabian village of Prevorst in 1801. After marrying a distantly related merchant, Gottlieb Hauffe, at nineteen, this young woman began to suffer from high fever and daily recurring cramps. An illness started, which caused her to be in a so-called 'magnetic' or mesmeric trance state almost permanently until her death in 1829. The last three years of her life she was treated by the physician dr. Justinus Kerner, known for his previous successes with so-called somnambulic patients. She came to live permanently in Kerner's own house. During this period, stories about her miraculous abilities spread widely, causing Friederike Hauffe to become known as 'the Seeress'. Kerner, who became more and more impressed by Friederike's phenomena, especially by her capacity to commune with spirits, took the opportunity to 'study' his patient intensively and to observe the occult *in concreto*. Soon after her death, Kerner published a detailed account of his observations and his experiments with Friederike Hauffe, titled *Die Seherin von Prevorst: Eröffnungen über das innere Leben des Menschen und über das Hereinragen einer Geisterwelt in die unsere*.

To this day, overviews in the English language of the history of psychiatry, parapsychology, occultism and related fields duly mention the pioneering importance of Justinus Kerner and 'his' Seeress, but none of them goes beyond a brief presentation based on secondary sources. In this article Hanegraaff intends, firstly, to provide the English speaking reader with a more complete and accurate picture than is currently available, taking advantage of older as well as recent German research. Secondly, Hanegraaff addresses the practical and theoretical problems involved in an attempt to disentangle 'myth' from 'reality', in a story which owes its very fame to its 'miraculous' and therefore historically problematic aspects. And thirdly, he addresses some problems of interpretation deriving from the relationship (personal, professional, literary) between the male poet and physician Justinus Kerner, on the one hand, and his female patient Friederike Hauffe, on the other.

Kerner's role in the 'beatification' of Friederike Hauffe, Hanegraaff concludes, can be traced with far more clarity than her own. As a sick patient, Friederike Hauffe had been a frustration to Kerner the physician; as the Seeress of Prevorst, she ended as a blessing for Kerner the Romantic poet. The process of 'beatification', by which Friederike Hauffe was to be transformed into 'The Seeress of Prevorst' took place under the decisive influence of Justinus Kerner. But already long before that, Friederike Hauffe had entered a circle, and fallen under a spell, out of which she would not be able any more to escape for the remainder of her life. This circle was woven in a complicated pattern, fabricated from various strands of her native culture, and it had begun to be spun from the moment of her birth. It would have had far less power over her if she had been less sensitive by nature, if her urge for a deep spiritual fellowship had been less profound, and if she had been more fortunate in her personal life. As it was, however, the course of her life left her increasingly helpless to withstand the power of myth closing in on her.

The second article brings us to classical and recent Hindu miracle stories from South India. Anne van Voorthuizen, who took a degree in Religious Studies at Utrecht University, based her article on a combination of the study of literature and field research. It is entitled "Māriyamma<u>n</u>'s *Šakti*: The Miraculous Power of a Smallpox Goddess."

Māriyamma<u>n</u> is a goddess worshipped primarily in South India. Her power to cause and cure diseases, especially smallpox, gives Māriyamma<u>n</u> the capacity to directly influence people's lives. This ability accounts for the countless miracles she performs. Tales about Māriyamma<u>n</u> explain how she became the goddess of smallpox. Interestingly, versions of the story vary widely; some are passed down through the popular and primarily oral tradition of folk Hinduism, others are Sanskrit texts with great authority in the orthodox Brahmin tradition. In this article, Van Voorthuizen compares different versions of the story for the first time, focusing on how they reflect their social, religious and gender-specific context. After sketching the main features of the Māriyamma<u>n</u> cult in South India, Van Voorthuizen analyses a version of the Māriyamma<u>n</u> story orally passed down in Tamil Nadu, a second one written in Sanskrit, and thirdly an interpretation of the story by a Māriyamma<u>n</u> priestess and medium from Madras.

To study the gender-related differences between these stories, the following questions are raised: How do the stories differ? What differences are there in gender-specific themes? Is there a link between gender-specific themes and the significance of gender in social reality? Can women's voices be detected beneath or behind the androcentric tale? How much influence did women have on the telling and recording of these stories, and what impact did this have on the narratives? And finally, do women appropriate Māriyamma<u>n</u>'s miraculous powers in a gender-specific manner?

A comparison of the various versions shows that the oral tradition of folk Hinduism credits Māriyamma<u>n</u> with miraculous powers, while the male-dominated Sanskrit tradition makes no mention of these abilities. Van Voorthuizen ascribes this to the greater influence women have had on the development of folk Hinduism. The Māriyamma<u>n</u> stories from the oral tradition are, in the terminology of literary theorist Elaine Showalter, double-voiced; within their subculture, women redefine reality from their own perspective. In this instance, a kind of hidden resistance can be detected. While in Christian tradition miracles are positive by definition, the miraculous powers of Māriyamma<u>n</u> are ambivalent; they are both curative and lethal. This, too, can be ascribed to women's position in Indian society. The ambiguous power of minor goddesses in Hinduism, seen in light of their suffering and anger, is yet another double voice reflecting women's marginalized position.

The last two contributions focus on miracle stories in contemporary literature written by women. The authors examined material which enabled them to deal with the questions: Why, and to what end, do women in contemporary Western culture write miracle stories? Ilse N. Bulhof, former associate professor of Philosophy at the Catholic Theological University in Utrecht and professor emeritus of Philosophy at Leiden University studies the relationship between women and miracles in the stories of Austrian novelist Ingeborg Bachmann. She reasons from the perspective of cultural philosophy.

According to Bulhof, miracles have become 'utopic' in the context of modern western culture: there is no place for them any more. In the modern period the dualistic worldview of God and world slowly gave way to a one-dimensional world from which miracles in the literal sense and Transcendence as the origin of the miraculous have been excluded. Yet some events in daily reality—such as a birth or a full recovery from a sickness—are still experienced as truly wonderful, even as miraculous, as when we speak of 'the miracle of love'. Small-talk and poetry have become the 'non-serious' dwelling places of miracles in this figurative or metaphoric sense, closely associated with the language of somewhat marginalized people like artists, children and women.

To Ilse Bulhof, the Austrian writer Ingeborg Bachmann (1926–1973) shows that even the miraculous in this poetic sense is threatened by a worldview that excludes the truly Other, Transcendence. The marginalization of the miraculous and of the others who are women, Bachmann discovered in a painful process, are two sides of the same coin. Bachmann was born in Klagenfurt, Austria, thirteen years before the *Anschluss* between Austria and Hitler's Germany. After defending her doctoral thesis on the philosophy of Martin Heidegger (1949), she decided that her future lay in literature rather than philosophy and its 'pitiful' jargon. She wrote poetry, short stories, and a novel which remained unfinished.

In this article Bulhof analyzes the development of Bachmann's thinking on women and miracles. Although Bachmann herself does not use the words 'miracle' and 'miraculous' in her text, Bulhof believes her fiction can be read as a woman's struggle to rescue a sense of the miraculous from a darkening world by bringing into focus various shapes of 'figurative' miracles. To demonstrate this, four of Bachmann's literary texts are discussed here: first, the short story "The Thirtieth Year," in which the literally and figuratively closed world of modernity (closed because one cannot escape its one-dimensionality) excludes miracles—and implicitly, women; second, the short story "Everything," in which a (poetically speaking) miracle occurs—the type that is allowed in the context of modernity: democratic solidarity between a woman and a man; third, the novel *Malina* in which the expectation raised by the possibility of miracles in the figurative sense is denied; and fourth, *The Case of Franza* (posthumously published) in which both literal and metaphorical miracles are left behind in a new and hopeful experience of what is most common and most ordinary: the elemental. The absence of the Absolute 'out there' frees one for a new experience of the world: not as an ontologically or historically lower realm (a vale of tears or a 'not-yet') but as the realm of the elemental, the material, the concrete, the sensuous that simply is what it is—the miracle of the elemental as a sacred dimension in human life. But in *The Case of Franza* Bachmann leaves open the question whether women or anyone else for that matter can ever feel at home in this experience of the elemental. Perhaps it was not by accident, Bulhof concludes, that this volume of Bachmann's trilogy *Todesarten* ("Ways of Dying") has remained unfinished.

The final article in this book is called "Miracles of Desire: Transfigurations in Rhoda Lerman's *The Book of the Night*". Its author, Inez van der Spek, is a researcher at the Faculty of Humanities of the University of Amsterdam. Her contribution deals with the postmodern science fiction/fantasy novel *The Book of the Night* (1984) by American writer Rhoda Lerman (*née* Sniderman, 1936). Both in style and content this novel reflects many of the themes dealt with in other articles in this anthology. The novel is pervaded with miraculous events and reflections on miracles as conceived of in widely divergent 'worlds'. Lerman's writings cannot be pinned down to a particular literary genre but are a patchwork of generic styles. Lerman utilizes satire and the fantastic to examine sexuality and sexual relationships, (sub)urban anxieties, and religion. She frequently combines elements of realism, mythology, and theology to comment upon the position of women in history and contemporary society. In *The Book of the Night*, all of these elements are mingled idiosyncratically with metaphors from cosmological science. In particular the 'order out of chaos' model inspired by thermodynamics (I. Prigogine) feeds the understanding of miracle in *The Book of the Night*.

This novel tells the story of the girl Celeste who comes with her father to the Isle of Iona (off the Scottish western coast, as we already learned from Borsje's research on St. Colomba), where the tenth century coexists with the nineteenth and the twentieth, ancient polytheisms with Jewish and Christian monotheisms, medieval magic and sorcery with modern science. Celeste is brought up as a boy, and, at reaching puberty, is sent to the monastery by her father to become a novice. Everything takes a dramatic *and* miraculous turn when she falls in love with the abbot.... Celeste changes from a girl into a cow. In the story, this event is conceived of as a wonder and debate-evoking miracle. But pivotal in this miracle story is, as Van der Spek shows, not the young girl's transformation into a cow, but her anxious desire to transfigure into a woman.

In this article, Van der Spek reads *The Book of the Night* as a miracle story in the context of a postmodern outlook on life and literature. According to Van der Spek *The Book of the Night* is an example of 'ontological poetics', in which the coexistence and mingling of different worlds, or modes of being, offers a fertile climate for the miraculous to thrive in. As postmodernist fiction, rather than raising the question *what* is a miracle, and how we are to recognize one, it deals with the ontological question of *where and when* a miracle is, of its space and time. Its very title points in the right direction: the *when* of miracles is the dark, the nightside of life. In what seem bizarre and exotic scenes in *The Book of the Night* Van der Spek detects imaginative explorations of sexuality and sexual difference, the formation and collapse of language, the limits of will and grace, and the site of the sacred in late twentieth century Western culture. The breakdown of time/language in *The Book of the Night* implies that self-evident and fixed categories of 'nature', 'woman', 'human' and 'holy' are undermined. In the end, a beautiful yet muted girl-cow transfigures into a woman. Celeste has experienced a miracle realized by her own intense desire to become a female sexual subject. This desire is not opposed to grace, but constitutes a redefinition of grace as the gift of transformation of religious and cultural order.

In the "Epilogue" I will elaborate on a number of the conclusions which can be drawn from these studies. The articles in this anthology show us that it is unproductive to presume that women resort to miracles mainly because they lack autonomy, power and rationality. Miracles have a unique function in religious expression and communication—and women's involvement in miracles should be explored from this angle. It is true that miracles, and stories about them, can evoke every conceivable stereotype of 'woman'. Yet, through miracles women have also shaped and transformed religious discourses and practices. Miracles are able to empower women, giving them not only religious influence and authority, but also the ability to identify and relieve personal and communal suffering. Furthermore, miracles can help women to confront and to overcome the stigmas of corporeality which mainstream monotheistic religions have assigned to the female body. I will illustrate these conclusions by drawing upon the individual studies in this book.

Translation: Mischa F. Hoyinck

2

MAGIC, MIRACLE AND MIRACLE WORKERS IN THE *ACTS OF THECLA*[1]

MAGDA MISSET-VAN DE WEG

That which remains inexplicable may fascinate even more than what is intelligible.[2]

Introduction

In many or most respects, formative Christianity did not differ or distance itself from the worlds in which it originated. For instance, with people from every level of society Christians shared belief in or fear of magic, the *magos* and the 'reality' of miracles, all of which formed an integral part of culture and society.[3] Not surprisingly therefore, miracles were an important feature of Christianity from its very

---

[1] I should like to express my gratitude to Pieter van der Horst, Ab de Jong, Anne-Marie Korte en Anke Passenier for their comments, ideas and criticism.

[2] J. Goldin, "The Magic of Magic and Superstition", *Aspects of Religious Propaganda in Judaism and Early Christianity*, ed. E. Schüssler Fiorenza (Notre Dame, 1976), pp. 115–147, esp. p. 126.

[3] See for example D.E. Aune, "Magic in Early Christianity", *Aufstieg und Niedergang der römischen Welt* II.23.2 (1980), pp. 1507–1557, esp. pp. 1518–1519; E. Schüssler Fiorenza, "Miracles, Mission, and Apologetics: An Introduction", *Aspects of Religious Propaganda*, ed. Schüssler Fiorenza, pp. 1–25, esp. p. 6; P.J. Achtemeier, "Jesus and the Disciples as Miracle Workers in the Apocryphal New Testament", *Aspects of Religious Propaganda*, ed. Schüssler Fiorenza, pp. 149–186, esp. pp. 152–153 and pp. 173–174; G. Poupon, "L'accusation de magie dans les Actes apocryphes", *Les Actes apocryphes des apôtres: Christianisme et monde païen*, eds. F. Bovon et al. (Genève, 1981), pp. 71–85, esp. pp. 80–82. In this article I shall not concern myself with or pretend to contribute to paradigm or terminology debates on "magic" or any other (larger) subjects in the same field, such as the dichotomy between magic and religion. A considerable number of studies have been published on these subjects. For example Aune, "Magic in Early Christianity"; H.S. Versnel, "Some Reflections on the Relationship Magic-Religion", *Numen* 38 (1991), pp. 177–197; H.D. Betz, "Magic and Mystery in the Greek Magical Papyri", *Magika Hiera: Ancient Greek Magic and Religion*, eds. Ch.A. Faraone and D. Obbink (New York/Oxford, 1991), pp. 244–259; A.F. Segal, "Hellenistic Magic: Some Questions of Definition", *Studies in Gnosticism and Hellenistic Religions Presented to Gilles Quispel*, eds. R. van den Broek et al. (Leiden, 1981), pp. 349–375; and cf. M. Douglas, *Purity and Danger: An Analysis of the Concepts*

inception and occur in profusion in both canonical and extracanonical traditions.[4] Like their contemporaries, Christians translated social concerns and problems into miracle stories and/or used these tales as a means of propaganda when faced with competition and slanderous attacks. Christian apologists emphasized the superiority of the miracles performed by Jesus and relegated pagan miracles to the realm of evil spirits.[5] Of course not everybody was convinced, and Celsus, for his part, called the New Testament miracles 'monstrous tales', and 'the practices of wicked men possessed by an evil daemon'.[6]

In the *Acts of Thecla* (*AThe*) too, as in the other *Apocryphal Acts of the Apostles* (*AAA*), miracles function as a rhetorical mode for raising the matter of the legitimacy of Christianity as a new religion and the credence of its propagators. The miraculous events fulfil an instru-

---

of Pollution and Taboo (Repr. London/New York, 1992), p. 18, p. 19 and p. 58 ff.; F. Graf, "Prayer in Magic and Religious Ritual", *Magika Hiera*, eds. Faraone and Obbink, pp. 188–213; F. Graf, *Gottesnähe und Schadenzauber: Die Magie in der griechisch-römischen Antike* (München, 1996); eds. P. Schäfer and H.G. Kippenberg, *Envisioning Magic: A Princeton Seminar and Symposium* (Leiden, 1997). For an overview of the different connotations of the term *magos* and, among others, the development in a derogatory sense, including further references, see A.F. de Jong, *Traditions of the Magi: Zoroastrianism in Greek and Latin Literature* (Leiden, 1997), pp. 387–403.

[4] Magic and miracles also have, of course, a legitimate place in the literary canon and even in historical reports. See for example R. Reitzenstein, *Hellenistische Wundererzählungen* (Leipzig, 1906), p. 16: "Daneben dringt die Wundererzählung, und zwar gerade diejenige, welche lehrenden, d.h. religiösen Zweck verfolgt, auch in die große Literatur und strebt nach prunkvoller Form"; A. Jensen, *Thekla-Die Apostelin: Ein apokrypher Text neu entdeckt* (Freiburg/etc., 1995), p. 98: "(. . .) gewisse mirakulöse Beigaben auch in die Berichte von Martyrien eingegangen (. . .) deren Historizität in keiner Weise bezweifelt werden kann"; G.W.H. Lampe, "Miracles and Early Christian Apologetic", *Miracles: Cambridge Studies in Their Philosophy and History*, ed. C.F.D. Moule (London, 1965), pp. 203–218, who notes that even 'serious' authors reproduce legends, for example Eusebius (*Historia Ecclesiastica*. I.13).

[5] Outperformance of non-Christian miracle-workers is not an issue in the *Acts of Thecla*. For a striking example thereof, see the controversy between Simon Magus and the apostle Peter in the *Acts of Peter*. On the aspect of propaganda and miracle as a sign of the true apostle see for example, Schüssler Fiorenza, *Aspects of Religious Propaganda*, and J.-M. van Cangh, "Miracles évangéliques – Miracles apocryphes", *The Four Gospels 1992: Festschrift Frans Neirynck* III, eds. F. Van Segbroeck et al. (Leuven, 1992), pp. 2277–2319, esp. p. 2279, who refers to the miraculous in *Pistis Sophia*, which, according to Van Cangh "sert donc à la fois à la 'production de la foi' et à la légitimation de la parole des apôtres". Lampe, "Miracles and Early Christian Apologetic", pp. 206–208, refers among others to Peter's speech on the day of Pentecost: 'Jesus, a man attested of God by mighty works and wonders and signs' and Athanasius' *De incarnatione* 15 and 18: 'His miracles demonstrate that he is God'.

[6] That is to say, Origin records Celsus saying these words in his apologetic work *Contra Celsum* I.6 and II.32.

mental role in what might be summarized as: convincing and converting prospective adherents and consolidating the faith of the communities represented in the narratives. From the perspective of the teller(s) of the tales activities within this sphere meet, of course, with approval. The miraculous is as it were a sanctioning device. The 'unbelievers', of course, are ascribed a different perception of the activities of the apostle. In their misunderstanding eyes, for example, the apostle Paul resorts to magical practices in order to convert people to the Christian belief. The ambiguous attitude, known from many ancient literary texts, towards 'magic' which could be labeled either as good or as bad, is thus represented and identifying who says what about whom and why comes to the fore, not least because it functions as a marker of difference. The aim of this paper is, firstly, to delineate how this finds its expression in the narrative.

Secondly, in the ancient world view the realm of the natural and the supernatural were interrelated:

> A tree could not build a house, but a person could. A person could not make it rain, but a god could. A normal human being could not heal the sick with a word or a touch, or cast out an evil demon, or bring the dead back to life, but a divine human could. Such a person stood in a special relation to the gods (...) For most ancients the question was thus not whether miracles were possible (...) the only questions for most ancient persons were (a) who was able to perform these deeds and (b) what was the source of their power?[7]

With this in mind and in view of the major role which is accorded to women in this narrative, I will seek to visualize what the miraculous events as related in the *AThe* reveal regarding the situation and status of women in (at least some, ascetic) Christian communities, or: what does the fact that women are cast as active agents in and during the miraculous events tell us about the validation, legitimacy and credence of their actions and position?

The Acts of Thecla

In the early centuries of Christianity the *Acts of Thecla*, also known as the Acts of Paul and Thecla and/or as a part of the *Acts of Paul*,

---

[7] B.D. Ehrman, *The New Testament: A Historical Introduction to the Early Christian Writings* (New York/Oxford, 1997), p. 199.

was a popular and widespread text. After the church rejected the work and branded it as apocryphal,[8] it hovered on the margins of the Christian churches. But of late these Acts, together with a number of other 'forgotten novels of the Church', are no longer pushed aside as 'silly stories believed by the common herd' but are again attracting their due attention.

The *AThe* probably date from the middle of the second century C.E. The early Christian writer Tertullian designates (circa 200) as the author a presbyter in Asia Minor, who, according to him, fabricated writings which he attributed to Paul. The presbyter, according to Tertullian, acted out of love for Paul and finally had to resign from office.[9] Despite the problematic manuscript tradition of Tertullian's treatise *De baptismo*,[10] most experts do not doubt Tertullian's statement concerning the author. Nonetheless some caution is called for, not only because pseudepigraphy was a known and accepted phenomenon in the ancient world, but especially with a view to the context of the statement itself, namely Tertullian's polemic against women's claim, on the precedence of Thecla's 'acts', to the right to preach and to baptize. Tertullian's treatise does however provide a terminus ante quem of some time before the end of the second century C.E.,[11] and constitutes a witness to women's ecclesiastical activities and authority in the 2nd century C.E. There are many more

---

[8] The 'Liber qui appellatur *Actus Theclae et Pauli*' is rejected in the Gelasian Decree (6th Century, but the Decree may contain older parts); the *Travels of Paul* (*Acts of Paul*) in the Stichometry of Nicephorus (probably 4th Century), and the *Acts of Paul* in the Catalogue of the Sixty Canonical Books (7th Century). See for example J.K. Elliott, *The Apocryphal New Testament: A Collection of Apocryphal Christian Literature in an English Translation* (Oxford, 1993), pp. xxiii–v and p. 350.

[9] *De baptismo* 17, written between 198 and 206 C.E.

[10] See for example S.L. Davies, "Women, Tertullian and the *Acts of Paul*", *Semeia* 38 (1986), pp. 139–143 and the "Response: Thomas W. Mackay", *Semeia* 38 (1986), pp. 145–149; W. Rordorf, "Tertullien et les Actes de Paul (à propos de *bapt.* 17,5)", *Autour de Tertullien: Hommage à René Braun II* (Nice, 1990), pp. 151–160, and recently, A. Hilhorst, "Tertullian on the Acts of Paul", *The Apocryphal Acts of Paul and Thecla*, ed. J.N. Bremmer (Kampen, 1996), pp. 150–163.

[11] For a date in the first half of the second century, see W. Rordorf, "In welchem Verhältnis stehen die apokrypen Paulusakten zur kanonischen Apostelgeschichte und zu den Pastoralbriefen?", *Text and Testimony: Essays on New Testament and Apocryphal Literature in Honour of A.F.J. Klijn*, eds. T. Baarda et al. (Kampen, 1988), pp. 225–241, pp. 227–237; on the arguments for allowing a large period of time (A.D. 140–200) within which to date the *AThe*, see for example Hilhorst, "Tertullian on the Acts of Paul".

witnesses to Thecla's popularity and importance, for example a host of references to the story in various writings,[12] and in tributes paid to her in archaeological monuments and iconography.[13]

Ever since interest in the *Apocryphal Acts of the Apostles* (*AAA*) has been revived, their genre and social background have been important areas of study, but in neither of these fields a consensus has been reached. The hypotheses that the *AAA* are (oral) narratives which originated in ascetic circles of women, or that the *AThe* is written by a woman, have elicited criticism.[14] I shall limit myself here and now to the suggestion that the author who wrote the *Acts of Paul* based his composition of this specific narrative on more than one tradition. As the Antioch episode, in which the interests of women are the decisive factor, differs from the other episodes of the *AP*, it seems very likely that this tradition originated in a group in which women occupied an important place. The author may have inserted this anomalous tradition in his Paul-oriented framework in order to defend the position of women because dissension arose regarding their status in ascetic communities.[15]

---

[12] For example Ps. Chrysostom's *Panegyric to Thecla*; Augustin, *Contra Faustum* 30.4; *De virginitate* 44; *Sermones* 354.5.5; Ambrose, *De virginibus* 2.19.21; Jerome, *Epistulae* 22.41; Methodius, *Symposium* esp. logos 11,56–58.

[13] See C. Nauerth and R. Warns, *Thekla: Ihre Bilder in der früh-christlichen Kunst* (Wiesbaden, 1981); R. Warns, "Weitere Darstellungen der heiligen Thekla", *Studien zur frühchristlichen Kunst* 2 (Wiesbaden, 1986), pp. 75–137.

[14] See for example S.L. Davies, *The Revolt of the Widows: The Social World of the Apocryphal Acts* (London, 1980), who suggests that the *AAA* not only originated in communities of women/widows but must have been written by a woman. For the hypothesis of an oral (folk)tradition of women and/or the possibility of female authors, see R.S. Kraemer, "The Conversion of Women to Ascetic Forms of Christianity", *Signs* 6 (1980), pp. 298–307; D.R. MacDonald, *The Legend and the Apostle: The Battle for Paul in Story and Canon* (Philadelphia, 1983); V. Burrus, *Chastity as Autonomy: Women in the Stories of the Apocryphal Acts* (Lewiston/Queenston, 1987). For a critical reaction, see for example P. Dunn, "Women's Liberation, the *Acts of Paul*, and Other Apocryphal Acts of the Apostles: A Review of Some Recent Interpreters", *Apocrypha* 4 (1993), pp. 245–261 and J.-D. Kaestli, "Fiction littéraire et réalité sociale: Que peut-on savoir de la place des femmes dans le milieu de production des Actes Apocryphes des Apôtres?", *Apocrypha* 1 (1990), pp. 279–302, who concludes: "En définitive, les divers arguments avancés par les tenants d'une lecture 'féministe' des Actes apocryphes s'avèrent insuffisamment fondés. Sauf dans le cas des *AcThecl*, on ne peut pas situer la genèse de ces récits dans une communauté de 'veuves'. Seule une étude de chaque texte dans sa singularité et dans sa totalité pourra évaluer à sa juste mesure la contribution des Actes à la connaissance historique du christianisme ancien, et du rôle qu'y ont joué les femmes".

[15] For further arguments see M. Misset-van de Weg, *Sara & Thecla: Verbeelding van vrouwen in 1 Petrus en de Acta Theclae* (Utrecht, 1998).

A Brief Outline:

The *AThe* centres on a young woman, Thecla, who becomes fascinated both by the Christian message of asceticism and resurrection and the bearer of that message, the apostle Paul. Her decision to answer Paul's call to renounce the ways of the world, leads her to severing all ties with her family and her fiancé and to join Paul. This 'act of Thecla' has severe consequences. In her home town, Iconium, she is condemned to be burned alive because she refuses to be married. She is, however, miraculously saved from being burned to death at the stake and joins Paul again. He takes her to Antioch, where he abandons her to cope for herself. She fights off a prominent citizen who sexually harasses her, but this results in her condemnation to be thrown before wild animals. During the entire ordeal she receives much support from the women of Antioch and the queen Tryphaena in particular. Thecla survives the fight with the wild animals in the arena through a chain of miraculous events. Finally, she joins Paul for the third and last time. She then takes her leave and goes her own way after she has been authorized to go and teach the word of God.

The 'Magos' and the 'Anomos'

The main event of the opening scene of the *AThe* is the arrival of the apostle Paul in Iconium, accompanied by two impostors Demas and Hermogenes. Paul is explicitly introduced as a charismatic person, as a man 'full of charisma' (*charitos plêrê*) [3]. He is warmly received by Onesiphorus, an Iconian Christian, and his family, who escort him to their house. In the *ekklêsia*, gathered together in the house of Onesiphorus, Paul speaks 'the word of God concerning self-control and resurrection', in the form of a series of beatitudes [5, 6]. Thecla, a young unmarried woman (*parthenos*), who lives next door to Onesiphorus, sits at her window and hears Paul speak. She is fascinated by his words and when she sees many married and unmarried women entering Onesiphorus' house, she very much wants to join them and see Paul in person. When Thecla continues to sit motionless, listening day and night at the window, her mother, Theocleia, becomes increasingly worried. She seeks the help of Thamyris, Thecla's fiancé and relates to him how her daughter is completely mesmerized, confused, 'bound (*dedemenê*) to the window like a spider by his words' [9], captivated by the words of a stranger and how a strange passion seems to have a hold on her, in short how a spell has been cast on her.

Theocleia's interpretation of her daughter's emotional state, brings to mind the notion of the 'wonderful' power or irrational impact of speech (*logos*), which was believed to stir passions and to deceive.[16] Such features as the repetition of 'Blessed are . . .' in the beatitudes—the 'words of God' spoken by Paul—the contents of which startle and enchant Thecla, might substantiate this association.

Allusions to magical motifs and practices or the results thereof, are also discernable in such elements as closed doors that cannot be an obstacle; the invocation of the name of (a) God; the elements water and fire; the sign of the cross; and the reference to Paul as a stranger (*xenos*) [8, 13, 19 and cf. 12] which might contain the implicit allegation that he is a *magos*.[17] A core term, especially in chapter 8 is, however, 'binding' (*deô*, and the related terms *atenizô, proskeimai, kratô*) by which Theocleia suggests that Thecla has fallen prey to an erotic magic spell.[18] This theme of 'binding' is taken up again on another symbolic level after Paul has been arrested. Paul is brought before the Governor who listens to him carefully, and is thrown in prison where he has to remain until the Governor has more time to listen to him. Thecla, meanwhile, who up and until that moment had been virtually comatose, gets up and takes action:

---

[16] J. de Romilly, *Magic and Rhetoric in Ancient Greece* (Cambridge/London, 1975), esp. pp. 75–88, argues how the old alliance between magic and rhetoric, embodied in, for example, Gorgias, was revived in the first two centuries C.E. It concerns (sublime) speech that produces enchantment and ecstasy, startles (*sun ekplêxei*) and acquires an influence and power that is irresistible.

[17] The status of the magician as a 'stranger' was a known concept, which did not represent a xenophobic reaction but corresponded with the social status of the *magos*, who 'is always the other, not us'—F. Graf, "How to Cope with a Difficult Life", in: eds. Schäfer and Kippenberg, *Envisioning Magic*, p. 112. It should of course be noted that not every *xenos* was considered a *magos*. For the accusation of '*magos*' see for example Poupon, "l'Accusation de Magie", pp. 73–76.

[18] Cf. Poupon, "l'Accusation de Magie", p. 73: "Or, l'on sait que l'un des pouvoirs revendiqués par tout magicien était précisément de faire naître ou mourir à son gré la passion amoureuse. Il faut bien reconnaître que le spectacle de Thècle à sa fenêtre, dans une immobilité hypnotique, avait de quoi légitimement inquiéter ses proches."; J.N. Bremmer, "Magic, Martyrdom and Women's Liberation", *The Apocryphal Acts of Paul and Thecla*, ed. Bremmer, p. 42. On fettering and unfettering, see W. Burkert, *Creation of the Sacred: Tracks of Biology in Early Religions* (Cambridge/London, 1996), pp. 118–121; and see for example the magic song of the Erinyes (*hymnos desmios*) and the magic formulas (*katadesma*), better known as *defixiones*.

> But Thecla during the night,
> having taken off her bracelets,
> gave them to the doorkeeper.
> And when the door had been opened for her
> she went to the prison.
> And giving a mirror made of silver to the jailer
> she went in to Paul.
> And sitting at his feet
> (...)
> her faith increased and she kissed his fetters. [18]

Both the gestures and the items (bracelets, mirror, fetters) may symbolize that Thecla lays aside the ties that bind her to and 'mirror' her former image which was related to marriage and 'the world' (*kosmos*), both of which ascetics are encouraged to renounce.[19] The symbolism is at its height when, sitting at Paul's feet, Thecla kisses his fetters and thus embraces new chains, binding herself as it were to Paul and the Christian faith.

Another suggestion of erotic magic, again connected with binding, occurs when Thecla's family discovers her disappearance. They set out to look for her and finally find her in the prison with Paul 'as it were bound together (*sundedemenên*) in loving affection' [19]. The readers cannot miss the erotic overtones, nor are they meant to miss it, especially because it can be the making of an exciting story. However, it seems that the suggestion of erotic magic is deliberately relegated to the (shortsighted) eyes of the beholders: Thecla's family.[20] In other words, the readers may for some time be in two minds, but are little by little steered towards leaving the erotic interpretation to the pagan onlookers and are at the same time guided towards grasping and adjusting to the ascetic (over)tones and message.

Meanwhile, Theocleia's assessment of Paul, amounting to her allegation that he is a magician, reverberates throughout the entire episode. First, when Thecla's fiancé Thamyris bribes Demas and Hermogenes in order to wring information from them by asking them who the deceiver and stranger is who is so much loved by his fiancée [13, 15]. Demas and Hermogenes reply that they do not know who the man is and succeed in convincing Thamyris to get

---

[19] See in the *AThe*: 'Blessed are they who renounced this world'; 'blessed are they who, because of love of God, have departed from the ways of the world'; 'blessed are the bodies of the virgins' [5, 6].

[20] See Theocleia's interpretation of Thecla's 'conversion'.

Paul arrested and convicted [12]). The result is that the opinion of the Iconian crowd is manoeuvred towards accusing Paul of being a *magos* and to bring pressure to bear on the Governor:

> And the whole crowd spoke:
>   Lead the magician away
>   because he has seduced all our women.
> And the crowds let themselves be persuaded
> (...)
> Now when Paul was brought forward
> again the crowd shouted even louder:
>   He is a magician,
>   away with him. [15, 20]

Whereas forms of unsanctioned religious activity mostly met with tolerance and the evidence for legal actions against *magoi* is sparse, they could be at risk. In fact, although magic was commonplace, magic and the magician were generally considered illegal throughout the history of the Roman empire. Magicians could face capital punishment, they might either be burned at the stake, thrown before wild animals or crucified. A conflict over magic was usually not dominated by believers versus rationalists, but was often related to social tensions and asymmetries of power, albeit intertwined with religious matters, and in that sense a conflict between two sorts of believers. For instance, from the standpoint of the accuser the magician could be in league with 'wrong' powers or the demonic, while from the standpoint of the supporter, he or she sanctioned the 'right' powers. In other words, the labelling is relative and depends upon who responds to whom. Hence, the accusation of the practice of magic could be used as a means to exert social control, and a *magos* was often condemned on primarily social grounds. Literary sources in which the charge of magic appears often reveal such primarily polemical programmes.[21] In the *AThe* we encounter an example of such a

---

[21] See E.R. Dodds, *Pagan and Christian in an Age of Anxiety* (Cambridge, 1965), p. 124; Aune, "Magic in Early Christianity", pp. 1518–1519 and p. 1522; A.M. Tupet, "Rites magiques dans l'antiquité romaine", *Aufstieg und Niedergang der römischen Welt* II.16.3 (1986), pp. 2591–2675; Poupon, "l'Accusation de Magie", p. 83; C.R. Phillips III, "*Nullum Crimen sine Lege*: Socioreligious Sanctions on Magic", *Magika Hiera*, eds. Faraone and Obbink, pp. 260–276, esp. p. 261 and his "The Sociology of Religious Knowledge in the Roman Empire to A.D. 284", *Aufstieg und Niedergang der römischen Welt* II.16.3 (1986), pp. 2677–2773, esp. p. 2719, who also refers to later Christian developments when ostensibly Christian practices of which the institutional Church did not approve were labeled as 'magic' and 'Theological and political triumph

programme, namely the strategy of labelling Paul, the opponent, as a morally suspect *magos* in order to get rid of him.

The interpretation and attitude of Thecla's mother might, however, also reflect a known mechanism to save the face and more importantly the honor of her family. A girl who eluded parental control, could be the cause of a social tragedy and a fall in the fortunes of a house.[22] The claim that a *magos* made her do it could alleviate the pain or was less hurtful then a girl's voluntary wantonness.[23]

After Thecla and Paul are found together in the prison, they are both put on trial. The Governor, who is said to be extremely vexed, ordered Paul to be flogged and expels him from the city. The grounds for the verdict are not mentioned, but it seems likely that the Governor meets the demands of Thamyris and the crowd, which would mean that Paul is indeed punished as a *magos* who seduced the women of Iconium and Thecla in particular. At first glance, the pleasure with which the Governor listens to Paul's explanation of who he is and what he teaches, makes it seem likely that the main reason for Paul's conviction is not the contents of his teaching as such (see [17] and [20]). Moreover, when Demas and Hermogenes try to convince Thamyris to accuse Paul of being a Christian, it is clearly expressed that the Governor 'kept his wits about him' [16]. However, when it is Thecla's turn to be tried Theocleia's words do link the daughter's *anomia* with the apostle's teaching:

> Theocleia, her mother, cried out, saying:
> Burn the lawless one,
> burn her that is no bride
> in the middle of the theatre,
> in order that all the women who have been taught by this (man) may be afraid. [20]

---

intermingled as repressive measures were instituted against those Christians and pagans perceived to be in league with the Dark Powers and hence disloyal to Church and State'.

[22] The last paragraph of the *AThe* may very well be an indication of an awareness of such a catastrophe awaiting parents whose daughters, in the manner of Thecla, left them: "And after she had sent for her mother, she said to her: 'Theocleia, mother, are you able to believe that a Lord lives in the heavens? Because if it is money you desire, the Lord shall give it to you through me, if it is the child you desire, I am standing here beside you'" [43].

[23] Cf. J.J. Winkler, "The Constraints of Eros", *Magika Hiera*, eds. Faraone and Obbink, pp. 214–243, esp. p. 233.

In the end it becomes clear that the Iconian authorities are less disturbed by the male *magos* than by the female adherent of a life of celibacy. The *magos* does not get away scot-free, but it is his 'victim' who has to bear the brunt of severe repressive measures. Why? Because she committed the crime of discarding the customs of the Iconians and breaking the laws which they considered of vital importance for the welfare of the city.[24] We might conclude today that given the fact that the 'seducer' is punished mildly while the 'seduced' receives capital punishment, we detect here a clear case of 'blaming the victim'. Another (possibly anachronistic) observation might be that the absence of a father, a brother or any other male relative and the disappearance of Thamyris from the narrative, shifts a disproportionate amount of blame on the woman, Theocleia. Finally, this disturbing scene might be interpreted as an effort of a desperate woman who had already distanced herself from and even mourned her daughter. After Thecla's social death she is now, in view of the family honor, trying to salvage what she can by demanding Thecla's physical death for the well-being of the city.

Metamorphoses

Following the trial the Governor and the crowd immediately leave for the theatre, awaiting the spectacle, but

> Thecla, like a lamb in the wilderness looks around for the shepherd,
> so she was seeking Paul,
> and when she was looking at the crowd
> she saw the Lord sitting there in the shape of Paul. [21]

An account of metamorphosis is a well-known element of Hellenistic magical belief and a recurring feature in Greek literature of old. As a theme it surfaces frequently in the *AAA*.[25] Jesus appears in many different forms, for example as one of the apostles, as a child or as a sailor.[26] In the *AThe* Jesus's appearance clearly supports Thecla,

---

[24] On the protection of marriage in a society with a population 'grazed thin by death', see P. Brown, *The Body and Society: Men, Women and Sexual Renunciation in Early Christianity* (New York, 1988; Repr. London/Boston, 1991), p. 5 ff.

[25] On aspects of metamorphosis in the *AAA*, see P.J. Lalleman, "Polymorphy of Christ", *The Apocryphal Acts of John*, ed. J.N. Bremmer (Kampen, 1995), pp. 97–118.

[26] For Jesus in the form of an apostle, see for example the *Acts of Andrew* 47: 'Maximilla, led by the Lord disguised as Andrew, went to the prison again with

who is receiving her first reward for choosing the ascetic lifestyle: 'Blessed are the pure in heart, for they shall see God'.[27] The effect is amazing: she is transformed from a frightened lamb into a woman radiating strength (*dynamis*):[28]

> when she was brought in naked,
> the Governor wept and marvelled at her inner strength
> (...)
> And she, assuming the shape of the cross mounted the pyre. [22][29]

The betrayal by someone close to her, the Pilate-like attitude of the Governor during the trial, the theme of the lamb, the shape of the cross are elements that, when added up, may be pointing towards another narrative 'metamorphosis' of Thecla into a Christlike figure. The re-presentation of the crucified Christ became a common theme in Christian martyrological texts. The representation of Jesus's death and crucifixion functioned as a coping mechanism. In order to endure the horrific pain, the martyrs were able to reconfigure its meaning by transforming the otherwise annihilating pain into the molding of the body to the suffering of Jesus and the assurance of heavenly reward.[30]

Iphidama'; the *Acts of Peter* 22: "In my sleep I saw you (...) you cried even more loudly, 'Come, our true sword, Jesus Christ (...)' And at once a man who looked like you, Peter, came with a sword"; the *Acts of Thomas* 11: "And he saw the Lord Jesus talking with the bride. He had the appearance of Judas Thomas, the apostle".

[27] As has been pointed out by S. McGinn, "The Acts of Thecla", *Searching the Scriptures II: A Feminist Commentary* ed. Schüssler Fiorenza (New York, 1994), pp. 800–828, esp. p. 815.

[28] *Dynamis* can mean power, the ability to do anything, authority, but has also spiritual connotations, such as magical power and the manifestation of divine power (see Matt. 11:20–21).

[29] For the translation of the last part of this sentence, and the connotation of triumph in assuming the shape of the cross, see Bremmer, "Magic, Martyrdom", p. 49. I have also duly noted P. Cox Miller's warning in her "Desert Asceticism and 'The Body from Nowhere'", *Journal of Early Christian Studies* 2/2 (1994), pp. 137–153, to weigh such theologically motivated interpretations which associate "one of the least comprehensible forms of ascetic display with a most orthodox Christian theology of the cross" (p. 145).

[30] On the subject for example R. Valantasis, "Narrative Strategies and Synoptic Quandaries: A Response to Dennis MacDonald's Reading of Acts of Paul and *Acts of Peter*", *The Society of Biblical Literature 1992 Seminar Papers* (Atlanta, 1992), pp. 234–239, esp. p. 238; A. Jensen, *Gottes selbstbewußte Töchter: Frauenemanzipation im frühen Christentum?* (Freiburg/etc., 1992), pp. 245–252; M. Tilley, "The Ascetic Body and the (Un)Making of the World of the Martyr", *Journal of the American Academy of Religion* 59/3 (1991), pp. 467–479.

Saved by the Miracle

The second miraculous event occurs after Thecla has mounted the pyre and the fire is lighted and blazes. At that moment God takes pity. He makes the earth rumble and causes hail and rain to come down in large quantities, so that the fire is extinguished. Many people die as a result of this violent event, but Thecla is saved. God is undoubtedly the agent of this miracle. However, in the ensuing episode in the open tomb, much of the credit goes to Paul, for Thecla's salvation is described as the answer to his prayers.

> When she was brought to the tomb to Paul,
> bending his knees and praying and saying
>> Holy Father, Jesus Christ, let not the fire touch Thecla but stand by her, for she is yours,
>
> she, standing behind (him), cried out
>> Father, who made the heaven and the earth,
>> Father of the holy child,
>> I praise you because you have saved me that I might see Paul.
>
> And when he stood up Paul saw her and said
>> God, knower of hearts,
>> the Father of our Lord Jesus Christ,
>> I praise you because you hastened to grant me what I asked. [24]

This somewhat surprising turn manoeuvres Paul into a special position. The miracle as a result of Paul's prayer accentuates that he is a true apostle who had been operating in Iconium under divine sanction.[31] At the same time a misunderstanding is rectified: Paul is not the kind of magician the Iconians took him for. He is not a *magos* who seduces women, but he is what he claimed to be: the teacher of the things revealed to him by the living God who sent him to carry out that task.[32] Thecla's thanksgivings, directed to God, for saving her, for delivering her from the fire, convey the conviction that is maintained throughout the narrative: it is ultimately God who works all miracles via others.[33]

---

[31] The view that the performance of miracles is one of the signs of the true apostle can also be deduced from the New Testament letters of Paul. See Goldin, "The Magic of Magic", pp. 122–3; Achtemeier, "Jesus and the Disciples", 150–152.

[32] "(...) The living God (...) has sent me (...) If then I teach the things revealed to me by God..." [17].

[33] "Father (...) I praise you, because you saved me [from the fire] [24]; Lord God (...) who rescued me from the fire [31]; My God and God of this house, where the light shone for me, Christ Jesus, the son of God, my helper in the prison,

A few other remarkable aspects that characterize the salvific miracle need to be mentioned. Firstly, in striking contradistinction to the extensive descriptions of the events that are soon to take place in Antioch, the attention paid to the miracle as such and the ensuing effects, is quite minimal. No mention is made of the reaction of the people of Iconium, which could mean that no missionary effect is assigned to this particular miracle. This is amazing, because even punitive miracles—after all this miracle does not only save, but kills as well—usually produce converts, or one might say frighten people into conversion. It seems that-again different from the Antioch episode—the emphasis in this episode is conversion through the word.[34] Nevertheless, when all is said and done, Paul's entire mission to Iconium seems to result in one explicit convert only: Thecla. The only response of the Iconian authorities to Thecla's miraculous rescue appears to be her expulsion from their and her city:

> because I did not want to be married to Thamyris
> I have been driven out of the city. [26]

Secondly, Thecla's choice not to marry Thamyris, to break with her family, thereby breaking the law of the Iconians, is divinely sanctioned through the miracle. The propagandistic side of the miracle might thus be that women are called to choose an ascetic lifestyle and to endure the consequences, because, although they may have to suffer and their family may declare or wish them dead, God will be on their side. The blessings that await them are spelled out in the beatitudes.

> Blessed are the bodies of the virgins:
> they shall be pleasing unto God,
> and they shall not lose the reward for their chastity.
> For the word of the father shall become for them a work of salvation
> in the day of his son
> and they shall find peace for ever and ever. [6]

---

helper before the Governors, helper in the fire, helper among the wild animals, you are God, and to you be the glory for ever, amen" [42].

[34] See c. [7] and [9].

On the Road to Antioch

Following the trial, Paul, together with Onesiphorus and his family, has gone to an open tomb on the road from Iconium to Daphne. After six days, one of Onesiphorus' children is buying food and meets Thecla who is trying to find Paul. The child takes her to him. When Thecla has been reunited with Paul, she announces that she wishes to follow him. He will not have it, because, as he says, there is wickedness all around and she is beautiful. His additional remark that she might not be able to resist another temptation is astonishing and a debasement of this young woman who just bore the worst test. But sure enough, such a woman does not let herself be put off and it is thus that Thecla tries another approach in answer to the stereotypical gender biased reaction and says: 'Just give me the seal in Christ and no trial will touch me' [25]. Thereupon Paul tells her to have patience. Does a suggestion of a magical protective power of baptism resound here, and does this second reaction of Paul indicate a rejection of such a notion? Perhaps, but the narrative does not leave it at that: Paul will be proven wrong on both counts. In the following episode in Antioch, Thecla will amply demonstrate that she is indeed quite capable of resisting temptation and the moment Thecla has baptized herself, she will be surrounded and protected by fire.

> But she had indeed thrown herself into the water
> in the name of Jesus Christ
> (...)
> and a cloud of fire surrounded her
> so that the wild animals did not touch her
> nor could her nakedness be seen
> (...)
> And they tied her by the feet between the bulls
> (...)
> but the flame surrounding her burned through the ropes [34 and 35]

Upon their arrival in Antioch, a prominent citizen, named Alexander, desires Thecla at first sight. He offers Paul money and presents because he wants to have her. The answer of the charismatic apostle, who has been sent by God to draw people away from corruption and immorality [17], is that he denies Thecla altogether by saying: 'I do not know the woman of whom you speak, nor is she mine' [26]. Alexander, who is identified as 'being a powerful man', apparently feels free to accost her right there and then in the middle of the street. Thecla

> however did not put up with it
> but was looking for Paul,
> and she cried out bitterly, saying
>> Do not violate the stranger,
>> do not violate the servant of God.
>> I am a prominent (woman) of the Iconians
>> and because I did not want to be married to Thamyris
>> I have been driven out of the city.
> And grabbing Alexander she tore off his cloak
> and she took the crown off his head
> and made him stand there as an object of ridicule. [26]

Thecla is brought before the Governor, who finds her guilty of sacrilege, and condemns her to be thrown before wild animals. The women of Antioch react immediately and strongly. They are shocked and protest most vehemently against this appalling and unholy judgment, but protests of women are of no avail. Thecla, who begs the Governor that she might 'remain pure' [27], which means to be spared rape, is taken in *custodia libera* and as a comfort by a wealthy woman named Tryphaena whose daughter has died. The day before the animal fight, Thecla, according to custom, is paraded in the streets together with the animals. She has been tied to a fierce lioness, but contrary to what the public must have assumed, the lioness does not harm her, but instead licks her feet. The onlookers are astounded [28], which is a known and welcome acclamation of the crowd to a miraculous event.[35]

A Dream-vision and the Miraculous Power of Prayer

After the parade, Tryphaena takes Thecla back to her house. This time the reason is made even more explicit. Tryphaena's daughter, Phalconilla, who had died, appears to her mother in a dream-vision and tells her:

---

[35] Prof.dr P.W. van der Horst kindly pointed out to me that the lion, licking the feet of the saints is known as a motif in hagiographical literature. In 3rd–6th century hagiography it represents the return to a paradisiacal situation.

> Mother you shall have Thecla,
> the desolate stranger,
> in my place
> that she may pray for me
> and I may be transferred to the place of the righteous. [28]

Upon Tryphaena's request Thecla asks God to grant the queen her wish that her daughter may have eternal life [28, 29]. Tryphaena in turn asks Thecla's God to save Thecla:

> God of Thecla my child,
> come to the aid of Thecla. [30]

Dreams, visions and metamorphoses qualify as miracles,[36] but can these prayers be counted as miraculous events? As has been noted, miracles in a Christian context are considered acts performed through God's power; prayer and the invocation of the name of God or Jesus are considered to be the empowering act.[37] The miracle that saved Thecla in Iconium is ascribed to Paul, or to be exact, described as an answer to his prayer. Thecla and Tryphaena's prayers can and ought to be appreciated in the same manner. Just like Paul, the women perform this empowering act, or, judging from the results, have been granted the same saving powers. Phalconilla is saved—transferred to the place of the righteous, or as is summarized later, raised from the dead!—Thecla is saved a second time and this has been preceded by Tryphaena's prayer.

Even though in the narration of the events that take place in Antioch the subject of teaching the word of God has not yet been raised, Tryphaena's words 'Now I believe that the dead are raised, now I believe that my child lives' [39], underline Phalconilla's 'salvation' as the result of a miracle, and hence Thecla as the agent. Awakening faith as a particular and important aspect or the intended effect of a miracle is of course a known element of *Christian* miracle stories.

---

[36] On visions, dreams, etcetera, as miracles, see *e.g.* Reitzenstein, *Hellenistische Wundererzählungen*, p. 9 n. 4: "Vision und Traum gehören in antiker Betrachtung (bei Christen wie Heiden) immer zum Wunder; sie zeigen das Wirken und die Kraft Gottes".

[37] See for example, Achtemeier, "Jesus and the Disciples as Miracle Workers", p. 170 and p. 174. An interesting view on the power of Christian prayer, that reveals parallels with the *AThe*, is expressed by Tertullian (*De oratione* 29), who believes that prayer can "extort the rains of heaven, recall the souls of the departed from the very path of death, transform the weak, restore the sick, purge the possessed, open prison bars, loose the bonds of the innocent".

To be sure, Tryphaena makes her statement after she has witnessed many more prodigies, which undoubtedly contributed to her 'belief'.

A Chain of Miraculous Events

'When dawn came', on the day of the execution, Thecla is literally taken from Tryphaena, who accompanies her to the arena—a most unusual act for a queen to perform. Thecla is stripped and thrown into the arena. Lions and bears are driven towards her. A first wondrous event, however, occurs: a lioness lays herself down at Thecla's feet, defends her against a she-bear and a lion, but is killed while wrestling with the lion. The women, who remain present, protesting continuously, lament the death of Thecla's helper, the lioness. Many more animals are driven into the arena. Thecla, even though she is labeled a '*thêriomachê*' [30] does not fight. On the contrary, she prays.[38] She turns around, sees a pit filled with water (and seals) and decides it is time for her to be baptized. She throws herself into the water and baptizes herself, while the women and this time the whole crowd are begging her not to throw herself into the water. The Governor bursts into tears. The seals in the pit are killed by lightning and a cloud of fire surrounds Thecla so that she is not only protected from the animals, but also shielded from people gazing at her naked body. Her body is no longer public property!

However, the end result of the sudden compassion of the crowd and the Governor is that more fearsome animals are let loose. When that happens only the women are again or still frantic. They take action by throwing herbs into the arena which anesthetize the animals. Alexander does not give up and convinces the Governor to have Thecla tied by her feet between fearsome bulls. But the flame that now surrounds Thecla burns through the ropes and again she remains unharmed. Tryphaena can no longer endure the horrific sight and faints. Her handmaidens, who may have anticipated that their message might intimidate the authorities, announce that the queen has died. Although it remains anybody's guess whether they did or did not plan their diagnosis, they are most certainly taken at

---

[38] The attitude of (total) surrender, is known from martyrology, see for example the *Passio Perpetuae* (19–21).

their word. The announcement frightens Alexander out of his wits. He begs the Governor to release Thecla lest the Emperor, upon receiving the message that and under which circumstances his relative Tryphaena has died, destroys him and the city.

The Governor orders Thecla's release and finally shows an interest in her identity by asking her who she is. Vouaux pointed out that the Governor's second question: "And what is there around you, that not even one of the wild animals touched you?" shows that the Governor reacts in accordance with the 'habitudes d'esprit' of his time, so that he must have anticipated an explanation in the sphere of magic.[39] Thecla, however, interrupts this line of thinking and testifies that her protection is connected with (her) faith in the living God and his Son, 'the refuge to the tempest-tossed; solace to the afflicted; shelter to the despairing' [37], whose servant she is.[40] Thereupon the Governor acknowledges and confirms her status of servant of God (*doulê tou theou*), to which she had already appealed when Alexander assaulted her in the street. The Governor issues a decree, saying:

> Thecla,
> the servant of God,
> the god-fearing woman,
> I release to you. [38][41]

Thecla is thus rehabilitated: she is a woman who honours God. Since new cults were often confronted with the accusation of *asebeia*, the opposite of *theosebeia*, Thecla's rehabilitation can also, albeit implicitly, be interpreted as serving the interests of the Christian community; it may be meant to hint at the official political approval of the religious movement to which Thecla belongs. The resounding cheer of the women of Antioch who are elated and praise God, saying: 'There is one God, he who has saved Thecla', in such a manner

---

[39] L. Vouaux, *Les Actes de Paul et ses lettres apocryphes* (Paris, 1913), p. 217: "il ne peut croire qu'à l'intervention de la magie; plusieurs textes latins ont avec justesse précisé sa pensée dans ce sens". One of the Latin versions of the *AThe* even records Thecla's response: *ego non sum maga, ut vos putatis sed*. . . .

[40] On the development of the image of God in the *AThe* as the helper of the powerless, see Misset-van de Weg, *Sara & Thecla*, p. 184.

[41] The decree resembles the laudatory speech (*laudatio*) expressed by Governors in order to clear the name of the accused. Cf. W.L. Schutter, *Hermeneutic and Composition in I Peter* (Tübingen, 1989), p. 16 n. 72.

that the city was shaken by the sound [38], might thus serve the same twofold purpose.[42]

The series of events in the arena reveals many intriguing and interesting aspects. From the beginning, the women of Antioch, including the queen Tryphaena, ventilate their anger, but the authorities are obviously in a position to ignore them.[43] The women, however are persistent and refuse to bow to their position of social disadvantage and lack of authority to influence the course of events. They resort to their own means of power.[44] They throw herbs into the arena with the miraculous result that all the animals 'are overcome as if by sleep'. They do not touch Thecla (cf. 22 and 34: *ouch hêpsato autês to pyr* (...) *hôste mête ta thêria haptesthai autês*) and the animals, moreover, are neither harmed nor killed.[45] The women's conspicuously nonviolent action is very much in contrast with the violence instigated by the men. Non-violence also characterizes Tryphaena's interventions. In an early stage, she had already tried to safeguard Thecla by crying out in order to frighten away Alexander [30], whereupon the Governor sent soldiers (!) to fetch Thecla. Tryphaena

---

[42] On the accusation of *asebeia* and the cheer *Eis theos*, see H.S. Versnel, *Inconsistencies in Greek and Roman Religion I. Ter Unus: Isis, Dionysos, Hermes. Three Studies in Henotheism* (Leiden/etc., 1990), p. 117, pp. 123–131 and p. 135.

[43] Under Roman law women were not allowed to represent another party, unless they were pursuing their own interest and/or profit. Cf. Y. Thomas, "The Division of the Sexes in Roman Law", *A History of Women in the West I: From Ancient Goddesses to Christian Saints*, ed. P. Schmitt Pantel (Cambridge/London, 1992), pp. 83–137, esp. p. 136.

[44] Useful definitions of authority and power are quoted by N. Steinberg, "Israelite Tricksters, Their Analogues and Cross-Cultural Study", *Semeia* 42 (1988), pp. 1–13, p. 6, from a passage of M.G. Smith, *Government in Zazzau, 1800–1950* (London, 1960), pp. 18–19: "Authority is, in the abstract, the right to make a particular decision and to command obedience (...) Power (...) is the ability to act effectively on persons or things, to make or secure favorable decisions which are not of right allocated to the individuals or their roles".

[45] A sophisticated command of drug compounding was common knowledge. It was not unusual for women (and men!) to know the magico-religious connotations of plants or herbs. Drugs were even considered to function as 'the hands of the gods'; see J. Scarborough, "The Pharmacology of Sacred Plants, Herbs, and Roots", *Magika Hiera*, eds. Faraone and Obbink, pp. 138–174, esp. p. 163. An interesting comparison can be made with Medea who used herbs to lull the guardian reptile of the golden fleece to sleep in Apollonius of Rhodes, *Argonautica* IV.156–158. In view of the above, I cannot endorse Achtemeier's conclusion in his "Jesus and the Disciples as Miracle Workers", pp. 169–170, that the Apocryphal Acts never so much as hint at the use of herbs or incantations, or magical devices in the description of the miracles. Apparently he does not consider the actions of the women to be magical acts, which might be due to his focus on the apostles as the mighty men of wonders.

still 'did not shrink away' (31), but not even her status of queen, which would evidently not be one of social or political disadvantage, did carry enough weight. She had to resort to supporting Thecla by escorting her to the arena and finally, analogous to the action of the lioness, she lays herself down, so to speak. Neither the actions of the lioness, nor the actions of the women of Antioch, nor even divine protection and intervention in the form of a cloud/flame of fire could impress the authorities or induce them to put a stop to the fight. It is finally Tryphaena's fainting in combination with the ploy of her handmaidens which terminates the ordeal. [36]

Female Wit

The actions of the women who do not have access to legitimate means of power are instigated by the desire to promote the well-being of those who lack authority, and prompted by their wit, which means the intelligence and understanding to make the right decision or take the right action in a particular situation. The women's wit calls to mind the quality called *mētis*, the cunning intelligence that is, for example, Odysseus' heroic characteristic, or the clever, resourceful, major element in his strategy that 'gives him a fuller understanding of the circumstances in which he and the other characters of the poem are operating and a greater power to shape the course of events.'[46] It is this particular manifestation of female wit which, in the *AThe*, is valued when the chain of miraculous events reaches its climax. And, the effect is such that Thecla is not only saved from the wild animals but also released. Subsequently, when Thecla in her concluding thanksgivings attributes her salvation undiscriminately to God's help, divine lustre is lent to the actions the women had the wit to take:

My God,
(...)
Christ Jesus,
son of God,
my helper in the prison,

[46] S. Murnaghan, "Penelope's *Agnoia*: Knowledge, Power, and Gender in the *Odyssey*", *Rescuing Creusa. New Methodological Approaches to Women in Antiquity*, ed. M. Skinner, A Special Issue of *Helios*, New Series 13/2 (1987), pp. 103–115, esp. p. 104.

helper before the Governors,
helper in the fire,
helper among the wild animals,
you are God
and to you be the glory for ever,
Amen. [42]

Thecla speaks these words when she has returned to Iconium. Prior to her return, she is invited back to Tryphaena's house, where she rests and teaches the word of God, 'so that the majority of the female servants also believed.' [40] When she has found out that Paul is in Myra, she joins him there and tells him that she is now baptized and that she is going to Iconium. Thereupon Paul commissions her to 'go and teach the word of God' [41]. The queen Tryphaena supplies her with the material requirements which allow her to be of independent means. Back in Iconium she thanks God in the house of Onesiphorus (see above) and sends for her mother to whom she offers her support.

And when she had given this witness
she went to Seleucia
and after enlightening many with the word of God
she fell into a beautiful sleep. [43]

In Conclusion

The results of conjoining the miraculous events and women in the *AThe* and the implications of this relation for an understanding of the position of women in (some, ascetic) early Christian communities, can now be summarized.

In the *AThe* the miraculous events serve the purpose of raising the matter of the legitimacy of the new religion of the ascetic Christians and its propagators and within this framework sub-aims can be distinguished. Firstly, when Paul is accused of being a *magos*, implying that he is an evil sorcerer because he seduces women, the charge is cleverly refuted and made to function as a propagandistic means to reveal Paul's or the apostle's divine empowerment. Hence, whereas the conclusion might be drawn that as far as the praxis is concerned magic and miracles interlock, a clear distinction is made when it comes to labelling the activities. Non-Christians are ingeniously saddled with magic in a pejorative sense; they are cast as being preoccupied with (erotic) magic and thus cannot but identify the apostle as a dangerous *magos*; there is nothing positive in the wake of 'magic'. Miraculous actions and events as opposed to magic validate the Christian message and messengers, lead to faith and praise of the one and only God; and ultimately the Christian faith leads to eternal life.

Secondly, in and through the miraculous events, an answer is provided to the problem of social tensions resulting from the conversion of women to an ascetic form of Christianity, which appears to be inextricably bound up with the problem of women's suffering as a result of asymmetry of power. In the Iconium episode both the metamorphosis, meant to support Thecla, and the miracle by which she is saved from the pyre, sanction a woman's decision to detach herself from her family and the societal norms and values she is supposed to embody. During the Antioch episode the legitimacy of women's right to a certain form of autonomy, including the inviolability of women's bodies, is confirmed in the chain of miraculous events that result in women's victory over a host of 'wild animals'. Thecla/woman, 'unbound' both from the things of the world and in the end from the apostle Paul, is set free and commissioned to pursue her apostolic activities. Therefore, the most important implication of the relation between women as both performers and beneficiaries of miracles and their position in the Christian community and society at large, is the validation of Thecla as a *doulē tou theou*, and thus of women's position of (apostolic) authority.

Thirdly, miracle working must be modified in the sense that the activity of the Christian miracle workers is mostly one of mediation or a manifestation of the power of God who is the 'true' miracle worker. With this in mind it can nevertheless be established that women are portrayed as important participants in effecting the miracles; they do indeed work miracles and/or need to work their own miracles. Thecla equals Paul as wonder worker as far as both means and effect are concerned; in fact she, and the women of Antioch outshine him. The chain of miracles in which the women function as intermediaries shows that the women 'produce' many converts, whereas in the *AThe* Paul can be credited with one convert only.

The women of Antioch resort to their own means-gendered and stereotypical, but effective-to achieve the miraculous termination of a situation of injustice and suffering. Their acts, revealing solidarity and wit, are successful and 'divine'. Above all they fulfil a critical function: the denouncement of asymmetry of power, or men's power over women. The success of their actions positively asserts and validates these women's commitment and underscores that women are not powerless, but sometimes even divinely empowered. Wonders never cease!

> Après qu'elle eut annoncé l'évangile de salut, qu'elle eut catéchisé, baptisé et enrôlé dans l'armée du Christi un grand nombre,
> qu'elle eut fait aussi beaucoup de miracles (...) elle ne mourut nullement.[47]

---

[47] Quoted from: A.-J. Festugière, *Sainte Thècle Saints Come et Damien Saints Cyr et Jean (Extraits) Saint Georges* (Paris, 1971), p. 19.

3

FATHERLY AND MOTHERLY CURING IN SIXTH-CENTURY GAUL: SAINT RADEGUND'S *MYSTERIUM*

Giselle de Nie

Introduction

In Poitiers, probably around the year 590, the Italian-born poet and priest Venantius Fortunatus (c. 540–c. 605) wrote one of the first biographies of a holy woman in the West: that of his intimate friend, the then just-deceased nun Saint Radegund (c. 520–87).[1] She was a Thuringian princess, captured on the battlefield, who had become a Frankish queen, but had later managed to leave her royal husband to embrace the religious life and found a convent in the above-mentioned city. Although she had been revered by most people as a saint already during her lifetime, her powerful personality and independent interpretation of the monastic life-style prescribed by the Rule of her convent—Fortunatus' poems show that, instead of strict withdrawal from the world, she cultivated religious friendships and literary tastes—had alienated the city's bishop; he resented being unable to assert his rightful authority as the convent's ecclesiastical supervisor. When the nuns' revolt after Radegund's death called the headstrong queen's reputation into question,[2] it was probably to restore the latter that Fortunatus undertook to write his encomiastic biography, in which we see only ascetic piety, humility and loving care.

---

[1] Venantius Fortunatus, *Vita sanctae Radegundis*, ed. B. Krusch, Monumenta Germaniae Historica (= MGH), Auctores Antiquissimi (= AA) 4.2 (Berlin, 1885), pp. 38–49. Tr. J.A. McNamara and J.E. Halborg, *Sainted Women of the Dark Ages* (Durham-London, 1992), pp. 70–86. On Fortunatus' life and career see: B. Brennan, "The career of Venantius Fortunatus", *Traditio* 41 (1985), pp. 49–78, and J. George, *Venantius Fortunatus: A Poet in Merovingian Gaul* (Oxford, 1992), pp. 4–34.

[2] Gregorius Turonensis, *Historiae* (ed. B. Krusch and W. Levison, MGH Scriptores rerum Merovingicarum (= SSrM) 1.1, editio altera (Berlin, 1951)) 10.16.

At approximately the same time that Fortunatus was writing, his friend and patron, the historian and hagiographer Bishop Gregory of Tours (539–94) included some holy women in his numerous brief notices on Gallic saints and their miracles, and wrote a biography of one: Monegunde. But he also wrote brief, admiring, passages about Radegund, stressing her queenly as well as her saintly qualities.[3] About fifteen years later, Baudonivia, a nun in Radegund's convent, wrote another biography of the saint to supplement that by Fortunatus, who is mentioned in her preface as then being bishop of Poitiers. Baudonivia presents Radegund as a queenly personality and a teacher, aspects which Fortunatus had, it seems intentionally, omitted.[4]

Although Greek women saints' miracles were being reported at least since the fourth century, in the West sainthood and miraculous curing had up to then been attributed only to men,[5] and the latter's cures tended to resemble those of their model, the fourth-

---

[3] Gregorius Turonensis, *In Gloria Confessorum* (ed. B. Krusch, MGH SSrM 1.2 (Hannover, 1885), pp. 484–561) 5, 16, 18, 24, 33, 42, 89, 102, 104, 107; Saint Monegunde: idem, *Vita Patrum* (MGH SSrM 1.2, pp. 661–744) 19. About Radegund: *Historiae* 3.4, 7; 6.29, 34; 7.36; 9.2, 42; and *In Gloria Confessorum* 104.

[4] Baudonivia, *Vita sanctae Radegundis*, ed. B. Krusch, MGH SSrM 2 (Hannover, 1888), pp. 377–95. Tr. McNamara and Halborg, *Sainted Women of the Dark Ages*, pp. 86–105. This biography reports only one other direct cure—in a manner which is not indicated, of a woman's eye-ailment—during her lifetime (c. 11), and an unspecified number through her tomb, especially of possessed and fevers but including that of an abbot's toothache (c. 25–8). On Radegund's life and career, see: B. Brennan, "St Radegund and the early development of her cult at Poitiers", *Journal of Religious History* 13 (1985), pp. 340–354. Recent studies of Radegund include: (Comité du XIVe Centenaire), *La riche personalité de Sainte Radegonde: Conférence et homilies* (Poitiers, 1988); Jean Leclercq, "La sainte Radegonde de Venance Fortunat et celle de Baudonivie", *Fructus Centesimus: Mélanges offerts à Gerard J.M. Bartelink*, eds. A.A.R. Bastiaensen et al., Instrumenta Patristica 19 (Steenbrugge, 1989), pp. 207–216; S. Gäbe, "Radegundis: sancta, regina, ancilla. Zum Heiligkeitsideal der Radegundisviten von Fortunat und Baudonivia", *Francia* 16 (1989), pp. 1–30; C. Papa, "Radegonda e Batilde: modelli di santita regia femminile nel regno Merovingio", *Benedictina* 36 (1989), pp. 13–33; R. Folz, *Les saintes reines du Moyen Age en Occident (VI–XIIIe siècles)*, Subsidia hagiographica 76 (Brussels, 1992), pp. 13–24. On the position of women in Frankish Gaul, see also: H.-W. Goetz, *Weibliche Lebensgestaltung im frühen Mittelalter* (Cologne, 1991), pp. 7–44.

[5] Cf. A. Rousselle, "La sage-femme et le thaumaturge dans la Gaule tardive. Les femmes ne font pas de miracles", *La médecine en Gaule. Villes d'eaux, sanctuaires des eaux*, ed. A. Pelletier (Paris, 1985), p. 248. On Greek women saints performing miracles, see: E. Giannarelli, "Women and miracles in Christian biography", *Studia Patristica* 25 (1991), pp. 376–380. See also: H.-W. Goetz, "Heiligenkult und Geschlecht: Geschlechts-spezifisches Wunderwirken in frühmittelalterlichen Mirakelberichten?", *Das Mittelalter* 1 (1996) 2, pp. 89–111.

century Saint Martin of Tours. Fortunatus and Gregory are thus the first to tell us about women's cures in Gaul, both during their lives and through their tombs after death. As far as we can tell from the reports, most of these cures do not differ significantly from those by men. Since the two women saints that we know most about, Monegund and Radegund, lived in a cloistered sphere, this must be one reason why they are reported as healing more women than men: very few men had access to them. Another reason is likely to be that women patients tended to feel more comfortable with a woman healer.[6] Not surprisingly, both saints also associated themselves closely with the memory of Saint Martin. Monegund established her monastic community in the *atrium* of his very church in Tours, and Radegund visited his various shrines before establishing herself in Poitiers, close to a Martinian monastery. One of her last reported acts was to request an official in a dream to rebuild a chapel for the saint.[7]

All three authors describe Radegund as an independent and unconventional, as well as a forceful, personality. As I hope to show in what follows, Fortunatus' biography contains indications that she may have innovated in her exercise of the existing male curing tradition as well. Focusing upon a notion that keeps recurring in crucial places—that of *mysterium*—, I shall place his stories of Radegund's cures alongside his descriptions of those by a contemporary living male saint (whom he also knew personally), Bishop Germanus of Paris (555–76). In this way, what may be her unique contribution will become visible.

The Term Mysterium

What, however, is a *mysterium*? The term occurs in the following story about a cure by Radegund which is significantly qualified as 'a new kind of miracle'. Fortunatus tells us that

> the nun Animia was so completely swollen with dropsy that she had reached her end. The appointed sister nuns were around her, expecting her to expire at any moment, when she saw in her sleep that the

---

[6] As also Goetz, "Heiligenkult und Geschlecht: Geschlechtsspezifisches Wunderwirken in frühmittelalterlichen Mirakelberichten?", p. 104.
[7] Gregorius, *Vita Patrum* 19.2; Fortunatus, *Vita sanctae Radegundis* 33–34, 87–89.

blessed Radegund, with the venerable abbess, ordered her to descend nude into a bath (*in balneo*) without water. Then, with her own hand, the saint was seen to pour oil over the head of the sick woman, and to cover her with a new robe. After this mystery had been enacted (*peracto mysterio*), she awoke from sleep and nothing of the illness was left; she had not lost the water through perspiration but it had been consumed within. By this new kind of miracle (*novo sub miraculo*) the illness left no trace in her womb (*uterus*). For she who had been believed to be ready to be carried to the grave (*tumulum*), lifted herself at once from her bed, with the scent of the oil remaining upon her head and the fact that there was nothing harmful in her belly (*venter*) as a testimony (*testimonium*) [to the truth of the event].[8]

What we see here is that the *mysterium* is the hinge event in this story: the transformational moment. In the Gospels, the term is used by Christ to refer to manifestations of the invisible presence and working of the Kingdom of God in the human life-world.[9] According to the authoritative dictionary of early Christian Latin, the term later came to denote: a symbol of a divine truth or its content; a revealed divine doctrine; the effectuation of Christ's redemption of man; a (pagan or) Christian rite or mystical celebration, especially that of the transformation of bread and wine into the body and blood of Christ: i.e. the Eucharist; and the (ritual) Eucharistic prayer.[10]

The term 'mystery', then, was used to indicate a pattern of transformational divine action in the human life-world, an event which cannot be rationally analyzed or understood; it can only be pointed to in a specific event or metaphor functioning as a symbol, and entered into through ritual symbolic action. According to the then already established church tradition, certain Old and New Testament events could be identified as such 'mysteries'. For they could have more than only an empirical meaning in that their contours were perceived to manifest the archetypal patterns or 'figures'[11] of transtemporal modes of divine interaction with humankind. With this in mind, Bible exegesis flourished, and particularized meanings of the term *mysterium* emerge. Thus, two hundred years before Radegund, bishop

---

[8] Fortunatus, *Vita sanctae Radegundis*, 80–81.
[9] As in Matthew 13:11, Luke 8:10, and John 1:3, 9; 9:5.
[10] A. Blaise, *Dictionnaire Latin-Français des Auteurs Chrétiens* (Turnhout, 1954), pp. 547–548. Gregory of Tours refers to the Eucharist as a *mysterium* in his *Virtutes sancti Martini* (ed. B. Krusch, MGH SSrM 1.2, pp. 584–661) 2.1.
[11] As E. Auerbach, "Figura", *Archivum Romanicum* 22 (1938), pp. 436–489.

Hilary of Poitiers had written the *Tractatus mysteriorum*, which lists and explains a number of visible biblical events as revealing specific divine prophecies about the future of the Church and its members.[12] As we shall see, this tradition is reflected in Fortunatus' writing, and Radegund must also have been aware of it.

Another fourth-century treatise, Bishop Ambrose of Milan's *Liber de mysteriis*, describes the symbolic actions involved in the ritual of baptism and explains how they effect the catechumen's rebirth into a new life.[13] Here, then, *mysterium* is a symbol as enacted and effectuated in and through human ritual. Although Radegund may have read Ambrose's treatises on virginity,[14] she would not have been likely to have known this one; as a priest, however, Fortunatus would. These two treatises show that in this period *the term 'mysterium' could be understood as pointing to the effective operation of (biblical) symbols or 'figures' of divine activity in present sensory reality through their ritual enactment*. In what follows, I hope to show that Fortunatus may have used the notion of 'mystery' in a striking new way: to indicate both the symbolic ritual through which Radegund precipitated a miracle as well as the event itself as a visual manifestation of an invisible divine transformational dynamic or pattern of action. It seems to me that Fortunatus would have had no reason to invent her new curing rituals, and thus that it was very likely Radegund herself who was, more or less consciously, innovating here.

In the story above, her 'new kind of miracle' took place during another's dream, and a dream—in late Antiquity—was regarded as the privileged manner in which an objectively existing spiritual reality could be perceived.[15] As we saw, the successive acts of descending into a bath, and being anointed and clothed with a new robe that, together, appear to have precipitated the cure are referred to as an *'enacted* mystery'. This phrase appears to refer to the performance of a ritual that actualizes and activates the religious symbol. The symbol here could be that of baptism, because all the acts

---

[12] Hilaire de Poitiers, *Traité des mystères*, ed. and tr. J.P. Brisson, Sources chrétiennes (= SC) 19bis (Paris, 1967).

[13] Ambroise de Milan, *Des mystères*, ed. and tr. B. Botte, SC 25 (Paris, [1950]), pp. 107–128.

[14] Ambrosius Mediolanensis, *De virginibus Libri Tres*, ed. E. Cazaniga, Corpus Scriptorum Latinorum Paravianum (Torino, n.d.).

[15] As also P.C. Miller, *Dreams in Late Antiquity: Studies in the Imagination of a Culture* (Princeton, 1994), p. 40.

described in this story also appear in the late antique north Italian and Gallican rites of baptism which, as we saw, was designated as a *mysterium*.[16] But, as we all know, dreams can condense various symbols into one. Thus, the presence of the abbess alongside Radegund may indicate that the dream acts were at the same time the equivalents of the ritual profession of a nun as the bride of Christ.[17] (Since the fourth century, the veiling of a religious woman was celebrated as her affiancing to Christ.)[18] Gregory of Tours reports a dream of another of Radegund's nuns in which the abbess brings her a bridal robe, sent by 'the Bridegroom' (i.e. Christ), in a setting that can only be Paradise.[19] This dream event made such an impression upon her that she asked to be walled in as a recluse, which was ceremonially carried out, Radegund presiding. Significantly, both of these events, then, have a ritual dimension, both take place in the imaginative or spiritual world, and both effect a transformation. In the curing dream, however, there is almost certainly another dimension that is specifically connected to its status as a cure: that of an associative overlap with the apostolic (and contemporary) ecclesiastical ritual of anointing the sick,[20] another ritual of transformation.

It remains to explain why the whole event is designated as 'a new kind of miracle'. As we see elsewhere in Fortunatus' biography, Radegund—as the first sainted queen and a pioneer in miracle-doing holy womanhood in the West—is *explicitly* compared only to male models of saintliness and exercise of holy power.[21] However, her non-miraculous actions resemble those of some earlier ascetic women, with whom Fortunatus compares her explicitly in one of his poems.[22]

---

[16] See: "Baptême", *Dictionnaire d'Archéologie chrétienne et de Liturgie* (= DACL) 2.1b, col. 318–320, 325–326; "Bains", Ibid., col. 98, and "Huile", DACL 6.2, col. 2779–2783.

[17] In the rite of the late antique consecration of virgins, as Duchesne describes it, there is only a veiling and no anointing: L. Duchesne, *Christian Worship: Its Origin and Evolution*, Tr. M.L. McClure, 4th ed. (London/New York, 1912), pp. 422–427.

[18] J. Bugge, *Virginitas. An Essay in the History of a Medieval Ideal*. International Archives of the History of Ideas, series minor 17 (The Hague, 1975), pp. 59–67, esp. p. 66.

[19] *Historiae* 6.29.

[20] Mark 6:13; James 5:14–17.

[21] Fortunatus, *Vita sanctae Radegundis* 4 (Israel), 7 (Samuel), 13 (three youths in Babylon), 37 (Germanus), 84 (Martin). In chapters 11 and 44 her actions imitate those of Saint Martin without his name being mentioned.

[22] Venantius Fortunatus, *Carmina* (ed. F. Leo, MGH AA 4.1 (Berlin, 1881)) 8.1.41–46. See on this topic: G. de Nie, "'Consciousness fecund through God': from

The only explicit female model—consonant with the self-effacing image of the saint that Fortunatus, to restore the saint's reputation, is here concerned to present—is the very humble one of Martha, who served Jesus and his disciples while her sister Mary sat and listened to their conversation.[23] We shall see, however, that Fortunatus may be slipping in one part of his subject's innovations in a less conspicuous manner, and that this could be what he meant with the qualification 'new kind of miracle'.

In what follows, I shall first examine the male curing tradition as Fortunatus describes it in the acts of Saint Germanus of Paris. Then I shall attempt to show that the contours of the events in the dream cure cited above may imply and involve, alongside the traditional Christian symbolism already mentioned, a new image that highlights woman's role in a cure. For in this and in one other 'new kind of cure'—which Fortunatus also explicitly designates as such—, a symbolic dimension appears to become visible which displays a new powerful role model for Christian women. And I shall argue that, in these, the term *mysterium* points precisely to *the transformation of the human body through the ritual enactment of a powerful image, archetypal pattern of transformational divine action, or symbol*. But we must begin by a brief look at some more general preconceptions underlying the view of cures in this period.

Late Antique Views of Healing

A late twentieth-century layman's view of healing tends to be couched in terms of a purely empirical conception of the material world inherited from the nineteenth century. In this world view, a 'miracle' is theoretically impossible: it is assumed that each phenomenon or event must have a 'natural' explanation, even though it has not yet been found. The late antique person, however, whether pagan or Christian, looked at the human life-world from a different perspective. First, although the material and the spiritual dimensions were conceptually distinguished, they were not perceived as being in fact separated

---

male fighter to spiritual bride-mother of Christ in late antique female sanctity", *Sanctity and Motherhood: Essays on Holy Mothers in the Middle Ages*, ed. A.B. Mulder-Bakker (New York/London, 1995), pp. 139–151.

[23] Luke 10:38–42. Fortunatus, *Vita sanctae Radegundis* 42.

from each other. Quite the contrary. Throughout material objects, animals and human persons good and evil *spiritual forces and powers* were thought to be present and active; there was no neutral territory or vacuum.[24] Illness too, therefore, was not only a physical thing; we see in Gregory of Tours' stories that it is frequently described as the effect of a malign power which had invaded the person from without, and which needed to be driven out again.[25]

A second crucial difference from modern views is that for sixth-century Christians contemporary events, and especially miracles, could also be interpreted—like those in the Bible—as signs revealing divine action patterns. Their internal contours or 'figures', too, were thought to reveal archetypes of spiritual truth which were being divinely replicated since biblical times. In fact, the whole palpable and visible world was thought to be a veil that covered the *archetypal forms or figural patterns of the 'really real' spiritual world*, which could sometimes be perceived in dreams or visions. The central example of such an archetypal form or pattern of spiritual truth was, of course, the visible event of Christ's death and resurrection as imaging or 'figuring' the victory over all evil and the entrance into eternal life; this was the central Christian *mysterium*.

A last, essential, difference with modern thinking is that—in pagan as well as in Christian circles—*all phenomena in the cosmos were thought to participate in each other through resemblance in form*.[26] This meant that the ritual enactment of a particular symbolic form would effect the celebrant's participation in (the power pattern of) the archetype at the place of action. Thus, even Augustine regards the human sounding of the word of God as effecting its actual presence: Christ as the divine Logos or Word is actively present in and working through the human words of the preacher.[27] Two centuries later, Gregory of

---

[24] As A. Angenendt, "Die Liturgie und die Organisation des kirchlichen Lebens auf dem Lande", *Cristianizzazione ed organizazzione ecclesiastica delle campagne nell'alto medioevo: espansione e resistenze*, Settimane di Studio del Centro Italiano di Studi sull'alto medioevo 1 (Spoleto, 1982), p. 186. On the intellectual background, see: L. Thorndike, *A History of Magic and Experimental Science*, vol. 1 (New York, 1923), pp. 540–547.

[25] As in his *Virtutes sancti Martini* 4.37. Cf. G. de Nie, *Views from a Many-Windowed Towe: Studies of Imagination in the Works of Gregory of Tours*. Studies in Classical Antiquity 7 (Amsterdam, 1987), pp. 230–237.

[26] G.B. Ladner, *Handbuch der frühchristlichen Symbolik* (Stuttgart/Zürich, 1992), pp. 19–20.

[27] Based upon 1 Thessalonians 2:13 and John 1.1–4, 9; Augustine, *De magistro*

Tours reports that the pronouncing of a saint's name precipitates the presence of his holy power, and that even reverent contact with the written letters of the miracle stories of a saint (who happened to be his uncle) healed someone's blindness.[28] To sum up, the coalescence of the material and the spiritual and the participation of phenomena in each other through the resemblance of 'figured' patterns and/or analogy were the underlying reasons that late antique medical practice, pagan and Christian, tended to combine physical remedies with symbolical acts. The latter were intended to invoke and bring to the spot beneficent spiritual powers or power-patterns to drive out the disease-causing spirit as well as its bodily effects.[29]

In the Christian tradition which we see in late sixth-century saints' lives and miracle stories, the saint's healing action tends to follow a similar pattern. For here too, the use of spiritual 'power' is often, but not always, simultaneous with practical therapy. Generally speaking, an act of prayer to ask for power from Christ usually came first. Then, touching or anointing to transmit this healing 'power', and/or symbolical gestures such as the sign of the Cross, the invocation of the divine name, or the speaking of ritual words followed. All this is not infrequently combined with cleansing, and herbal or other physical treatment of the patient.[30] Something like the Old Testament view that "unless the Lord builds a house those who work on it labor in vain" may be said to underlie these therapies.[31]

(ed. K.D. Daur, CCSL 29 (Turnhout, 1970), pp. 156–203) 11.30 and 12.40. Cf. G. de Nie, "Die Sprache im Wunder—das Wunder in der Sprache. Menschenwort und Logos bei Gregor von Tours", *Mitteilungen des Instituts für Österreicheische Geschichtsforschung* 103 (1995), pp. 1–25.

[28] Gregorius, *Virtutes sancti Martini* 23 and *Vita Patrum* 8.12. The latter resembles the use of amulets—along with herbs and potions—in Marcellus's pagan magical medicine; see: A. Rousselle, "Du sanctuaire au thaumaturge: la guérison en Gaule au IVe siècle", *Annales* 31 (1976), p. 1093.

[29] See: "Médecins", DACL 11.1, col. 109–180. On pagan women doctors: col. 119–20; the Merovingian period and healing saints: col. 149–154, and Rousselle, "Du sanctuaire au thaumaturge: la guérison en Gaule au IVe siècle."

[30] A. Rousselle, *Croire et guérir: La foi en Gaule dans l'Antiquité tardive* (Paris, 1990), pp. 83–96, 114–128. Cf. idem, "Du sanctuaire au thaumaturge: la guérison en Gaule au IVe siècle."

[31] Psalm 126 (127).1.

Male Cures: 'The Miracle-Doing Doctor'

The male curing tradition in sixth-century Gaul becomes most visible in Saint Germanus of Paris, because of all the male saints whose deeds Fortunatus records, he effected by far the most cures: including indirect ones, forty-eight, against seven by his nearest male rival.[32] Accordingly, the saint is repeatedly referred to as a "doctor",[33] and praised as a "miracle-doing doctor (*mirificus medicus*)", a "healing leader (*medicabilis praesul*)", and one who "outdoes all the art of doctors (*omnem artem medicorum ... superasse*)".[34] As may be expected, ordinary physicians are therefore disparaged.[35] Although Radegund's cures number fourteen, she is only once referred to as a 'doctor', perhaps as a reminiscence of the Roman tradition of women doctors.[36]

In what follows, I shall focus upon the curing methods that appear to be similar to Radegund's, but also indicate accents that differ. The cures through anointing and washing will be looked at first, and the stroking and holding which this involved have been included also when these occur by themselves. I shall begin by putting alongside Radegund's above-quoted cure of Animia's dropsy (which will be further analyzed in the section on Radegund's cures) the single similar one by Germanus, and then survey his rituals of anointing, stroking and washing. This section will be concluded by looking at the use of the term *mysterium* for one of Germanus' miracles, and its meanings elsewhere in Fortunatus' prose saints' lives.

Dropsy

The one cure of dropsy recorded of Germanus tells us that Daningus,

> given up by the doctors, and at the end of his strength, turned to the holy man for a remedy (*remedium*). When the patient had taken off his clothes and the saint had anointed him with his sacred hands (*sacris manibus peruncto*), the fluid of the dropsy inside his body was at once consumed by the fluid on the outside, and the infusion of water was

---

[32] Saint Albinus (in: Fortunatus, *Vita sancti Albini* (ed. B. Krusch, MGH AA 4.2, pp. 27–33)).
[33] Fortunatus, *Vita sancti Germani* (ed. B. Krusch, MGH AA 4.2, pp. 11–27) 72, 109, 137, 146, 149, 157, 185.
[34] Ibid. 137, 141, 109.
[35] Ibid. 146, 159.
[36] Fortunatus, *Vita sanctae Radegundis* 29; Roman female physicians: DACL 11.1, col. 119–120.

dried up by the oil. In this astonishing manner (*modo admirabili*) neither did the humor come out nor was it held inside, and a humor was dried up by a humor in a praiseworthy manner.[37]

The here evident trope of the inversion of everyday reality or paradox is not infrequently stressed by Fortunatus; it points to Christianity's more general inversion of everyday values.[38] But, as I hope to show later, paradox is likely to have played a central role in the healing processes themselves too. In the above story, the oil and the touching by the saint's 'sacred hands' are highlighted. As I have already indicated, it is of course the treatment which the apostolic letter of James had prescribed:

> If anyone among you is ill, let him call for the priests of the church, and let them pray over him (*super eum*), anointing him with oil in the name of the Lord. And the prayer of faith shall save the ill man, and the Lord will raise him up. And if he has committed sins, they will be forgiven.... The assiduous prayer of a just man is very powerful, for Elijah was a man of like nature with ourselves....[39]

This prophet not only averted as well as brought on rain, as James writes, but had also healed and revived the dead.[40] We may assume that, in Fortunatus' story, the prayer is taken for granted. Early in the sixth century, Bishop Caesarius of Arles had repeated these instructions for healing in one of his sermons, and added the ingestion of the Eucharist.[41] Concerned with the healing of the soul as well as

---

[37] *Vita sancti Germani* 146–147. On the importance of humors in the ancient and medieval view of illness, see: R. Fahraeus, "Grundlegende Fakten über die Pathologie der Körpersäfte und ihre Relikte in Sprache und Volksmedizin", *Volksmedizin. Probleme und Forschungsgeschichte*, ed. E. Grabner, Wege der Forschung 63 (Darmstadt, 1967), p. 448.

[38] Centrally, of course, through that of life through death and power through humility. Inversion in general is stressed, for instance, in *Vita sancti Germani* 67: "in inverted order (*versa vice*)". And see on its corollary, the inversion of emotions: Fortunatus, *Vita sanctae Radegundis* 11: "believing she would lose whatever she did not give to the poor (*hoc se reputans perdere quod pauperibus non dedisset*)", and 17: "she was fulfilled by a long fast with tears as though she were satiated with delicious food (*quasi repleta deliciis sic longo ieiunio satiaretur in lacrimis*)." And G. de Nie, "Visies op St. Radegunde's 'vlammende geest'. Zesde- en twintigste-eeuwse gevoelspatronen in ideaal, verhaal en beeldspraak" [Views of Saint Radegund's 'flaming spirit'. Sixth and twentieth-century patterns of feeling in ideals, narratives and imageries], *Emoties in de Middeleeuwen* [Emotions in the Middle Ages], ed. R.E.V. Stuip and C. Vellekoop, Utrechtse Bijdragen tot de Mediëvistiek 15 (Hilversum, 1998), pp. 49–78.

[39] James 5:14–17.

[40] 1 Kings 17:1, 18:1, 41–35; 17:17 ff.; 2 Kings 4:32–34.

[41] Caesarius, *Sermones* (ed. G. Morin, Corpus Christianorum Series Latina (= CCSL) 104 (Turnhout, 1953)) 184.5.

of the body, he says that the priest's prayer will effect divine forgiveness of the patient's sins—also a central issue in some of Christ's cures.[42]

Anointing

Anointing is involved in twenty-one of Germanus' cures. Preceded by prayer, he treats in this way: paralysis, cramped open mouths, lacerations by a wolf and temporary insanity, blindness, gout, muteness, gangrene, and, as we saw, dropsy.[43] Sometimes the touching and stroking is highlighted. In the case of a woman whose mouth stood open, the saint is said to "have touched her head all around (*palpato undique capite*)".[44] Another time, however, the same malady was cured in this manner while calling upon Christ's name.[45] But the power of the oil itself, too, may be the center of attention. When someone's contracted hand "had touched the oil, the latter's power poured the remedy into it (*Qua contacta oleo virtus infudit remedium*)"; the right hand is said to have been "purged" of its disability (*purgata vitio*).[46] Something, then, was driven out, and the cure is therefore also a kind of exorcism. In another case, a paralytic is healed by having

> sanctified oil poured over him: when it had touched his whole skin, strength entered his inner parts (*sanctificati olei liquore perfuso, cum cutem summam tetigisset, vigor medullas introiit*).[47]

The adjective "revived (*redivivus*)" is here used of his hands, and it is said that "the whole fabric of his limbs was restored (*tota membrorum fabrica reparatur*)". In this case, then, the model of death and resurrection is made explicit. When a withered hand "revived (*revirescit*)" and "bloomed again (*reflorescit*)", through contact with "sacred oil" and Germanus' hands,[48] the same association appears to be evoked, but here the saint's hands are evidently a parallel conduit of holy power.

---

[42] Loc. cit.; Matthew 9:2, Luke 7:48.
[43] *Vita sancti Germani* 47, 49, 50, 55, 56, 72, 74, 75, 82, 103, 106, 109, 121, 131, 133, 137, 138, 141, 145, 147, 157.
[44] Ibid. 49.
[45] Ibid. 56.
[46] Ibid. 50–51.
[47] Ibid. 106–107.
[48] Ibid. 157.

The common sense remedy of hot water and cabbage leaves, in combination with the anointing with 'blessed oil', cured gangrene. Significantly, this cure is said to have taken place through the "poultice (*malagmate*)".[49] The saint, then, combines practical remedies of independent efficacy with the holy power of the oil. It is not impossible that he used oil or an ointment with special ingredients prepared by himself, like the ointments of pagan doctors.[50] Neither here nor anywhere else is there any suggestion of an incompatibility between 'natural' and 'holy' medicine: it is in fact here that the saint is designated as a 'miracle-doing doctor'.

Washing

Germanus is nowhere described as washing anyone's whole body, but he does clean and wash parts of it as needed. In one case, the bishop makes the sign of the Cross over an old woman's blind eyes and, the next day, when they are seen to be bleeding, washes them with warm water.[51] Elsewhere, a blind slave girl's eyes were anointed and prayed over; then she was given bread and salt over which the sign of the Cross had been made, and told to go home; the next day, Germanus cleaned and washed her then bleeding eyes with warm water (*fovens et abluens*). One was thereupon healed; the other, anointed once more, bled again at night, and was healed the next day, probably by another washing.[52] Here, it looks as though symbolic gestures—the sign of the Cross, the anointing with the blessed oil, the consumption of blessed bread (the Eucharist?)[53] and salt—triggered a somewhat slower healing process which was aided by nutrition and washing. For, like so many others in Gaul in this period, the woman was probably undernourished and ill cared for.[54]

Touching

There are a few cases of anointing in which not the oil or the dressing is highlighted, but the quality of Germanus' touch itself. When

---

[49] Ibid. 137.
[50] Rousselle, "Du sanctuaire au thaumaturge: la guérison en Gaule au IVᵉ siècle", p. 1099.
[51] *Vita sancti Germani* 112.
[52] Ibid. 73–75.
[53] Cf. Caesarius, *Sermo* 184.5.
[54] Cf. "Médecins", DACL 11.1, col. 149–150.

a man was brought to the saint who had been lacerated by a wolf, contracted gangrene and slipped into insanity through the shock and pain, Germanus

> turned to the support of his [healing] art (*suae artis*); when he had anointed the arm all around with the blessed liquid of the oil, and had stroked the man in a healing manner with his holy fingers, that illness which had invaded his heart with violent pain fled from the obsessed places (*sacris eo digitis medicabiliter adtrectato, pestis illa quae viscera dolore grassante pervaserat loca fugit obsessa*). The flesh which had already been dissolved in rotting was restored to its pristine vigor, [and] without delay—as though he were awakening from sleep—the pain receded and his [right] mind returned.[55]

Here, not only is the gangrenous arm anointed but the whole, crazed, man is stroked (rubbed or massaged?) 'in a healing manner', and thereby cured and brought back to his right mind. The story may present a longer healing process in a condensed manner. As we see in the wording, the stroking was thought to have driven out a possessing, disease-causing agent who had taken over the patient's mind as well. Germanus elsewhere cures a possessed person also by the imposition of hands.[56] In another case, when he has first applied saliva,[57] and then oil, his touching as such is praised:

> For the holy man, in the matter of illnesses, curing is the same as touching (*Nam causas infirmitatis hoc erat sancto viro curare quod tangere*).[58]

Elsewhere, when he has only made the sign of the Cross—but evidently thereby touching the skin of the mute, paralytic girl—it is said that "for the saint touching was reviving (*hoc fuit apud sanctum vivificare quod tangere*)".[59] Finally, in one case, someone's withered hand is said to have been healed "between the hands of the doctor (*inter manus medici*)".[60]

Christ, of course, had touched to heal.[61] And Saint Martin had healed a mute and completely paralyzed girl through prayer, pouring oil into her mouth, and stroking her limbs.[62] A holy man is per-

---

[55] *Vita sancti Germani* 72.
[56] Ibid. 78.
[57] As Christ had done to heal blindness in John 9:6 ff.
[58] *Vita sancti Germani* 82.
[59] Ibid. 127.
[60] Ibid. 157.
[61] For instance, in Matthew 8:3.
[62] Sulpicius Severus, *Vita sancti Martini* (ed. J. Fontaine, SC 133 (Paris, 1967)) 16.

ceived as powerful because, through continuous prayer, he is 'filled with God (*plenus Deo*)' or Christ—a description of Saint Martin, the apostle of Gaul, which can also be used for holy men in the sixth century.[63] At the same time, however powerful Germanus' touch is perceived to be, it is evidently also—as all the examples show—warmly caring. For he once healed a mute paralytic servant boy by "anoint[ing] him continually for three days with sacred oil (*quem continuatim per triduum sacro liniens oleo*)".[64]

Mysterium

In two cases, however, Fortunatus qualifies a cure through anointing as a 'mystery'. In one story, the anointing of a contracted hand with blessed oil is described as:

> When the liquid of the blessed oil had been poured out, or rather the ointment of the mystery had been spread about (*mysterii potius unguento resperso*), [the saint] restored him to health by another prayer.[65]

The term here appears to point, in one way or another, to the transforming power of the anointing ritual as precipitating the cure. In the second story, taking place in the city of Nantes, the lady Tecla asked the bishop for help for her husband, the merchant Damianus. First, a deacon was sent who 'touched' the patient; evidently to no effect. For

> the next day, the bishop himself, having been asked to do so, went to the ill man, who was to be pitied, for he was shamelessly oppressed by the double torture of great pain from gout [in both hands and legs]. At the same moment that the priest of the Highest [Deity] anointed the sick man with blessed oil, he at once snapped (*prosiliuit*) completely out of the illness by the straightening of his hands and the strengthening of his legs.
>
> But, so that the mystery (*mysterium*) should be duplicated in one house . . ., Maria, his daughter, who was blind, deaf and dumb, was presented to him. They placed the living corpse (*vivum cadaverem*) before the feet of the saint, saying: 'Good shepherd (*bone pastor*), apply to this

---

[63] Sulpicius, *Vita sancti Martini* 3.1; about Gregory of Tours: Baudonivia, *Vita sanctae Radegundis* 23. Saint Martin as the apostle of Gaul: Gregorius, *Historiae* 1.39: "then our sun too arose . . . for it was in this time that the most blessed Martin began to preach in Gaul (*tunc iam et lumen nostrum oritur . . . hoc est eo tempore beatissimus Martinus in Gallias praedicare exorsus est*)."

[64] *Vita sancti Germani* 109; the case in chapter 58 is perhaps similar.

[65] Ibid. 138.

ill girl whatever remains of your medicine (*medicina*) [i.e. the oil]. For we believe her to have been reserved for you, so that you would receive the praise, and so that, given back to her family, she would acquire from the priest what she lacks from her parents.'

When their outstanding piety was supported by tears, the warrior at once turned to the arms of his warfare, and the powerful orator offered prayers to obtain the victory (*ad militiae suae belliger arma convertitur et ad obtinendam victoriam preces offert fortis orator*). Thereupon the holy man rose from his prayer, anointed all places of the girl's head with blessed oil, and drove out the illness three times in the name of the Trinity. At once, the paths of the ears and the eyes were opened, and while, everyone applauded, the mute girl was given the faculty of speech. When this had been done, each merchant of the city of Nantes gave or sent as much as he could for this healing to the holy man to be devoutly dispensed to the poor.[66]

The terms in which the above cure is described may be said to make it into an embodied miniature of the central Christian belief of life as death except when revived to eternal life through the power of One who had himself entered the true life through death. We saw that this redemption itself could be termed a *mysterium*: a hidden but actively powerful dynamic pattern or archetype of spiritual truth. In this story, the term *mysterium* appears to point to that redemption itself as well as to the manner in which its pattern was replicated in the curing ritual of anointing. Here, then, the *mysterium* is the empowering truth of a transforming archetype or symbol as activated by its re-enactment in a ritual.

A few other uses of the term *mysterium* in Fortunatus' saints' lives are possibly relevant to our argument.[67] In the story of a beacon of light rising from the church of Saint Hilary to hang over the Frankish king Clovis (486–511) as he was about to give battle (c. 507) to the Arian king Alaric and his Visigoths,[68] Fortunatus speaks of it as a "sign of light (*signum luminis*)" and a "royal mystery (*regalis mysterium*)"; but he also writes: "I should like to know why there was a hidden mystery of such fire (*tanti ardoris secretum mysterium*) and so clearly revealed (*manifestum prolatum*)". And then he explains that it is a replication and re-enactment—in visual form—of Saint Hilary's verbal

---

[66] Ibid. 130–133.
[67] The meaning of the term in Fortunatus' *Vita sancti Hilarii* (MGH AA 4.2, pp. 1–7) 12 is unclear to me, and that in ibid. 34 appears to indicate something like a vision or revelation.
[68] Fortunatus, *Virtutes sancti Hilarii* (ed. B. Krusch, MGH AA 4.2, pp. 7–11) 20–23.

battle against the Arian emperor Constantius, approximately a hundred and fifty years earlier. Here again we see the early medieval tendency to transpose the contours of events and notions into images. The terms "prodigy (*prodigium*)" and "miracle (*miraculum*)" also designate the phenomenon, however, and it is compared to the pillar of fire preceding the Hebrews in the desert.[69] Gregory of Tours refers to this pillar (again an image) as "the archetype (*tipus*) of the Holy Spirit"[70]—a very clear example of the contemporary habit of thinking in terms of images rather than of concepts. Fortunatus, however, says that by this beacon Saint Hilary "showed (*ostenderet*)" what he also expressed in words[71]—presumably through an apparition or in a dream. Here, then, 'mystery' appears to mean a visual manifestation of an actively present, but ordinarily hidden, dynamic pattern of spiritual reality.

But Fortunatus also uses the term for the strange behavior of a candle given to Saint Hilary's tomb by two merchants, one of whom did not really want to give it; it split in two, and one half rolled away: the saint had rejected it as an unwilling gift.[72] The incident is thereupon designated as a "judgment (*iudicium*)", probably meaning that the event functioned as an ordeal. For, if we are to believe Gregory's stories, false oaths on saints' tombs in this period tended to be followed by an instant, visible punishment.[73] Here again an event in the invisible dimension is revealed by a visible one; or, to approach it from the other side: the contours of a visible event are perceived and understood as revealing an already known, invisible and significant pattern.

Finally, in his Life of Saint Marcellus of Paris, Fortunatus uses the term 'mystery' twice. One of these cases, the saint's victory over a dragon, will be discussed in another context. The other is when the young Marcellus' sinful bishop is punished by the loss of his voice, and the future saint cures him through asking him to say, 'in the name of the Lord' (a ritual formula, invoking the Lord's power),

---

[69] Exodus 13:21.
[70] *Historiae* 1.10.
[71] *Virtutes sancti Hilarii* 21: "It would not have been enough for [the saint] to show this sign to support the king if he had not added [in a dream or apparition] a clear warning with his voice (*Parum illi fuit pro solatio regis signum ostendere luminis, nisi aperte monitus addidisset et vocis*)."
[72] Ibid. 30–33.
[73] E.g. Gregorius, *In gloria martyrum* 19.

what he wishes him to do. Fortunatus comments—showing the crucial importance of the spoken word as a means of pastoral care and ecclesiastical government—:

> Truly worthy is the blessed Marcellus' speaking (*sermo*), so that the one who gave his shepherd health should rule the flock of the Lord.[74]

The *mysterium* here is the indirect manifestation of the then still hidden, but in the spiritual sphere evidently already present, reality of Marcellus' future as bishop. In sum, then, also in his other saints' Lives, Fortunatus uses the term to mean both a transforming symbolic ritual and the visible manifestation and operation of a transcendent divine reality pattern.

Male Curing: The ideal Father

The manner in which Fortunatus describes his subject tells us a great deal about the author's perceptions of the role of the Christian bishop in mediating holy power. As we have seen, in the patriarchal society of sixth-century Gaul, Germanus is continuing an established tradition of the holy bishop as a father, a shepherd, an orator, and a 'warrior' against the evils threatening his flock.[75] In addition, he is elsewhere compared to Moses.[76] Over against such an impressive figure, complete subjection and dependence is the only adequate attitude, and we see this reflected in the stories. Fortunatus is certainly writing propaganda for an unarmed church depending upon the general belief in its monopoly of spiritual power to survive as an institution in a violent, inadequately ordered society, one in which every self-respecting man could and did defend his interests with physical weapons. Conversely, however, the insecurity which such a situation engendered among the weak and helpless cannot but have created a pressing need for protection by someone of power. The ideal figure of the saint as we find it in the biographies being written in this period is tailored to satisfy this need.[77] Accordingly, at the end of the biography, Fortunatus refers to the bishop as "the father and the shepherd of the people (*pater et pastor populi*)".[78] I have shown

---

[74] Fortunatus, *Vita sancti Marcelli* (MGH AA 4.2, pp. 49–54) 27–35.
[75] See on the perceptions and duties of bishops in this period: G. Scheibelreiter, *Der Bischof in merowingischer Zeit* (Vienna, 1983).
[76] *Vita sancti Germani* 22–25.
[77] Cf. De Nie, *Views from a many-windowed tower*, pp. 251–287.
[78] *Vita sancti Germani* 205.

elsewhere that others in this period sometimes ascribed explicitly 'motherly' qualities to contemporary holy men as well.[79] Fortunatus, however, chooses to describe Germanus' loving care of his patients as that of a father figure.

Tomb-Bath-Womb: The 'Doctor' as Mother?

As already mentioned, Radegund had no tradition of holy women performing miracles behind her (Monegund was a contemporary, and probably only known in and around Tours), and was therefore perceived as following male clerical role models—especially that of Saint Martin. We see this perception most clearly in a letter addressed to her by a council of bishops during her lifetime, in which she is spoken of as his 'companion'—the greatest compliment that could be given.[80] Although, Fortunatus' biography stresses her deference to males, including saints,[81] the number of her miracles (fourteen) shows that her power to do these was evidently not perceived as inferior to theirs. But how could a woman be described as 'powerful'? In his preface to the Life, Fortunatus refers to the "strong victories (*fortes victoriae*)" won by holy women of 'fragile bodies' through the "power of a distinguished mind (*virtute mentis inclitae*)".[82] These words recall the male model of the 'warrior', evidently the most conspicuous one indicating strength and power in holiness.[83] But, further on, Fortunatus appears to present his subject also in terms of another, only indirectly expressed, model.

In his friendship poems to her, Radegund appears as a strong-spirited and warm-hearted spiritual mother to her nuns and to the poet himself.[84] Spiritual motherhood was a late antique Christian

---

[79] As in *Vita sancti Caesarii* (MGH SSrM 3, pp. 457–501) 1.53: "for he loved them not only with a fatherly but also with a motherly affection (*ille tamen eos non solum paterno, sed etiam materno diligebat affectu*). Cf. also: G. de Nie, "Is een vrouw een mens? Voorschrift, vooroordeel en praktijk in zesde-eeuws Gallië" [Is a woman a human being? Precept, prejudice and practice in sixth-century Gaul], *Jaarboek voor Vrouwengeschiedenis* 10 (1989), pp. 72–73, and idem, "'Consciousness fecund through God'. From male fighter to spiritual bride-mother in late antique female sanctity", pp. 101–102.

[80] Gregorius, *Historiae* 9.39.

[81] As in Fortunatus, *Vita sanctae Radegundis* 19–20, 30–32.

[82] Ibid. 1.

[83] Cf. De Nie, "'Consciousness fecund through God': From male fighter to spiritual bride-mother in late antique female sanctity", pp. 116–123, 139–151.

[84] As Fortunatus, *Carmina* 8.8.1: *O regina potens*; 11.1: *Mater opima*. Gregory, *Historiae*

ideal for monastic men as well as women who had renounced physical procreation. For, replicating the 'figure' or archetype of the Virgin Conception, spiritual 'children' were thought to be conceived and born through the pouring of the word of God into others' hearts.[85] Although, as far as we know, Radegund never had children of her own, her actions may indicate that this ideal was a central one for her.[86]

For in his biography, Fortunatus appears to show that, from the beginning, she embodied this ideal in acts of practical, loving care: washing, stroking and anointing were prominent in Radegund's relations to others; this is evident, too, in the cure we have already looked at. When she was being educated at the estate of Athies before her marriage, she founded a hospital for poor, sick women, in which she "washed them in baths".[87] Later at Saix, when she had left her husband, she again cared for the poor and the sick: she bathed them on Thursdays and Saturdays, cleansed their sores, deloused hair, treated infected wounds, extracted worms, and (in a reference to James) "in the evangelical manner, overcame illness through the pouring out of oil". Here, the oil itself appears to be doing the curing. But elsewhere, "lying", says Fortunatus, "that it would be of use to her", she uses a vine leaf over which she has made the sign of the Cross to cure an ulcer.[88] He means that she is trying to hide her miraculous healing under the guise of a herbal remedy. And she uses an apple to heal unspecified illnesses, equally miraculously.[89] For the rest, the practices here mentioned appear to be a medical kind of care rather than miraculous healing. Women were bathed with soap from head to foot; when necessary they were given new clothes and, in any case, meals. In implicit imitation of Saint Martin, Radegunde embraced and kissed leprous women with

---

9.39, quotes a letter of a council of bishops to Radegund telling her that her nuns "leave their parents and choose you whom grace, not nature, makes their mother (*relictis parentibus, te sibi magis elegant, quam matrem facit gratia, non natura*)."

[85] Cf. De Nie, "'Consciousness fecund through God': from male fighter to spiritual bride-mother in late antique female sanctity", pp. 101–102.

[86] Ibid., pp. 139–151.

[87] Fortunatus, *Vita sanctae Radegundis* 12. She may have been imitating the fourth-century Fabiola's hospital, known through a letter of Hieronymus (Jerome): *Epistolae* (ed. J. Labourt, vol. 4 (Paris, 1954)), 77.6. But Bishop Caesarius had also founded a hospital in Arles: *Vita sancti Caesarii* 1.20.

[88] Fortunatus, *Vita sanctae Radegundis* 47.

[89] Ibid. 49. Cf. 78, in which an absinth leaf she had carried against her chest cures an ulcer.

joy.⁹⁰ As we saw, all this earns her the somewhat dubious praise of the epithet "new Martha".⁹¹ There simply was no traditional role model for a holy healer who happened to be a woman!

When she was settled in Poitiers, however, something happened which Fortunatus describes as follows:

> A certain nun shivered with cold by day and burned with fire by night through an entire year. And when she had lain lifeless (*exanimis*) for six months, unable to move a step, one of her sisters told the saint about her infirmity. Finding her almost lifeless (*perinanis*), she bade them prepare warm water and had the sick woman brought to her cell and laid in the warm water. Then she ordered everyone to leave, only the sick woman and the doctor (*medica*) themselves remaining for almost two hours. She held the whole form of the body in her arms and [stroked] the weak limbs from head to foot (*Quantum est corporis forma a capite usque ad plantam infirma membra conbaiulat*). Through which, wherever her hand touched, the pain fled from the patient. And she who had been placed in the bath by two persons, came out of it in full health. The woman who had previously been disgusted by even the smell of wine now accepted it, drank it and was refreshed. What more shall I say? The next day, when she had been expected to migrate from this world, she came forth (*processit*) cured into the community.⁹²

Ostensibly, a persistent fever has been stopped by the application of heat and stroking. As we have seen, the latter also occurs—without a bath—in Saint Martin's cure of the paralyzed girl, and in cures by her older contemporary Saint Germanus.⁹³ Radegund's holding and stroking for two hours of 'the whole form of the body" and "the weak limbs from head to foot" are reminiscent of Saint Martin's "gradually, at his touch, her individual limbs began to revive (*paulatim singula contactu eius coeperunt membra vivescere*)".⁹⁴ To raise an actually dead person, Martin had—in imitation of Elijah—placed his body upon that of the deceased, perhaps to transmit vitality and warmth (or did he already practice artificial respiration?), and prayed.⁹⁵ Radegund's treatment of a warm bath and holding is perhaps another way to do this. Although prayer is part of the proceedings in

---

⁹⁰ Ibid. 39–42.
⁹¹ Ibid. 42.
⁹² Ibid. 68–70.
⁹³ *Vita sancti Germani* 109.
⁹⁴ Sulpicius, *Vita sancti Martini* 16.8.
⁹⁵ *Vita sancti Martini* 7; 1 Kings 17:21. Cf. L. Bieler, "Totenerweckung durch synanáchrosis", and O. Weinreich, "Zum Wundertypus der synanáchrosis", *Archiv für Religionswissenschaft* 32 (1935), pp. 228–245, 246–264.

Radegund's other cures, it is not mentioned here. Probably, it is assumed. After having thus been 'recreated', as it were, in the warm bath by Radegund's hands, the nun 'came forth' again into the community.

The saint's treatment resembles the therapeutical bathing and massage which were part of the pagan water sanctuaries' care for women, the care which was taken over after their demise by 'wise women' or birth-helpers, about whom we unfortunately know very little.[96] Radegund appears to be acting in this tradition. At the same time, however, there are symbolical and spiritual dimensions to her act. One is that the pain is said to have 'fled' upon her touch. Such a notion must be based upon the holy person as 'filled with God', an epithet that, as we saw, had been used of Saint Martin, Radegund's model.

Martin's earthly remains, and therefore the center of his cult, were at Tours. What Fortunatus prudently omitted, and Baudonivia, when the danger has passed, reveals is that from 568 on—much to the annoyance of the city's later bishop Maroveus—Radegund created her own center of spiritual power in Poitiers. For, like certain other late antique women,[97] she managed to associate herself with another even more prestigious and hence presumably more powerful relic: that of the Holy Cross, a particle of which was sent to her at her request from Constantinople by the reigning Emperor and Empress;[98] after its installation there, Radegund renamed her convent after the Holy Cross. Radegund herself is supposed to have said that, with the relic, "Christ will visibly live here".[99] And with that fact, Radegund's convent must have become something close to the spiritual center of the Frankish kingdoms. Her second biographer accordingly speaks of her ruling "a heavenly rather than earthly kingdom".[100] But Radegund's appropriation of the Holy Cross relic also associated her with Christ's presence in a special way. This special way may give an added dimension to Fortunatus' introduction of Radegund's cure

---

[96] Rousselle, "La sage-femme et le thaumaturge dans la Gaule tardive: Les femmes ne font pas de miracles", pp. 249–250.

[97] Ibid., p. 246.

[98] Baudonivia, *Vita sanctae Radegundis* 16; Gregorius, *Historiae* 9.40.

[99] Baudonivia, *Vita sanctae Radegundis* 16.

[100] Ibid. 10: "where she seemed to reign, she prepared for herself a kingdom that was more heavenly than of this earth (*ubi dum regnare videretur, sibi magis caeleste quam terrenum praeparavit regnum*)."

of Animia's dropsy as one of the "wondrous events which the compassionate mercy of Christ effects (*mirabilia quae Christi misericors operatur clementia*)".[101]

The therapeutic immersion we saw in the cure just quoted resembles that in our very first story: Animia's being anointed and thereupon newly clothed in an empty bath. To recapitulate the latter story: the phrase *peracto mysterio* there seems to assimilate these acts to a religious ritual, possibly the purificational liturgy of baptism, in which anointing took place before and after the immersion. In the sources of the time we find that the unbaptized were thought to be *ipso facto* possessed by the Devil.[102] As already mentioned, however, invasion by the Devil or one of his demons was also held to be responsible for illness. And the anointing and clothing by the abbess as well as Radegund, finally, may point to the ritual of a nun's ceremonial entrance into the religious life. In contemporary symbolism, however, a new robe can also be a symbol of a new body.[103] This symbolism, in turn, appears to point to still another dimension: that of the whole event as, at the same time, an enacted ritual of a (Christlike) death and burial in a tomb—Animia is said to have been on the point of death and sleeping—, and a resurrection. Such a comparison is far from unusual; Gregory, too, not infrequently couches his descriptions of cures in terms of death and resurrection, pointing towards the last heavenly one to come.[104] In Radegund's cure, it is the combination of a densely symbolic ritual with the sensory replication of central Christian events and symbols, then, which appears to be indicated by the term *mysterium*.

One word, however, appears to point to the possibility that Animia's illness was not so much in her belly as in her womb: the word *uterus* can mean both.[105] It is tempting to suspect a hysterical pseudo-pregnancy here in connection with what appears from other sources about the convent to have been very lively—even physical—imaginations there of being the beloved bride of Christ.[106]

---

[101] Fortunatus, *Vita sanctae Radegundis* 80.
[102] Angenendt, "Die Liturgie und die kirchlichen Organisation auf dem Lande", p. 185.
[103] See on this subject: A. Kehl, "Gewand (der Seele)", *Reallexikon für Antike und Christentum* 10, pp. 945–1025.
[104] As in *Vita sancti Martini* 2.3 and 4.34.
[105] Blaise, *Dictionnaire latin-français des auteurs chrétiens*, p. 862.
[106] Fortunatus, *Carm.* 8.3.125–128, and Appendix 23.19, 23–4 (to the abbess): "If

This brings us to the possibility that there could be yet another symbolic dimension. For the uterus and the bath are analogical or congruent images. Thus the whole ritual may also point symbolically to something like the patient's new conception (through the oil), gestation (her presence in the bath, being anointed there, and clothed, while asleep, in a new robe—as we saw, a late antique symbol for a new body), and birth (she arose from her bed, and came forth from seclusion in the cell). If so, the structure of Animia's cure—that of rebirth—is remarkably similar to the one in which the feverish nun was restored through holding and stroking in a real warm bath.

A third story is similar. It shows us how Radegund revived a dead girl, probably an oblate in her convent. The whole event is explicitly introduced as a repetition of a model miracle of Saint Martin, but Christ too is mentioned:

> Let the model of an ancient miracle in the manner of Saint Martin in the present time (*more beati Martini tempore praesenti antiqui norma miraculi*) be proclaimed in praise of Christ.[107]

This is again an indication of the importance then accorded to doing things in a (male-dominated) recognizable tradition. The somewhat obscure wording in this story appears to indicate that the bath in which the girl's dead body was about to be washed was already warm (*Quae mortuam sororem nuntiavit infantulam et, frigida qua lavaretur, paratam esse iam calidam*). Upon her hearing of the death, Radegund commanded the corpse to be brought into her cell and secluded herself with it, sending everyone away. Did she also ask for the bath, as she did in the earlier story? While everyone outside was preparing for the girl's funeral, she stroked (*tractat*) the body in her cell for almost seven hours—in the warm bath, as in the first story? We are not told. Its use as an indication of the time elapsed since the girl's death does not exclude its also being used by Radegund, as in the other cures. It is tempting to suspect that the author took its use to be self-evident. It is not clear, however, what is so Martinian about this cure; perhaps the revival as such, or the prolonged stroking, as

---

sleep overtakes you, keep Christ in your heart... let yourself go legitimately in his embrace: for whoever holds him need fear no sin (*Si sopor obripiat, retinendo in pectore Christum/ . . . /huius in amplexu te totam effunde licenter:/ Illum quisquis habet crimina nulla timet*)." Cf. Hieronymus, *Epistolae* (ed. Labourt, vol. 1 (Paris, 1949)) 22.26.

[107] Fortunatus, *Vita sanctae Radegundis* 84.

in the previous story. However that may be, Fortunatus concludes by saying that Christ, seeing the saint's faith, gave the girl her health again: "as the saint arose from her prayer, the girl arose from death". The saint, therefore, from time to time also prostrated herself in prayer. Again, the paradox of the Christian religion of new life—or rebirth—through death is made visible here.

In the three stories we have just looked at, the core elements are a warm bath, or the strong suggestion of one, and the stroking or anointing's effecting of a new body. Is it only the dressing-up of the effect of ordinary bathing and massage as a miracle? Or should these experiences be understood as being formally analogous to being conceived and formed in the womb, and emerging through birth? This view accords with their all being said to have passed from (near-)death to a new life. Although the latter is a frequent motif in sixth-century cures, the combination of bathing and stroking with this motif which we see in Radegund's miracles is unique. It looks as though she is continuing the tradition of gynecological therapy and the birth-helper's craft, but in the spiritual dimension.

If the above sounds far-fetched, it should be noted that this symbolism can also be recognized in the curing rituals of certain present-day oral societies. Thus Felicitas Goodman identified in the different acts of touching in South American Indian healing rituals—previously analyzed only by men:

> the ritual transmutation of the mother's labor pain, the newborn's issuing from her womb, its being welcomed, attended and finally placed at the mother's breast to draw nourishment.[108]

But a male anthropologist who is also a psychologist reports similar structures in an African curing ritual. René Devisch describes the Yaka concept of illness as a disconnecting and disordering of psycho-physical energies which blocks a person's vital source.[109] The ritual curing process undertakes to undo this through the enacting of paradoxes: 'the simultaneous deployment of one connotation and its reverse', for instance, death and birth.[110] The bodily enactment of such a paradox would precipitate the actual healing.[111] And so, in

---

[108] F. Goodman, *Ecstasy, Ritual and Alternate Reality: Religion in a Pluralistic World* (Bloomington/Indianapolis, 1988), p. 32.

[109] R. Devisch, *Weaving the Threads of Life: The 'Khita' Gyn-Eco-Logical Healing Cult Among the Yaka* (Chicago, 1993), pp. 132–133.

[110] Ibid., p. 269.

[111] Ibid., pp. 266–267.

Yaka ritual, death and rebirth or revival become different aspects of the same event. We have seen the same thing happening in sixth-century cures.

And, just as in the late antique period, here too dream consciousness is observed to play a central role. For the ritual enactment of metaphors of liminal situations in present-day oral societies, Devisch says, induces a state of dream-awareness in which discursive reasoning is temporarily put aside for iconic 'thinking', and images are preverbally experienced as affect-laden realities[112]—just as in Animia's dream. He writes:

> ... the actualized trance and concomitant acts have a metamorphic effect. The cathartic trance arouses a deeply lived and bodily enacted experience of freeing and channeling life-bearing in the body, therapy group, and life-world in unison.[113]

In this context, then, ritual symbols are not just mental images; they are

> corporeal devices, processes and methods or patterns that ... arise from a potential which, akin to the dream, unconceals both images and inner energy woven into the texture of the body.[114]

And "ritual metaphor [is] a performance that does actually effect the innovative interlinking that it exploratively signifies. . . .".[115] This kind of healing is founded in imaginative dreamwork—including such processes as condensation, fusion, figuration—that is largely beyond dialogue and discursive reality. It can not be verbalized but only experienced, acted out.[116] This, too, we have seen happening in Radegund's cures.

Is all this peculiar only to oral societies? Apparently not, for in western countries certain schools of modern psychotherapy use guided waking dream methods that effect clinically attested psychic, and even physical, healing in exactly the same way: through imaginatively enacting, and/or interacting with, either spontaneous or induced *images as metaphors for non-verbalizable affective states and patterns*. For the *human mind-body continuum is observed to imitate, affectively, internally, what*

---

[112] Ibid., pp. 255, 257.
[113] Ibid., p. 211.
[114] Ibid., p. 280.
[115] Ibid., p. 43.
[116] Ibid., p. 282.

it sees. Expressed in medical terms: affect-laden mental images are observed to behave as though they were bio-electrically charged patterns through which, in the hypothalamus, revitalizing—or killing—messages are given to the body's autonomous systems.[117]

These modern views show the central function of the mind's symbolizing for bodily well-being and, I suggest, make Radegund's apparently exotic symbolic ritual something we might begin to understand. Apart from the medical terminology, however: how can the seeing of an image be understood to transform the beholder? From personal experience most people will know that one can 'fall in love' at first sight with a face, a house, a landscape, a vase—perhaps unconsciously, affectively recognizing the contours of a dream image of happiness. Marcel Proust's Swann fell *back* into love through the hearing of Vintueil's musical phrase, which had previously seemed to coincide with—and thus affectively represent or 'figure'—the contours of his then blossoming love for Odette.[118] Experiencing a visual image in such a manner, then, as an affective, dynamic pattern, might precipitate a transformation in mind and body.

To return to Radegund: the effect of ritually enacting death and birth metaphors in the sixth century then, I suggest, is likely to have resembled that in today's oral societies. As Fortunatus describes it, Radegund appears to have acted just as intuitively with her womb-like baths and creative stroking—as it were metaphorizing an imminent tomb into a bath which becomes a recreating womb. As far as I know, it is a ritual that occurs nowhere else in late antique saints' lives. The fact that Fortunatus uses the term 'new kind of miracle' for the dream bathing ritual seems to indicate that he was aware of this. In his intricate and many-layered poems he shows himself to be a master of imagistic allusion. The hagiographical genre in this period, however, required unadorned, colloquial speech. Nevertheless, alongside the largely implicit symbolism of the rituals of a nun's profession, baptism and anointing of the sick, as well as that of Christ's death and resurrection, he appears to be subtly pointing to a womb

---

[117] B.S. Siegel, *Love, Medicine and Miracles: Lessons Learned About Self-Healing from a Surgeon's Experience with Exceptional Patients* (New York, 1986), pp. 66–69.

[118] M. Proust, *À la recherche du temps perdu*, vol. 1: *Du coté de chez Swann* (Paris, 1954), p. 283: "the little phrase of Vintueil's sonata ... continued to remind Swann of the love he had for Odette (*la petite phrase de la sonate de Vinteuil ... continuait à s'associer pour Swann à l'amour qu'il avait pour Odette*)."

symbolism that reveals Radegund's acting out and realizing her ideal of spiritual motherhood.

Trampling the Serpent Underfoot: Christian Woman as the New Eve?

Radegund's second kind of innovative cure involves a different ritual: that of an exorcism in which the possessing agent appears as a serpent. Only one of Germanus' cures resembles it. Here, the saint heals a possessed person who was a member of the clergy in a manner about which we are not told—perhaps by prayer and/or the imposition of hands[119]—and "the bystanders saw the spirit (*umbra*) that was driven out emerge from the possessed man's head like a small bird".[120] When it was caught,

> the holy man himself crushed it with his feet (*contrivit vestigiis*). When he stepped upon it (*cum pede comprimeretur*), the False One was at once turned into blood in a double praise, so that it would not be trampled underfoot (*nec calcaretur*), and so that, by the testimony of his fall (*sui casus indicium*), the omnipresent Artificer would be shown up as the bloodstained perpetrator of murders.[121]

That the bird, as the visible manifestation of the possessing agent should be killed is obvious. Showing the 'figurative' habit of mind in this period, Fortunatus assimilates the saint's catching and crushing the bird to the 'fall' of the evil angel Satan from heaven,[122] and its turning to blood as a manifestation of its murderous nature. He does not highlight the gesture of grinding underfoot. In Psalm 90 (91):13, however, we read: "You will tread upon (*calcabis*) the adder and the basilisk; you will trample the lion and the dragon underfoot (*conculcabis*)". These animals are, of course, figures of spiritual evil.[123] Jesus' perhaps derivative statement that the apostles have been given the power to tread upon serpents[124] may resonate as well. The

---

[119] As in *Vita sancti Germani* 53 (prayer: *exorante*), and 78 (hands on head).
[120] Ibid. 142. Cf. P. Dinzelbacher, "Der Kampf der Heiligen mit den Dämonen", *Santi e demoni nell'alto Medioevo occidentale (secoli V–XI)* Settimane di Studio del Centro Italiano di Studi sull'alto Medioevo 36 (Spoleto, 1989), pp. 675–682.
[121] Ibid. 143.
[122] Revelation 12:9.
[123] Cf. "Serpent", DACL 5.1, col. 1353–1356; and "Dragon", DACL 4.2, col. 1537–1539.
[124] Luke 10:19.

figure of Christ trampling upon Satan as a serpent and/or dragon has been found in early Christian iconography.[125] But these associations are evidently not the author's focus of attention in the context of a cure.

Outside that context, however, the overcoming of serpents is a well-known motif in male saints' lives. Saint Martin had commanded water snakes to retreat.[126] And Fortunatus himself reports in his Life of Saint Hilary of Poitiers that the man of God had chased snakes off a certain part of an island. He did this with the sign of the Cross and the invocation of the name of the Lord. These acts must have accompanied a command however because, in the same passage, Fortunatus praises Hilary for "commanding serpents" and confining them through his "speech" to a certain region, making the rest of the island safe for human habitation. The author's subsequent stress on Hilary's "charm (*dulcedo*)" in all this, however, appears to point to the event as a metaphor for containing evil in the bishop's human community.[127] The story shows again that speaking was a typically male power role. But Fortunatus here also explicitly and significantly contrasts the first Adam's being overcome by a serpent with Hilary, as a servant of Christ—the new, second Adam—overcoming them. Elsewhere, he recounts a similar event in Saint Marcellus' "triumphal mystery (*triumphale mysterium*)", in which the saint tamed and drove away the dragon who had been infesting the suburbs of Paris "in the spiritual theatre (*in spiritale theatro*)" in front of all the people.[128] The male saint, then, is presented as overcoming the serpent through the power of the word, and not through physically treading upon him. Gregory and Fortunatus' writings abundantly show that rhetoric—as an instrument of power—was highly prized in men in this period, but never attributed to women.[129]

Two of Radegund's cures, however, show a trampling of the disease-causing agent underfoot, and in one case the latter looks like a serpent. In both cases, the illness is possession without other physical symptoms. Here is the first story:

---

[125] See: "Serpent", DACL 5.1, col. 1353; and "Dragon", DACL 4.2, col. 1537.
[126] Sulpicius Severus, *Dialogi* (ed. C. Halm, Corpus Scriptorum Ecclesiasticorum Latinorum (= CSEL) 1 (Vienna, 1866), pp. 152–216) 2 (3).9.4.
[127] *Vita sancti Hilarii* 35–39.
[128] *Vita sancti Marcelli* 40.
[129] For instance: Gregorius, *Historiae* 2.22 and Fortunatus, *Carmina* 3.4.

> A certain woman labored so heavily under an invasion by the Enemy that the rebellious Foe could scarcely be brought to the saint. She commanded the Adversary that he should prostrate himself with his fear on the pavement. At the very moment that the blessed lady spoke he threw himself upon the ground, and the one who had been feared was now himself afraid of her. When the saint, full of faith, stamped upon his neck, he came out in a flux from her belly (*cum calcasset in cervice, fluxu ventris egressus est*).[130]

In late antique possession stories, the actions and speech of the person concerned are not their own but those of the possessor.[131] The curing of possession by purgation in one way or another was a late antique medical prescription, and is also reported in one of Saint Martin's cures.[132] But this ritual of a, presumably rather uncomfortable, stamping on the possessed's neck is not found elsewhere. The specific mention of the neck seems to me to point to the passage in Genesis in which it is said that the seed of the woman—and, in this context, Eve's descendants must be meant—will crush the head of the serpent who is the image of Satan: "she shall bruise your head (*ipsa conteret caput tuum*)".[133] As we saw, Radegund was a dominating figure, through her prayers and miracles said to 'rule' Gaul as 'a spiritual kingdom' alongside the secular government of her stepsons. It is tempting to believe that she is here, against the patriarchal ordering of society, pointing to a woman's version of world history: to the descendants of a new, independent and powerful Eve alongside the new Adam who was Christ—now 'living' in her chapel at Poitiers—, and who had also acted through male saints such as Saint Hilary, whose tomb was not far from the convent. Was she, as spiritual queen, spiritual mother, teacher and custodian of the relic of the Holy Cross, in fact providing an intrinsically female role of power over against that of the male father, shepherd, doctor, warrior and orator?

The second story, just as the one about Animia, announces innovation, but Fortunatus cautiously calls it "a new healing of Christ (*nova Christi curatio*)". He tells us that when Radegund was still at her

---

[130] Fortunatus, *Vita sanctae Radegundis* 71–72.
[131] As P. Brown, *The Cult of the Saints: Its Rise and Function in Latin Christianity* (Chicago, 1981), p. 111.
[132] *Vita sancti Martini* 17.5–7. Cf. Rousselle, *Croire et guérir*, p. 116.
[133] Genesis 3:15. Cf. DACL 5.1, col. 1353.

country estate, a woman called Leubila, in the countryside, was also greatly "troubled (*vexaretur*)" by the Adversary; but

> the following day, while the saint prayed, she was publicly healed through a new cure of Christ. For the skin of her shoulder opened with a rustling sound and a worm came out. She reported that when she trampled that same worm underfoot, she was liberated.[134]

The worm is, of course, a kind of serpent. Gregory's story of another woman's cure shows that violent intestinal illness incurred through sorcery (*maleficium*) could be, probably correctly, diagnosed as 'serpents'—meaning worms—in the belly, which eventually became visible after purgation.[135] In the Third World today, there are diseases in which worm-like larvae of certain kinds of flies can penetrate the skin, incubate in the underlying tissue for days or weeks, and emerge again and drop on the ground. These diseases are not described as happening in Europe today.[136] The possibility that they occurred in the extremely unhygienic conditions of the sixth-century Gallic countryside cannot, however, be excluded.[137] Such a worm-like larva could easily be perceived, and treated as, the serpent who is Satan. Crucial, however, is that Leubila overcame the 'serpent' not by words, but by means of a visible symbolic ritual that seems to enact the biblical promise.[138]

If—as seems to be the case—the saint indeed only prayed and the girl enacted her own ritual, this is an uncommonly active role for a patient in this period. For in all other reported contemporary miracles, the living saint—man or woman—always does, or is always regarded as doing, everything for a passive, powerless sufferer. Radegund's life story shows, however, that she was capable of almost anything: like—against all custom—leaving her royal husband, getting

---

[134] Fortunatus, *Vita sanctae Radegundis* 67.

[135] Gregorius, *Vita patrum* 19.3.

[136] Subcutaneous myiasis, Dermatobia hominis, and Dermal myiasis: P.E.C. Manson-Bahr and D.R. Bell, *Manson's Tropical Diseases*, 19th ed. (London etc., 1987), pp. 911–917.

[137] Quartan fever, which is also frequently mentioned by Gregory, is designated as a kind of *paludisme* or malaria by M. Rouche, "Miracles, maladies et psychologie de la foi à l'époque carolingienne en Francie", *Hagiographies, cultures et sociétés IV–XIIe siècles* (Paris, 1981), p. 322.

[138] Cf. G. de Nie, "Text, symbol and 'oral culture' in the sixth-century Church: The miracle story", *Mediaevistik* 9 (1996), pp. 115–133.

herself consecrated as a deaconess when not only she was still legally married to the king, but the female diaconate was already abolished, and persuading her rejected husband to support and finance her founding of the convent.[139] In this last cure, too, she was acting independently and innovating.

The 'Mysterium' of the New Eve

At the end of Fortunatus' story of Radegund's life, he tells us that a tribune severely suffering from a constriction of his throat had a dream in which Radegund comes to visit him. As will be seen, the discomfort may have been connected with his resisting popular pressure to perform certain actions. Radegund does three things. First, she takes him by the hand and shows him a place in which there were 'relics' of Saint Martin, and in which, according to the wish of the people of the region, a church should be built in his honor. Fortunatus goes on: "What a mystery (*Quale mysterium*)! The fundament and pavement [of an older church?] were found, where the church was built."[140] Here, the dream image appears to be the 'mystery'—showing something that is hidden but real, and which, when found, will transform people's lives. The next thing Radegund did was to stroke the tribune's jaws and throat for a long time, finally saying: "I came so that God might confer better health upon you". Finally, she requested him to release, for her sake, those whom he held in his prison—which he carried out after his awakening. A messenger later confirmed that she had died at the very hour of the tribune's dream, and, as Fortunatus writes,

> through the triple mystery (*triplici mysterio*) of the opened prison, the tribune cured and the temple built, the oracle of the saint was confirmed (*sanctae probavit oraculum*).[141]

The dream about the saint, then, was an 'oracle' whose truth was proven by the occurrence of the events it had announced. Why are these events themselves designated as 'a triple mystery'? Because, I

---

[139] Fortunatus, *Vita sanctae Radegundis* 26–28; Baudonivia, *Vita sanctae Radegundis* 5. On the abolition of the female diaconate in Gaul, see: S.F. Wemple, *Women in Frankish Society: Marriage and the Cloister 500–900* (Philadelphia, 1981), pp. 138–141.
[140] Fortunatus, *Vita sanctae Radegundis* 87–89.
[141] Ibid. 90.

would suggest, they are all manifestations and effects in sensory reality of 'figural' patterns or symbols of the Kingdom of God: those of Christ's salvation of man from sin and from illness (the latter is likely to be perceived as a punishment as well as an manifestation of the former), and of the building up of the Church. As so often, here again the contours of the visible events are perceived as those of biblical images and 'figures'.

To summarize and conclude: focusing upon the concept of *mysterium*—meaning the human enactment of a divine symbol as well as its manifestation in the sensory sphere—, a comparison between Fortunatus' descriptions of Saint Germanus' and Saint Radegund's cures reveals many similarities between them. But it also brings out the uniqueness of two of the latter's healing rituals for women. For whereas Germanus is presented as behaving in a quintessentially male and patriarchal manner, Radegund is seen to exploit her ideal of spiritual motherhood and experiment with the specific potential of Christian womanhood. She transforms the image and symbol of Christ's death and resurrection—through whose contours miraculous cures were then not infrequently perceived—, and makes the Old Testament prophecy of woman's treading upon the serpent a present reality. In the first ritual—which is designated as 'an enacted mystery'—, the bath in which the patient is laid symbolically turns from a tomb (into which everyone else was about to lay her) into a womb from which the patient emerges, as it were, reborn: the event mimics and replicates woman's natural reproductive capacity. The second ritual appropriates the biblical 'figure' highlighting woman (one which is, as far as I know, not mentioned anywhere else in this period) and expels the disease-causing agent—imaged as a serpent—by enacting and thereby fulfilling the prophecy. What we see happening here also occurs in oral societies today: a patient's affective enacting of a significant metaphor or symbol can precipitate a real physical transformation through what one might call 'iconic alchemy'.[142]

That Radegund was indeed especially remembered as a spiritual mother seems also to be evident in Baudonivia's report that, just after her decease, Gregory of Tours was startled to see in her face

---

[142] Cf. G. de Nie, "Iconic alchemy: imaging miracles in late sixth-century Gaul", *Studia Patristica* 30 (1997), pp. 158–66.

a reflection of that of "the Mother of the Lord".[143] Fortunatus' other, overlapping, image of Radegund as the new Eve is also—if dimly—visible, however, in what a mid-sixth-century religious poet in Rome, notwithstanding the grinding inequality of women in everyday life, presented as the official church view:

> Mary ... the gateway of God, the virgin mother of her own Creator. ... The second virgin put to flight the woes of Eve's crime; ... she restored what the first took away. ... [Eve] begetting mortal things and [Mary] bearing divine, she through whom the Mediator came forth into the world (*mortalia gignens/Et divina ferens, per quam Mediator in orbem/ Prodiit*). ...[144]

---

[143] Baudonivia, *Vita sanctae Radegundis* 23.
[144] Arator Subdiaconus, *De actibus apostolorum* (ed. A.P. McKinlay, CSEL 72 (Vienna, 1951)) 1.57–60, 66–68. Tr. R.J. Schrader et al., *Arator's On the Acts of the Apostles (De actibus apostolorum)*, Classics in Religious Studies 6 (Atlanta, 1987), pp. 26–27.

4

WOMEN IN COLUMBA'S LIFE, AS SEEN THROUGH THE EYES OF HIS BIOGRAPHER ADOMNÁN

Jacqueline Borsje

Introduction

This article[1] will explore the role of women in Adomnán's *Vita Sancti Columbae*, 'The Life of St Columba' (VC). The first part of the article will give an introduction to early Irish narrative texts and miracles. The second part is devoted to a short description of the saint, the *Life* and its author. The third part summarises all episodes of VC in which women are mentioned and, in addition, provides an analysis of the role that some[2] women play, focussing upon the relationship between Columba and these women, and its portrayal by Adomnán.

Early Irish Texts and 'Miracles'

There is a huge amount of early medieval Irish texts extant, written in (Hiberno-)Latin, Irish or a mixture of these two languages. These texts represent several genres, such as hagiography, sagas, place-name lore, etymologies, genealogies, annals, law texts, texts related to biblical and deutero-canonical books, commentaries, and so on. These texts were either composed or written down in monasteries and their environment. This means that sagas which could have their roots in the pre-Christian past are only available to us in manuscripts that

---

[1] This article was started at the Department of Theology of the Vrije Universiteit in Amsterdam and finished at the School of Celtic Studies of the Dublin Institute for Advanced Studies. I would like to express my thanks to Bob Ordish for correcting my English. Moreover, I am indebted to Proinsias Mac Cana, Karen Jankulak, and to the research group 'Women and Miracle Stories'—especially to Anne-Marie Korte—for their comments on an earlier draft.

[2] Sometimes women are only referred to without there being any narrative context about them that can be analysed.

were produced in a Christian milieu. The methodological problems and the possibilities that this textual material offers have been dealt with elsewhere;[3] it is beyond the scope of this article to go into this.

I would like to focus here on a narrative motif in early Irish texts. In this literature, one often encounters the phenomenon in which changes are brought about by employing invisible, supernatural or extraordinary forces. For instance, water is changed into wine or a woman takes on the shape of a bird. The name given to this phenomenon depends on the genre of the literature in which it is found: in hagiography, it is called a miracle; in sagas, it is called magic.

This dualistic way of naming the same phenomenon has its roots in Christian ideology. In Christian literature, a supernatural phenomenon in a Christian context is evaluated as good, having its source in God. Outside of the Christian context, in the hands of non-Christians, it is condemned and is sometimes explicitly connected with the forces of evil, like the Devil and demons. This non-Christian power called magic is, moreover, often supposed to work evil: to bring destruction, disease and death. One can find this dualism in VC, the text central here, where the supernatural acts of the protagonist Columba are called miracles. His human antagonists on the supernatural level are the *magi*, the magicians or druids. An example of how they perform the same supernatural act is given in VC II.34. Both a druid and the saint change the weather. The druid raises an adverse wind and creates a mist of darkness in order to prevent Columba from departing from the land of the Picts. Adomnán, the author of VC, tells us explicitly that this is done by the art of demons. He then narrates how Columba sails fast *against* the wind, and after a while he performs the same trick as the druid: he changes the direction of the wind. It is thus made clear that Columba's 'magic' is superior to that of the druid. This message is emphasised by the terms used: Columba's art is called a miracle and his power springs from the Divine—God and Christ.[4]

---

[3] For an extensive survey, see K. McCone, *Pagan Past and Christian Present in Early Irish Literature*, Maynooth Monographs 3 (Maynooth, 1990). For an attempt to distinguish between native Irish and Christian motifs, see J. Borsje, *From Chaos to Enemy: Encounters with Monsters in Early Irish Texts. An investigation related to the process of Christianization and the concept of evil*, Instrumenta Patristica XXIX (Turnhout, 1996), especially chapter 1.

[4] Although this dualism is ideological, I will follow the terms used in my source in the course of this article: miracles connected with the saint, and magic related to the druids. For more about magic as a religious phenomenon, see J. van Baal, *De magie als godsdienstig verschijnsel* (Amsterdam, 1960).

The Saint and his Biographer

St Columba, the Irish monk who performs the miracles central to this study, is regarded as one of the major Irish saints.[5] He lived in the sixth century.[6] He left Ireland in 563 with twelve companions and founded a monastery on the Scottish island of Iona. This became an important centre of the Irish church.[7]

Vita Sancti Columbae[8] was composed by Adomnán (c. 628–704),[9] a relative of Columba and his ninth successor as abbot of Iona. VC was written at the request of the monks of Iona, as Adomnán himself tells us (VC, first preface).[10] Adomnán collected and arranged stories about the miracles that Columba performed both during his life and after his death. Adomnán experienced some of the posthumous miracles himself (VC II.44–46); for most of them, however, he relied upon sources, both oral and written (VC, second preface). The stories are not told chronologically; Adomnán carefully selected the narratives and arranged them thematically. He divided the miracles into three categories, which he made the subjects of the three books of VC. These categories are: first, miracles of prophecy; second, miracles of power; and third, miraculous angelic visions and apparitions of light and fire. These three books are preceded by two consecutive prefaces.[11]

---

[5] Other famous Irish saints are St Patrick, St Brigit, and St Brendan.

[6] He was born between 519 and 522 and died on 9 June 597; see A.O. and M.O. Anderson, *Adomnán's Life of Columba* (Edinburgh and London, 1961; revised edition by M.O. Anderson, Oxford, 1991), p. xxviii (page citations are to the revised edition).

[7] J.F. Kenney, *The Sources for the Early History of Ireland: Ecclesiastical. An Introduction and Guide* (1929; reprint, Dublin, 1979), p. 224.

[8] The text is found in the following manuscripts: Msc. Generalia I, Stadtbibliothek Schaffhausen, fol. 1–136, 713; ms. I, Grand Séminaire Metz, fol. 1–79, 9th century; Add. 35110, British Library, fol. 96^v–143^r, c. 1195; Cottonian Tiberius D III, British Library, fol. 192^r–217^r, end-12th to very early 13th centuries; and Royal 8 D IX, British Library, fol. 1^r–70^r, 15th to early 16th centuries. For an edition of this Latin text and its translation, see Anderson, *Adomnan's Life of Columba*; for a more recent translation, see R. Sharpe, *Adomnán of Iona. Life of St Columba* (Harmondsworth, 1995).

[9] Anderson, *Adomnán's Life of Columba*, pp. xxxix, xli.

[10] Opinions about why the monks requested the production of the *Life* differ. See J.-M. Picard, "The Purpose of Adomnán's *Vita Columbae*", *Peritia* 1 (1982), pp. 160–177, and M. Herbert, *Iona, Kells and Derry. The History and Hagiography of the Monastic Familia of Columba* (Oxford, 1988), pp. 142–148.

[11] For more about the literary models that Adomnán used, see G. Brüning, "Adamnans *Vita Columbae* und ihre Ableitungen", *Zeitschrift für celtische Philologie* 11

VC is a lengthy work: the (latest) edition and translation by Marjorie Ogilvie Anderson runs to 235 pages, the translation by Richard Sharpe (a Penguin pocket) to 134. The first Book comprises 50 chapters, the second 46, and the third 23. Each chapter deals with at least one miracle. It should be noted that the majority of the people playing a part in these anecdotes about miracles are male. Viewed quantitatively, women play a marginal role in VC.[12] The fact that Columba lived in a male monastic community is not totally satisfying as a possible reason for this because Columba's adventures among lay people in Ireland and Scotland are related as well. This article will not attempt to address the issue of the quantitative role but seeks instead to analyse the qualitative role of women in this *vita*.

The Stories about Miracles involving Women

Another document written by Adomnán is the *Lex Innocentium* (697 A.D.), also known as *Adomnán's Law*. This is a law for women, clerics and youths (i.e. boys), who by this law are exempted from military service. *Adomnán's Law* was thoroughly analysed by Máirín Ní Dhonnchadha.[13] She concludes that in this law Adomnán addresses women mainly as wives and mothers:

> In fact, one can discern a clear subtext in the Law whereby Adomnán calls on all laywomen (and men) to accommodate themselves to christian marriage and abandon unorthodox unions. Remarkably, the Law makes no reference whatsoever to women in religious life. (...) By excluding all reference to virgin nuns and formerly married women who entered the church, Adomnán gives a new emphasis to women's *militia Christi*. (...) Adomnán's Law calls on women to serve not in ascetic denial but in marriage and motherhood. The Law implies an opposition between men as takers of life (with just cause) and women as givers of life.[14]

(1917), pp. 213–304: pp. 229–255. For more about the structure of VC and its background in classical biography, Christian hagiography and Irish narratives, see J.-M. Picard, "Structural Patterns in Early Hiberno-Latin Hagiography", *Peritia* 4 (1985), pp. 67–82 (cp. Borsje, *From Chaos to Enemy*, pp. 95–97).

[12] The second preface mentions one woman; Book I mentions women in nine chapters, Book II in twelve and Book III in three.

[13] See M. Ní Dhonnchadha, "The *Lex Innocentium*: Adomnán's Law for Women, Clerics and Youths, 697 A.D.", *Chattel, Servant or Citizen. Women's Status in Church, State and Society*, eds. M. O'Dowd and S. Wichert, Historical Studies XIX (Belfast, 1995), pp. 58–69.

[14] Ní Dhonnchadha, "The *Lex Innocentium*", p. 67.

At the end of her analysis of the *Law of Adomnán*, Ní Dhonnchadha adverts to VC, which "undoubtedly was also a vehicle for Adomnán's own views".[15] She points out that Adomnán presents his view of Christian marriage with the endorsement of Columba, referring to a story in which a woman suddenly loves her ugly husband.[16] She draws attention to the fact that this story is preceded by the miracle in which Columba helps his relative in childbirth,[17] and as Adomnán has good reasons for the way he organises his material this story sequence is not without meaning. Her conclusion is that Adomnán saw Christian marriage as in the best interests of women and that, although he must also have had respect for ecclesiastical or solitary living women, there is no evidence that he was willing to see real power in their hands.[18]

As the *Law of Adomnán* was the focus of her study, Ní Dhonnchadha only summarises her findings about VC briefly. I would like to posit that it is worthwhile to have another look at the women in VC. A first glance at the material shows us that Ní Dhonnchadha is right in the quantitative way: most of the women figuring in VC are wives and mothers. But the stories about Columba's miracles reveal more about them. I would like to attempt to lure these women out of the shadow of Columba. We have to look at them through the eyes of Adomnán. Being conscious of that we may perhaps learn more when we focus our attention upon the way he describes them and Columba's relationship with them.

Let us now have a closer look at the women who figure in Columba's *Life*. What kind of women are they?[19] What role do they perform? What function do they have in the stories? What kind of relationship do the women have with Columba—do they cooperate with him or obstruct his work? Does he help or punish them? How does Adomnán describe the women—which explicit terms and implicit images does he use? In the light of Ní Dhonnchadha's last conclusion, it is interesting to ask: do they have no power whatever, or can we detect a certain degree of power?

---

[15] Ní Dhonnchadha, "The *Lex Innocentium*", p. 69.
[16] For more about this and the next example, see below.
[17] Ní Dhonnchadha, "The *Lex Innocentium*", p. 69.
[18] Ibid.
[19] In this description I shall include only those references that speak of women *expressis verbis*. I leave out inclusive designations such as, for instance, 'people' and 'parents'.

In order to gain a clear view of the material, I have divided the stories into three categories: first, anecdotes in which women seem to have a neutral role; second, anecdotes about women who co-operate with Columba or are helped by him, and third, women who obstruct his work or are punished by the saint. I will describe each miracle-story and examine the women's relationship with Columba and its description by Adomnán. Because not every reader will be familiar with Irish hagiography in general and Adomnán's VC in particular, I will quote three chapters[20] completely, so that one can savour the style and read the narrative directly.

Stories about women who play a neutral role

Adomnán not only arranged Columba's miracles in the three Books according to the three categories mentioned above but also made small divisions within the Books.[21] Thematically related material is often grouped together. Examples are the clusters of Columba's acts of vengeance upon enemies (II.22–25) and his encounters with beasts (II.26–28).[22] I believe that the two chapters that I shall deal with now also form such a cluster (I.38–39). In the first episode Columba visits Ireland and sees a cheerful cleric travelling in a chariot over the plain of Brega.[23] This man, Lugaid the Lame, is said to be wealthy and respected among the people. Columba comments that he sees the man differently and he adds the prophecy that on the day of his death he will be wretched and poor. While reclining on a couch with a prostitute, he will choke to death on a piece of meat. This indeed happens in due course. The word used to refer to the woman is *meritrix*.[24] Anderson[25] translates this 'a harlot', Sharpe[26] as

---

[20] I chose these three from a selection the research group 'Women and Miracle Stories' made which were of particular interest to them.
[21] For more about this technique of *divisio*, see Picard, "Structural Patterns", pp. 77–78.
[22] See also below, where II.25 is quoted. The last paragraph of II.25 is an instance of how Adomnán explicitly marks his way of clustering.
[23] For more information about places and people mentioned in VC, see Sharpe, *Adomnán of Iona*. I follow the spelling of the names as given in Sharpe's translation.
[24] One would expect here *meretrix*; for more about the Hiberno-Latin spellings in VC, see J.-M. Picard, "The Schaffhausen Adomnán—A Unique Witness to Hiberno-Latin", *Peritia* 1 (1982), pp. 216–249.
[25] Anderson, *Adomnán's Life of Columba*, p. 73.
[26] Sharpe, *Adomnán of Iona*, p. 142.

'his[27] whore' (I.38). Another *meritrix* occurs in I.39. Neman mac Guthriche is rebuked by Columba for his bad deeds, but the man mocks the saint. Columba replies that this man will be discovered by his enemies while he is lying with a prostitute. They will kill him and his soul will be dragged to Hell by demons. Some years later, in the district of *Cainle*,[28] the prophecy is borne out.

Columba appears to be neutral towards these women: the two prostitutes just happen to be present at the deaths of men. The mention of these women is purely incidental; their presence in the anecdotes is not pivotal. The point of the story is Columba's prophetic knowledge of the future. It is, however, also important to look at Adomnán's portrayal of the story—he might be conveying a message through details. It should be noted that, according to Sharpe,[29] the word *meritrix* "reflects Adomnán's attitude to loose liaisons in a polygamous (and sometimes promiscuous) society; it does not suggest a commercial relationship". If Sharpe is right then Adomnán uses *meritrix* as a term of abuse rather than to designate a profession. Sharpe does not, however, tell us upon which facts he bases this supposition, which is why I take the word at its face value. The order of II.38 and II.39 shows a line of escalation, from a cleric[30] with a hidden evil to an obviously evil man. Columba discloses his vision to the first man's friends, and the contrast between the view of the 'world' and the view of the saint is described in a neat opposition in chiasmus: the world sees the man alive, rich and honoured (*homo dives et honoratus*); Columba sees him on his day of death: a little man, miserable and poor (*homuncio miser et pauper*). The first man was a cheerful, respected type of person; the second is chided for his evil deeds (*de malis*). This second man's end is prophesied to himself. The

---

[27] The possessive pronoun in Sharpe's translation stems from his interpretation of the *meritrix* (for more about this, see below).

[28] Places which Sharpe was not able to identify are given in italics. I follow him in this.

[29] *Adomnán of Iona*, p. 300, n. 172.

[30] There is no explicit comment in VC about the fact that a cleric has sexual contact with a woman, unless we should read the term *meritrix* as a form of criticism, as Sharpe does. Lisa Bitel ("Sex, Sin, and Celibacy in Early Christian Ireland", *Proceedings of the Harvard Celtic Colloquium* 7 (1987), pp. 65–95: pp. 81–83) points out that celibacy was more an ideal—found in the penitentials and hagiography—than a fact: "Prominent ecclesiastical leaders were often, even usually, married men with dynasties to build and maintain" (ibid., p. 83). Sharpe (*Adomnán of Iona*, p. 300, n. 169) writes about this instance: "the point is probably that clerical orders were merely an adjunct to a man of high secular status".

fact that these two men are on a couch with a prostitute does not seem to be particularly important: no additional detail, image or comment are added.[31] This does, however, not rule out the reading of these scenes as another aspect of the evilness of the two men, because prostitution is generally condemned within Christianity.

There is another anecdote in Book I in which a woman is mentioned in the context of a prophecy about the circumstances of the death of a man. In this instance it is, however, not the saint who mentions her, but her husband. Guaire mac Áedáin asks Columba what kind of death he has to expect (I.47). He will die neither in battle nor at sea, the saint responds. Instead his death will be caused by a companion of his journey, from whom he suspects nothing. Guaire assumes that he will be killed either by a friend or by his wife: "*aut marita ob alicuius iunioris uiri amorem me maleficio mortificare*",[32] 'or my wife, to contrive my death by magic art, for love of a younger man'.[33] This is not the case, says Columba, who refuses to be more specific. The death actually occurs by his own knife which accidentally wounds his knee, the wound causing his death several months later.

Columba appears to be neutral towards this woman as well. It is her husband who maligns her and not the saint. It should be noted that Jean-Michel Picard[34] attaches great importance to Guaire's statement. Picard connects this with the mythological motif of wooing a young woman who sets the hero impossible tasks[35] and reconstructs an archaic mythological complex which could be characterised as 'the death of the old, impotent king'. Picard believes that Adomnán used a story from this older, different genre[36] and adapted it to his purposes. Although Picard offers interesting material and insights, some methodological observations make it difficult to accept his suppositions. He builds extensively upon the Finnish epos *Kalevala*,

---

[31] I see no reason to characterise each of these women as 'the harlot of the Apocalypse', as Ní Dhonnchadha ("The *Lex Innocentium*", p. 69) does.

[32] Anderson, *Adomnán's Life of Columba*, p. 84.

[33] Anderson, *Adomnán's Life of Columba*, p. 85.

[34] J.-M. Picard, "The Strange Death of Guaire Mac Áedáin", *Sages, Saints and Storytellers. Celtic Studies in Honour of Professor James Carney*, eds. D. Ó Corráin, L. Breatnach and K. McCone, Maynooth Monographs 2 (Maynooth, 1989), pp. 367–375.

[35] For more about this and other elements involved in this complex, see Picard, "Strange Death", p. 370.

[36] See Picard, "Strange Death", pp. 371–372.

and even though he adverts to older layers and variant versions in traditional folkore,[37] it seems problematic to me to use a literary production from the 19th century as an important basis for the reconstruction of a mythological complex that should be older than VC itself.[38] As we are dealing here with the role of the woman, it is also important to note that the woman's role in this posited complex shifts with each textual tradition with which Picard is dealing.[39] More study—especially into the function and identity of the women mentioned—is needed to do justice to the material collected by Picard, but this is beyond the scope of this article.

I would like to offer another attempt at understanding this story, based on Adomnán's choice of words. The wife of Guaire is depicted as capable of murder out of passion, which she would achieve by *maleficium*, 'an evil deed', or 'magic art',[40] 'witchcraft'.[41] This word is indeed used in such a context in VC II.17, where the *maleficia* of a *maleficus* are described: this sorcerer milks a bull, but this is done by demonic imposture and diabolic art, as Columba shows. The milk is in fact the bleached blood of the bull, which almost dies. Columba reveals the truth and heals the bull. This is part of the opposition evident throughout VC: Columba sides with God, good and life; the druids or magicians (*magi*) and evil-doers (*malefactores*)[42] side with devils, evil and death.[43] The application of the word *maleficium* to the woman thus has a pejorative sound within the context of VC. However, Columba has nothing to do with her, nor does Adomnán go into details about her. It is Guaire who uses the word *maleficium* and he turns out to be wrong. This story gives an example of a possible source of female power, but this is neither important to Columba, nor does it pertain to the point Adomnán wants to make.

Closely related to the themes of I.38–39 and I.47 is the following anecdote: a woman is mentioned in a prophecy about the circumstances of a man's grave (I.20). Báetán, a descendant of Nia

---

[37] "Strange Death", p. 368.
[38] For more about *Kalevala* see, for instance, H. Pihlajamaa, "Kalevala. Finlands nationale epos", *Bzzlletin* 10 (1982) 92, pp. 35–38.
[39] See Picard, "Strange Death", pp. 368–369.
[40] Anderson, *Adomnán's Life of Columba*, p. 85 (n. 111: 'sorcery' or possibly 'poison').
[41] Sharpe, *Adomnán of Iona*, p. 149.
[42] It should be noted that Adomnán designates evil-doers who are magicians as *magi* and, in the case of II.17, *maleficus*; evil-doers who are robbers or otherwise violent men are designated *malefactores* (see II.22 and II.24).
[43] See, for instance, II.11, II.17, II.22–25 and II.34.

Taloirc, goes to Columba to ask the holy man's blessing before departing and seeking a place of retreat in the sea.[44] When Báetán leaves, Columba prophesies that he will not be buried in such a place, but where a woman (*femina*) will drive sheep across his grave. It turns out that this man does not find his place of retreat and returns to Ireland, where he becomes the head of a small church. When he dies he is buried at Derry. At that time there is an attack of enemies, with laymen, women and children ("*plebicula cum mulieribus et paruulís*")[45] taking refuge in the church. On one particular day during that period it is seen that a woman (*mulier*) drives her sheep across the place where Báetán has recently been buried, and someone concludes that Columba's prophecy of many years ago has come true (I.20).

Here again, we can see the mention of a woman as merely an incidental detail, miraculously known by Columba. It is possible that more is intended by the contrast of a faraway, desolate, silent, peaceful island and a noisy place in Ireland where people and cattle are fleeing from enemies. Perhaps the mention of the woman's feet on the grave of the man who wanted to be a hermit signifies a contrast of sexuality versus celibacy, but Adomnán does not make this explicit. In fact, this example from VC does not tell us anything about the woman with her sheep. The only hint might be aimed at the man: he is not holy enough for a desert place in the sea, and therefore is buried in the noisy, busy 'world'. The case of this woman resembles the examples described above (I.38–39): she happens to be present. One could compare this with a prophecy in I.17: Columba tells a man that when he sees his butler swinging a pitcher, he will know that he is soon to die. This says nothing about either butler or pitcher: it is a matter of fact, occurring as the circumstances of a man's death.

There is a woman who is mentioned only as a relative of a witness to a miracle. III.19 relates how a young man, called Fergnae, sees angelic light descending upon Columba. He relates this vision

---

[44] This refers to the Irish custom of *peregrinatio*: following the example of the hermits in the East who retreated into the desert to be alone with God, some Irish people sought an island in the sea as a retreat from the world, a wilderness (*eremus, desertus*). For more about this, see K. Hughes, "The Changing Theory and Practice of Irish Pilgrimage", *The Journal of Ecclesiastical History* 11 (1960), pp. 143–151, and Sharpe, *Adomnán of Iona*, pp. 280–281, n. 109.

[45] Anderson, *Adomnán's Life of Columba*, p. 46.

to his sister's son, the priest Commán, who in his turn passes on the information to Adomnán. We know nothing about the woman: her only function is to be the link between these men as their relative, as sister and mother.

Another woman is mentioned in a prophecy about sins committed in the past and about the future and death of a man (I.22). Columba makes the monks pray in the church in the middle of the night, for in that hour an outrageous sin has been committed. The saint announces that the unhappy sinner will arrive a few months later on Iona. When that time is near, Columba sends his servant Diarmait to the harbour with the command that the wretch is not to set foot upon the island. The unhappy man replies to this message that he will not take food until Columba has spoken with him. This makes the saint go to the harbour. Baithéne[46] intercedes for the man, quoting from the Bible. Then Columba replies that this man has killed his brother like Cain and has committed incest with his mother (*mater*; designated *genitrix* in the title).[47] The wretch kneels upon the shore and vows to do the penance that Columba will impose. The saint tells him that if he does penance with wailing and weeping among the British for twelve years, and never returns to Ireland for as long as he lives, God may perhaps forgive him. Columba prophesies to his own people, however, that the man is a son of perdition: in a short while he will return to Ireland where he will be killed by his enemies. What Columba says happens accordingly to this man, who belonged to the Uí Thuirtri (I.22).

Columba does not make any reference to the sinfulness of the mother, which makes one wonder whether she underwent the sex with her son unwillingly. This seems all the more probable as another one of her sons had been killed by the incestuous son. Neither does Adomnán comment on the woman, but it is significant that his title for I.22 refers to the incest but not to the fratricide. The punishment that Columba announces for the man is in accordance with the penitentials,[48] and the emphasis on the incest might also be in keeping with those texts. As Bitel has commented:

---

[46] Baithéne is the monk who will succeed Columba after his death.

[47] "*De infelici quodam qui cum sua dormiuit genitrice*" (Anderson, *Adomnán's Life of Columba*, p. 48).

[48] See T.M. Charles-Edwards, "The Social Background to Irish *Peregrinatio*", *Celtica* 11 (1976), pp. 43–59: p. 51.

To churchmen the worst kinds of sexual sins were incest with one's mother, and, for women, adultery and breaking the vow of celibacy. Confessors imposed some of their heaviest penances on men who violated their mothers.[49]

It seems, therefore, that this woman suffered violence at the hand of her son, as otherwise one would expect comment from Columba or Adomnán upon her sin, which could perhaps be designated adultery. However, the focus is upon the man, who is described in biblical terms: he is like Cain[50] and is a son of perdition (*filius perditionis*).[51]

Finally, there are two examples of prophecies about women addressed to men (I.28 and I.46). By his miraculous prophetic qualities, Columba knows of a divine punishment taking place far away and tells this to a man who sees the saint's flushed face. Sulphurous fire has come down from Heaven upon a Roman city in Italy. The saint knows that almost three thousand men have perished. The Latin text then reads: "*excepto matrum puerorumque numero*",[52] 'not counting the number of women and children'[53] (I.28). Understandably both Anderson and Sharpe[54] translate *matres* as 'women' here, but it should be noted that the main meaning of *mater* is 'mother'.

As Columba's face becomes marvellously red when he beholds the fearful vision of the Roman city on fire he probably has compassion for all people involved, even though it does not seem to be necessary to state the number of women and children. I will not dwell upon this all too familiar characteristic of historical and sometimes contemporary texts in overlooking certain groups of people. The fact that Adomnán uses the word *matres* for women might be a symptom of his posited view of women primarily as wives and mothers.

In I.46, Columba is a guest at *Coire Salcháin*. One evening there is a certain layman among his visitors. Columba asks him where he lives and when the man answers *Cruach Rannoch*, the saint tells him

---

[49] Bitel, "Sex, Sin, and Celibacy", p. 75.

[50] Gn 4:8. All references to the Bible in this article are to the Vulgate. See T. O'Loughlin, "The Latin version of the Scriptures in Iona in the late seventh century: the evidence from Adomnán's *De locis sanctis*", *Peritia* 8 (1994), pp. 18–26.

[51] This expression is found twice in the Bible: Jo 17:12 which refers to the disciple Judas, who will betray Jesus Christ, and II Th 2:3 which refers to a figure who is characterised as an opponent of the divine powers, and who ultimately claims to be God. I am indebted to Tjitze Baarda for information about this latter matter.

[52] Anderson, *Adomnán's Life of Columba*, p. 54.

[53] Anderson, *Adomnán's Life of Columba*, p. 55.

[54] *Adomnán of Iona*, p. 132.

that his home district is being plundered. The man begins to lament his wife (*marita*) and children (*filii*). Columba comforts him, saying that the 'little man' should go home. His 'little family' has fled to the mountain and thus escaped the robbers, who have stolen all his 'little cattle' and household furniture. The man returns home and finds everything as the saint predicted.

Columba communicates with the man; nothing can be read about his attitude towards the family. The saint addresses the man as 'little man' (*homunculus*) and he refers to his little family (*familiola*) and little cattle (*pecuscula*). These diminutives also occur elsewhere in VC (for instance, II.20 and II.21), where they refer to poor people. Anderson interprets this as perhaps Columba's "kindly patronage towards their lowly condition".[55] Diminutives like this, however, also occur in other contexts in VC, such as for instance in the case of the rich cleric, mentioned above. In order to find the meaning of this style figure, more research should be done. One might also wonder whether it has its origin in the saint or in his biographer.

Stories about women who cooperate with Columba or are helped by him

The second category consists of stories about women who have a positive relationship with Columba. Three examples—II.20 and II.32–33—describe women who are helped by Columba on his initiative. A very poor man called Nesán the Crooked who lives in Lochaber receives Columba hospitably for one night. The saint blesses his five cows, whereupon they increase in due course to one hundred and five cows. In addition, as Nesán is a layman with wife and children ("*cum uxore et filiis*"),[56] his seed is blessed in his sons and grandsons ("*in filiis et nepotibus*")[57] by the holy man (II.20).

II.20 forms a cluster with II.21 since they deal with the same kind of miracle: in II.21 Columba also blesses a poor man who has received him hospitably, the cows therefore increasing in number (from 5 to 105) and the family becoming fruitful in sons and grandsons. It is beyond doubt that Columba was received hospitably by the wife in each case, but no special reference is made to the contact

---

[55] Anderson, *Adomnán's Life of Columba*, p. 121, n. 149.
[56] Anderson, *Adomnán's Life of Columba*, p. 120.
[57] Ibid. Perhaps one should translate 'children and grandchildren'.

between the saint and the woman. In the similar episode of II.21 she is not even mentioned, but the woman must be present there too because she is necessary for the blessing of descendants. These miracles are inherently inclusive of women; no conclusions about the women can be drawn from them.[58]

The incidents described in II.32–35 take place among the Picts; II.32–34 deal with encounters between the Christian saint and the Pictish druids. In II.32 Adomnán tells us that a Pictish layman was converted to Christianity when he heard Columba preaching the word of life, and was baptised together with wife (*marita*), children and servants. A few days after the conversion of this family, a son becomes severely ill. When the boy is dying the druids begin to taunt the parents and belittle the God of the Christians. Columba hears about this and, out of zeal for God, he travels to his friend. The father leads Columba to the building where his dead son lies and Columba prays all alone, upon which the boy is restored to life. The people of the household rejoice and glorify the God of the Christians. Adomnán concludes that Columba performed the miracle that the prophets Elijah and Elisha and the apostles Peter, Paul and John also performed.

The story abounds with interesting oppositions, such as for instance the development from mourning to rejoicing and the belittling of the God of the Christians by the druids to the glorifying of the God of the Christians by the household. However, the Pictish woman is only mentioned as a wife and a mother (*mater* in the summary of Columba's miracles of power in I.1); no further details are given about her, which is why her role cannot be analysed. She is a passive recipient of Columba's aid.

In II.33 the following story is told. The druid Broichan, who is foster-father of the Pictish king Bridei, has an Irish slave (*serva*; referred to as *ancella* in the title)[59] and Columba wants him to liberate her out of human kindness. Broichan refuses and Columba threatens him

---

[58] II.20 ends with an additional anecdote, not present in all manuscripts and forming an opposition with the first part. It relates how a rich man was inhospitable towards Columba. This man becomes poor and his son runs away. There is no mention of a wife.

[59] "*De Broichano mago ob ancellae retentionem infirmato, et pro eius liberatione sanato*", 'Concerning the magician Broichan, who was smitten with illness because he retained a female slave; and was cured, when he released her' (Anderson, *Adomnán's Life of Columba*, pp. 140–141).

that if he does not release this pilgrim captive (*perigrina captiva*) before Columba's departure from the province he will die. This conflict happens at Bridei's court, in the presence of the king. Columba leaves and takes a white stone from the river Ness, prophesying that the stone will heal the illnesses of many 'heathens' (Pictish people). He then goes on to announce that a heavenly angel has struck Broichan. Columba prophesies that the glass from which Broichan was drinking has broken into many pieces and the druid is almost choking to death. The king will soon send two messengers for help. Therefore, this terribly stricken man is now ready to release the young female slave (*ancellula*). The two men indeed arrive on horseback and relate all the events, prophesied by Columba, including the intended release of the slave-girl (*servula*). Columba sends two of his own men with the white stone. Broichan first has to promise that he will release the handmaid (*famula*) and then they are to dip the stone into water. The druid must drink the water, which will heal him. If he refuses to release the slave (*serva*), he will die at once. Columba's two envoys go to the royal dwelling and repeat the saint's words. The king and the druid are very afraid. The handmaid (*famula*) is set free and the stone is dipped into water. Miraculously, the stone floats like an apple or a nut. This is because the saint's blessing cannot be submerged. The druid drinks and returns from the brink of death to full bodily health. The stone is kept among the king's treasures. Many people are healed from their diseases by drinking water in which it is dipped, but when it is anyone's destined day of death the stone cannot be found. This also happens on the day of the king's death (II.33).

Like II.32, II.33 describes a power struggle, here between Columba and the druid Broichan. In II.33 the freedom of an Irish woman[60] is at stake. Adomnán uses many words to refer to the woman, designating her status as a slave although we gain no further insight into the woman herself. Both the Pictish woman and the Irish slave remain in the shadows. The miracles deal with hostile encounters between men with a supernatural function and help offered to the women involved, the point being Columba's miraculous power which is superior to the powers of the druids.

---

[60] For other examples of Irish women as slaves to magicians, see D.A. Bray, "Motival Derivations in the *Life of St Samthann*", *Studia Celtica* 20–21 (1985–86), pp. 78–86: p. 82.

The following two examples describe women helped by Columba at the request of someone else. The sister (*soror*) and foster-mother (*nutrix*) of Colgu mac Cellaig is suffering from a very severe inflammation of her eyes. Colgu asks Columba for a block of salt which has been blessed by the saint for her benefit. She hangs the blessing on the wall above her bed. After some days the village is burned down by some misfortune, as is the woman's (*femina*) cottage, but the small part of the wall where the blessing hangs remains. The fire has not dared to touch the two pegs on which the block of salt is suspended (II.7).

Nothing is said about Columba's relationship with this woman. Adomnán does not mention whether the woman was healed, although we can presume she was. He uses this anecdote as a link between two clusters of miracles. II.4–6 describe healing miracles; II.7 starts with the request for a healing miracle and ends with the miracle that the piece of salt blessed by Columba could not be burned by fire. II.8–9 continue this line, although focussing upon the element opposite to fire: water. II.8 relates how a book falls into water. All the pages are rotten, but for the one written by Columba. II.9 will be described below: a book fallen in water remains unharmed because it was written by Columba. One can only admire Adomnán for his eye for structure. At the same time, in the context of this study, we have to conclude that the woman with her sore eyes is dealt with only very summarily. Obviously she is less important than the saint and her relative Colgu mac Cellaig, who is at least named.

The second example gives Columba's help in the form of revenge. This chapter will be quoted entirely:

De alio itidem innocentium persequutore

CVM uir beatus adhuc iuuenis diacon in parte Lagenensium diuinam addiscens sapientiam conuersaretur, quadam accedit die ut homo quidam innocuorum inmitis persequutor crudilis quandam in campi planitie filiolam fugientem persequeretur. Quae cum forte Gemmanum senem supra memorati iuuenis diaconi magistrum in campo legentem uidisset, ad eum recto cursu quanta ualuit uelocitate confugit. Qui tali perturbatus subitatione Columbam eminus legentem aduocat, ut ambo in quantum ualuissent filiam a persequente defenderent. Qui statim superueniens, nulla eis ab eo data reuerentia, filiam sub uestimentis eorum lancea iugulauit, et relinquens iacentem mortuam super pedes eorum auersus abire coepit.

Senex tum ualde tristificatus conuersus ad Columbam: 'Quanto', ait, 'sancte puer Columba hoc scelus cum nostra dehonoratione temporis spatio inultum fieri iudex iustus patietur deus?' Sanctus consequenter hanc in ipsum sceleratorem protulit sententiam, dicens: 'Eadem hora qua interfectae ab eo filiae anima ascendit ad cae-

los, anima ipsius interfectoris discendat ad inferos.' Et dicto citius, cum uerbo, sicut Annanias coram Petro, sic et ille innocentium iugulator coram oculis sancti iuuenis in eadem mortuus cicidit terrula. Cuius rumor subitae et formidabilis uindictae continuo per multas Scotiae prouincias cum mira sancti diaconi fama deuulgatus est.

Hucusque de aduersariorum terrificis ultionibus dixisse susficiat. Nunc de bestiis aliqua narrabimus pauca.[61]

[ii.25] Concerning yet another oppressor of innocents

WHILE the blessed man, still a young deacon, was living in Leinster,[62] studying divine wisdom, it happened one day that a certain cruel man, a pitiless oppressor of the innocent, was pursuing a young girl, who fled upon the level surface of the plain. When by chance she saw the aforesaid young deacon's master, the aged Gemmán, reading on the plain, she ran straight to him for protection with all the speed she could. Alarmed by this sudden happening he called to him Columba, who was reading at a little distance, so that together they might to the extent of their power defend the girl from her pursuer. But as soon as the man came near, showing them no reverence he killed the girl with a spear, under their robes. And he left her lying dead upon their feet, and turning away began to depart.

Then the old man in great distress of mind turned to Columba, and said: 'For how long, holy boy, Columba, will God, the just judge, suffer this crime, and our dishonour, to go unavenged?' Thereupon the saint pronounced this sentence upon the miscreant: 'In the same hour in which the soul of the girl whom he has slain ascends to heaven, let the soul of her slayer descend to hell.' And more quickly than speech, with that word, like Ananias before Peter, so also before the eyes of the holy youth that killer of innocents fell dead on the spot. The fame of this sudden and dreadful vengeance was immediately spread abroad throughout many provinces of Ireland, with wonderful renown of the holy deacon.

Let it suffice to have told so much of terrible vengeance upon enemies. Now we shall tell some few things about animals.[63]

This scene is thought-provoking: the innocent young girl, literally 'the little daughter' (*filiola*), is terrified while she hides under the robes of the clerics who with their bare hands are powerless or impotent to protect her from the spear of the cruel man. Her corpse lies at the feet of the two dishonoured[64] men. Only when Gemmán expresses

---

[61] Anderson, *Adomnán's Life of Columba*, p. 130.
[62] Anderson gives 'the region of the Lagin'.
[63] Anderson, *Adomnán's Life of Columba*, p. 131.
[64] For more about honour and dishonour in this context, see Sharpe, *Adomnán of Iona*, p. 329, n. 268, and Borsje, *From Chaos to Enemy*, pp. 170–171.

his distress does Columba act. He condemns the man to death and Hell. Why did he not do so earlier, when the girl was still alive? II.25 is the last chapter in a cluster of miracles about Columba's 'terrible vengeance upon enemies' (II.22–25). However, chronologically, this could be the first time that Columba experienced this miraculous power,[65] as he is still a student in Ireland. Perhaps this miracle is his initiation into using 'very terrible words' (II.22) with their striking effect. Adomnán compares the way the killer falls down dead before St Columba with the way Ananias fell before St Peter, thus referring to Act 5:5.[66] Ananias, however, is not said to descend to Hell, as the soul of the killer would. Here, Adomnán again works with oppositions: the soul of the innocent little daughter goes up to Heaven whereas the soul of the savage killer of innocents goes down to Hell. The anecdote also deals with two of the groups that Adomnán tries to protect from violence in his *Law of Innocents*: women (represented by the girl) and clerics (represented by Gemmán). Could it be that Columba, the young deacon and pupil of Gemmán, himself stands for the third group, the youths? In any case, the girl in this anecdote has the function of representing innocent victims who should be protected and are rewarded by God. Her function is as a symbol; we cannot find out anything more about her identity as a creature of flesh and blood.

The third subcategory consists of two examples of women who are helped by Columba at their own request: II.5 and II.40. The first relevant chapter (II.5) concerns an ecclesiastical woman (*sancta virgo*, once designated *sacra virgo*). Her name—Mogain, Daiméne's daughter—and the place where she lives—Clochar Macc nDaiméni—are announced in the title.[67] Columba summons Brother Lugaid *Láitir*, 'the strong', and sends him to Ireland because the holy virgin Mogain has had an accident during the night while returning home after the night office. Stumbling, she has broken her hip in two. She calls Columba continuously in the hope that she will receive relief from the Lord through the saint. Lugaid takes with him a lit-

---

[65] The first evidence of his power was changing water into wine (II.1), but this miracle is harmless compared to what we are dealing with here.

[66] In II.23, belonging to this same cluster about vengeance, there is a paraphrase from St Peter's words in Act 5:4, uttered by St Columba.

[67] "*De Maugina sancta uirgine Daimeni filia quae inhabitauerat hi Clochur filiorum Daimeni*" (Anderson, *Adomnán's Life of Columba*, p. 100).

tle box of pine-wood containing a blessing.[68] He is to dip the blessing in a vessel of water and pour the water over the hip, while invoking God's name. Then the hip bone will be joined and the holy virgin will be healed completely. In addition, Columba writes on the lid of the box the number of years (23) that the sacred virgin will live on after the cure. Lugaid carries out these orders for the benefit of the holy virgin, who is very glad and grateful for his coming to her. She lives on for twenty-three years, continuing to do good works.

Mogain is one of the two women who are named[69] and the only ecclesiastical woman mentioned in VC. This chapter is found in the above-mentioned cluster of healings and describes a double miracle: a miracle of power (the healing) and a miracle of prophecy (the number of years of her life). This combination of miracles is also found and explicitly mentioned in II.4. Moreover, there is another parallel between II.4 and II.5 in that the healing of the illness takes place in Ireland, with Columba on Iona and sending a messenger with the instrument for the healing. In II.4 and II.6 a number of people are healed; in II.5 a woman is healed and in II.7 another woman receives the piece of salt to heal her eyes. This short survey gives another example of Adomnán's eye for structure. As for the contents of II.5, Mogain seems to know Columba as she calls repeatedly for him and expects to be healed by the Lord through him. The message from Adomnán seems to be that this nun is an example of piety. He mentions her name, ecclesiastical status and dwelling place, which I interpret as a sign of her importance. He shows her going home from a church service, her faith in God through Columba and he tells us that she continued doing good works after her healing. Therefore, we have here a woman who is neither wife nor mother (at least, as far as we know), but who is at the same time presented as an admirable woman.

The second woman asking for Columba's help is definitely known to the saint: she is related to him through his mother's family (II.40). This chapter is entitled "*De quadam muliercula magnas et ualde dificiliores parturitionis ut Euae filia tortiones passa*",[70] 'Of a certain young woman,

---

[68] This is an object blessed by Columba; Anderson (*Adomnán's Life of Columba*, p. 103, n. 134) suggests here a written prayer.
[69] The other one is Eithne, Columba's mother (see below).
[70] Anderson, *Adomnán's Life of Columba*, p. 162.

who was suffering, as a daughter of Eve, great and very hard pangs of childbirth.'[71] Columba is reading on Iona but suddenly announces that he must go to the oratory to pray for a woman (*femina*) in distress in Ireland. She is suffering from the pangs of a very difficult birth and calls out to Columba for divine help through him. The woman is related to Columba: her father belongs to Columba's mother's (*mater*) kin. Moved by pity for the young woman (*muliercula*), Columba runs to the oratory and kneels, praying to Christ born from humankind (*de homine natus*). He then leaves the oratory and tells the brothers that the Lord Jesus, born of woman (*de muliere progenitus*), now shows favour: the sufferer has received help in time and has safely borne a child; she will not die at this time. In that same hour the poor woman (*misella femina*) is restored to health, as is afterwards told by people coming from the district in Ireland where the woman (*mulier*) lived.

There are clear references to Columba's feelings towards this woman: when he realises her condition, he smiles (*subridens*); he is moved by pity (*motus miseratione*), runs to the church and kneels in prayer. The woman hopes for divine assistance because she is family of Columba. Her hope is not in vain: she gives birth and is restored to health. Adomnán refers to her in the title as a daughter of Eve, which has its source in Gn 3:16 where Eve is told that she will bring forth children in pain. This is the only place in VC where Adomnán uses the name of a woman from the Bible. As we have seen above (for instance, in II.32), he refers to the names of prophets and apostles to compare them with Columba. Here, he is specific in his various designations of Jesus—Christ and the Lord Jesus—of whom he says that he is *de homine natus* and *de muliere progenitus*, referring to his mother Mary although without naming her. Adomnán names men far more frequently than women, a fact that also pertains to biblical characters. It is, furthermore, interesting to note that Columba's mother is mentioned in this chapter because there is reason to compare her with Jesus's mother (see below, in the discussion of III.1). There is no reference to the young Irish woman being helped because of her belief (compare, for instance, the monk Baíthéne being safe when faced with a sea-monster because of his belief; I.19):[72]

---

[71] Anderson, *Adomnán's Life of Columba*, p. 163.
[72] Cp. Borsje, *From Chaos to Enemy*, pp. 168–169.

she is aided because she is Columba's family and asks his help. Adomnán has placed this miracle about the young woman giving birth between two other miracles involving women: II.39 about a virtuous wife, and II.41 about a woman who refuses to have sex with her husband (see below). The women could be seen as receiving Columba's admiration (II.39), endearment (II.40), and admonition (II.41).

This last chapter (II.41) represents the fourth subcategory: cooperation with Columba, which happens through the saint himself. This chapter will also be quoted completely:

> *De quodam Lugneo guberneta, cognomento Tudicla, quem sua coiux odio habuerat ualde deformem, qui in Rechrea commorabatur insula*
>
> ALIO *in tempore cum uir sanctus in Rechrea hospitaretur insula quidam plebeus ad eum ueniens de sua querebatur uxore, quae ut ipse dicebat odio habens eum ad maritalem nullo modo ammitebat concubitum accedere. Quibus auditis sanctus maritam aduocans in quantum potuit eam hac de causa corripere coepit, inquiens: 'Quare mulier tuam a te carnem abdicare conaris; domino dicente, "Erunt duo in carne una"? Itaque caro tui coiugis tua caro est.' Quae respondens: 'Omnia', inquit, 'quaecumque mihi praeciperis sum parata quamlibet sint ualde laboriosa adinplere, excepto uno, ut me nullo conpellas modo in uno lecto dormire cum Lugneo. Omnem domus curam exercere non recusso, aut si iubeas etiam maria transire, et in aliquo puellarum monasterio permanere.' Sanctus tum ait: 'Non potest recte fieri quod dicis. Nam adhuc uiro uiuente, alligata es a lege uiri. Quod enim deus licite coniunxit nefas est separari.' Et his dictis consequenter intulit: 'Hac in die tres, hoc est ego et maritus cum coiuge, ieiunantes dominum precemur.' Illa dehinc: 'Scio', ait, 'quia tibi inpossibile non erit, ut ea quae uel dificilia uel etiam inpossibilia uidentur a deo inpetrata donentur.'*
>
> *Quid plura, marita eadem die cum sancto ieiunare consentit, et maritus similiter. Nocteque subsequente sanctus in somnis pro eis deprecatus est. Posteraque die sanctus maritam praesente sic conpellat marito: 'Ó femina, si ut hesterna dicebas die parata hodie es ad feminarum emigrare monasteriolum?' Illa: 'Nunc', inquit, 'cognoui quia tua a deo de me est audita oratio. Nam quem heri oderam hodie amo. Cór enim meum hac nocte praeterita quomodo ignoro in me inmotatum est de odio in amorem'.*
>
> *Quid moramur? Ab eadem die usque ad diem obitus anima eiusdem maritae indesociabiliter in amore conglutinata est mariti, ut illa maritalis concubitus debita quae prius reddere rennuebat nullo modo deinceps recussaret.*[73]

---

[73] Anderson, *Adomnán's Life of Columba*, pp. 164, 166.

[ii.41] Concerning a certain Luigne, a pilot surnamed 'the little hammer', who lived in the island of Rathlin, and whom his wife held in aversion because he was very ugly[74]

AT another time, when the holy man was a guest in Rathlin island, a certain layman came to him and complained regarding his wife, who, as he said, had an aversion to him, and would not allow him to enter into marital relations. Hearing this, the saint bade the wife approach, and began to chide her as well as he could on that account, saying: 'Why, woman, do you attempt to put from you your own flesh? The Lord says, "Two shall be in one flesh." Therefore the flesh of your husband is your flesh.' She replied: 'I am ready to perform all things whatsoever that you may enjoin on me, however burdensome: save one thing, that you do not constrain me to sleep in one bed with Luigne. I do not refuse to carry on the whole management of the house; or, if you command it, even to cross the seas, and remain in some monastery of nuns.' Then the saint said: 'What you suggest cannot rightly be done. Since your husband is still alive, you are bound by the law of the husband; for it is forbidden that that should be separated, which God has lawfully joined.' After saying this, he continued: 'On this day let us three, myself, and the husband with his wife, pray to the Lord, fasting.' Then she said: 'I know it will not be impossible that things appearing difficult or even impossible may be granted by God to you, when you ask for them.'

In short, the wife agreed to fast on the same day, and the husband also, with the saint. And on the night following, in sleep, the saint prayed for them. On the next day the saint thus addressed the wife, in the presence of her husband: 'Woman, are you today, as you said yesterday, ready to depart to a monastery of nuns?' She said: 'I know now that your prayer concerning me has been heard by God. For him whom I loathed yesterday I love today. In this past night (how, I do not know) my heart has been changed in me from hate to love.'

Let us pass on. From that day until the day of her death, that wife's affections were indissolubly set in love of her husband; so that the dues of the marriage-bed, which she had formerly refused to grant, she never again denied.[75]

We have here a chapter which centres on a woman. The heart of the episode is a lively debate between the saint and the woman; the husband functions as the initiator when he voices his complaint. In contrast, he is a silent witness at the end of the story. The debate starts with Columba summoning and reproaching the woman. He

---

[74] Anderson has Lugne, Tudicla (instead of 'little hammer') and Rechru respectively as names of persons and places.

[75] Anderson, *Adomnán's Life of Columba*, pp. 165, 167.

quotes the Bible against her behaviour, saying: "*Erunt duo in carne una*", 'Two shall be in one flesh'.[76] As Columba mentions 'the Lord' as his source, this quotation is from either of the Gospels. The woman replies with a proposal: she wants to continue her celibacy, either as the head of the household or by entering a monastery, even by way of *peregrinatio*, as she says that she is prepared to cross the seas if necessary. Columba rejects this proposal: "*Nam adhuc uiro uiuente, alligata es a lege uiri*", 'Since the man is still alive, you are bound by the law of man'.[77] Sharpe[78] rightly comments that here is an allusion to the words of St Paul.[79] Columba then goes on paraphrasing the Bible: "*Quod enim deus licite coniunxit nefas est separari*",[80] 'for it is forbidden that that should be separated, which God has lawfully joined'.[81] Columba is quoting Jesus here again as the paraphrase gives the next line spoken by Jesus after his quotation of the 'one flesh' sentence from *Genesis*.[82] Columba then makes his proposal: a fast and prayer by the two persons involved and the saint himself. At this point the woman shows her faith and trust in Columba by cooperating.[83] The next day, when the three gather together, it becomes clear that the conversation on the previous day had the character of a debate, because Columba enquires about the woman's feelings. If the conversation had taken the form of a saintly command, he would not have done so. It is evident that a miracle has occurred: hate has been replaced by love, which will last till the day

---

[76] Gn 2:24; Mt 19:5; Mc 10:8; I Cor 6:16; Eph 5:31.

[77] Anderson (*Adomnán's Life of Columba*, p. 165) and Sharpe (*Adomnán of Iona*, p. 195) translate *vir* in this sentence as 'husband'. Adomnán, however, refers to the husband in this chapter by *coiux* and *maritus* (and when he introduces him, he uses *plebeus*). The term *vir* comes from Adomnán's source: St Paul. It should be noted that the expression *lex viri* gives the impression that this is a distinct law, but the law St Paul refers to is the same as the one that Jesus refers to in Mt 19 and Mc 10: the law of Moses.

[78] *Adomnán of Iona*, p. 341, n. 322.

[79] See Rom 7:2 ("*nam quae sub viro est mulier vivente viro alligata est legi si autem mortuus fuerit vir soluta est a lege viri*") and also I Cor 7:39 ("*mulier alligata est quanto tempore vir eius vivit quod si dormierit vir eius liberata est cui vult nubat tantum in Domino*").

[80] Anderson, *Adomnán's Life of Columba*, p. 164.

[81] Anderson, *Adomnán's Life of Columba*, p. 165.

[82] "*quod ergo Deus coniunxit homo non separet*" (Mt 19:6); "*quod ergo Deus iunxit homo non separet*" (Mc 10:9), both phrases following "*erunt duo in carne una*" (Mt 19:5; Mc 10:8).

[83] Sharpe (*Adomnán of Iona*, p. 341, n. 321) refers to a variant version of this miracle in the *Life of St Brigit*, but in this case the woman does not cooperate. The complaining husband sprinkles the house with blessed water during her absence and the miracle happens afterwards.

of the woman's death. Sharpe[84] comments upon the Christian view of marriage, as expressed in this chapter. He points out that it is uncertain whether the marriage had been consummated or not. I believe Adomnán shows—again by his choice of words—that it was not. On the day before the fast and prayer the woman refers to the monastery as "*puellarum monasterio*",[85] 'a monastery of girls'; the next day Columba asks whether she still wants to go to 'a little monastery of women': "*feminarum (. . .) monasteriolum*".[86] As Adomnán chooses his words with care, there must be a meaning behind this shift. Apparently the woman first sees herself as a girl, a virgin, and after the miracle she has turned into a 'woman'. This shows that it is difficult to envisage 'the' Christian view of marriage. St Paul could have encouraged this woman to remain celibate,[87] but St Columba and Adomnán apparently see celibacy and *peregrinatio* as an ideal fit for men; the place of a woman is, according to them, next to her husband. This reinforces Ní Dhonnchadha's conclusion (see above) about Adomnán's view of women that they are primarily wives and mothers. At the same time, we see here a woman of flesh and blood. She is independent, not having sex against her wish. She does not immediately give in when the saint quotes the Bible against her, but enters into debate with him. She remains within Christian discourse when she proposes celibacy or even pilgrimage as solutions. She chooses alternatives from the Irish social-religious context. Had the woman been schooled in Scripture she might have found in the context of I Cor 7 (to which Columba alludes) an argument for her case: it says in I Cor 7:11 that if a wife departs from her husband, she should either remain unmarried or be reconciled to him. Columba pleads for the second solution; the woman suggests a solution which corresponds with the first one. With the means that are at her disposal, this woman shows herself to be a person of independent judgment, being a match for the biblical knowledge of the saint, and in the end changing her view not because of coercion but because of a miracle.

The fifth subcategory shows women cooperating with Columba

---

[84] *Adomnán of Iona*, p. 341, n. 321.
[85] Anderson, *Adomnán's Life of Columba*, p. 164.
[86] Ibid. Anderson (p. 165) translates the two instances as 'monastery of nuns'; Sharpe (*Adomnán of Iona*, p. 195) gives 'some woman's monastery' and 'a monastery of women' respectively.
[87] See, for instance, I Cor 7:7–8.

on their own initiative: in II.9 in a very subtle way, and in II.3 and II.39 by way of wives who give their husbands advice.

A boy accidentally drops a book, handwritten by Columba, in a river in Leinster. The book lies in its satchel in this river from Christmas till Easter. After Easter some women (*feminae*) are walking along the river bank, where they find it. They carry it to a Pictish priest called Éogenán, who was the owner of the book. The priest opens the sodden, rotted satchel and finds the book inside undamaged, clean and dry (II.9).

In II.9 the saint himself is absent. The point of the miracle is the divine esteem that Columba enjoys: things blessed or written by his hand are miraculously safe from destruction by either fire (II.7) or water (II.8–9). The women are only a link in the chain of events, but thanks to them the miracle becomes public. Again, these Irish women are anonymous whereas the Pictish priest is named. He functions as the figure of authority who identifies the book, as he is its former owner. Adomnán furthermore refers to testimonies of truthful and blameless men (*viri*), who, admittedly, also remain anonymous.

In II.3 the monks of Columba are sent by the holy man to a field owned by a layman, called Findchán, in order to collect bundles of wattle for the building of a guesthouse. They fill a freight-ship with this material but on their return they tell the saint that the layman is very distressed at this loss. Columba orders the monks to bring twice three measures of barley to the man, which he should sow in ploughed land. Findchán is glad to receive the barley but wonders at the command: how can a crop sown after midsummer succeed? It is against the nature of the land. His wife (*marita*) reacts by advising him as follows: "*'Fac', ait, 'secundum sancti mandatum, cui dominus donabit quodcumque ab eo postulauerit'*",[88] 'Do according to the bidding of the saint, to whom the Lord will grant whatever he may ask of him'.[89] The messengers of Columba recount the saint's injunction: Findchán should trust in the omnipotence of God. The crop, sown after the first fifteen days of June, will be reaped in the beginning of August. The man obeys: he ploughs and sows. In the beginning of August the harvest is fully ripe. This happened in *Delcros* (II.3).

In this episode without a preceding prophecy by Columba, the layman's wife advises her husband to obey the saint, for Columba

---

[88] Anderson, *Adomnán's Life of Columba*, p. 96.
[89] Anderson, *Adomnán's Life of Columba*, p. 97.

receives what he asks from God. The story centres on the dealings between the saint and the layman, but the spontaneous advice of the wife is noteworthy. She cooperates with the saint on her own initiative, enabling the miracle to take place. The messengers, by contrast, are only carrying out Columba's command. Adomnán seems to present here a woman who is an example to be followed because of her faith in the saint.[90]

In the final example a man called Librán travels in pilgrimage from his home, the province of the Connachta, to Columba on Iona. He confesses all his sins to the saint, who declares that he must live seven years in penance in Tiree. Librán is willing to carry out this command, but it is in conflict with an oath he swore earlier. He had killed a man in Ireland and, instead of being condemned to death, he had been released by a wealthy relative. In his gratitude Librán swore that he would serve this man during the rest of his life but after some days he decided that he preferred to serve God and deserted his relative, thereby breaking his oath. This notwithstanding, Columba sends him away to do penance and orders him to return at Lent after the seven years in order to receive the Eucharist at Easter. This indeed happens. After the Easter celebration Librán goes to Columba, who tells him the prophecy that his earthly master is still alive, and so are his father, mother (*mater*) and brothers. Columba gives him a decorated sword that he should offer to his master in return for his freedom. However, Columba prophesies, the relative will not accept the sword.[91] The reason for this is the following:

> *Habet enim bene moratam coiugem, cuius salubri obtemperans consilio té eadem die gratis sine pretio libertate donabit, cingulum ex more captiui de tuís resoluens lumbís.*[92]

For he has a virtuous wife, and yielding to her sound advice he will on that day grant you liberty, freely and without recompense, unloosing according to custom the captive's belt from your loins.[93]

---

[90] It should be noted that in the later version of the Middle Irish *Life of Columba* (see Herbert, *Iona, Kells and Derry*) this story is to be found as well (§33), but here the woman has disappeared from the story. This *Life* is dated to not much later than 1169 (ibid., p. 193).

[91] This phrase is omitted in Sharpe's (*Adomnán of Iona*, p. 190) translation.

[92] Anderson, *Adomnán's Life of Columba*, p. 156.

[93] Anderson, *Adomnán's Life of Columba*, p. 157.

Columba foretells Librán that when he is free from this worry another responsibility will arise. His filial duties towards his father will need to be fulfilled, which his brothers will bring pressingly to his attention. Columba orders him to take care of his aged father, even though it may seem burdensome to him. It will be a duty of short duration, because after a week his father will die. After the burial, the brothers will urge him to fulfill his filial duties to his mother. But from this duty he will be freed by a younger brother, who will serve their mother on his behalf. After these words, Librán departs with the sword and the saint's blessing. In Ireland, everything happens in accordance with the prophecy of Columba. His master is willing to receive the sword, but:

> *refragans uxor: 'Ut quid nobis', ait, 'hoc accipere quod sanctus pretium misit Columba? Hoc non sumus digni. Liberetur ei pius hic gratis minstrator. Magis nobis sancti uiri benedictio proficiet quam hoc quod offertur pretium.' Audiens itaque maritus hoc maritae salubre consilium continuo gratis liberauit seruum.*[94]

> the [master's] wife refused, saying: 'How can we take this price that Saint Columba has sent? We are not worthy of this. Let his pious servant be released for him without payment. The holy man's blessing will profit us more than this price that is offered.' When the husband heard this salutary counsel of his wife, he immediately released his slave without payment.[95]

The events concerning his father and mother develop likewise in accordance with Columba's prophecy. That Librán is now completely absolved is, in my opinion, to be deduced from the ending of his story: he returns to Columba and his voyage is marked by miracles he performs in Columba's name. He narrates to Columba what has happened to him—also mentioning the wife (*uxor*) of the master with her salutary advice and his mother (*mater*)—and returns the sword. Librán becomes a monk and—as Columba prophesies—he lives long and dies in Durrow, one of Columba's Irish monasteries. He is buried among Columba's elect monks (II.39).

In II.39 two women play a role: a wife and a mother. I will begin the analysis with the latter, whose role is smaller. The mother of Librán is helped by Columba as the saint points out the filial duties of the son, even though they are taken over by Librán's brother.

---

[94] Anderson, *Adomnán's Life of Columba*, p. 158.
[95] Anderson, *Adomnán's Life of Columba*, p. 159.

This anecdote is centered on the fulfilment of duties—to God, to a benefactor and to parents. Columba helps Librán to meet these duties in order to be a free man again, that is: a servant of God. In this status, the former killer becomes a miracle worker himself. The function of the mother (and father) is to represent duties that children have towards their parents; no further conclusion can be drawn about the woman herself.

Concerning the role of the wife in II.39, it is important to note that Adomnán emphasises the fact that her advice is beneficial (*salubris*). He mentions this three times explicitly: in Columba's prophesy, in the story when she actually gives the advice and in Librán's account of his doings to Columba. The woman in II.39 seems to symbolise a new morality. According to early Irish ideas about compensation,[96] her husband would have been perfectly right in accepting the sword. He had paid compensation for the death penalty on Librán, who in his turn offered his life, or his services for life, to compensate for this. Had the relative accepted the sword, this would have been the compensation for the loss of Librán's services. However, the woman breaks the chain of compensation by refusing the sword. Or perhaps one should say that she changes the method of compensation: instead of material recompense she wants immaterial recompense: the blessing of the saint instead of his beautiful sword. The choice of a blessing instead of a sword might also be seen in the light of the new morality: peace and well-being instead of war and violence. Finally, it should be noted that she is referred to as *bene morata*. In this, she is preceded and will be followed. A woman who keeps her sin hidden is believed to be *bene morata* (I.17; see below), but Columba sees through this. In the example central here (II.39), Columba prophesies that the woman will be *bene morata* and the Third Book supplies the last woman who is *bene morata* (III.10; see below). No doubt, these women are given in a climactic line. The first woman seemed of good character, but was hiding something; the second woman was indeed of good character and cooperated on her own initiative with the saint, thereby symbolising the new Christian morality, and the last woman is herself part of a miracle of power when she fights in the sky with the forces of evil.

---

[96] For more about early Irish ideas about compensation see, for instance, Sharpe, *Adomnán of Iona*, p. 338, n. 312, and Borsje, *From Chaos to Enemy*, pp. 65–90.

The last subcategory deals with women who are the subject of a miracle themselves. They are both from the Third Book: one is a vision experienced by a woman (III.1) and the other a vision seen by Columba (III.10).

The first example deals with Columba's mother, Eithne daughter of Mac Naue. Adomnán gives her name in the second preface when he points out that the saint was born of noble parents. He does not mention her name in II.40 and III.1, which chapters also refer to her. I will quote III.1 entirely:

> *ANGELUS domini in somniis genitrici uenerabilis uiri quadam nocte inter conceptum eius et partum apparuit; eique quasi quoddam mirae pulchritudinis peplum adsistens detulit, in quo ueluti uniuersorum decorosi colores florum depicti uidebantur. Quodque post aliquod breue interuallum eius de manibus reposcens abstulit; eleuansque et expandens in aere dimisit uacuo. Illa uero de illo tristificata sublato sic ad illum uenerandi habitus uirum: 'Cur a me', ait, 'hoc laetificum tam cito abstrahis pallium?' Ille consequenter: 'Idcirco', inquit, 'quia hoc sagum alicuius est tam magnifici honoris, apud te diutius retenere non poteris.'*
>
> *His dictis supra memoratum peplum mulier paulatim a sé elongari uolando uidebat, camporumque latitudinem in maius crescendo excedere, montesque et saltus maiore sui mensura superare. Vocemque huiuscemodi subsecutam audierat: 'Mulier, noles tristificari. Viro enim cui matrimoniali <copula> es iuncta talem filium editura es floridum qui quasi unus profetarum dei inter ipsos connumerabitur; innumerabiliumque animarum dux ad caelestem a deo patriam est praedistinatus.' In hac audito uoce mulier expergescitur.*[97]

[iii.i] AN angel of the Lord appeared to the mother of the venerable man in a dream, one night between his conception and his birth; and standing there, gave her, as it seemed, a robe of marvellous beauty, in which there appeared embroidered splendid colours, as it were of all kinds of flowers. And after some little space, asking it back, he took it from her hands. And raising it, and spreading it out, he let it go in the empty air. Grieved by losing it, she spoke thus to that man of reverend aspect: 'Why do you so quickly take from me this joyous mantle?' Then he said: 'For the reason that this cloak is of very glorious honour, you will not be able to keep it longer with you.'

After these words, the woman saw that robe gradually recede from her in flight, grow greater, and surpass the breadth of the plains, and excel in its greater measure the mountains and woods. And she heard a voice that followed, speaking thus: 'Woman, do not grieve, for you will bear to the man to whom you are joined by [the bond] of marriage a son, of such grace that he, as though one of the prophets

---

[97] Anderson, *Adomnán's Life of Columba*, pp. 182, 184.

of God, shall be counted in their number; and he has been predestined by God to be a leader of innumerable souls to the heavenly country.' While she heard this voice, the woman awoke.[98]

This episode brings to mind the parallel of the angelic visitation of Mary, the mother of Jesus.[99] Mary is visited before the conception and the message she receives is straightforward, without symbolism, but all the same it seems that here we have a biblical precedent after which III.1 is modelled, albeit with its own images and message. One could add to this the observation noted above that Columba's mother is alluded to in II.40, in which Jesus's mother is also hinted at. Just as Columba follows in Christ's footsteps by certain miracles (for instance, changing water to wine in II.1), so does his mother follow Christ's mother in receiving a vision of an angel. In both cases the point is of course the importance of the son to be born. However, more is to be deduced from Adomnán's structure of the text. III.1 forms a cluster with III.2–4, in which people other than Columba see miraculous apparitions. His foster-father, the priest Cruithnechán, sees a fiery ball of light above the sleeping child Columba (III.2). The famous St Brendan sees a fiery pillar moving in front of Columba, and angels in his company (III.3). His master Uinniau sees the youth Columba in the company of an angel (III.4). It is remarkable that a woman is found among this eminent vision-receiving company. Moreover, Eithne is the only one in this group who talks with the angel—just as her model Mary.

A woman is the subject of a vision of Columba in III.10, which is headed by the title "*De angelorum simili uisione quos uir beatus aspexerat alicuius bene moratae feminae animam ad caelum ferre*",[100] 'Concerning a similar vision of angels whom the blessed man beheld carrying to heaven the soul of a certain virtuous woman'.[101] On a certain day on Iona, Columba suddenly looks at the sky and addresses a woman (*mulier*) who is happy (*felix*) and virtuous (*bene morata*) and whose soul is being carried by divine angels to Paradise at that moment. These words are heard by one of the brothers, Genereus the Englishman (*Genereus Saxo*). A year later the saint tells Genereus about another marvellous thing he sees. The soul of the woman (*mulier*) now meets

---

[98] Anderson, *Adomnán's Life of Columba*, pp. 183, 185.
[99] See Lc 1:26–38.
[100] Anderson, *Adomnán's Life of Columba*, p. 196.
[101] Anderson, *Adomnán's Life of Columba*, p. 197.

the soul of her husband, a pious layman, in the air and fights together with holy angels against the hostile powers for the man's soul. Thanks to the angelic help and aided by the righteousness of the man himself, they are able to snatch the soul away from the demons and bring it to the place of eternal rest.

Two journeys of souls to Heaven seen by Columba are described. The first journey of the soul of the happy woman happens without any opposition; the second, of her husband's soul, yields a fight with demonic powers. There are three chapters in VC where such a fight over the destiny of a soul between angelic and demonic forces can be found.[102] In III.6, angels and demons fight over the soul of one of Columba's monks; in III.10 the husband's soul is at stake, and in III.13 the fight concerns the soul of a guest of a monks' community. In all three cases additional assistance is given: the soul of the monk goes to Heaven thanks to Christ; the soul of the husband joins his wife's soul thanks to her and his own righteousness; and the visitor's soul survives the demonic attack because Columba and his monks pray so that the souls of the other monks are aided by the angels. The closest parallel to III.10 is III.13, because in both cases a human soul or human souls join in the combat: the soul of the woman and the souls of drowned monks respectively. Adomnán's main concern is the presentation of Columba as an extraordinarily holy person who sees these fights take place in the sky above. The anecdote shows however also the importance of being righteous and presents the woman called *bene morata* as an example to follow. It is furthermore important to note that although she is a wife, Adomnán designates her *femina* and *mulier*. I see this as further evidence of her importance.

Stories about women who obstruct Columba's work or are punished by him

The third category of women playing a role in Columba's miracles concerns women who are punished by the saint or obstruct his work. Two chapters of VC fall into this category: I.17 (a woman punished) and II.37 (an obstructing woman).

---

[102] For more about this combat, see Borsje, *From Chaos to Enemy*, p. 110, n. 273.

The title of I.17 already refers to the hidden sin of the mother (". . . *et de quodam occulto matris eius peccato* . . .")[103] of Colgu mac Áedo Draigniche, from the Uí Fiachrach. Columba asks Colgu, who also lives on Iona, whether his mother (*genitrix*) is a religious woman (*relegiosa*) or not. Colgu answers that to his knowledge his mother (*mater*) is of good character and reputation ("*bene moratam et bonae famae*"),[104] whereupon the saint sends the man to his mother in Ireland to question her about a very grave sin that she keeps hidden. Colgu leaves to interrogate his mother; she denies the sin at first but then confesses.[105] She must do penance as instructed by Columba and is then restored (*sanata*). She marvels greatly at the miraculous knowledge of the saint. The second part of I.17 deals with prophecies concerning Colgu himself, about how he will be the head of a church in Ireland and about the circumstances of his death.

Elsewhere in VC (I.40) there is a male parallel to this event. On Sunday, Columba goes to celebrate the Eucharist in a small church, where a priest leads the service. This man is very religious (*valde relegiosus*) in the eyes of the brothers present. However, Columba sees through this and utters terrible words: clean is being mixed with unclean. A man who keeps a great sin hidden is performing the sacred rite. This man is forced to confess in public and the end of the story is that the people present marvel greatly at Columba's divine knowledge. These two anecdotes supply parallels and oppositions. Both people hiding their sin live in Ireland but the first mentioned is a woman—a mother, to be precise—and the second is a man—a priest. The woman is visited by her son and is forced to confess in private. The man is visited by Columba and is forced to confess in public. The point in both stories is that either an individual or a group marvel at Columba's prophetic knowledge. We have here an early medieval example of the split—later so well-known—between private and public, where woman stands for the first and man for the second. This is emphasised by the fact that the woman is defined by her family status as a mother and the man by his public function as a priest.

In II.37 Columba performs a miracle for a man, but a woman also plays a central role in the events. A very poor layman from

---

[103] Anderson, *Adomnán's Life of Columba*, p. 40.
[104] Ibid.
[105] W. Reeves (*The Life of St. Columba, Founder of Hy; written by Adamnan, ninth abbot*

Lochaber goes to the saint. Columba feels sorry for him, because he cannot feed his wife (*marita*) and children. The poor man receives alms and the command to bring a wooden stick from the forest. The saint sharpens the stick into a spike, blesses it and gives it to the man. The spike will hurt neither humans nor cattle but only wild beasts and fish. As long as he has the spike, there will be abundant food in his house. The man places the spike in a wild place and the next day he finds a stag of marvellous size transfixed upon it. This happens every day thereafter: a stag, hind or other beast falls upon the spike, to such an extent that he can even sell meat to the neighbours. However, this ideal state does not last:

> *Sed tamen diabuli inuidia per sociam ut Adam et hunc etiam miserum inuenit, quae non quasi prudens sed fatua taliter ad maritum locuta est: 'Tolle de terra ueru. Nam si in eo homines aut etiam pecora perierint, tu ipse et ego cum nostris liberis aut occidemur aut captiui ducemur'.*[106]

> But the malice of the devil reached this wretched man, as it did Adam, through his wife. She, not like a wise woman but as a fool, spoke to her husband thus: 'Take up the spike from the ground. For if people, or if cattle, should perish upon it, you yourself and I, with our children, will either be put to death, or be led into slavery'.[107]

The husband objects with a reference to the words of the saint: neither human nor cattle will be hurt by the spike. However, he yields to his wife (*uxor*) and places the spike inside his house, beside the wall. Then his house dog falls on it and is killed. His wife (*marita*) reacts with fear that one of the children may fall upon it and die that way too. The husband carries the spike into the forest and puts it in a very dense thorn-brake, where no living being could fall on it. However, the next day, the death of a she-goat is caused by it. He then puts the spike in a river. The next day he finds a salmon of marvellous size impaled on it. He puts the spike on top of the roof of his house, where a raven is pierced by it. Then the man, led astray by the advice of his foolish wife (*coiux*), chops the spike into small pieces and burns them. After this, the man becomes a beggar again. For a short while he had been enriched but the remaining days of his life he and his family are poor.

---

of that Monastery (Dublin, 1857), p. 46, n. d) says that her sin is adultery, but there is no ground for this in the text.

[106] Anderson, *Adomnán's Life of Columba*, pp. 148, 150.
[107] Anderson, *Adomnán's Life of Columba*, pp. 149, 151.

In II.37, Columba does not speak to or about the woman involved; he pities the beggar and gives him a miraculous spike. It is, therefore, Adomnán who is responsible for the images found in this anecdote. In his subtle, implicit way, he describes the blessed situation after the encounter between the saint and the beggar and in doing so calls forth the image of Paradise. Joy and excess mark the state of the beggar and his family when he possesses the spike. Moreover, as in Paradise, they do not need to work for their food: every day there is a fresh catch of meat. In his choice of words when announcing that things are going wrong Adomnán draws an explicit parallel with the story from *Genesis* 3. He equates the serpent with the Devil (without mentioning the serpent explicitly), compares the man with Adam and points out the pivotal role of the woman who—not wise but foolish—brings about 'the Fall'. Things go wrong because of her fear of an accident that will lead to tragedy for her family. The man brings the spike into the house and the prevailing order is disrupted. When the dog dies after falling on the spike the woman utters her fear—now concerning her children—for a second time and this time she is probably right: the spike is no longer safe. Here, we have, therefore, a woman's advice that obstructs Columba's work. It is worthwhile comparing this anecdote with the other two instances of female marital advice in VC: II.3 and II.39, dealt with above. The woman in II.3 gives her husband advice and thus cooperates with Columba, bringing about the miracle of the barley harvest. The woman in II.37 gives her husband advice and thus hinders Columba, causing the miracle of abundant food to end. All three chapters deal with the idea of compensation: the wattle is recompensed by barley in II.3; the death penalty is paid off by the relative, which is recompensed by voluntary slavery in II.39. When this arrangement breaks down because the slave absconds the saint offers payment in the shape of a sword, which is then replaced by the saint's blessing. In both these cases the woman involved urges her husband to trust and obey the saint; the two women therefore think and speak according to the Christian ideal. In II.37 the idea of compensation is present in the woman's fear of someone suffering injury from the spike, the family subsequently being unable to pay and therefore condemned to either slavery or death in order to compensate for the damage.[108]

---

[108] Cp. Sharpe, *Adomnán of Iona*, p. 337, n. 305.

The sequence in this story is, first, the state of poverty, which then changes into a state of abundance thanks to the saint's blessing. Finally, the state of poverty returns because of the fear, or the absence of trust. The woman thinks according to the 'old ways', the law of compensation. The absence of the Christian ideal of trust in and obedience to the saint is condemned by Adomnán, who not only characterises the woman as foolish but also puts the story into a biblical framework by summoning the image of Eve (without mentioning her name) and Adam, and by mentioning the source of all evil: Satan.

Conclusions

Vita Sancti Columbae comprises 121 chapters (the two prefaces included), of which only twenty-five deal with women. Of all the women mentioned in VC only two of them are specified by their own name: Eithne the mother of Columba and Mogain the holy virgin. They are shown to be important women: Eithne is to a certain extent modelled after Mary; Mogain is a woman whose status is not defined by men, because she is neither a mother nor a wife but a nun, a woman with a respectable religious status. Adomnán mentions many names of men and places in VC but most of the women in his anecdotes are not named. This is also the case with reference to people from the Bible. It should be noted that this is in contrast with Irish sagas in which women are usually named. Nevertheless, Adomnán gives various general designations to women: *marita*, *uxor*, *coiux* and *socia* for wife; *mater* or *genitrix* for mother; *ancella*, *serva*, *peregrina captiva*, *ancellula*, *servula* and *famula* for female slave; *femina*, *mulier* and *muliercula* for woman, and *filiola* and *filia* for girl. Adomnán apparently did not think women very important. Despite their anonymity, we do catch glimpses of the women, which tell more about them than their just being wives and mothers. On the basis of the second category of women being the largest (women who cooperate with Columba or are helped by him), we can conclude about the relationship between Columba and women that they were usually on good terms. Adomnán describes women as persons of flesh and blood, as examples and as symbols. He shows women as examples of innocence, of being in need of protection or liberation, of piety and of trust in the saint. These instances are rather stereotypical, and they are consistent with the way women are offered protection in the *Law of Adomnán*. Women are not found among Columba's public opponents: neither the druids nor the perpetrators of violence. One woman is mentioned in connection with magic, but she is the victim of a false accusation. The only female opponent of Columba is a wife and mother, who bases her resistance upon care for her family. She obviously is a woman of flesh and blood, but she also is a symbol for the older order based upon compensation. With her 'foolish advice', she can be seen in contrast with the two other wives who give their husbands 'sound advice'. These latter two stand for the new religious order based upon trust in the saint and God. Another example of a woman of flesh and blood is the woman who enters into debate with Columba. She draws upon the social-religious context for arguments for her case, in which she shows herself to be an independently thinking person. A few examples of power of women are economic (prostitution, herding sheep); psychological (influence upon husbands by giving advice with good and bad outcome), and finally, cosmic power (fighting with demons in the sky). This last statement should be complemented by an analysis of the roles of men in VC, but this comparison is matter for further research.

5

FRESH WATER FOR A TIRED SOUL: PREGNANCY AND MESSIANIC DESIRE IN A MEDIAEVAL JEWISH DOCUMENT FROM SICILY

Marcel Poorthuis & Chana Safrai

Introduction

Among the many treasures found in the *Geniza* of Cairo—a *Geniza* is a stockroom for manuscripts that have become unusable—one document is of particular interest within the framework of 'Women and Miracle Stories': the so-called 'Messianic document'. Thanks to the eminent scholar Jacob Mann this text was rescued from oblivion and published in 1931 with a brief commentary.[1] Since its appearance it has attracted some interest in the scholarly world, and was edited a couple of times. This present study, while based upon previous editions of the text as well as upon previous historical analysis,[2] wants to push research one step further. In determining the historical circumstances of this text its significance is by no means exhausted. Strangely, the fact that in this text a woman receives a Messianic revelation, while she is making priestly gestures and is covered with a *Talit* (prayer shawl), has not received due attention. This narrative may shed new light upon the position of women within Judaism in relation to prophecy and charismatic authority.

---

[1] J. Mann, "Messianic excitement in Sicily", in: *Texts and Studies in Jewish History and Literature* 1 (Israel, 1970), pp. 34–44. In his collection of Messianic texts from the Geniza: "The Messianic Movements in the Period of the First Crusades", *Collected Articles* 1 (Israel, 1971), pp. 182–224, Mann reports eight cases of Messianic upheaval in Germany, France, Spain, North Africa, Palestine, Yemen and Kurdistan. Most of these upheavals are preserved in letters from the Geniza.

[2] N. Zeldes, "Ma'aseh muflah beSizilia. Hosafot uBirurim leIinyan Ha-Tenuat HaMeshihit beSizilizah", *Zion* 58/3 (1993), pp. 347–363. S. Krauss, "Zu Dr. Manns historischen Texten", *Hebrew Union College Annual* 10 (1935), pp. 274–287. A.Z. Aescoly, "Al HaTenua haMeshihit beSikilia", *Tarbiz* 11 (1940), pp. 207–217. J.N. Epstein, "LaTenua haMeshihit beSikilia", *Tarbiz* 11 (1940), pp. 218–219. A.Z. Aescoly, *HaTenuot haMeshihiot beIsrael* (Jerusalem, 1956), pp. 240–247. N. Cohn, *The Pursuit of the Millennium: Revolutionary Millenarians and Mystical Anarchists of the Middle Ages* (London, 1970), p. 69.

The major thrust of this article is the analysis of the document as a story, told by two narrators concerning a miraculous event in which a certain woman plays a major role: her pregnancy is viewed as a Messianic sign for things to come. At the same time this woman's actual position outside the revered space and institutional authority of Judaism confirms her eccentric position. This fact shows that miraculous events are not always authorised by religious authorities, but sometimes take place on a more basic level or even 'on the fringes'.

History is no mere collection of facts that can be studied as 'objective' data, but it is structured as a narrative. This document is no exception to that. The miraculous events are embedded in a story written by a particular person for a specific circle of readers. It follows that this document can be studied in terms of rhetorical devices, stage-setting and dramatic effect. Departing from the perspective of the text as a narrative that uses miracles as a special device to convince readers of the Messianic urge of its content, this article charts the roles of the different personages, their speech-acts, their staging and localisation, and the overall gender patterns in this story.

The document is damaged but includes a title, and is written as a full-fledged story. Unfortunately the end is missing and the story is cut in the middle. Most of the first part, however, including the miracle story, has been preserved, which enables a careful analysis. Three interconnected stories can be distinguished and for convenience's sake we divide the document into three corresponding parts: A, B and C. Part A tells the story of a certain charismatic woman in Sicily who has been pregnant for more than nine months and performs wondrously. Signs, letters and even the image of a small human being appear on her body and upon her clothes. The story ends up with her prayer for repentance and with an admonition to avoid fiery catastrophe, sword and persecutions. Part B is shorter; the scene takes place inside the synagogue of Catania and involves two men who receive a vision of an angel with a sword and a fire. They flagellate themselves. Part C contains another account by the same narrator about an imminent redemption. It relates the story of the hidden king who is waiting with his troops for a Messianic battle. This story is beyond the scope of this study, but is important as a further indication to the provenance of the text and the message contained in it. The first two parts of the document, though not equal in length, seem to complete each other and as such call for a careful literary comparison.

The Messianic Text from Sicily

Genre

Our text is a travel account by a non-professional writer who may have written his story to inform people at home. The writer writes a poor Hebrew with occasional miss-spellings. The description of his itinerary may have been part of a letter meant to be dispatched.[3] Both letters[4] and accounts of itineraries[5] are suitable vehicles for Messianic reports because of the sudden character of the Messianic events and owing to the necessity to spread the rumours as quickly as possible. Quite often these reports themselves tell about other letters that are to be dispatched, just as in our document (story A and C). Messianic rumours combine a small-scale event in a remote corner of the world with a larger political framework, in which even the non-Jewish kings and rulers may play an important part.[6]

These letters are often full of Messianic expectations that were frustrated afterwards. Hence one may assume that these documents were either quite embarrassing for the Jewish community at large, or dangerous as they may add new fuel to Messianic fervour. Both possibilities seem to be valid reasons for suppressing those kinds of texts. Their preservation in the *Geniza* is solely due to the occurrence of the sacred Name of God in the texts. Documents that take a more critical stand toward Messianic phenomena have a greater chance to survive in printed form, like Maimonides' famous *Letter to Yemen* or Benjamin of Tudela's *Itinerary*. Our text however, differs

---

[3] Most scholars agree that the document represents a letter. However, Zeldes, "Ma'aseh muflah beSizilia", p. 348 disagrees and considers it the remains of a book.

[4] Cf. the collection of Messianic texts from the Cairo *Geniza* in Mann, "The Messianic Movements", pp. 182–224.

[5] Cf. Benjamin of Tudela's famous twelfth century account of the pseudo-Messiah David Alroy who called himself king of the Jews and escaped from a closed prison and walked upon water. Eventually his own father-in-law killed him. See M.N. Adler (ed.), *The Itinerary of Benjamin of Tudela* (New York, repr. of the 1907 edition), pp. 54–57.

[6] In case the writer himself believes in the Messianic upheaval, the non-Jewish ruler is pictured as a witness to the Messianic truth 'à contre coeur'. Cf. the letter from the Cairo *Geniza* about a Jewish woman in twelfth century Baghdad, to whom Elijah, the Messiah's precursor, appeared in a dream during a period of serious oppressive measures by the Moslem government. The chief Qadi warned the Caliph not to harm the Jewish people for this should not remain unpunished. However, the Caliph ignores the advice after which Elijah appears to him as well! Cf. S.D. Goitein, "A Report on Messianic Troubles in Baghdad in 1120–21", *Jewish Quarterly Review* 43 (1952–1953), pp. 57–76.

from these, both in literary quality and in the uncritical adherence to the Messianic phenomenon that is described.

Historical background

Jacob Mann rightly stated that it is extremely difficult to ascertain the period in which our text was written. He cautiously relegates the manuscript to the twelfth century, primarily for palaeographic reasons. The historical data in the text do not offer a definitive clue as to the date, but they are nevertheless significant. After publication, this text was hotly debated.[7]

A historical background emerges in part C, where our text tells about upheavals in different parts of Europe. Especially the last reference to a persecution of Jews in Germany, where priests intervened on their behalf, seems noteworthy to us. One gets the impression that these events happened in the not too distant past. Although this offers no definite clue for a date, some scholars claim that reference is made to the plight of the German Jews during the Crusades in the twelfth and thirteenth centuries.[8] Other scholars, however, argue in favour of the fifteenth[9] or even the sixteenth[10] century.

Another possible clue to the background may be sought in similarities between our text and the Messianic movement of the mystic Abraham Abulafia. Abulafia (born 1240) lived in Sicily from 1279 to 1291. The Messianic aura around his person is evident, although he may not have been explicit about his Messianic aspirations.[11] Abulafia's

---

[7] A clear overview of the historical possibilities is offered by Zeldes, "Ma'aseh muflah beSizilia", pp. 347–363. She argues strongly in favour of the fifteenth century, connecting it to a Sicilian document from 1456, which deals with Sicilian Jews who attempted to emigrate from Sicily to Jerusalem.

[8] J.N. Epstein, "Latenuat haMeshihit beSikilia", *Tarbiz* 11 (1940), pp. 218–219. The historian A. Ashtor agreed with Epstein. Cp. D. Berger, "The Attitude of St. Bernard of Clairvaux Toward the Jews", *Proceedings of the American Academy for Jewish Research* 40 (1972), pp. 89–108; Cohn, *The Pursuit of the Millennium*, p. 69.

[9] Krauss, "Zu Dr. Manns historischen Texten", pp. 274–287. See J. Mann, "Rejoinder", *Hebrew Union College Annual* 10 (1935), pp. 302–305, who strongly rejects Krauss' suggestion, stating that the Jews had already been expelled from Sicily at that time. Krauss' option for the Messianic activities of David Re'ubeni is rejected by Mann, who argues that the Jew had already been expelled from Sicily at that time and that David Re'ubeni had only loose connections with Marocco.

[10] Aescoly, *HaTenuot hameshihiot beIsrael*, pp. 240–247.

[11] His adversaries depicted him as such and if Abulafia did not claim to be the Messiah he was very close to it. Cf. M. Idel, *The Mystical Experience in Abraham Abulafia* (New York, 1998), p. 140 and literature in notes 329–30.

visit to pope Nicholas III[12] in 1280 to plead for improvement of the plight of the Jews may not be Messianic as such,[13] but nevertheless reflects a high religious-political vocation similar to our document. The hidden Messianic troops in our text are somewhat similar to Abulafia's vision in *Sefer Ha'ot*: "I saw a man coming from the west with a great army, the number of warriors of his camp being 22.000 men".[14] Of course the idea of hidden Messianic troops of either a militant or a spiritual nature is ancient indeed and rather widespread.[15] Again, however, the fact that Abulafia and our text share a location as well as similar ideas and pictures may be significant.[16]

Historically speaking both the thirteenth century and the late fifteenth century were periods of major persecution and suffering as well as heightened Messianic fervour in Sicily and southern Italy. From 1278 onwards, a vehement anti-Jewish campaign by the Dominican inquisition guided by the inquisitor-general Bartolomeo de Aquila is attested. High taxes for Jews and ample rewards for apostate

---

[12] Pope Nicholas III was the author of *Vineam Soreth* (1278), in which the new orders of the Franciscans and Dominicans are charged with the mission to the Jews. He threatened to burn Abulafia but died the night before the latter's arrival at Rome! After a month's imprisonment by the Franciscans Abulafia was released.

[13] G. Scholem, *Major Trends in Jewish Mysticism* (New York, 1974), p. 128 regards it as Messianic: the Jewish Messiah's connection with the city of Rome is a traditional element in rabbinic literature. Nahmanides had affirmed in the Barcelona disputation of 1263 that the Messiah would go to Rome to ask for the liberation of his people.

[14] Corresponding with the 22 letters of the alphabet. Cf. Idel, *The Mystical Experience in Abraham Abulafia*, p. 95; "Tribes, Lost Ten," *Jewish Encyclopedia* 12, p. 249.

[15] Cf. Mt. 26,53: 'twelve legions of angels'. Troops with these symbolic numbers are known from Qumran as well. Evidently these ideas are inspired by the Biblical account of the Israelite camps in the desert (Num. 31,4–5). Where our text speaks about the troops staying near the river one may be reminded of the rabbinic story about the lost tribes hidden across the river Sambatyon. Likewise the fifth century Church Father Commodianus refers to the return of Christ at the head of a host consisting of the lost tribes of Israel. This hidden, holy people is singularly virtuous. At the same time these saints will show themselves to be fierce warriors. See Cohn, *The Pursuit of the Millennium*, p. 28.

[16] The connection between this mystic Abulafia and our text is not only of a geographical nature; Abulafia's description of mystical phenomena bears a striking resemblance to those in our text. Experiencing letters, colors and liquid substance, as well as the mystic's trembling and shaking, are familiar phenomena to Abulafia and his circle. Cf. Idel, *The Mystical Experience in Abraham Abulafia*, pp. 96–97 (letters of blood), p. 75 (trembling, sense of oil). Idel does not note the similarity between Abulafia and our text. Elsewhere Idel advocates a connection between our text and that curious Messianic figure of gentile birth, Solomon Molko (sixteenth century). Admittedly, phenomena like "the form of a man clad in clothes white as snow" and a Talit covered with holy names, reveal a remarkable similarity.

Jews caused mass conversions.[17] Royal restrictions upon the inquisition—it was not allowed to banish the Jews from society—could not prevent the downfall of Jewry in Southern Italy. In 1290 the Dominican friar Bartolomeo repeated the old accusation against the Jews of having murdered a Christian child. The result was a large-scale persecution and more mass conversions.

At the beginning of the fourteenth century, Jewish life on the main land of Southern Italy seems to have disappeared except for the peculiar position of the *neophyte*, Jews converted to Christianity, comparable to the Marranos in Spain. Although the island of Sicily remained outside these vicissitudes, it cannot but have been affected by it. The expulsion of the Jews from Spain in 1492 meant the end of Sicilian Jewry as well, for Sicily had been under Aragonese rule for two centuries already.[18]

For the present it suffices to underline that our document, if it is indeed a letter from Sicily, may be an indication for the spiritual climate in lower social strata. Various elements in our document seem to correspond with elements from books and documents from 'higher' cultural circles, though differing precisely in their less sophisticated nature.[19] Our document testifies to a hardly known popular culture in which the role and function of the charismatic woman is to be located. In this type of document, one finds her in full colours, although even here or maybe precisely here, she is veiled and hidden behind conventional forms and norms.

---

[17] Cf. J. Cohen, *The Friars and the Jews* (London, 1982), p. 87.

[18] In 1455 Jews from Catania and other towns in Sicily attempted to emigrate to Jerusalem but were discovered by the authorities and punished. C. Roth, *The History of the Jews of Italy* (Philadelphia, 1946), p. 243. In 1457 many Jews threatened to leave the town and in 1466 taxes were reduced by half. The Catanian Jews were finally expelled with the rest of Sicilian Jewry in 1492. Zeldes connects this event to our document; cf. note 7 above.

[19] For high culture in Sicily compare S.M. Stern, "A Twelfth Century Circle of Hebrew Poets in Sicily", *Journal of Jewish Studies* 5 (1954), pp. 60–79; pp. 110–113. Although the physical phenomena of our text and those in Abulafia are remarkably similar, Abulafia offers a much more sophisticated explanation, while our text remains crudely 'materialistic'.

Fresh Water for a Tired Soul—The Manuscript

A
(fol. 1, recto) Fresh water for a tired soul
When we, Michael the son of Samuel, and [. . .][20] came [to] Sicily, we came to a Jewish community, and the name of the place was Catani[a and we heard that there was] a woman, who had been prophesying in San Torbo,[21] and we w[ent to that place to see] her, and she was pregnant, and her nine months' time had passed. And her husband's name was R' Hayim, and we went to the synagogue and we experienced[22] a good smell, [while she] was standing outside. And after the prayer, a trembling seized her and she went home, and she fell upon her face. And she sent for us, as we were in the synagogue, and we went with her husband, and she told her husband: Thus was decreed[23] over me by the Holy One, namely that all the community should come and see me. And we saw her falling upon her face pleading and crying, and she said to her husband: Let them bring me a shawl,[24] and throw it upon me. And they brought a shawl, and as the shawl was brought from the house, the following letters appeared on the shawl she had already upon her: אני (ani = I) [and] after it three *yods* (:::) appeared thus, and in addition, on another edge of the cover appeared אחד (eḥad = one),

And the writing was saffron, and the letters were humid, and each and every one standing there put his finger into it and nothing from the humidity stuck on our hands. And she screamed: Cover me with a shawl, [and they brought the shawl]. And we saw that shawl and there was nothing on it, but once it was put on her, the letters א ס and further א ו and further ס ו appeared, and they said: take another (shawl). And they took it and brought another one, and on it appeared once more ה ז ה ד[25] And she [was lying down] in fear and trembling, and she stretched out her lef[t] hand.

---

[20] Mann reads another name here, but Zeldes checked the manuscript and left the name out. Hence there are two persons: Michael the son of Samuel and the anonymous writer.

[21] Zeldes, "Ma'aseh muflah beSizilia", p. 348, identifies this place as Centorbi, a small village near the eastern coast of Sicily.

[22] Lit.: We heard.

[23] Possibly passivum divinum, meaning either 'decreed' or 'destined'. The Holy One is God rather than some Messianic person like the sixteenth century Solomon Molko. See Aescoly, *HaTenuot hameshihiot beIsrael*, pp. 243–244.

[24] Lit. טלית (Talit): covering or praying shawl. See discussion below.

[25] For a possible interpretation of the various Hebrew letters see Mann, "A Messianic Excitement in Sicily", pp. 39–40, notes 13–14.

Hiding[26] in that hand a human image was seen, and something similar to saffron was flowing down. And we all who stood there, took it and tasted it, [and it tasted] like the taste of oil cakes,[27] and its smell was good as flowing myrrh,[28] and we heard in [her prayer]: Hear O Israel, the Lord is our God, the Lord is One, God is longsuffering and full of grace and [truth].

(verso) . . . . [we] all of us were pleading with [her and then] she lifted her hands [as] priests lift (their hands) [when they step upon the pulpit] and blood appeared on the shawl and then letters appeared . . . appea[red] a stroke of blood, and in the stroke a circle . . . . [and] we saw with our own eyes (א) the signs and the letters [that were on the s]hawls. And she told us: Give praise and thanks to the Lord, and repent [fully] you as well, and in all the places wherever you go through you will show the written words [and] the shawls and they will repent, because thus did the Holy One command me.

And on the Sabbath day after the prayer, we went with her husband to her house to eat together. Before we said grace after the meal, we saw her going up to her upper chamber and she fell upon her face and she was suffering. And we went up with her husband with his permission to see her, and we saw her as if she was eating, and her hands were in her lap. Then we saw her three fingers and they were oozing something similar to oil, and her husband took and gave each and everyone and we ate and it had the taste of honey and its smell was like flowing myrrh. And then she wiped her fingers in her headkerchief, and the entire headkerchief was humid as if it had been dipped [in water], and it had the taste of honey and its smell was very good, incomparable with any other smell [in the world]. And then she sat and started to pray: Lord hear, Lord our God [have mercy and compassion. And] she moaned and said: Woe to the wicked, and woe to them that do not [repent], since thus swore the Holy One before the angels and before Moses [our teacher]: The End is near, and if the wicked will not repent, behold [ma]ny [will perish in s]word and in famine and in persecution, and if they will repent [they will escape] since My salvation[29] is near to come. And that which I have been eating . . . the Holy One Blessed be He will give to Israel.

B
And she told us: Go to the synagogue, [and say the] prayer. And we went and prayed and we saw the curtain as if? . . . . . . good and strong and we saw also a fire entering the synagogue. (fol. 2, recto) And (it) went to the other corner, and two men from those [praying fell on the flo]or, and were beating themselves against the ground, and later when they [stood up from the ground] we asked them each separately:

---

[26] מלטה; Mann suggests: המליטה (cf. Is. 66.7) = she delivered.
[27] Num. 11:8.
[28] Ex. 30:23.
[29] Or: my salvation.

What did you see? And the one [spoke and his friend] did not hear it. He said to us: We have seen the angel with [a sword in his hand, and in his] other hand a huge fire, and he intended to strike me. Similarly [the other was telling] and saying likewise.

C
Rejoice and be happy and return [fully], and fast and supplicate because of the message that came to us on the twenty eighth of the month of *Tishrei* on a Sunday. As I was writing these prophecies, not yet having completed them, behold, a stranger from Morea came . . .

After this the writer relates the story of how this stranger, a non-Jew from Morea (Southern Greece) told a local Jew, Leon, about the arrival of the ambassadors of the 'hidden king'. This Leon told the Jewish community about it and eventually this Leon, Eliah the leader (*Parnas*) of the community, the teacher David and the writer interviewed this stranger. The man told that the hidden king had sent letters to the king of Spain, of Germany and all the other kingdoms with the command to aid his ambassadors on their mission to gather all the Jews and to take them to Jerusalem. The Jews should support each other financially and sell whatever they possessed without any concern as to their living in Jerusalem. These ambassadors were due to arrive at Sicily, according to this non-Jew. In addition to that he had been an eyewitness to an upheaval in Spain where a certain bishop (*hegemon*) did not consent to the departure of the Jews for Jerusalem unless they had parted with their money first. They agreed. The ambassadors, he explained further, belong to the hidden ones, two hundred horsemen and twelve leaders, with credentials signed with twelve golden seals. Each of them represented twelve thousand warriors. The kings of Spain, Germany, Hungary and France were sorely afraid and brought together both money and soldiers to buy off the 'hidden ones', or else to fight them. Upon the ambassadors' arrival in Spain the king received them with great pomp in the company of local Jews riding on horseback. However, the ambassadors refused to enter the city but remained outside near the river, supplied with food and drink by the king.

All this the non-Jew declared to have witnessed himself and he said that the 'Marchese' would bring instructions to the leaders (of Sicily) how to act. In addition to that he told about an uprising of Germans to kill the Jews, which, however was averted by priests who warned the mob that great evil would befall all the world if the Jews were attacked. After another interview the next day this non-Jew assures that the 'Marchese' will arrive (in Sicily) together with the ambassadors.[30]

Here the manuscript breaks off.

---

[30] See about this section S. Bowman, "Messianic Expectations in the Peloponnesos", *Hebrew Union College Annual* 52 (1981), pp. 195–202.

Formal Features

Narrative Devices

There is a remarkable difference between story A about the charismatic woman and story B about the two men, the first being considerably longer and thus more complex. The two men report only briefly their unanimous vision of the angel with a sword in one hand and a huge fire in the other. The story about the woman portrays a more subtle experience and contains several elements of revelation. Although one would perhaps expect to find a subtle, but hidden and shortened account of a female charismatic event over against a more dominant, longer and highlighted male charismatic event, the size and presentation of our document displays the contrary. Obviously the woman's account is much more elaborate than that of the men.

A closer comparison of comparable details in the two stories is illuminating. The revelation in story A is much more physical and of a more bodily nature than the revelation in story B. Over against the fiery angel's apparition, the woman "stretched out her lef[t] hand. Hiding in that hand a human image was seen". Furthermore, the story features a complex and somewhat miraculous childbirth scene, including a variety of signs: the woman is over nine months pregnant, she is suffering from pain, lying in her suffering, palpitating and oozing liquids with a certain 'good smell', with a particular colour and of an oily quality. A perceptive reader will be reminded of a situation of childbirth although the final results remain mysterious. The image seen on her left hand is an image of a man, not of a baby.[31] Nevertheless it seems safe to conclude: a small image became visible, accompanied by mysterious circumstances taking place in the intimate realm of the inner part of the home.

Acting Persons

Whereas story A is considerably longer than story B, in both stories the visionary persons remain anonymous. The two travellers present themselves: Michael the son of Samuel and the writer, whereas in story A the charismatic woman is the anonymous wife of R' Hayim.

---

[31] See also note 38.

In story B both charismatic men remain anonymous, whereas in story C the local leaders are mentioned by name. Apparently the stories emphasise communal authority over against the authority of the actual visionary persons, or in other words: the leaders of the community are better known than its charismatic members. The visionaries are rather channels of the prophetic message and they carry no personal mark.[32]

Both the woman and the men fall on their faces upon receiving their message. In story A, the act of falling precedes a dramatic scene, possibly of ecstasy or perhaps a scene of actual childbirth. The woman falls twice, first as she enters her home returning from the synagogue and once again after lunch as she goes to her upper chamber. Both men in story B fall and they do so within the synagogue precincts following the fire vision there. From a literary perspective there is a certain symmetry in the two stories (1 person × 2 falls / 2 persons × 1 fall).

Locations

Regarding the change of locations, the stories are again mutually illuminating. The two men function within the synagogue, they receive their vision as well as its interpretation within the same location. The woman's story on the other hand emphasises several times that the woman's actions pertain to the home sphere. After prayer she goes home, and invites her husband and the visitors to come from the synagogue to her home. At the end she sends her entire audience back to the synagogue, which sets the scene for story B. In the middle of story A, the woman retreats even more by ascending to the upper chamber. The travellers get permission to intrude into her private realm. Does this difference merely reflect a difference in appropriate social behaviour according to gender? Or should one assume a contextual difference? The fact that the woman calls from the private realm to the multitude outside might have a special meaning. Although the three stories are each of them Messianic, the locations differ. The home-oriented inner message of the woman in story A may serve as a literary foil for story C, which is internationally and even universally oriented.

---

[32] For a similar phenomenon, see Goitein, "A Report on Messianic Troubles in Baghdad", pp. 73–74, where most actors in the story (father, matchmaker) bear a name whereas the prophetess remains anonymous.

Pursuing this track further, one might even read the whole document as tripartite, developing from the inner private sphere, through the communal synagogue to the universal world, as a dynamically structured trilogy. Of course the story of the charismatic woman would then be reduced to a mere literary device, but this does not seem to be justified. The stories convey the impression of a historical account and of a series of events that have really taken place. Perhaps the writer used conventional patterns of gendered behaviour to 'cloak' his own Messianic prophecy.

Speech-Acts

Let us now turn from the images to the actual verbal messages in the first two stories of the document. In story B, the two men report their personal impressions and fears. Each in his turn says: "He intended to strike me". The woman in story A, on the other hand, is introduced in the beginning of our document as a woman who prophesies. In the course of the story she utters many words of wisdom and direction. She calls for her husband; then she explains to him that the Holy One has decreed that her intimate events and their meaning should be revealed to the world. In her ecstasy or suffering, she orders to bring the shawls, she prays the *Shema*, connecting it to the mercy qualities of God (Ex. 34:6), and she calls for praise and repentance in the name of the Holy One. Eventually she once again invokes the name of the Holy One and of other heavenly figures (angels and Moses) and prophesies against the wicked, calls for repentance and gives some concrete practical instructions to return to the synagogue.

The men, although in the public realm of the synagogue, use private and personal words, in contrast with her more oracular performance. She manages to co-ordinate the whole scene, not unlike some women are able to do during childbirth, and she experiences her vision in an articulated national scope, or even as a cosmic struggle between good and evil. She is a messenger of the Holy One by her powerful words, which are accepted by both the narrator and the leaders of the community. In this respect her revelation is transferred from the private sphere to the utmost public realm.

Ironically, the female role turns out to be much more universalistic and powerful than the roles of the two men. The two revelations are described as dual, opposite scenes. One is tempted to think of a carefully constructed story which uses male/female oppositions to highlight the Messianic message. Perhaps, however, it is rather a testimony of the community's acceptance of an extraordinary revelation by an exceptional woman in a time of heightened Messianic fervour.

Gender-Relations

The overall impression throughout the entire document is of conventional gender patterns. In this story a traditional husband/wife relation is central. As it was pointed out above, the woman bears no name, she being presented as secondary to her husband. Throughout the entire wondrous event the husband maintains his masterly, landlord position in his house. The visitors accompany him to his home. His wife addresses him, as if to get his permission, in order to reveal her private condition. Though she claims a vision and instructions from heaven, the story does not suggest in this respect a breach in the conventional gender relations. The same constellation of relations is repeated at dinner, where the visitors join the husband inside the house. The wife is in charge of the home, but male visitors come at his invitation, and not due to her prophecy, though the narrator suggested in the beginning that their visit to the town is due to rumours about her visionary capacities.

Then they join him at his permission to see her in her upper chamber, and again the husband offers each visitor a taste of her oily fluids, as if offering a dessert after dinner. A similar sense of conventional gender relations can be detected in the placid division between the female realm outside the synagogue and at home, and the clearly male realm within the synagogue. This division is not challenged, but rather becomes part of the dynamics in the Messianic message. In the end the males are sent out of the female visionary space back to the synagogue, i.e. to the male realm as if to carry out in the appropriate place what has been ordered.

One should keep in mind that this vision is presented against a traditional background devoid of any critical attitude as to gender relations. Only then the following questions become relevant: do the actual gender relations in our story reflect more than androcentric story telling? Can we detect here traces of a female protagonist's strategy to be seen and heard? Did the woman refrain from assuming full authority (as would befit a prophetess) as a conscious strategy, or should this be explained as a well-known phenomenon of women often failing to assume authority and adapting themselves to dominant gender division without criticism? In other words: to what extent does this story reflect—consciously or unconsciously—a woman's 'own' voice? These questions are important even when no definite answer can be provided.

Special Themes

Pregnancy and Childbirth

Central in story A is the woman being pregnant. What is the meaning of this fact that so strongly determines the images and sensory perceptions of her revelation? The metaphor of pregnancy indicating Messianic expectation combines both the elements of 'the signs of the time' (suffering, birth pangs) and of calculation: a fixed time, a kairos (birth). It explains why this metaphor is firmly rooted in Messianic religious imagery. The Messianic contrasting experience of the present pain and the expectation of new life in the near future are embodied in pregnancy and childbirth. Without pain no birth; the pain is in itself an announcement of redemption.[33] Paul uses the same metaphor when he speaks about "the creation that groans in birth pangs" (Rom. 8,22). The Talmud knows of the expression חבלי המשיח (*chevlei Ha-Mashiah*), the birthpangs that precede the Messiah's advent. "The son of David will come after the tyranny will have unfolded Israel for nine months", the Talmud states[34] in symbolic language. Roman idolatry and tyranny that embitter Israel's life are compared here with the period before giving birth, in which no new life is yet to be seen. Curious rabbinic statements become more comprehensible, if we understand this idea of the birthpangs that precede the Messianic advent: "Let the Messiah come, but I don't want to see him!" In a more elaborate passage the Talmud interprets the text in Jer. 30,6: "See, if a man gives birth? Why do I see every man putting his hands on his loins like a woman in labour?" Obviously Jeremiah does not intend to say that a man can be in birthpangs, but in a remarkable gender-bending the Talmud

---

[33] In Dutch the word 'verlossing' means both 'redemption' and 'giving birth', similar to 'delivery, deliverance' in English.
[34] Bab. Talmud Sanhedrin 98b.

explains: The 'man' that gives birth refers to God! The Almighty is like a woman in labour, suffering because of the plight of the people of Israel and because of all the injustice on earth. But this same suffering points towards the Messianic future. These rabbinic examples demonstrate clearly the possible Messianic connotations of the childbirth metaphor.

Our text uses pregnancy as a metaphor for Messianic expectations, but at the same time as an actual event, as if the woman is really pregnant, her pregnancy being no mere symbolism for Messianic expectations, but in itself a Messianic sign. Very striking in this respect is the story of a Messianic upheaval in Baghdad in the twelfth century referred to above.[35] The prophet Elijah appeared to a woman and told her that Israel's redemption was near at hand. This woman led an ascetic life and consented to be married only after considerable pressure. She resumed celibacy prior to her vision.[36] Our document should be contrasted with this idealisation of celibacy, which may be common in Christianity but is rare (although not wholly absent) in Judaism. Despite some similarities our text is very remote indeed from these ascetic trends as it regards pregnancy (hence: being bodily, female and fruitful) as a suitable vehicle for divine messages.[37]

Questions remain concerning the actual event. Is this woman in labour or in ecstasy? Is she experiencing an imaginary delivery, or is she setting the stage to prophesy? Does she perhaps transform a sad miscarriage into a Messianic sign?[38]

---

[35] See above note 6.

[36] Goitein, "A Report on Messianic Troubles in Baghdad", p. 58, p. 66, p. 73.

[37] In encratitic and ascetic Christian sources celibacy is a condition sine qua non. Time and again young women on the eve of their marriage are prevented from 'consummation' by a saint or an apostle (e.g. *Acts of Thomas* 6–16; The Story of the Saints Nereus and Achileus, in the *Legenda Aurea*). However, there are some remnants of this ascetic tradition in Judaism as well: cf. the traditions about Moses' abstention from intercourse from Sinai on (Sifre Numeri § 100), though Moses' example is not to be emulated according to the Rabbis. For ideas of celibacy within mediaeval Judaism, see A. Maimonides, *Highways of Perfection*, ed. S. Rosenblatt (Jerusalem, 1979), p. 147: "it is an error to think of someone or of oneself as a saint because he gives up marriage or fasts continually . . . while he is remiss in certain commandments". Does Abraham Maimonides disapprove of celibacy in general here or only if one should be neglecting the commandments?

[38] It was interesting to note that female readers of previous drafts of this article were inclined to read it as a miscarriage or an unfortunate childbirth, while male readers were quick to jump on to the symbolic meanings of pregnancy and childbirth.

The Talit – Clothing and Covering

The shawl is a prominent feature in our story, and contains elements that may constitute a direct challenge to conventional religious attitudes concerning woman's behaviour. The story has two words for the clothing and covers that are put upon the woman during her vision. The one is the טלית (*Talit*). Later on in the narrative the woman wipes her fingers with her מנדלין (*Mandalin*).[39] The *Talit* was translated by 'shawl' and the *Mandalin* by 'headkerchief'. Wearing a *Talit* is customary for men during prayer. Ever since the early rabbinic literature it is generally accepted that women do not wear it though it is not explicitly forbidden.[40]

Furthermore, one of the peculiarities of the Sicilian *Geniza* documents is the long list of various sorts of textiles known and used in the Jewish local language.[41] Bearing those facts in mind, may one assume that the choice of this particular word *Talit* for the covering contains specific religious overtones? Does the woman turn to this garment as a sign and a symbol of her particular position?

The *Talit* as a symbol for eschatological expectations is not unknown. The excited Jews in Byzantium gathered wearing their *Talits* and did not do any work, i.e. they simulated a long Sabbath.[42] But in our text the symbolic function of the *Talit* would be strongly determined by the woman wearing it. Does this woman resort to this male symbol as a means to provoke, or should one understand it as a mere popular eschatological symbol?

---

[39] This Greek word is probably one of the many traces of Greek introduced to Sicily via the Arabic occupation of Sicily until the eleventh century.

[40] Tosefta Kiddushin 1:8; Sifre Num. 115; Bab Talmud Menahot 43a; Jer Talmud Berakhot 3:3 (6b); Jer Talmud Kiddushin 1:8 (61c). In a thirteenth century discussion the Talit is mentioned as an example of goods, that a man may give to his bride as a symbol of their marriage, marriage being a kind of 'acquisition'. (*Responsa Chachmei Provence*, Vol. I, b, Lema: Teshuva al.). It is curious that a woman receives a Talit as a present. The Talit may denote a useless property of no value for the woman, since she does not wear it. However, even as a 'useless' gift the Talit is still legitimate as a present in the official marriage ceremony. According to the ruling of Hillel, who established the regular custom ever since, the marriage ritual is valid even by the exchange of one penny.

[41] M. Ben Sasson, *The Jews of Sicily between 825–1068: Documents and Sources* (heb.) (Jerusalem, 1991), pp. 659–660, index s.v. בד (bad = cloth). Cf S. Simonsohn, *The Jews of Sicily* (Leiden, 1997). See also: Y. Stillman, *Female Attire in Medieval Egypt according to the Trousseau Lists and Cognate Material from the Geniza*, Dissertation (Philadelphia, 1972).

[42] Bod. Ms. Me. Heb.3. a 27. Cf. Mann, "The Messianic Movements", p. 196.

M.T. Wacker maintains that the procedure of covering oneself, taking off and piling up many veils constitute a strong symbolic performance for women's conscious claims to power and participation.[43] Is one justified to read a similar motive in this present account? Even if one accepts the *Talit* as an emancipatory symbol, it should be admitted that in our story this symbol remains well hidden behind conventional veils.

The Priestly Gesture

The priestly raising of the hand deserves attention as well. Once again one encounters in the story a specific gesture reserved to men but in this case attributed to the woman during her vision. Just like the *Talit*, the priestly blessing accompanied with a specific posture of the fingers is the prerogative of male priests and not of priestesses or daughters of priests.[44] The priestly gesture is one of the specific synagogue or public realm activities, to be carried out only in a full community with a minimum of ten men (*minyan*). The rabbinic discourse even deliberates whether women are to be included in receiving the priestly blessing.[45] Should one interpret the woman's gesture as a sign of consciously breaking away from conventional gender roles? Or should one understand it as part of the androcentric story using well-known symbols for this charismatic event, while forgetting or ignoring the fact that the protagonist is a woman?

The Reading of the Shema

As the woman produces or gives birth to the little image in her left hand, she is heard to be praying. Her prayer includes the first verse of the *Shema* (Dt. 6:4), and a part of what is called the thirteen qualities of God (Ex. 34:6). Here we elaborate upon three elements concerning the reading of the *Shema*.

a. Although the reading of the *Shema* could be a private prayer, the reading of the divine qualities belongs definitely to a community service. The reading of the *Shema*, too, could be a formal public

---

[43] M.T. Wacker, "Gendering Hosea 13", in B. Becking and M. Dijkstra (eds.), *On Reading Prophetic Texts: Gender-Specific and Related Studies in Memory of Fokkelien van Dijk-Hemmes* (Leiden, 1996), pp. 265–282.
[44] Sifrei Num. 39; Num. Raba 11:4.
[45] Sifrei Num. 39; ibid. 43.

prayer activity namely the so-called פורס על שמע (*pores ʿal Shemaʿ*), when a leader reads one verse at a time and the community responds.⁴⁶ The document shows a small break here, followed by the descriptive statement: "[we] all of us were pleading with [her]". Does this imply her activity being public or private?

b. Rabbinic tradition from the Tannaic period throughout Jewish history attributes to the *Shema* an ecstatic mysterious potential. The *Shema* is understood as the declaration of the kingdom of heaven;⁴⁷ for Rabban Gamaliel it is the key to the kingdom of heaven.⁴⁸ The *Shema* is recited at the end of the Day of Atonement and is the summit of the religious experience of the day. It constitutes the last words of any dying person.

Hence the occurrence of the *Shema* in our story is no mere accident. Does the story mean to tell us that the woman is acting as a leader in prayer as she communicates her vision to her audience? Or do they all join in her private moment of childbirth or 'birth of prophecy'? The recital of the *Shema* can be seen as a public ceremony, but also as a private voice of intimate prayer.

c. Furthermore, rabbinic law knows of restrictions as to the leaders of the ceremonial *Shema* reading. Small children and the blind are officially disqualified,⁴⁹ though not all rabbinic authorities agree in this respect.⁵⁰ Tractate *Soferim* possibly even implies that women are part of the restriction.⁵¹ If one understands our story as referring to a formal occasion, one cannot but underscore the implications for the challenging of traditional gender roles and relations. Does this account imply a critique of male religious prerogatives? Or is this an example of an androcentric story about an exceptional woman which is devoid of revolutionary potential precisely because of its exceptional nature?

---

⁴⁶ Maimonides, Mishne Tora Hilkhot Tefila uNesiat Kapaim, 8:5.
⁴⁷ Mishna Berachot 2:2; Sifrei Num.,115; Deut. Raba, 2:28; Tanhumah, Lech Lecha 1.
⁴⁸ Mishna Berachot 2:5.
⁴⁹ Mishna, Megila 4:4; 4:6; Tosefta Megila 3:16.
⁵⁰ Tanhuma, Toldot 7. See the exhaustive treatment in T. Marx, *Halakhah and Handicap: Jewish Law and Ethics on Disability* (Utrecht, 1993), passim.
⁵¹ Tractate Sofrim 10:7. It may be argued, however, that the mentioning of women there does not refer to the beginning of the passage.

The Rhetoric of Miracles

Miracles are embedded in stories, and every miraculous event is told as a miracle story. Our research on this text about a miracle occurring to a woman requires taking the story-element into account as well. Miracle stories have a strong rhetorical potential and serve to persuade the listener of a religious truth.[52] The miracle's proof is an essential element in the story. Hence one of the rhetorical elements in the composition of a miracle story is the investigation and probing of any event before declaring it miraculous. The proof is an intrinsic part of the story telling in any miraculous event, and it plays a very prominent part in the present document as well. Considering we are dealing with a tripartite story, comparison of the different proofs enables us to get a clearer picture of the woman's story. Let us first make an inventory of the proof elements.

In story A, one of the bystanders puts his finger in or on the appearing wet letters, but nothing seems to stick to it. Later on the speaker testifies and says: "We saw the *Talit* and nothing was on it, and then letters appeared". Yet further on they taste from the saffron-looking moisture and the storyteller claims: "we saw with our own eyes". In the upper chamber the woman's husband gives the visitors once more a bit to taste. Thus the proof consists of a concrete employment of various senses, touch, smell, taste and sight. Likewise the prophetess charges them to take with them the *Talits* as well as the testimonies that they were supposed to write in order to show them together, so that people from far away should see and repent.

In story B, the people see the vision, but the main proof is the fact that both men, while interrogated separately, tell the same story. One may regard this as a quasi-juridical proof.

Story C is dealing with written material and henceforth the nature of the proof changes. The writings are sealed with ten seals, the letters are written in *Yehudit*, presumably Hebrew, as a proof of authenticity. At the end the messenger takes a vow of truth, and there is an attempt to identify these writings with previous secret information from the so-called *Genuzim*, the 'hidden ones'. Here the type of proof is legalistic in nature rather than personal.

---

[52] Convincingly argued by B. Blumenkranz, "Juden und Jüdisches in christlichen Wundererzählungen", *Juifs et Chrétiens: Patristique et Moyen Âge* (London, 1977). The author demonstrates how mediaeval Christian miracle stories serve as a strong polemical tool against Judaism.

An ascending scale in the presentation of the miracles becomes patent. The scale runs from the private realm through the interpersonal to the written and impersonal, and from sensory perception to the more constructed, non-sensory perception. One is even tempted to say there is a shift from nature to culture, and from the direct and simple to the indirect and complex. However, this deserves some additional reflection. Precisely the dichotomy between nature and culture is hotly debated nowadays, as these elements often presuppose unconscious gender dualism in combination with scales of value.[53] The unconscious equation of nature with female and of culture with male is precisely one of the ideologies of male dominance irrespective of how the 'call of nature' is perceived, negatively or utopian. One should be careful then to apply the distinction nature-culture to our story. Abulafia's mysticism demonstrates that sensory elements are not lacking in male religious experience either! It would be a mistake to conclude that the woman's prophecy is considered less elevated and less legitimate than the other two prophecies. Her prophecy takes place in the private realm, but the proof of her wondrous behaviour is concrete, direct and generally accessible. What is more, the woman herself orders the evidence of proof to be showed and spread to the outside world.

As has been said before, in this document men and women move along conventional guidelines. The demand for proof in this possibly popular document does not break away from traditional gender roles and stereotypes. Nevertheless one should pay special attention to one type of proof in the female protagonist's story. The prophetess herself calls for the audience to collect her shawls and carry them with a written story (כתבים). In other words, the storyteller probably suggests that the woman herself is not satisfied with her private set-up. Should one attach particular importance to that element by assuming here two different levels of participation? On the one hand the storyteller presents a conventional reading of the woman's situation. On the other hand and in spite of himself he testifies to her wish that her prophecy be written down and spread over the world. Unwittingly, he allows a female voice to come through and to be heard.

---

[53] Sherry B. Ortner, "Is Female to Male as Nature is to Culture?" in: M. Zimbalist Rosaldo and L. Lamphere (eds.), *Woman Culture and Society* (Stanford, California, 1975), pp. 67–87.

Conclusions

The analysis of characters and activities is dependent on the storytelling structure of the document. If the document is a letter to be dispatched and multiplied in various Jewish communities, there may be some significance in the fact that the woman's story is longer and more detailed and the first one in this short series of three stories. Would our story carry a different significance if it were a chapter in a book or part of a longer story?

However, the story is told by an eyewitness as part of a sequence of events, not as a separate story. Part A occurs first, and practically invites the following short event B. The third event C occurs simultaneously. We noticed the movement from intimate privacy to the public realm. The question at hand is: To what extent is the woman's story part of a rhetorical device? Does the woman only serve the overall purpose of the story, or does she herself direct the story? She may, however, just as well be considered a tool serving as an opening to the 'real important' world prophecy. But she may as well be regarded as the embodiment of the relevance of world history and of national agitation. In that case she is the real agent and catalyst of the story.

If our document is part of a lost book, as Zeldes claims, it would be slightly more probable that the story is fiction. The female element might then be interpreted as a literary device, using conventional gender images. If, however, one is rather inclined to regard the document as a letter, preserved in the *Geniza* not because of its content but only for religious reasons, then one may give more credence to the woman's actual performance as a prophetess. However, both as a literary fiction and as a historical event, the significance of this female protagonist remains undisputed.

Here then is a story of a woman with a strong vocation but without any official means to share her insights with the community, for she belongs and remains outside the synagogue. She interprets her concrete or imaginary pregnancy as a Messianic sign. Her charismatic behaviour appears to be an adequate channel, since her claim is heard and recognised by the community. In her excitement she is pushing her traditionally determined limitations as far as possible by permitting unsolicited intimate contacts (with permission of the husband, her own consent or refusal remaining unknown), as a means to spread her vision and message. She may even resent this intrusion, which may explain her screaming and her asking to be covered by extra shawls. During this private affair she applies some other strategies to widen her horizons by adopting specific male gestures, hereby perhaps claiming more credibility and authority. This in turn gives her the opportunity to speak up and to be heard in her own circles and beyond. True to her vision she attempts to break through her cultural limitations by exploring wider horizons. We do not know if the storyteller noticed this message. Still, the fact that he delivered it is remarkable. It shows at least that emancipatory stances may have been imagined and reverberated earlier and more often than we usually think.

6

THE LIFE OF CHRISTINA MIRABILIS MIRACLES AND THE CONSTRUCTION OF MARGINALITY[1]

Anke E. Passenier

Introduction

In the Life of Christina Mirabilis (1150–1224)[2] by the devout and learned Dominican Thomas of Cantimpré[3] the miraculous plays such a prominent role, that it must have baffled even medieval readers.

---

[1] The research for this article was supported by the Foundation for Research in the Field of Philosophy and Theology in the Netherlands which is subsidized by the Dutch Organization for the Advancement of Research.

[2] Thomas of Cantimpré, *Vita Beatae Christina Mirabilis Virginis*, ed. J. Pinius, *Acta Sanctorum Iul.* V (1868), pp. 637–660, hereafter cited as *VCM*, followed by page and paragraph number; translated by Margot H. King, *The Life of Christina of Saint-Trond* (Toronto: Peregrina Publishing Co., 1989). Important recent studies on Christina of Saint-Trond are: M.H. King, "The Sacramental Witness of Christina Mirabilis: The Mystic Growth of a Fool for Christ's Sake", *Peaceweavers. Medieval Religious Women* 2, eds. L.T. Shank and J.A. Nichols (Kalamazoo: Cistercian Publications, 1987), pp. 145–164 and R. Sweetman, "Christine of Saint-Trond's Preaching Apostolate: Thomas of Cantimpré's Hagiographical Method Revisited", *Vox Benedictina: A Journal of Feminine and Monastic Spirituality* 9, 1 (1992), pp. 67–97. Christina also received attention in Brenda Bolton's article on the Lives of women saints: B.M. Bolton, "Vitae Matrum: A further Aspect of the *Frauenfrage*", *Medieval Women*, ed. D. Baker (Oxford: Basil Blackwell, 1970), pp. 253–273; in the studies of Caroline Walker Bynum, *Holy feast and Holy Fast: the Religious Significance of Food to Medieval Women* (Berkeley: University of California Press, 1987), especially pp. 120–123 and pp. 273–274; *Fragmentation and Redemption: Essays on Gender on the Human Body in Medieval Religion* (New York: Zone Books, 1992) especially pp. 236–237 and *The Resurrection of the Body in Western Christianity, 200–1336* (New York: Columbia University Press, 1995) especially pp. 221, 224, 333 and in Amy Hollywood, *The Soul as Virgin Wife. Mechthild of Magdeburg, Marguerite Porete and Meister Eckhart* (Notre Dame: University of Notre Dame Press, 1995), pp. 41–49 passim, pp. 233–238 passim.

[3] Thomas of Cantimpré (1201–1270/2), native of Liège, was an Augustinian canon, who moved to the Dominican order about 1230 and studied in Cologne under Albertus Magnus and in Paris. His best known works are the *Bonum Universale de Apibus*, ed. Georgius Colvenerius (Douai: B. Belleri, 1627) and the *De Natura Rerum*, ed. H. Boese (Berlin/New York: Walter de Gruyter, 1973). Moreover, he wrote the *Vitae* of four women saints: Christina of Saint-Trond, Margaret of Ypres, Lutgard of Aywières and Mary of Oignies in a supplement to the life by Jacob of Vitry. On Thomas's biography, see the articles of A. Deboutte, "Thomas van

From the hagiographer's repeated warnings that the extraordinary occurrences, as related in the *Vita*, were incomprehensible to human reason and against the ordinary course of nature, it appears that he himself was clearly aware of this. However, instead of diminishing the credibility of the *Vita*—as it might to modern readers[4]—the miraculous could rather heighten it, because it manifests the presence and power of God himself. Undoubtedly, divine intervention would be more convincing than the actions of feeble and fallible men. Therefore, miracles can function as a kind of divine signature on a saint's Life.[5] In the case of Christina's Life the divine signature of the miraculous seems to have been written all over it, covering like a veil the human Christina, who remains hidden from the inquisitive eyes of ordinary mortals. Whereas the other *Vitae* of women saints by Thomas of Cantimpré[6]—although not devoid of extraordinary events either—can be considered as spiritual biographies religious women could model their own lives after,[7] Christina's *Vita* can hardly serve as such

---

Cantimpré zijn opleiding te Kamerijk", *Ons Geestelijk Erf* 56 (1982), pp. 283–299 and "Thomas van Cantimpré als auditor van Albertus Magnus", *Ons Geestelijk Erf* 58 (1984), pp. 192–209.

[4] Since the Bollandists seriously questioned the authority and historical value of the *Vita* at the turn of the 19th century, it became generally relegated to the realms of pious folklore. The *mirabilia* the *Vita* is suffused with compelled scholars to judge it the work of an incompetent, credulous biographer, a fable of no historical worth. See King, "Sacramental Witness", p. 147 and Sweetman, "Christine of Saint-Trond", pp. 77–78.

[5] On miracle-working as a criterion for sainthood see, for example, D. Weinstein and R.M. Bell, *Saints & Society: The Two Worlds of Western Christendom, 1000–1700* (Chicago/London: University of Chicago Press, 1982), pp. 143–153.

[6] Thomas also wrote the biography of Margaret of Ypres (1216–1237): *Vita Margarete de Ypris (VMY)*, ed. G. Meersseman, *Archivum Fratrum Praedicatorum* 18 (Paris/Rome, 1948), pp. 106–130, translated by M.H. King, *The Life of Margaret of Ypres by Thomas de Cantimpré* (Toronto: Peregrina Publishing Co., 1996); of Lutgard of Aywières (1182–1246), *Vita Lutgardis Virgine (VLA)*, ed. G. Henschenius, *Acta Sanctorum Jun. IV* (1867), pp. 187–209, translated by M.H. King, *The Life of Lutgard of Aywières by Thomas de Cantimpré* (Toronto: Peregrina Publishing Co., 1991); and a supplement to Jacob of Vitry's *Vita* of Mary of Oignies (1177/78–1213): *Vita Mariae Oigniacensis, Supplementum*, ed. A. Rayssius, *Acta Sanctorum Jun. V* (1867), pp. 572–581, translated by H. Feiss, *Matrologia Latina* 9 (1987, 1989).

[7] Simone Roisin, who wrote a landmark study on Cistercian hagiography, has argued that Thomas's *Vitae* of Margaret of Ypres and of Lutgard of Aywières should be interpreted as promoting a new concept of religious perfection, as it emerged in Cistercian spirituality at the time, focussing on inner asceticism and contemplative introspection. They are essentially mystical biographies, culminating in the *Vita* of Lutgard of Aywières as the masterpiece. The *Vita* of Christina, which does not fit in with the pattern of the spiritual biography, lacking a division according to mystical stages of the soul and concentrating on 'faits extérieurs', according to Roisin is a still immature work of Thomas, not yet imbued with the Cistercian ideal:

a model.[8] It is too much wrapped up in the miraculous that enfolds her life from the beginning until the end like an ultimate accolade.

Christina's Life practically opens with her dying from exhaustive contemplation, which her body could not endure. The next day, however, during her funeral mass, she returns to life and rises from the coffin to levitate to the ceiling rafters of the church. Only the priest can, by the power of the Sacrament, force Christina to descend (651,5). Afterwards, she tells her dumbfounded sisters and spiritual friends how she had visited purgatory, hell and heaven and that she had returned to life with a special mission from the Lord. She would suffer the torments of purgatory in her mortal body without any harm or injury, delivering agonizing souls from purgatory and exhorting the living to turn aside from their sins. Christina warns her friends not to be troubled by the things they were going to see in her, because they would surpass human understanding and were never seen among mortals before (651/52,6–8). Indeed, after the stunning opening of the *Vita* many astounding miracles follow. As Christina, shortly after her resurrection, flees the presence of men into remote desert forests to be alone with God, she is saved from starvation by sweet milk dripping from her virginal breasts (652,9). Another mammary wonder occurs when she is languishing in prison, bound with a wooden yoke, which caused terrible wounds on her body. Then, at a certain moment her virginal breasts begin to flow with a liquid of the clearest oil, which she uses to soften the course prison-bread with and as a healing ointment for her festering limbs. This miracle finally convinces Christina's sisters and spiritual friends, who, deeming her possessed, had chased and imprisoned her, that God is at work in her (654,19). Quite spectacular and miraculous too, are the expiatory sufferings Christina takes upon herself after her stay in the deserted places. She throws herself into hot ovens

---

S. Roisin, "La méthode hagiographique de Thomas de Cantimpré", *Miscellanea historica in honorem Alberti de Meyer* (Louvain: Bibliothèque de l'Université, 1946), pp. 546–557. See also Simone Roisin, *L'Hagiographie cistercienne dans le diocèse de Liège au XIIIe siècle* (Louvain: Bibliothèque de l'Université, 1946).

[8] Margot King's interpretation of the *VCM* as a mystical biography, with a division of Christina's feeding, education and her acts (gesta) following William of Saint Thierry's description of the growth of the soul according to the animal, rational and spiritual levels, I find not entirely convincing. In my opinion the purpose of this Life is not so much the presentation of a novel model of spiritual life, but rather the exhortation to penance in view of future punishment and the propagation of theological notions on important topics of the time.

and roaring fires, she jumps into cauldrons with boiling water (652,11). In winter she stays under frozen rivers for days and she stands upright on revolving mill-wheels in icy waters (652,12). Although she suffers her pains loudly and dramatically, howling as with the pangs of childbirth, her body always remains unscathed, not showing any trace of injury or mutilation. A further manifestation of the miraculous are the effects of contemplation and ecstatic rapture on Christina's body. Sometimes she would unexpectedly be ravished in the spirit and her body would roll and whirl around with such extreme violence that her limbs could no longer be distinguished (653,16; 656,35). Furthermore, when in ecstatic rapture a kind of angelic singing would resound from her breast and her throat (656,35). In the last year of her life, when she was frequently withdrawing into remote deserted places again, the spirit had gained such control over her body, that she would barely touch the ground and people could scarcely tell, whether a spirit or a material body had passed by (658,46; 659,50). The ending of Christina's life is as stunning as the beginning. After the quiet and unconspicuous death she had been hoping and praying for, she is called back to life by the priores of St. Catharine's, who desperately wants her to reveal the answers to some burning questions (659,52–53). Thus, death and subsequent resurrection mark the beginning as well as the end of the *Vita*.

From these examples we may conclude that the miraculous plays an exceptional role in the *Vita* of Christina. Christina's exploits are even so extreme, that, at a certain moment, her relatives and fellow religious pray God that he would moderate his works in the holy woman, lest evil might come out of it (654,20). After Christina had thrown herself into a baptismal font this moderation is effected, enabling Christina to live among humans (654,21). Obviously, the miraculous is of an ambivalent nature; its disturbance of the ordinary might prove disruptive and destructive. In this article I intend to analyze the function of miracles and the miraculous in the specific context of the *Vita* of Christina. Firstly, the function of the framework of the text, marked by Christina's death and resurrection, which sets the scene for the entire *Vita*, moving it to a supernatural and other-worldly level, shall be discussed. Secondly, attention will be given to Christina's spectacular re-enactments of purgatorial torments, which are illustrative for women's ministry to the dead and the development of new theological concepts on purgatory. Thirdly, we will look into the mammary wonders of lactation and oil-exuding and the miraculous somatic phenomena accompanying states of contemplation and ecstatic rapture, which express certain theological views on the relation of body and soul, contemplation and action, earthly and heavenly life and, on the function of the sacraments. The analysis of specific miracles will serve to address more general questions. Notably, in what way and to what extent can the miracles in this *Vita* be regarded as empowering women and authorizing women's apostolate and ministry? Similarly, how and when do they appear to effect quite the opposite: favouring women's disempowerment and restriction of female religious ministry? Finally, the text being written by Thomas of Cantimpré, in what way does it serve the hagiographer to propagate his message?

Miracles and Marginality—A Borderline on the Threshold of the Beyond

Paradoxically, the Life of Christina Mirabilis practically opens with her death and the bargain struck between her and God that she would live purgatory on earth. The *Vita* also ends with a miracle of resurrection before Christina's final departure from the world of the living. The resurrection-miracles and Christina's odyssey into the beyond provide the framework for the whole *Vita* and are crucial to its interpretation. They qualify Christina as a traveller or even a wanderer between different worlds, realms and spheres: this world and the beyond, human society and the desert lands, the spiritual and the corporeal, contemplation and apostolic ministry. Only in the section of the *Vita*, where Thomas describes Christina's life and deeds (gesta) among men and her ministry within human society (654,22–658,45), she becomes 'real'. Her portrait obtains the recognizable traits of a 'religious woman' at the turn of the 12th century, who practises an apostolical life (vita apostolica) of poverty, prayer, continence, contemplation and compassion. Notably, she is active in an apostolate of correcting and converting sinners from their wicked deeds and in ministry to the dead, interceding and vicariously suffering for souls in purgatory. In her 'social' phase, dedicating herself with prayer, prophecy, preaching and penance to the salvation of sinful mankind—the living as well as the dead—she is a holy woman of great authority. Her advice and counsel are sought by many, including people of high standing, like the Count of Looz and the Benedictine nuns of St. Catharine's. Her ministry includes prophetic judgements on political events, expounding Scripture, hearing confession and admonishing sinning priests.

The section of the *Vita* dealing with Christina's deeds (gesta) in the world of men is conspicuously in contrast with the 'marginal' phases of her life that precede and follow it, in which the fantastical, the miraculous and the grotesque predominate. In the first and the last phase of her life Christina is literally levitated; like a ghost, a living dead, she floats in the clouds. In the course of the *Vita* we see her as it were descending from high to perform her task among men, and, after completing this, ascend again, becoming unapproachable to human beings. An intriguing explanation for the discrepancy between the different sections of the *Vita* has been offered by Robert Sweetman. He suggests that Christina's deeds defied an easy placement within the accepted patterns of feminine sanctity and that her exuberant idiosyncrasy demanded *apologia*. In response to this demand Thomas composed Christina's Life to represent her extraordinary behaviour as a living sermon on purgatory, as teaching by the example of her life.[9] Following this lead I argue that the 'miraculous framework' of the *Vita* probably served Thomas in the construction of marginality, paradoxically heightening and diminishing Christina's authority at the same time. A comparison of the 'miraculous sections' of the *Vita* with the presentation of Christina's active apostolate in society and with information other sources can supply on women's religious ministry, should support this assumption.

That Thomas conceives of Christina as living in the margin of society already appears from the opening of the *Vita*, where he devotes a few lines to her childhood and upbringing. Christina is introduced as the youngest of three orphan sisters, who after their parents death, desiring to live a religious life, arrange that the eldest sister devote herself to prayer, that the middle one take care of the household and that the youngest—Christina—watch the household flock (651,4). In other words, Christina is assigned the lowest and humblest office, but nonetheless it is she, unknown to all, who is secretly visited by

---

[9] Sweetman, "Christine of Saint-Trond", pp. 68–77. See also King, "Sacramental Witness", p. 158. B. Newman in her *From Virile Woman to Woman Christ: Studies in Medieval Religion and Literature* (Philadelphia: University of Pennsylvania Press, 1995), pp. 111, 122 claims to follow Sweetman, but when she calls the behaviour of Christina, which Thomas represents as a sermon on purgatory, 'bizarre, perhaps deranged', and speaks of her 'mental instability', she actually introduces a different interpretation I do not agree with.

Christ and experiences the inward grace of his sweetness. The universal motive of the youngest child rising to greatness (Cinderella, Jacob, King David) seems to be employed here. Furthermore, the passage seems to illustrate the borderline position Christina helds. Her elder sisters have already taken up the roles of the contemplative Mary, devoted to prayer and the active Martha, performing the household duties. Neither nun, nor housewife Christina resides outside of the social and religious household, 'unknown to all'. However, not the sister who was officially committed to prayer, but the humble shepherd Christina is the Lord's favourite.

Although the opening of Christina's Life seems to breathe the spirit of the legendary, it also subtly reflects the rise of the ideal of the *vita apostolica*. At the end of the twelfth and the beginning of the thirteenth century thousands of men and women throughout Europe were seized by a new religious fervour, marked by a heroic dedication to evangelical life.[10] The imitation of the Christ of the gospels in poverty, chastity and charity; apostolic zeal in preaching and pastoral activity; mystical striving to union with God and spiritual perfection were combined in the adage of the *vita apostolica*. Living religiously was no longer identified with monastic life within the safe boundaries of tightly organized religious orders, confined to an elite group set apart to perform religious duties. Instead, it became a universally proclaimed ideal, which especially in urban communities met with enormous response from people of all ranks of society. From the outset women were highly involved in the evangelical movement, particularly in the Low Countries, where 'mulieres religiosae' became its most powerful force. Some of these women became nuns or recluses, traditional forms of *vita religiosa*, others lived alone, or in loosely organized communities without an official religious rule as so-called beguines. Notably, in the diocese of Liège, within the confines of the principalities of Brabant-Flanders, a movement of 'religious women' emerged, whose renown was spread by an impressive series of hagiographical writings, to which also the Life of Christina belongs.[11]

---

[10] A first-rate study on this still is H. Grundmann's *Religiöse Bewegungen im Mittelalter: Untersuchungen über die geschichtlichen Zusammenhänge zwischen der Ketzerei, den Bettelorden und der religiösen Frauenbewegung im 12. und 13. Jahrhundert und über die geschichtlichen Grundlagen der deutschen Mystik* (Berlin: Emil Ebering, 1935). Neudruck mit dem Anhang: *Neue Beiträge zur Geschichte der religiösen Bewegungen im Mittelalter* (Darmstadt: Wissenschaftliche Buchgesellschaft, 1961).

[11] See, for example, S. Roisin, "L'Efflorescence cistercienne et le courant féminin

Christina of St. Trond,[12] a town near Liège, was one of the women, who in the first decades of the 13th century gave up the prospect of marriage and motherhood, renounced their earthly possessions and positions and took a religious habit to follow in the footsteps of Christ. Moreover, she belongs to the large number of women, who did not pursue the *vita apostolica* in a traditional way as nuns or recluses, but on their own terms, in novel, sometimes quite radical ways. Thomas's depiction of the young Christina, who lives in the margin of established institutions, and becomes the most intimate beloved of Christ, can be seen to reflect the concrete marginality of these religious women. At the same time it mirrors the high hopes invested in them by churchmen of high position, who expected evangelical renewal of the church from novel forces on the brink of established institutions.

Immediately following the description of Christina's childhood, Thomas proceeds with the scene of her death and resurrection, through which Christina obtains a marginality of a different order. We now see her entirely removed from the 'human household'. She journeys through purgatory, hell and heaven and when she returns she scarcely belongs to the human domain. Her spirit has become so sensitive, that it revolts at the foul smell of human bodies, unable to endure the stink of sinful humanity. She flees the presence of men and preferably resides in the desert or in lofty places, like trees and the tops of castles and churches (652,9). Her body is so light that like a sparrow she hangs suspended from the topmost branches of

---

de piété au XIIIe siècle", *Revue d'histoire ecclésiastique* 39 (1943), pp. 342–378; E.W. McDonnell, *The Beguines and Beghards in Medieval Culture* (1954, rpt. New York: Octagon Books, 1969); B. Degler-Spengler, "Die religiöse Frauenbewegung des Mittelalters. Konversen—Nonnen—Beginen", Albert Bruckner zum 13. juli 1984, *Rottenburger Jahrbuch für Kirchengeschichte* 3 (1984), pp. 75–88; B.M. Bolton, "Vitae Matrum", pp. 253–273; B.M. Bolton, "Some Thirteenth Century women in the Low Countries: A Special Case?", *Nederlands Archief voor Kerkgeschiedenis* 61 (1981), pp. 7–29; and U. Weinmann, *Mittelalterliche Frauenbewegungen: Ihre Beziehungen zur Orthodoxie und Häresie* (Pfaffenweiler: Centaurus, 1990).

[12] Contemporary historical testimony on Christina from other sources is scarce. We have a laudatory reference to her by Jacob of Vitry in his biography of Mary of Oignies (see below) and she features in the Life of Lutgard (see also below). There is a 15th-century testimony of Denis the Carthusian, who remembers that, when he went to school in St. Trond, he often heard Christina's name mentioned: Dionysius Cartusianus, *Liber de quator novissimis*, art. 50; *Dialogus de judicio particulari animarum post mortem*, art. 10; quoted by Pinius in his preliminary commentary on the *Vita* (*VCM* 638, 8). That Christina's renown soon was widely spread appears from early translations into Middle Dutch and Middle English. See on this point King, "Sacramental Witness", p. 160 n. 9.

the highest trees (653,15). When she prays she often stands erect on fence palings, where she would chant all the Psalms, 'for it was very painful indeed for her to touch the ground while she was praying' (653,16). It appears that during this time of liminality Christina was able to dwell in about every cosmic element, except earth. Not only does she ascend to lofty places like a bird, she also lingers in the waters like a fish. In her suffering of purgatorial pains, she even survives fire and ice. She seems to be anything but human. Often entering the graves of dead men to lament for the sins of men, her domain is that of the dead, rather than of the living (653,13). People, especially her embarrassed sisters and her spiritual companions, deem her possessed by demons and with great effort try to capture and imprison her, which, however, proves to be impossible (653,16f). Iron chains and fetters repeatedly fall off and a notorious bruiser hired to capture her can only catch her by breaking her leg (653,17). Subsequently, shut up in a narrow dungeon, she takes a stone from the floor and throws it with such force that she makes a hole in the wall. "Thus her spirit, which had been restrained more than was just, flew with her body in its weak flesh through the empty air like a bird, because 'Where the Spirit of the Lord is, there is liberty'", Thomas comments (653/654,19). The way Christina is violently stirred by the Spirit reverberates archaic notions, as they occur, for example, in the Old-Testament stories of Samson. The Spirit represents a wild, violent and uncivilized element, uncontrollable by and incompatible with any social order. Her belonging to the world of the Spirit makes Christina a non-human, a possessed, who is hunted like an animal by everyone, even by devout religious people, who fail to recognize her divine mission and the stirrings of God's Spirit. In the last year of her life, after completing her ministry to the living and the dead Christina is again driven into the desert and ascends to loftier realms. She barely seems to touch the ground and people can scarcely tell whether a spirit or a material body passes by (658,46). She belongs to the living and the dead at the same time. Even from her second death she returns once again (659,52,53). Thus, Christina is qualified as a homeless wanderer between different realms. She is a borderline-case, living on the threshold of the beyond. The miracle of her return to life makes her exceptional, gives her the position of an outsider, whose amazing exploits are solely justifiable and acceptable because they are divinely inspired.[13]

---

[13] The theme of the saint as an outsider, who fails to be recognized by the

The question is now, what motives Thomas might have had, composing Christina's Life as he did, providing it with a framework of such bizarre complexion. At any rate, it would be unjust to accuse him of mere phantastic confabulation. Actually, he constructs this section of the *Vita* on the basis of his sources, as he had promised to do in the prologue to the *Vita* (650,1–3). There, he begins by citing Jacob of Vitry's account of Christina's death and resurrection, her subsequent acts of penance to live purgatory on earth and her ecstatic ministry of leading souls to purgatory and to heaven.[14] Thomas asserts that without this testimony of the revered bishop he would never have presumed to have written the *Vita*. He had amplified this central account with the testimonies of straightforward witnesses from St. Trond. It is exactly this procedure, as accounted for in the prologue, which Thomas punctiliously follows in his biography. For his description of Christina's death and her suffering of purgatorial torments in the body he heavily relies on Jacob of Vitry's reference, adding the account of Christina's odyssey in the beyond, for which he could make use of the common literary genre of the other-worldly vision.[15] However, in the section of the *Vita*, in which Christina's ministry as a holy woman with an important position in society is described, Thomas is obviously relying on the testimony of inhabitants of the town of St. Trond and others, who had witnessed her public ministry. In the portrait Thomas draws of the 'moderate' Christina, who is, after her 'baptism', re-integrated in human society

---

people and is unjustly persecuted, but finally saved by a divine intervention, authorizing his/her apostolate is a common *topos* in hagiography. See, for example, M. Goodich, *Vita Perfecta: The Ideal of Sainthood in the Thirteenth Century* (Stuttgart: Anton Hiersemann, 1982), pp. 100–110. In the case of Christina, however, the splendid isolation of the saint is strongly reinforced by her death and resurrection, which qualify her as super-human, marginal and liminal. As to the scenes of Christina's persecution by relatives and spiritual friends, it is not unlikely that they are not merely an application of the topos of the suffering saint, but that they reflect actual resistance Christina might have encountered in the beginning of her ministry. We know from other sources, that solitary extra-regular religious women were often frowned upon by their contemporaries and that their biographers had to use all their cogency to exonerate them. See below.

[14] Jacob of Vitry describes Christina's death and resurrection in the prologue to his *Vita Mariae Oigniacensis (VMO)*, ed. D. Papebroeck, *Acta Sanctorum Jun. V* (1867), pp. 542–572; p. 543, 8.

[15] On this genre, widely spread and very popular in the Middle Ages, see, for example, H.R. Patch, *The Other World* (1950, rpt. New York: Octagon Books, 1970); P. Dinzelbacher, *Vision und Visionsliteratur im Mittelalter* (Stuttgart: Anton Hiersemann, 1981) and J. Le Goff, *La naissance du Purgatoire* (Paris: Gallimard, 1981).

we can recognize the religious aspirations of the numerous women, who at the time committed themselves to the *vita apostolica*. On the other hand, it represents us with an interpretation of apostolic life, which was not easily compatible with what the official church taught to be acceptable for women. From 13th-century legislative sources and polemic satire regarding 'religious women', as well as from the *Vitae* written by their (mostly) male admirers it can be inferred that clerical authorities were anxious to restrict women's practice of the *vita apostolica*.[16] Notably, semi-religious women, who committed themselves to the new ideal outside the enclosed sphere of a nunnery or convent, without taking vows or following an established rule, were subject to suspicion, slander and restrictive legislation. Criticism and disciplinary measures pertained to unauthorized mendicancy, vagrancy, and preaching activities, which in due time came to be exclusively male prerogatives.[17] Religious women, who did not live in settled communities, but moved about freely, begging for their livelihood, frequently conversing with monks and clerics, were suspect of idleness, frivolous play and scandalous flirts with the clergy. Ecclesiastical policy increasingly aimed at confining extra-regular religious women to their houses. Furthermore, women's engagement in preaching activities, expounding and reading Scripture, was not before long discouraged and prohibited.

At the time Thomas wrote his *Vita* of Christina, female mendicancy, vagrancy and preaching were not as yet entirely discredited, but they were neither in accord with officially promoted models of female sanctity, as can be implied from the general tenor of the *Vitae Matrum*. Writing Christina's Life on the basis of the testimony procured by witnesses of her public apostolate—as any painstaking biographer would—without causing offense obviously demanded great diplomacy. For example, he had to deal with the fact that Christina practised mendicancy in a very radical way (654/55,22–25). She had given up her rightful inheritance and everything she owned for Christ and used to beg for alms from door to door. Thomas explains that the Spirit of God had driven her to do so, because it might move sinners to mercy and make them turn away from their sins. Christina

---

[16] See on this A.E. Passenier, "'Women on the Loose': Stereotypes of Women in the Story of the Medieval Beguines", *Female Stereotypes in Religious Traditions*, eds. R. Kloppenborg and W.J. Hanegraaff (Leiden etc.: Brill, 1995), pp. 61–88.

[17] For the sources drawn on, see my "Stereotypes", pp. 65–81.

takes this mission so far that she even snatches away with force something when it is denied to her! When a sleeve was missing from her shredded gown, she would beg for one from anyone she met. When she was refused, she would simply take it and sow it on her garment.[18]

From the other *Vitae* of the early 'mulieres religiosae' it also appears that they were often attracted to the mendicant life, which seems to have been a common pursuit of all those in search of the *vita apostolica*, following Christ and the evangelical precepts. Margaret of Ypres, whose Life was composed by Thomas of Cantimpré as well, just like Christina went out begging after having given away all her possessions, so that she might share her alms with a beggar. She used to escape frequently from her house to beg: only the admonitions of her spiritual director, who pointed out the danger this might bring to a young woman, could keep her from doing so.[19] According to Jacob of Vitry also Mary of Oignies had a craving for begging and could only be dissuaded from a mendicant life through the insistent pleas of her relatives.[20] Obviously, hagiographers do not doubt that women's desire to pursue the mendicant life was motivated by their piety, but they do not want to present the mendicancy and vagrancy of their holy women as something to be emulated by other women. Although evangelical poverty and mendicancy were permitted by Innocent III (c. 1160–1216) and obtained an officially approved status in the mendicant orders, female mendicancy was never acceptable to the official church and had to be discouraged.[21] In the *Vita* of Christina, Thomas had to account for a radical pursuit of the mendicant life, which was even on the brink of criminal offense. The special mission to save souls from future punishment, which Christina according to Jacob of Vitry's testimony obtained from God himself during her visit to the other world, offers him a suitable justification for her forcibly taking food and clothes from stubborn and unwilling sinners. At the same time the uniqueness of

---

[18] It is exactly this kind of behaviour so-called Free-Spirits, proclaiming freedom of the Spirit for those who had reached spiritual perfection, were accused of in the course of the 13th century. See on this R.E. Lerner, *The Heresy of the Free Spirit in the Later Middle Ages* (Berkeley etc.: University of California Press, 1972).

[19] *VMY*, p. 117, 22.

[20] *VMO*, p. 557, 45.

[21] On clerical rejection of women's pursuit of mendicancy and its substitution by 'spiritual poverty', see Hollywood, *Soul as Virgin Wife*, pp. 42–44.

this ministry precludes that her example would be imitated by other women.

Another aspect of Christina's life that might have called for justification is her total independence. Obviously, Christina was not attached to any religious order nor to a beguine group. As Thomas possibly tries to illustrate with the story of her youth, she did not fit in with established female lifestyles. She seems to have been a solitary religious woman, who practised religious life in her own right, living in the family home, maintaining contacts with a loosely organized group of likeminded spiritual companions, lay people as well as *religiosi*. Such a solitary life was not exceptional, as the *Vitae* and other sources imply. Neither were changes of religious lifestyle, of orders or residence in order to realize a particular spiritual programme, frowned upon by ecclesiastical authorities at the time.[22] Thus, at a certain moment Christina left her own home and kin and went to Looz, on the border of Germany, to stay for nine years with a recluse called Iutta, 'who led a very religious life' (657,38). She also was very familiar with the nuns of St. Catharine's, who lived outside the town of St. Trond. She often visits them to engage in devout conversation and celebrates with them (656,35,36). At the end of her life she has her deathbed prepared with them and it is at the bidding of the nun Beatrice that she returns once again from death (659/60,51–53). Thus, she finally dies within the safe and solid confines of the monastery, quite in contrast with her unsettled life. However, it is not so much Christina's extra-regularity and her wandering between religious institutions that might have troubled Thomas, but her independent attitude. She does not seem to be under any supervision of the clergy. Although priests have the power to command her in the name of Christ and with the Sacrament, it is she who decides where and when she wants to receive communion. If she finds a priest unwilling, she hurries off to another, who will grant her what she wishes (652,10). Moreover, she reprimands priests for their sins, lest they blaspheme the name of Christ through their public excesses (657,40). Most of the time priests feature in the *Vita* as the baffled witnesses of Christina's dramatic performances and her astounding physical abilities (652,10; 658,47). Moreover, we seldom

---

[22] See Bolton, "Vitae Matrum", p. 260.

find Christina in church attending mass or praying at the official hours. At night after everyone has left she would go to church to sing angelic songs in a most wonderfully adorned latin (656/57,39).

Christina's relationship to the nuns of St. Trond shows a similar pattern: except for the moment of her death it is Christina who is in charge.[23] She sits with them in spiritual colloquies, which would sometimes lead to unexpected ecstatic rapture, with her body rolling and whirling like a hoop, producing a wondrous harmony from somewhere between her throat and breast. Afterwards, she loudly summons the nuns to assemble and join her in the praise of Christ for his miracles, which they happily do (656,35,36). That she had compelling authority with the nuns, can also be seen from them reinstating an apostate nun at her bidding (655,30). These examples may show that Christina's position with respect to the religious institutions and authorities must have been quite extraordinary. Of course, this is more or less inherent in her 'sanctity', which demands exceptional activities and behaviour and a certain degree of idiosyncrasy. Nonetheless, compared to the other *Vitae Matrum* of Thomas's hand, the kind of institutional freedom Christina displays is quite unusual. We may suspect that behind Thomas's depiction stands a woman, who developed a public ministry in her own right, without being supervised by the clergy or a spiritual director from regular orders. By describing her as an exceptional human being, incomparable to ordinary mortals, Thomas probably tries to prevent that the extraordinary liberties she takes would outrage the official church.

A third aspect of Christina's career, which will have required diplomatic handling, is her obvious involvement in activities associated with preaching. Robert Sweetman has convincingly pointed out that Thomas conceived of Christina's life as a preaching ministry, though not in ordinary terms.[24] She is, for example, portrayed as expounding the meaning of the Scriptures and explaining the most obscure religious questions to her spiritual friends (656/57,39,40). She assists the dying and exhorts them to confess their sins (655,27). She reprimands the Count of Looz, whenever he did anything against jus-

---

[23] That the nun Beatrice summons Christina back to life, saying: 'You were ever obedient to me in life!' might be an attempt of the hagiographer to make her more acceptable.

[24] Sweetman, "Christine of Saint-Trond", p. 68 ff.

tice or against the Church of Christ (657,41). To the Jewish community she proclaims the mercy of Christ the Lord to all those who wish to be converted to Him (655,27). On the other hand, as Sweetman notices, these activities take up relatively litle space within the *Vita* and they are overwhelmed by the many bizarre occurrences, which dominate the rest of the work. Far from delighting her hagiographer, they rather seem to cause him embarrassment. Given the fact that Christina, as a woman, lacked the ecclesiastical status to carry on a preaching ministry, this is not surprising.

Whenever Thomas portrays Christina acting in ways reminiscent of preaching, he seems at pain to restrict these activities and to keep them within certain boundaries. Sometimes explicitly, by asserting that, although Christina was able to expound the Scriptures, she was utterly reluctant to do so, because she felt that not she, but only the clergy were appointed to that task (657,40). Recounting her hearing the confession of the Count of Looz on his deathbed, he quickly adds, that the latter did not confess to Christina to get absolution, which she had no power to give, but rather to obtain that she would pray for him (657,44). Thus, he makes clear that the priesthood was not in danger from the zeal of the religious woman, whose words, as he asserts, had great persuasive power. Furthermore, Thomas seems to underscore this also in a more implicit way, by constantly stressing the supernatural and miraculous origin of Christina's knowledge of the divine and her preaching activities. For example, he presents her ability to understand all Latin and the full meaning of Scripture as miraculous, by stating that she had been completely illiterate from birth (657,40). He is apparently anxious to point out that Christina's teaching and preaching are not due to learning and studying, but to mystical experiences and ecstatic visitations. Here Thomas seems to employ a common *topos* in hagiography: the opposition of the simple religious woman, who has knowledge of the divine from ecstatic experience to the learned scholarly man, who knows them from reading books.[25] Also in the *Vitae* of Mary of Oignies and of Lutgard of Aywières this motive plays a role.[26] Whereas the permanent authority through priestly ordination was denied to women, charismatic, spontaneous and momentary authority through visions,

---

[25] See my "Stereotypes", pp. 75–81.
[26] *VMO*, p. 569, 99; *VLA*, p. 193, 12; p. 194, 15.

mystical experiences and intuitive knowledge apparently were not.[27] Not surprisingly, Thomas places them in the forefront of Christina's public ministry.

As Sweetman has demonstrated, equally important in Thomas's representation of Christina's preaching apostolate, is the emphasis on her teaching by example.[28] Whereas teaching by word, as one aspect of the preaching ministry—which Thomas will have conceived as a 'docere verbo et exemplo'[29]—was only open to ordained men, preaching in deed required no special ecclesiastical status. All believers, women as well as men, could teach by their deeds, by the example of their lives instruct, edify and exhort. That this was even a mode of preaching, thought especially convenient and appropriate for women, may be inferred, for example, from the words of the hagiographer Philip of Clairvaux. In his *Vita* of Elisabeth of Spalbeek (c. 1267),[30] he asserts that men should proclaim the gospel by writing and preaching.[31] Women, however, have a special ability to imitate Christ in his humanity, by representing his sufferings with their bodies and in visual, dramatic expression.[32] The stigmatic Elisabeth, who is portrayed dramatically re-enacting the scene of the crucifixion, is considered an icon of Christ by her hagiographer.[33] Also from other *Vitae* it appears that women were considered particularly apt to embody the divine, to incarnate the Word and to visualize the message.[34] This is exactly what Thomas makes Christina do in her public ministry. She visualizes and literally embodies the torments of purgatory as a living sermon, thus exhorting the living to repent

---

[27] On the male/female dichotomy of inspiration versus office see also Bynum, *Holy Feast*, pp. 282–288.

[28] Sweetman, "Christine of Saint-Trond", p. 72 ff.

[29] See on this C.W. Bynum, *Docere verbo et exemplo: An Aspect of Twelfth-Century Spirituality* (Missoula MT: Scholars Press, 1979) and her chapter 'The Sprirituality of the Regular Canons in the Twelfth Century' in *Jesus as a Mother: Studies in the Spirituality of the High Middle Ages* (Berkeley etc.: University of California Press, 1982), pp. 22–58.

[30] *Vita Elizabeth sanctimonialis (VES)*, *Catalogus codicum hagiographicorum bibliothecae Regiae Bruxellensis*, I (Brussels, 1886), pp. 362–378.

[31] *VES*, p. 372, 16.

[32] *VES*, pp. 363, 3–372, 15.

[33] See W. Simons and J. Ziegler, "Phenomenal Religion in the Thirteenth Century and its Image: Elisabeth of Spalbeek and the Passion Cult", *Women in the Church*, eds. W.J. Sheils and D. Woods (Oxford: Blackwell, 1990), pp. 117–126; p. 124.

[34] See A.E. Passenier, "The Suffering Body and the Freedom of the Soul: Medieval Women's Ways of Union with God", *Begin with the Body. Corporeality, Religion and Gender*, eds. J. Bekkenkamp and M. de Haardt (Louvain: Peeters, 1998), pp. 264–287.

and do penance while there is still time. That women did not always content themselves with the role of visual and dramatic illustration of Scripture and theological truth is testified indirectly in the *Vitae* of the religious women. In his *Vita* of Mary of Oignies Jacob of Vitry remarks that Mary wished to preach; however, since this was not possible for a woman, she had satisfied herself with the idea that Vitry would be her instrument.[35] Likewise, Christina's biography reveals that she engaged in preaching activities Thomas was anxious to keep within bounds. Notably, her evocative dramatic actions visualizing purgatory succesfully override these activities.

The miraculous framework of the *Vita*, characterizing Christina as a super-human, a wanderer between worlds, seems to function as a diversion, distracting the reader's attention from a religious woman, who practised a *vita apostolica*, comprising mendicancy, vagrancy and preaching in a way that was mostly deemed unfit for women.[36] The authority of the 'real' woman, living an 'extra-regular' religious life, is camouflaged by the authority of an extraordinary saint, who remains aloof from human society. Female religious ministry is carefully stylized to match established cultural codes and kept within boundaries. At the same time the *mirabilia* with which Christina's Life is suffused, make her an excellent vehicle for the message the Dominican preacher wants to convey to his readers. According to the homiletic principles to which he would have been committed, the bizarre, the fantastical and the grotesque were effective mnemonic devices in matters of spiritual instruction, leaving a lasting impression on the memory.[37] Far from diminishing the veracity of her story, they rather heighten its effectiveness in encoding a special message of repentance and penance, for which she is made the medium.

---

[35] *VMO*, p. 562, 69.

[36] A quite different explanation of the miracles in Christina's Life is offered by Paul Vandenbroeck, who holds that the miracles refer to shamanic practices—common in the popular culture of rural areas—, which Christina actually performed, P. Vandenbroeck, "'Dit raken van mij die onraakbaar ben...'", *Hooglied: De Beeldwereld van Religieuze Vrouwen in de Zuidelijke Nederlanden, vanaf de 13de eeuw*, ed. P. Vandenbroeck (Brussels: Snoeck-Ducaju & Zoon, 1994), pp. 20–27. In my opinion this stretches the definition of shamanism somewhat too far, making the concept applicable to all kinds of ecstatic and ascetic practices. Moreover, the concept of 'popular culture' as apart from learned culture, is much debated and does not seem to apply in the case of Christina, whose knowledge of Latin implies that she participated to some degree in learned culture.

[37] Sweetman, "Christine of Saint-Trond", pp. 79–80.

The 'Miraculous Body'—Suffering Purgatory on Earth

Thomas portrays Christina as living purgatory on earth, vicariously suffering the torments of the souls imprisoned there. On her journey into the beyond she had seen a dark and terrible place filled with the souls of dead men, recognizing many of them as people she had formerly known in the flesh. She had felt great compassion with the wretched souls, thinking that this place of cruel torment must be hell. But she was told that this place is purgatory and 'it is here that repentant sinners atone for the sins they committed while they were alive' (651,6). When she finally arrives in Paradise, the Lord offers Christina the opportunity 'to return to the body and suffer there the sufferings of an immortal soul in a mortal body without damage to it, and by these your sufferings to deliver all those souls on whom you had compassion in that place of purgatory, and by the example of your suffering and your way of life to convert living men to me and to turn them aside from their sins . . .' (652,7).

After her return from the desert, Christina sets out to fulfil her divine mission. She jumps into hearth fires, baking ovens and boiling cauldrons. In cold weather she submerges in the Meuse and revolves on a mill-wheel in icy water (652,11,12). Since alternating fire and cold were known as classical purgatorial pains, already featuring in Virgil's *Aenaeis* and in early Christian apocalypse and occurring abundantly in medieval other-worldly visions,[38] Christina's eccentric sufferings can be considered a literal re-enactment of these. Also her running through wood thick with thorns, chased by the dogs of Saint-Trond, which caused bleeding wounds all over her body (653,14), might be a traditional element, as a field of thorns also figures in other accounts of the beyond.[39] It seems that even the proverbial stench of hell is haunting Christina, who after her return from the beyond can no longer endure the awful smell of human bodies (652,9). Human society, it would appear, is literally turned into a purgatory on earth, where Christina's relatives and friends, who chase and torment her, thinking that she is possessed

---

[38] See on this Le Goff, *Naissance du purgatoire*, pp. 146–169, pp. 241–278 and passim.

[39] For example in the vision of Gottschalk (1189), edited by E. Assman, *Godeschalkus und Visio Godeschalci* (Neumünster: Wachholtz, 1979), p. 56: the souls on their way to the afterworld have to cross a field sown with sharp prickles, only leaving the feet of the pure uninjured.

by demons, become torturing demons themselves. Moreover, the cruel punishments society imposes on criminals, hanging them and breaking their limbs on racks, are shared by Christina as a part of her purgatorial penance. She stretches her arms and legs on the rack and suspends herself between the thieves on the gallows, sometimes hanging there for days (652,13).

Christina's purgatorial sufferings, as described in the first chapter of the *Vita* are of a highly miraculous nature. Again and again Thomas underscores that Christina survives her extreme torments without any harm to her body. She climbs out of ovens and boiling cauldrons unharmed and revolves on mill-wheels and racks without any fracture in her limbs. Even when her body is covered with bleeding wounds caused by scratching thorns, no trace of them remains after she has washed off the blood. The miraculous character of Christina's sufferings is obviously related to her particular mission of living purgatory *in via*. As Sweetman has argued, this was in fact (theo)logically impossible, since the pains of purgatory are suffered by disembodied souls and are of an intensity and severity, unknown in the world of human beings.[40] Thomas surmounts these problems through the miracle of Christina's resurrection, which provides her with a body, resembling the somato-morphic souls in the afterworld, who suffer the excruciating pains of physical torments with no harm to their indestructible bodies.[41] Thus, Christina, suffering loudly with chilling shrieks and howls, but without any visible harm, literally embodies the purgatorial pains, dramatizing and visualizing the future of every sinner.

It is important for us to bear in mind that these miraculous sufferings belong to the so-called 'marginal' stage of her life. They are situated before Christina's re-integration in human society and seem to be a 'supra-historical' elaboration of Jacob of Vitry's description of Christina's mission. Moreover, as we have observed before, the purgatorial penances, in which the hyperbolic and the grotesque predominate, characterize Christina's apostolate as teaching by example and turn the saint into a living sermon on purgatory. Other aspects

---

[40] Sweetman, "Christina of Saint-Trond", pp. 80–81.
[41] On somato-morphic souls and purgatory see C.W. Bynum, *The Resurrection of the Body in Western Christianity, 200–1336* (New York: Columbia University Press, 1995), pp. 279–305. On Christina's resurrected body as the explanation for her amazing asceticism and paramystical feats, see also Hollywood, *Soul as Virgin Wife*, pp. 44–46.

of her ministry, such as preaching and teaching, are overwhelmed by the miraculous purgatorial sufferings that set the scene for the *Vita*. However, nonwithstanding the phantastic traits of the opening episodes,—circumscribing the essence of Christina's apostolate, as Thomas wishes to present it—we may assume that Christina actually engaged in penitential activities for the dead, as there is corroborating evidence for this in other sections of the *Vita*. In the historically more reliable part that describes her public ministry in society, we see Christina sharing the purgatorial torments of the soul of her beloved friend Louis, Count of Looz. The Count of Looz, who plays an important role in the *Vita* and is referred to as 'a most noble man', was impressed by Christina's sanctity and followed her counsels and her advice. He called her his mother and like a mother she would reprimand him whenever he did anything against justice or against the Church and its ministers (657,41). Moreover, she advised him on political alliances, exposing traitors through the spirit of prophecy (657,43). Before his death he recited all his sins to Christina in order that she might pray for him. Finally, when all the counts were assembled in his bedchamber, he disposed of his goods, following Christina's advice. When the Count died Christina saw his soul being carried to purgatory and tormented there with the most bitter punishments (657/58,44). Feeling great compassion towards him, she then obtained from the Lord that she might suffer in her own body half of his purgatorial punishments. Thus, for a long time Christina tormented herself alternatingly with burning smoke and freezing cold, just like the Count's soul had to suffer in purgatory, until he was finally redeemed (658,45). This time, instead of barging into people's homes to jump in their hearth-fires, Christina seems to make deliberate use of ascetic techniques in her penitential activities on behalf of her friend's soul. Furthermore, she wets with her tears places where the Count had been accustomed to sin and she grieves in the places where he had been happy with a futile joy.

Here we see Christina engaged in a ministry of the dead, which was not at all exceptional, but shared by many devout women of her days.[42] From Saint's Lives and exempla as well as women's writings themselves it appears that intercession for the souls of the dead, especially of relatives, (spiritual) friends and fellow religious, played

---

[42] See on this especially Newman, *Virile Woman*, pp. 108–136.

a prominent role in the ministry of religious women. The Cistercian Lutgard of Aywières, called a purgatorial saint in Le Goff's landmark study on purgatory,[43] performed mortifications and fasts for a Cistercian abbot, who loved her dearly. She prayed for him so intensely, refusing any consolation from God, lest he would liberate the abbot's soul, that God finally releases him from his torments long before this was due.[44] Mechthild of Magdeburg, whose book *Das Fließende Licht der Gottheit*[45] contains many visions of purgatory, displays a similar insistence when pleading for the release of indigent souls. On one occasion she is so angrily disturbed by the sight of the tormented souls, that she 'takes purgatory in her arms', not willing to let go, although God warns her that the pain is too hard for her to bear. Finally, her request for mercy is granted: a thousand souls are released and as they are still too filthy to enter heaven, Mechthild bathes them in love's tears.[46]

In the general rise of purgatorial piety since the last third of the 12th century we see religious women take on a particular role as visionary intermediaries between the living and the dead and as intercessors, offering their prayers and sufferings to ease the pain of agonizing souls in purgatory. Their ministry of the dead is often high-lighted by their hagiographers and seems to have been encouraged by their spiritual directors. As Barbara Newman in her eminent discussion of the subject argues, this was partly due to the fact that such ministry constituted 'a safe, invisible, contemplative mission', expressing women's zeal for souls without violating gender taboos.[47] Moreover, laymen and religious males had options women did not have to put the growing concern for the dead to work, as the saying of masses— acknowledged to be 'the most effective suffrage for the dead'— was reserved for ordained religious males. As women's economic

---

[43] Le Goff, *Naissance du purgatoire*, pp. 434–436. It is quite striking that Le Goff does not mention the *Vita* of Christina as an example of the medieval development of purgatorial piety and theology.
[44] *VLA*, p. 197, 4.
[45] Mechthild of Magdeburg, *Das Fließende Licht der Gottheit*, ed. H. Neumann (Munich, Artemis, 1990), translated by C.M. Galvani, *Flowing Light of the Divinity* (New York/London: Garland, 1991).
[46] *Fließende Licht* II, 8, p. 46.
[47] Newman, *Virile Woman*, p. 11 f. On hagiographical emphasis on women's praying for, and—through ascetic feats and visionary advice—rescuing souls on earth and in purgatory at the cost of other aspects of women's *imitatio*, see Hollywood, *Soul as Virgin Wife*, pp. 44–50.

resources became increasingly limited, almsgiving and other meritorious acts that involved money often surpassed women's means. Jo Ann McNamara has suggested that devout women began 'to experiment with spiritual almsgiving to complement or replace corporeal charity'.[48] Prayers, tears and above all sufferings were the spiritual alms religious women could offer to ease the pain of the tormented souls in purgatory. However, whether physical suffering was something the women themselves put at the centre of their activities, is in my opinion questionable. Hagiography strongly emphasizes this aspect of women's purgatorial ministry, making intense compassion, expressed in physical suffering, whether self-inflicted through severe mortifications (fasting, cutting, burning) or involuntary through illness and distress (fevers, chills, bleedings) the central characteristic of women's apostolate to the dead. This concurs with the stereotypical notion of women's particular aptness to imitate Christ in his humanity through bodily suffering.[49]

Thomas's portraying of Christina's miraculous re-enactment of purgatory fits in with this tenor and can be interpreted as an effort to stylize women's purgatorial mission. The fact that in the middle part of the *Vita* bodily suffering plays a far less prominent role supports this assumption. It is merely one of the aspects of a general concern Christina displays with the dead and the dying. Her ministry among the people also comprised assistance of the dying, exhorting them to confess their sins, a mission she even extended to the large Jewish community of the town. Furthermore, Christina functioned as a kind of 'barometer of souls' in the town of Saint-Trond. She publicly announced the fate of the dying, whose future God had revealed to her, by expressing great distress for those who were to be damned and tremendous joy for those who were on their way to salvation. From her weeping, twisting and bending of her arms and fingers with sorrow and from her leaping and jumping high with joy, people knew what would happen to the dying in town (655,26). Bodily suffering, as vicarious penance for the dead, plays a role only in the episodes on Christina's relationship with the Count

---

[48] J.A. McNamara, "The Need to Give: Suffering and Female Sanctity in the Middle Ages", *Images of Sainthood in Medieval Europe*, eds. R. Blumenfeld-Kosinski and T. Szell (Ithaca/London: Cornell University Press, 1991), pp. 212, 221.

[49] See on this Bynum, *Fragmentation*, pp. 151–179. Bynum's position is criticized by Amy Hollywood in *The Soul as Virgin Wife*, p. 226 n. 8 and by myself in "Suffering Body", pp. 281–287.

of Looz. It is not unlikely, that the emphasis on physical pain in women's apostolate to the dead, as presented by hagiographers, derived at least partly from the wish to establish specific models of female religious ministry. A certain discrepancy in the representation of female apostolate to the dead between hagiographical texts and the writings of women themselves might suggest this also.

Although some women's writings concur with hagiographical representation, in most female-authored texts it is not so much physical suffering, which is at the centre of women's concern with the indigent dead, but psychological torment, the pain of love and compassion. As Barbara Newman observes, in their quest for union with God as unlimited, all-encompassing Love, women mystics like Mechthild of Magdeburg and Hadewijch declared themselves prepared even to 'reside in hell' if this would be God's will, thus proving the extremity of their love.[50] That God's love and compassion, infinitely surpassing their own, would not be able to conquer purgatory or even hell, was inconceivable to them. Mechthild angrily holds purgatory under her arm until God releases a thousand souls, who were imprisoned there. From the unrestrained charity for men God gave her, Hadewijch even went so far as to free souls from hell, claiming this as her right.[51] Although God had granted her her desire, she admits that she had been a Lucifer, ignorant of God's perfect justice, which caused her to sin and to suffer cruelty from men(!). In the writings of female mystics it is generally not so much physical suffering through self-mortification and illness, which releases tormented souls from purgatory by paying vicariously for their sins, as justice demands. Rather it is the mystic's love and the pain love causes her, which make God's mercy prevail over absolute justice.

Although hagiography allows also for the possibility of overriding God's justice through persistent pleading, as is the case in the Life of Lutgard, the *Vitae* generally keep to the paradigm of substitution and satisfaction. Justice is not overruled and the boundaries between hell and purgatory, reparable and irreparable sin are not blurred. From the discrepancy between hagiographical texts and some women's writings, the question arises to what extent the *Vitae* present us with

---

[50] Newman, *Virile Woman*, pp. 123–136.
[51] Hadewijch confesses this in the fifth vision of her *Visioenen*, see: *Het Visoenenboek van Hadewijch*, ed. H.W.J. Vekeman (Nijmegen: Dekker & Van de Vegt, 1980), pp. 75–79.

reliable information on women's ideas and activities.[52] They are obviously double-voiced texts, in which words and deeds of women are mediated through the perspective of male hagiographers, stylizing women's roles so as to fit officially accepted patterns. Nevertheless, there are slight indications in the *Vitae* that holy women like Christina Mirabilis and Mary of Oignies may have harboured desires and wishes which were not compatible with official standards. In his Supplement to the Life of Mary of Oignies, Thomas of Cantimpré recounts how Mary, who was 'extremely compassionate towards the souls in purgatory', was concerned about the soul of her deceased mother, whom she hoped to save through almsgiving and her honest way of life. One day her mother appears to her and tells her that her prayers could not help her, as she was eternally damned, because she had lived on goods acquired by usury and unjust commerce and did not restore them. After this Mary blesses God's judgement and does no longer weep about her mother; her reason triumphs over her 'carnal desire'.[53] From this episode we might infer that women's compassion with the indigent souls sometimes threatened to violate the boundaries of justice. In the *Vita* of Christina, Thomas represents his heroine as a strong advocate for divine justice, whose teachings on the world beyond strictly define purgatory as a separate place from hell (655,28). It is interesting, however, that Christina herself on her odyssey into the other world could not see the difference between hell and purgatory and had to be taught by the angels (651,6). Furthermore, in the *Vita* of Lutgard there is a striking passage on Christina, which could point to a view of hell resembling that of female mystics like Hadewijch. When Lutgard shows reluctance to enter the monastery of Aywières, as the Lord had commanded her, Christina says to her: 'I would rather be in hell with God than without Him in heaven with the angels'.[54] This statement which puts union with the Beloved's will before 'real union' in heaven and de-localizes divine presence, differs from Christina's literal expositions on hell, purgatory and heaven as places where the dead go

---

[52] On the discrepancy between the *Vitae* and female writings in general, see especially Hollywood, *Soul as Virgin Wife*, pp. 1–56. Hollywood points to the necessity of basing accounts of medieval women's spirituality and ministry on the writings of women themselves and of questioning the male-authored hagiographical texts, when they diverge from these.
[53] *SVMO*, p. 576, 12.
[54] *VLA*, p. 195, 22.

according to justice. The concept of the 'metaphorical' hell, here used by Christina, where one resides out of love at the pleasure of the Beloved, is hardly determined by justice. As such, it might blur the fixed boundaries between the different states of heaven, purgatory and hell, as it possibly did in the case of Hadewijch.

Moreover, it seems not unthinkable that Christina, whose compassion extended to the Jews, damnable in the eyes of society, and whose concern for souls drove her to the places of torture, where thieves and murderers were 'brought to justice', displayed a universalist tendency, reaching out even to the souls in 'real' hell! Thomas might have felt obliged to dissimulate this from the public and to put her apostolate in the right perspective by making her the mouthpiece and living example of sound doctrine on purgatory, as it was being developed at the time. Of course, here we venture into the realm of speculation. All we know is that women mystics sometimes, from empathy with the most wretched of souls and from the concept of God as unbounded Love, expressed a frank discomfort with the idea of damnation. Newman holds that the testimony of these female mystics is a-typical, since they were mostly 'irregulars' or solitaries, not representing the mainstream of feminine piety.[55] She points to the *Vitae*, like that of Mary of Oignies, which promulgate an orthodox purgatorial piety without expressing any doubts on the subject of eternal punishment. In my opinion, however, the reliability of the *Vitae*'s representation of female piety is questionable. Whether and to what extent Thomas's portrait of Christina reflects her actual ministry remains to be seen. Although sufficient proof on the subject is lacking, we cannot dismiss the possibility that the astonishing Christina of the *Vita*, embodying orthodox doctrine on purgatory, was deviced as a corrective of a female ministry of the dead, which threatened to violate doctrinal boundaries between hell and heaven, reparable and irreparable sin. Such ministry could be suspected of minimizing the importance of official means of expiation the Church offered, in which—as we should not forget—a lot of money was involved.

At any rate, whether or not she actually taught and lived purgatory as Thomas suggests, the miraculously resurrected Christina could serve him as a perfect example of sound doctrine on the hereafter,

---

[55] Newman, *Virile Woman*, pp. 134–136.

just as a devout Dominican would have propagated it. Whereas he himself, as a preacher and teacher, is engaged in the development and propagation of new concepts on purgatory[56]—one of the most important theological enterprises of that time—, the holy woman whose *Vita* he writes comes to embody this new theology. Moreover, the miraculously resurrected Christina endows purgatorial theology with a special divine authorization, since she had—as Thomas asserts—received her ministry directly from the Lord himself and had seen the world beyond with her own eyes. Perhaps even more than legitimizing female apostolate to the dead, the miraculous in the *Vita* stylizes it to match accepted patterns of female religious ministry and official theology on purgatory, as it was being developed at the time.

Miracles of Lactation and Oil-exuding: The Sacraments as Means of Divine Accommodation

Of all the miracles featuring in Christina's Life, two instances are of special importance to us because of their specifically female character: the mammary wonders of lactation and oil-exuding. Both miracles happen at a turning-point in the *Vita*, thereby changing Christina's relationship with human society. As Margot King has convincingly argued, these miracles are intended to be understood 'sacramentally', as referring to the grace of the sacraments, feeding, sustaining and healing humankind.[57] Moreover, as I would like to add, they convey certain notions on the relationship between body and soul, the spiritual and the physical world, contemplative isolation and social ministry.

When Christina, shortly after her resurrection, escapes her persecutors who deem her possessed, she flees into the remote desert forests, as she is horrified by the stench of human bodies. For a long time she lives in trees after the manner of birds. Even when she is very hungry and needs food, she does not want to return home, but 'she desires to remain alone with God in her hiding place in the desert'. She prays the Lord to have mercy on her and immediately her virginal dry breasts begin to drip milk against the law of nature.

---

[56] Thomas's concern with the fate of the dead and the hereafter expresses itself in his statement that he had primarily become a priest in order to save his father's soul from purgatory. See *Bonum Universale de Apibus*, II 53 par. 32.

[57] King, "Sacramental Witness", p. 150 ff.

A miracle unheard of since the Mother of God, Thomas adds. For nine weeks Christina is nourished with the milk from her fruitful, but virginal breasts, until she was captured again by the people (652,9). A similar miracle occurs when Christina is imprisoned by her sisters and friends and is bound tightly to a heavy wooden yoke, causing festering wounds on her limbs and such pain that she could not eat her bread. Again the Lord has pity on her and a great miracle happens: her virginal breasts begin to flow with a liquid of clearest oil. She takes this liquid to soften her coarse prison bread, so that she might eat and she smears it on the wounds of her festering limbs as a healing ointment. This miracle convinces Christina's family and friends that it is God, who is at work in Christina and begging her for forgiveness, they release her from her chains (653/54,19).

The essence of both of these miracles seems to be that God works in Christina and that she depends solely on God to save, feed and heal her. She is still dependent on food as an unbreakable tie to society and to human existence, but the miracle of lactation enables her to remain in her desert alone with God. Her hunger is stilled through divine intervention, so that she can do without normal nutrition. Also, the miracle of her breasts exuding oil proves that Christina in the torments she suffers from her persecutors, is saved and healed by God alone. In the preceding episode she tore off the medicated bandages with which the physician had bound her broken shin bone, because she thought it shameful to have any doctor for her wounds other than Jesus Christ (653,18). Natural cures she rejects, expecting only Jesus to cure her.

The miracles of lactation and oil-exuding both effect a change in Christina's relationship to society. Whereas the first one enables her to withdraw completely from the stinking world of men, the second one restores her to society and marks the beginning of her ministry among the people. As Robert Sweetman has observed, Christina is translated from a purely contemplative pattern of life to a mixed religious life, combining contemplation and apostolate. He has also pointed to the fact that this is an interesting parallel to the life of Thomas himself who, during the years he was working on Christina's biography, left the contemplative order of St. Victor to join the Dominican order, which held to a mixed life.[58] In the *Vita* of Christina,

---

[58] Sweetman, "Christine of Saint-Trond", pp. 81–82. From this parallel Sweetman

Thomas quite subtly addresses the burning question of how to combine contemplative contempt of the world with the apostolic attempt to save it. He clearly portrays Christina as a great contemplative, whose first death was even caused by excessive contemplation, which ruined her body. In her purely contemplative 'desert-period' she is able to survive entirely without human support.[59] Also in the 'moderate phase' of her life, working among the people, contemplation remains the heart of her activity. Already in this world Christina lives the life of the angels. She is often ravished in the spirit, which causes remarkable transformations of her body, no longer showing a human form. Without using her voice she produces wondrous songs, seeming to be the songs of angels. In the last year of her life the spirit controls almost every part of her corporeal body, so that she barely touches the ground and is hardly distinguishable from a ghost. All this makes Christina a champion of contemplation, whose astounding powers spiritualize the body and transport the spirit to the other world. Also from other *Vitae* of female saints it appears that holy women were especially venerated for their contemplative achievements. A propensity to ecstatic rapture—considered the summit of mystical union with God—producing paramystical psychosomatic phenomena, like compulsive singing and dancing, cramps, convulsions and paralytic seizures, is often considered the main characteristic of holy women.[60] As I have formerly argued, hagiographers tend to stress the ecstatic character of women's religious ministry so as not to violate gender boundaries, preserving official interpretation

---

raises the question to what extent Christina's biography must be considered as a projection of Thomas's own spiritual journey: 'Did Thomas construct the pattern of Christine's life from the many stories which circulated about her life and person so as to embody, in feminine guise, his own freshly realized Dominican ideal of the religious life, or does his account capture a religious project or calling which contemporary women religious themselves claimed as theirs?' (82). Another possibility could be that Thomas, rather than projecting his own ideal on Christina's life, stylizes a female form of mixed religious life, in which the contemplative aspect still predominates.

[59] Whether we will have to take Christina's stay in the trees literally and associate her with the stylitic branch of Syrian 'Dendrites', residing in trees and with the *gelta* (wild men) of the Irish church, as King helds, in my opinion is questionable, King, "Sacramental Witness", p. 162 n. 45.

[60] Thus, for example, Jacob of Vitry in the prologue to the Life of Mary of Oignies (*VMO*, 548, 7). See on this often-cited passage, for example, P. Dinzelbacher, "Europäische Frauenmystik des Mittelalters", *Frauenmystik im Mittelalter*, eds. P. Dinzelbacher and D.R. Bauer (Ostfildern: Schwabenverlag, 1985), pp. 11–17.

of Scripture and proclamation of divine truth to ordained males. However, it cannot be denied that women actually practised ecstasy as a means to obtain religious authority, albeit probably not to the degree hagiographers suggest. It is likely that Christina was one of the many ecstatic women who astounded their contemporaries by their mystical abilities.

Yet, Thomas obviously recounts the remarkable transformations of Christina's body not merely to characterize her as an ecstatic woman, but to address important theological themes concerning the relationship between the physical and the spiritual world. Christina exemplifies as it were the problem of the contemplative, entirely devoted to the spiritual, in moments of rapture already belonging to the hereafter, conversing with Jesus, Mary, the apostles and the saints, enjoying a fore-taste of eternity. How can one merge with the divine and at the same time live in the world and in the body? The answer Thomas gives in the *Vita* seems to be: through divine accommodation to human embodied existence, through the materialisation of spiritual grace in the sacraments. The miracles of lactation and oil-exuding as external, visible manifestations of grace, have a sacramental character. We find a parallel miracle in the Life of Lutgard, who, having spent some time in prayer and contemplation, was filled inwardly with such sweetness of spirit that oil dripped from her fingers 'as a manifestation of grace'.[61] Similarly, as Margot King has argued, the milk and oil flowing from Christina's breasts are to be interpreted as visible signs of invisible grace. Furthermore, they may remind us of the 'milk of the humanity of Christ',[62] which nourishes believers at the Eucharist. In medieval imagery the reception of the Eucharist could be symbolized as drinking from the breasts of Jesus.[63] The breasts of the lactating Virgin Mary, to whom Thomas explicitly refers in his account of the miracles, were likewise associated with the Eucharist.[64] That the milk dripping from Christina's breasts contains a reference to the Eucharist, is also confirmed by the passage

---

[61] *VLA*, p. 194, 16.
[62] *VLA*, p. 193, 13.
[63] See on this Bynum, *Holy Feast*, pp. 172–180, pp. 270–275; *Fragmentation*, pp. 93–97, pp. 106–108, pp. 205–206.
[64] See Bynum, *Holy Feast*, pp. 131–132, pp. 270–275; *Fragmentation*, pp. 101–114 passim. On the medieval association of breasts with food rather than with sexuality: *Fragmentation*, pp. 93–97.

following the miraculous lactation. After another escape from her family and friends, she does not flee to the deserts but runs to Liège instead, hungering 'for the sacred meat of the sinless Pascal Lamb' to strengthen her against the anguish she was suffering (652,10). Elsewhere Thomas says that the Sacrament of the Body and Blood of the Lord gave Christina strength of body and joy of spirit (654,22). Instead of ordinary food it is the food of the Sacrament, feeding, healing and sustaining body and spirit, which links Christina to the world of embodied humans and drives her back to society.

Caroline Walker Bynum has argued that abstinence of food to live (almost) entirely on the Host is frequently reported of medieval holy women, as they seek an essentially bodily union with Christ's humanity, especially with his Body. Sometimes their bodies are miraculously closed off to ordinary food, accompanied by holy exuding of breast-milk, blood or oil, which could be used to feed or heal others, their bodies becoming themselves a source of food.[65] Also in the case of Christina ordinary food is replaced by divine nourishment. The mammary wonders prove Christina's sole dependence on God and the operations of divine grace, enabling her to be completely independent from human society, except for the reception of the Eucharist.[66] Moreover, they seem to suggest that God's power can effect a miraculous reversal of the natural order. Thomas strongly stresses the fact that it is a *virgin*, whose dry breasts produce nourishing and healing effluvia. The chaste and barren virgin becomes fertile, just like the Virgin Mary. The lactation miracle refers to the miracle of Incarnation, Jesus born from a Virgin, God becoming flesh, which is prolongued and re-enacted in the Eucharist. The mammary wonders suggest that it is also the Sacrament, which produces Christina's incarnation, translating her from the summit of contemplation to the world of men. As we have noticed before, it was through the power of the Sacrament by which the priest com-

---

[65] Bynum, *Holy Feast*, pp. 113–129, pp. 190–207.

[66] Although the substitution of human by divine food plays an important role in the *VCM*, Christina does not seem to be a miraculous faster in the usual sense, as Bynum suggests (*Holy Feast*, pp. 120–121, p. 193, p. 274). On the contrary, Christina even drinks wine and snatches food from obstinate sinners. When, in the last year of her life, she hardly takes food anymore, this is not connected with living on the Host, but with the loosening of the tie to society and her ever increasing spiritualization. Neither is Christina, as Bynum repeatedly asserts (*Holy Feast*, p. 123, p. 211, p. 234) feeding and healing others with the effluvia from her breasts, unless we understand this metaphorically as referring to Christina's ministry.

manded her to come down from the ceiling rafters of the Church immediately after her resurrection.

Would it be mere coincidence then, that it is a baptism, which as a 'rite de passage' enables Christina to enter the world of humans and to live humanly? As she had started her ministry among men and people were gathering around her every day, her sisters and friends feared that the miracles God worked in her—especially her ascendence to lofty places like a bird and lingering in the waters like a fish—might exceed human senses and that 'the carnal minds of men might misinterpret them' (654,20). They then prayed the Lord that He would 'moderate his miracles in Christina in accordance with the usual state of men'. God generously answers their prayers: soon afterwards Christina, violently stirred by the Spirit, enters the church of Wellen and immerses herself completely in the baptismal font. Thereafter, 'her manner of life was more moderate with regard to society and she behaved more calmly and was more able to endure the smell of men and live among them' (654,21). The sacramental rite of baptism thus serves as a divine accommodation to the 'condition humaine', bridging the gulf between the carnal and the spiritual, body and soul.

That the relation of body and soul is a central theme in the *Vita* also appears from a dialogue in which Christina in a dramatic performance alternately identifies with her body or her soul (658/59,47–49). One morning in church a priest and his companion observed her secretly and saw how she threw herself down before the altar and, weeping loudly, began to beat her body and breast. Aggrieved she rebukes her body for tormenting her, keeping her wretched soul from returning to its Creator, delaying her from seeing the face of Christ. Then, however, she assumes the role of the body, crying and complaining bitterly and asking the soul why it is kept from returning to the earth from which it was taken and from resting until Judgement Day. After these words Christina changes her role again and, smiling joyously, she begins to caress and kiss the soles of her feet with great affection, saying: 'O most beloved body! Why have I beaten you? ... did you not obey me in every good deed I undertook to do with God's help? You have endured the torments and hardships most generously and most patiently which the spirit placed on you'. Then, she doubles her kisses and says: 'Now, O best and sweetest body, endure patiently. Now is an end of your hardship, now you will rest in the dust and will sleep for a little and then, at last, when the trumpet blows, you will rise again purified of all corruptibility and you will be joined in eternal happiness with the soul you have had as a companion in the present sadness'.

With this dramatic dialogue, belonging to the very popular genre of debates between Body and Soul,[67] Thomas advocates the importance of the body to human existence, now and in the world to come.[68] Sometimes we see him come close to Cathar dualism[69] with its rejection of the body and the physical as creations of a lesser God, for example, when he asserts that the thing for which Christina mourned the most was that humankind was corrupted by the 'seminal emissions, which would arouse the wrath of God' (659,50).[70] Corruptibility thus is closely linked with fertility and sexuality, as incorruptibility is with asceticism and virginity.[71] The dialogue, however, proves Thomas's firm orthodox stand and defies any 'heretical' dualistic tendencies, which were widely spread at the time. The *Vita* of Christina can be considered as a subtle argument on spiritual life, which does not entail complete disembodiment. Although the body can become spiritualized and transfigured like bread and wine are transformed into God's flesh and blood, it remains a body, which will even be saved at the end of times and restored to the soul so that they can be companions for ever. The stench of the human body haunting Christina is caused by its animality and its corruption through concupiscence, but it is not evil in itself. Through the sacraments as divine accommodation to human condition, Christina is able to overcome her deep reluctance and to perform her ministry among humankind, sinful as it may be. The contemplative leaves her secret desert and her splendid isolation to serve others. However, the presence of the saint—herself representing the divine—in society, requires a channelling of the spiritual, a taming of the free Spirit,

---

[67] On debates between personifications of Body and Soul, see for further references Bynum, *Resurrection*, pp. 329–334, where she also discusses the passage in the *VCM*.

[68] Here he is in accordance with Cistercian writers like Bernard of Clairvaux and William of St. Thierry. See Bynum, *Resurrection*, pp. 163–167.

[69] On Cathar dualism see, for example, A. Brenon, *Le vrai visage du Catharisme* (Portet-sur-Garonne: Éd. Loubatières, 1988), pp. 53–84.

[70] Unum erat, quod cum miro ejulatu saepius deplangebat, totum fere humanum generis in effusionibus seminum esse corruptum, et propter hoc iram Dei per vindictam toti fere Christianitati citius imminere.

[71] The patristic background of this theme is eminently discussed by Bynum in *Resurrection*, especially pp. 84–85, pp. 108–112.

a moderation of the miraculous and, so to speak a domestication of the saint. Thus, in the end Thomas relativizes the importance of wonders and miracles as signs of divine operation; not these, but the sacraments convey God's presence to ordinary humans, in need of (physical) mediation and intermediaries.

Conclusion

In the *Vita* of Christina Mirabilis the function of the miraculous is quite ambivalent. On the one hand, the miracles in the *Vita* authorize Christina's ministry, proving that she received her mission directly from God, without human intervention and even against the expectations and wishes of the most religious. The miraculous elevates Christina to the spiritual realm and places her high above ordinary mortals. On the other hand, we may observe that the miraculous restricts Christina's ministry by emphasizing her dramatic performance, bodily suffering and ecstatic abilities, thus stylizing a specifically female apostolate. Moreover, the miraculous episodes tend to override Christina's actual ministry and to marginalize her by stressing the uniqueness of her divine mission. The extraordinary powers and abilities ascribed to her conceal the powers she actually had. Furthermore, the miraculous can dissimulate idiosyncratic behaviour and modes of thinking, which did not fit accepted patterns of female religious ministry and piety. Thus, the endowment with miraculous gifts appears to be an ambiguous privilege. Lacking religious authority through ordination women in particular seem to have benefited from the 'miraculous' as a source of religious power. In this respect it is interesting to notice that in the *Vita* of Christina, Thomas keeps the 'miraculous' itself within certain boundaries. Sacraments and priests administering them set a limit to female 'miraculous behaviour', domesticating it to fit in with human society. The holy woman, sacrosanct as she may be, cannot escape entirely from social and ecclesiastical control.

Since the *Vita* of Christina is conceived by Thomas of Cantimpré, who stylizes her life into a 'sermon on purgatory' to edify his public, the question must be asked, whether it is Christina of St. Trond or rather her hagiographer, who benefits from the miraculous. In a way the miraculous life of Christina functions as a divine authorization of his own preaching ministry, exhorting people to penance and conversion and of his own theological views on purgatory, religious life, the sacraments and, last but not least, female apostolate. Christina's is the specifically female task of embodiment of something other than herself. Is the wonder-woman Christina of Thomas's *Vita* more than a vivid illustration in the margin, more than a medium to his message, providing it with a divine halo? Such considerations might prevent a naive espousal of the 'miraculous' as a strategy for women to gain religious power. In the *Vita* of Christina it proves to be Janus-faced: its other side is the construction of female marginality, the elevation to an other-worldly realm at the cost of a place in 'real' history.

7

IN PAIN YOU SHALL BEAR CHILDREN (GEN 3:16): MEDIEVAL PRAYERS FOR A SAFE DELIVERY[1]

MARIANNE ELSAKKERS

Introduction

Delivering a child was a risky business in the Middle Ages, the rate of mortality was high, and chances were that either mother or child or both would die in childbirth.[2] In our day and age we have become estranged from natural childbirth: it is the exception, not the rule.[3] Living in an almost 'over-medicated' society in which rationalistic solutions to problems prevail, and where a woman in labor is rushed off to hospital before any complication can arise, it is hard for us to imagine a society in which birth was so very closely linked to death. But, like us, medieval women must have wanted to rear their children, so the wish to survive childbirth must have been strong. And again, like us, people probably put their trust in professional healers. With a difference, however: while we make a clear distinction between religion, magic and medicine, i.e., between supernatural and medical healing, there was but a thin line between these two kinds of healing in the Middle Ages. Given the great risks to mother

---

[1] This paper is dedicated to my mother who never learned Latin, but nevertheless understood the Latin of the 'peperit' charm.

[2] Cf. Ronald C. Finucane, *The Rescue of the Innocents: Endangered Children in Medieval Miracles*. Draft version. (London: Macmillan, 1997), p. 24. The draft version of chapter 2 was kindly supplied by prof. Finucane; Christine Fell, *Women in Anglo-Saxon England and the Impact of 1066*. (London: Colonnade/British Museum, 1984), pp. 53–54 (archeological evidence); Henrietta Leyser, *Medieval Women; a Social History of Women in England 450–1500*. (London: Phoenix, 1996), p. 125, says that one in every forty women died in the 16th and 17th centuries; Clarissa W. Atkinson, *The Oldest Vocation; Christian Motherhood in the Middle Ages*. (Ithaca etc.: Cornell University Press, 1991), p. 84 & p. 210 where she quotes Luther, Estate of Marriage (WA 10–2.289, p. 40): "Work with all your might to bring forth the child. Should it mean your death, then depart happily, for you will die in a noble deed and in subservience to God".

[3] The situation in The Netherlands, with 30% of all mothers having their children at home, is exceptional compared to other Western countries, cf. Aleida Ineke Lidy Schoon, *De gynaecologie als belichaming van vrouwen, Verloskunde en gynaecologie 1840–1920*, Ph.D. Dissertation, University of Amsterdam (Zutphen: Walburg Pers, 1995).

and child, it is understandable that supernatural help, whether attributable to miracles or magic,[4] was just as welcome as the help of midwives or physicians—even though today we would probably file some of the help the latter were able to offer under the heading 'supernatural'. In the Middle Ages spiritual and medical healing often went hand in hand and the metaphors used in religious writings confirm this.[5] Stories of safe deliveries which were considered miracles are scattered throughout our medieval sources.[6] In the twentieth-century people don't expect miracles to happen any more. If a miracle is reported, rational explanations start pouring in; there is hardly any room for just plain belief in the unexplainable, the miraculous. To medieval men and women miracles were a distinct possibility, especially if one prayed for them. In medieval miracle stories we see that prayers and rituals can help to set the scene for the occurrence of miracles of healing.

Throughout the Middle Ages, we hear women who are about to deliver praying for a miracle. We not only hear their voices praying for miracles, but we also hear them giving advice to each other. A popular medieval childbirth charm—perhaps the most popular one—is the Latin '*peperit*' *charm*. Variant versions are found all over medieval Europe from the early Middle Ages until at least the beginning of the Renaissance.[7] The large number of extant versions suggests that the text was well-known and probably widely used. It is quite remarkable that the 'core' text of the charm does not sig-

---

[4] Magic in a 'pagan' context was forbidden, cf. John T. McNeill & Helena M. Gamer, eds. & trans. *Medieval Handbooks of penance; a Translation of the Principal Libri Poenitentiales and Selections from Related Documents*. (New York: Columbia University Press, 1990; repr. of 1938 ed.), pp. 305–306 (on magic and amulets) & passim.

[5] In religious texts medical metaphors are used when speaking of spiritual healing and vice versa, cf. Frederick S. Paxton, "Curing Bodies—Curing Souls: Hrabanus Maurus, Medical Education, and the Clergy in Ninth-Century Francia", *Journal of the History of Medicine and Allied Sciences* 50 (1995), pp. 230–252. Thinking along the same lines Burchard of Worms (11th-century) called Book XIX of his penitential *Corrector et medicus* 'the Corrector and the Physician'.

[6] Miraculous childbirth stories are especially prominent in the miracle stories collected by registrars at saints' shrines, cf. Ronald C. Finucane, *Miracles and Pilgrims; Popular Beliefs in Medieval England*. (London: Macmillan, 1995; repr. of 1977 ed.), passim, and Finucane, *The rescue of the innocents*, chapter 2, passim.

[7] In an edition of two early modern Flemish 'toverboeken' (books of magic) there are two remnants of the 'peperit' charm: *en dat bij adonay † Emanüel pepento maria periet* and *en de dat bij Adonij Emanuel perit marie perperit*, cf. Frans M. Olbrechts, *Een oud Mechelsch bezweringsformulier*, Koninklijke Vlaamsche Academie voor taal- en letterkunde, reeks, 6, nr. 150 (Gent: Vanderpoorten, 1925), pp. 183–184.

nificantly change, although there are many textual variants—differing in time and place.

The question we will try to answer is: Why was this prayer so popular in medieval Europe? After discussing the 'core' text and its structure, the text and some of the textual variants will be checked for characteristics of orality. Listening to the women's voices in the text and in the instructions which accompany it, we will analyse the language variation and the rituals to see if we can find out why, how and by whom the text was used, i.e. what the function of the text was.

Orality

Each performance of a text which is part of an oral tradition is unique and therefore different. This is why it is not unusual for there to be many variant versions of oral texts. The fact that we found more than sixty versions of the medieval 'peperit' charm—and there are probably many more versions waiting to be found—is the first indication that our text may have been part of an oral tradition.[8] The function of the 'peperit' text, as stated in the heading of many of our versions, for instance *ad difficultatem pariendi probatum* 'Excellent (or efficacious) for a difficult birth',[9] is the second indication of orality, because oral texts usually have some practical use or refer to a practical situation. Using the concepts developed by oral theorists[10] we will focus on these two aspects, i.e. the different types and levels of textual variation, and the practical function of the text. It is our

---

[8] Britta-Juliane Kruse, *Verborgene Heilkünste; Geschichte der Frauenmedizin im Spätmittelalter*, Quellen und Forschungen zur Literatur- und Kulturgeschichte, 5 (Berlin: De Gruyter, 1996), p. 49, remarks that there are 128 "Gebärmuttersegen" in the *Corpus der deutschen Segen und Beschwörungsformeln* in the Institut für deutsche Volkskunde der Deutschen Akademie der Wissenschaften Berlin.

[9] Ricardus Heim, "Incantamenta magica graeca latina", *Jahrbücher für classische Philologie. Supplementband* 19 (1893), pp. 463–576 at p. 500 (Bonn, Codex Bonnensis 218 (66a), MS formerly at the Maria Laach Monastery near Cologne, fol. 40r; 11th-century); Willy L. Braekman, "Magische experimenten en toverpraktijken uit een Middelnederlands handschrift", *Verslagen en Mededelingen van de Koninklijke Vlaamse Academie voor Taal- en Letterkunde* 1966, pp. 1–69 (53–118) at p. 22; Thomas Rogers Forbes, *The Midwife and the Witch*. (New Haven etc.: Yale University Press, 1966), p. 81. The charm was written in the margin.

[10] Cf. Dennis Green, *Medieval Listening and Reading; the Primary Reception of German literature 800–1300*. (Cambridge: Cambridge University Press, 1994) for a recent survey of oral theory.

intention to show that these texts functioned within an oral tradition.

Textual variation can take on the form of substitution, repetition or expansion. We shall see that there is variation on the word, phrase, formula and line level, i.e. words, formulas, phrases, and lines can be reworded or repeated without essentially changing in meaning. The text can also be expanded by the addition of a formula or formulas from other charms or prayers, or from church liturgy. Oral texts are flexible and stable at the same time, because rhythm, contents, and the simple syntactic structure do not significantly change. This prosodic, syntactic, stylistic and semantic stability combined with textual variation is characteristic of oral poetry. The use of a familiar structure or formula, and familiar sounds and rhythms enables people to remember a text and fill in the blanks. Thus a well-known structure can function as a mnemonic device: the rhythm of the occasion will remind you of the text, just as little girls spontaneously start to sing jump-rope songs as soon as the rope starts turning.

The function of an oral text can often be discovered by looking beyond the text and trying to visualize the performance of the text by the participants. In oral texts the link between performer(s) and audience is usually close; often audience and performer(s) coincide. The link between text on the one hand and performers on the other hand can be intensified by the so-called somatic component: actions, gestures, etc. to be performed by the participants during recitation. Analysis of the instructions, the language variation and the rituals involved will show us that the audience and performers of the 'peperit' charm consisted of the women present and the baby about to be born.

The 'Peperit' Charm

The structure of the 'peperit charm' will be illustrated using a 13th-century version from the Continent chosen for its simplicity.[11] The first two lines contain the heading and instructions; the purpose of the prayer: *pro dolore partus* is stated in line 1, and in the next line the speaker is instructed to recite the charm to the woman in labor.

---

[11] Adolph Franz, *Die kirchlichen Benediktionen im Mittelalter*. 2 Bde. (Freiburg im Breisgau: Herdersche Verlagshandlung, 1909), vol. 2, p. 200 nr. 6. (Vienna, Hofbibliothek, CVP 1064, fol. 17; 13th-century).

1   Pro dolore partus
2   dic ad mulierem

3   Anna peperit Samuelem
4   Elisabet genuit Iohannem
5   Anna genuit Mariam
6   Maria genuit Christum.

7   Infans,
8   siue masculus siue femina,
9   exi foras
10 Te uocat saluator ad lucem.

11 Sancta Maria peperit saluatorem,
12 peperit sine dolore
13 Christus natus est de uirgine.

14 Christus te uocat, ut nascaris
15 Exinanite. Exinanite. Exinanite.
16 Postea ter Pater noster.

The prayer itself (lines 3–15) consists of two formulas, the 'peperit' formula and the 'exi' formula, to which other formulas can be added at will. This version opens with the *'peperit' formula* (lines 3–6) in which instances of miraculous childbirth are enumerated: Mary who gave birth to Christ, even though she was a virgin, and (H)Anna, Elizabeth, and Anna who all had children when they were old and supposedly barren.[12] The births mentioned are considered miracles, not only miracles of conception, but also miracles of birth. Referring to these miracles, the speaker seems to beg for an analogous miracle. Analogy is a device frequently used in medieval charms and prayers to make the plea more powerful.

In the *'exi' formula* (lines 7–10) the prayer addresses itself directly to the infant. With the imperative, *exi foras*, it is commanded to come out and leave the womb. Christ, the savior or *salvator*, whose birth was perhaps the most miraculous in the series of births recalled in the 'peperit' formula, speaks to the child in the second person (*te*) and tells it to be born, using the metaphor *ad lucem* (line 10). The 'exi' formula contains two semantically identical commands: the 'exi' command and the 'vocat' formula. The first command is unambiguous and rather abrupt, almost staccato: *infans ... exi foras*, but the

---

[12] Cf. Matthew 1:18, Luke 2:5 etc.; 1 Samuel 1:20; Luke 1:7 & 1:13.

second command, using the words *te vocat ad lucem* '[the Savior] summons you to the light' seems to be gently coaxing the child out of the womb. The formulaic passage, *sive masculus sive femina* (line 8), is found in the middle of the 'exi' formula proper. While the meaning of this formula speaks for itself, its position in the sentence, in apposition to the adjuration *infans*, is remarkable. Its appositional function turns the phrase into a parenthetical statement in which the voice is lowered. Thus the syntactical position has acoustical consequences, and these seem to lessen the harshness of the imperative used in the 'exi' command.

An abridged version of the *peperit formula* is repeated in lines 11-13. The miraculous birth of Christ is referred to again, now stressing the fact that the virgin birth happened *sine dolore*. The implication is that the woman about to give birth wishes and hopes for a similar miracle, i.e. a painless and speedy delivery. In the last lines (14-15) the *exi formula* proper is repeated. Christ again speaks directly to the baby (*te*) and tells it to be born and make the mother's womb empty: *exinanite*.[13] Again, semantic variation is used: different words are used to express the same meaning. *Exi foras* 'come out' is replaced by *exinanite* 'make empty' and the vocat formula *te vocat ad lucem* is reworded: *Christus te vocat, ut nascaris*. The prayer ends (line 16) as it began with instructions: now telling those present, probably the midwife and other women attending the woman in labor, to pray three 'our fathers'.

This version of the charm has a rather tidy structure: it begins and ends with instructions and in between the two parts of the 'core' text, the 'peperit' formula and the 'exi' formula, alternate. The grammatical voice of the two main formulas is different, i.e. the formulas 'sound' different. In the first the declarative voice is used and in the second the imperative.[14] The 'peperit' formula is narrative in function and the 'exi' formula speaks directly to the listener. This alternation of 'voice' creates a rhythm of its own: soft, soothing phrases followed by short commands to the infant. The charm can be divided into two sections which differ in style. On the one hand

---

[13] Franz, Ohrt, Kruse and others have observed similar formulas in the Psalms and other biblical texts, see especially F. Ohrt, "Gebärsegen", *Handwörterbuch des deutschen Aberglaubens* Bd. 3 (1931), pp. 344-346.

[14] David Frankfurter, "Narrating Power: the Theory and Practice of the Magical *Historiola* in Ritual Spells", *Ancient Magic and Ritual Power*, eds. Marvin Meyer & Paul Mirecki (Leiden: Brill, 1995), pp. 457-476, uses the term 'directive' and 'declarative' utterance (esp. pp. 467-469).

the instructions with short matter-of-fact directions and on the other hand the prayer which in itself consists of two formulas:

INSTRUCTION		lines 1–2
'CORE' TEXT (the prayer)	} peperit formula (narrative section)	lines 3–6; 11–13
	} exi formula (imperative section) (adjuration, exi command, vocat formula, sive formula)	lines 7–10; 14–15
INSTRUCTION		line 16

Variation: The 'Peperit' Formula

Elizabeth, Mary and Anna, the mother of Mary, almost always figure in the 'peperit' formula. The name of Anna, mother of Samuel— the only Old Testament mother in the charms—comes up in several versions, and in other versions, two, probably more contemporaneous, births are added: Remigius and Elysa (*Cilina Remigium, Alheidis Elysam*).[15] What we see in the formula is functional and semantic repetition: analogous miracle stories or historiolae[16] are repeated. There evidently was a store of miracle stories to choose from. The length of the formula varies, i.e. the list of miraculous births, can be shortened and expanded. Sometimes the formula comprises several lines and gives several examples of miraculous births, sometimes it is reduced to a mere line: *Santa Maria peperit*,[17] or fragment of a line: *Santa Maria, libera ancillam tuam N.* and *virgo Maria natabit*.[18]

---

[15] See: Franz, *Die kirchlichen Benediktionen im Mittelalter*, vol. 2, p. 201 nr. 8 (Altovadensis, Cistercienserstift Hohenfurt, CAltov LXII, fol. 47) and Tony Hunt, *Popular Medicine in 13th-Century England*. (Woodbridge: Boydell & Brewer, 1990), pp. 302–303 nr. 36. (London, MS B.L. Sloane 3550, fol. 98r; early 14th-century). *Cilina* may be St. Caecilia, the mother of St. Remigius, the archbishop of Rheims who baptized Clovis in 497, cf. Forbes, *The Midwife and the Witch*, p. 89. The identity of *Alheidis* is not known, perhaps it is St. Adelaide, wife of Otto I (c. 931–999) although she is not known to have had a child named *Elysa*.

[16] The narrative section of a charm or prayer is also called a historiola. Cf. Frankfurter, "Narrating power", passim.

[17] Margaret Sinclair Ogden (ed.), *The 'Liber de Diversis Medicinis' in the Thornton Manuscript (Ms. Lincoln Cathedral A.5.2.)*, EETS, 207 (London: Oxford University Press, 1969; rev. repr. of 1938 ed.), p. 57 (MS Lincoln Cathedral-Thornton MS-A.5.2., fol. 303v; late 15th-century).

[18] Franz, *Die kirchlichen Benediktionen im Mittelalter*, vol. 2, pp. 201–202, nr. 1 (Vienna,

If we compare the versions line by line, we see that there is a great deal of variation on the word level, but that the length and structure of each line hardly vary at all. Synonyms are used and epithets take the place of names, e.g. '*genuit*' for '*peperit*', '*precursorem*' instead of '*Iohannem*' or '*Iohannem Baptistam*', and '*salvatorem*' for '*Christum*'. Sometimes the names mentioned are extended, i.e. an epithet is added in apposition. John the Baptist is called '*Iohannes*' or '*Iohannes Baptista*', Elizabeth '*sterilis*' and the titles '*beata*', '*sancta*', '*mater domini* etc.' or '*virgo*' are bestowed on Mary. Christ, the ultimate miraculous birth, is called '*salvator*', '*jesus salvator mundi*', and '*Christus filius dei*'. The list below gives an indication of the variation found in the line on Elizabeth, at the same time illustrating the flexibility of the formula.

Elisabeth			Iohannem
Elisabet	sterelis	peperit	Iohannem baptistam
Elisabeth		peperit	praecursorem
Elisabeth			precursorem
Elizabeth		genuit	precursorem
Elisabeth	uero	genuit	Iohanem

The construction employed in the 'peperit' formula is parallelism or syntactic repetition, a device which is characteristic of oral texts. As we see in these lines from an 11th- or 12th-century version from Germany,[19]

Anna	peperit	Samuelem
Elisabeth	[peperit]	Iohannem
Anna	peperit	Mariam
Maria	peperit	Christum

every line is syntactically and semantically identical: the same sentence structure and meaning are repeated over and over again with the minimal variation which is so characteristic of oral texts, in other words, the structure of each line in the 'peperit' formula is identical. Repetition combined with formulaic variation seems to enhance the wish for a safe delivery like the ones called to mind. The use of parallelism on every level (i.e. word, phrase, formula, line, syntactic and semantic) not only reinforces the woman's plea, but it creates

---

Hofbibliothek, CVP 2532, fol. 125; 12th-century), and Ogden, *The 'Liber de Diversis Medicinis' in the Thornton Manuscript*, p. 56, (MS Lincoln Cathedral-Thornton MS-A.5.2., fol. 303v; late 15th-century).

[19] Franz, *Die kirchlichen Benediktionen im Mittelalter*, vol. 2, pp. 198–199 nr. 1 (München, Staatsbibliothek, CLM 100, fol. 40, 40', 11th- or 12th-century).

a rhythm of its own. None of the expansions or abbreviations of the line seem to disturb the soothing, narrative rhythm of the text.

Variation: The 'Exi' Formula

The 'exi' formula can consist of a number of formulas or formulaic passages: the adjuration, the 'exi' command, the 'vocat' formula, and the 'sive' formula:

Adjuration	o infans
Sive formula	sive vivus sive mortuus
Exi command	exi foras
Vocat formula	quia Christus vocat te ad lucem[20]

Most of the variant versions contain at least some part of the 'exi' formula. There is remarkably little variation in the adjuration. We basically find either *adiuro te infans* or simply *infans*. In one version *infans* has been replaced by *Kamelle*,[21] and once or twice we find *creatura*,[22] or *o homo*.[23] In some versions the adjuration seems to be missing.[24] The reason for the stability of the phrase *adiuro te infans* is probably that *adiuro te* is a fixed phrase which is used in charms, prayers, benedictions, and exorcisms.[25]

---

[20] Hunt, *Popular Medicine in 13th-Century England*, pp. 302–303 nr. 36 (London, MS B.L. Sloane 3550, fol. 98r; early 14th-century).

[21] Franz, *Die kirchlichen Benediktionen im Mittelalter*, vol. 2, p. 199 nr. 2 (München, Staatsbibliothek, CLM 100, fol. 40'; 12th-century). *Kamelle* means 'Knabe' ('boy').

[22] Franz, *Die kirchlichen Benediktionen im Mittelalter*, vol. 2, p. 201 nr. 8 (Altovadensis, Cistercienserstift Hohenfurt CAltov LXII, fol. 47).

[23] Franz, *Die kirchlichen Benediktionen im Mittelalter*, vol. 2, p. 202 nr. 2 (München, Staatsbibliothek, CLM 7021, fol. 188'; 13th–14th-century).

[24] Often when the adjuration is missing, the exi command, too, is missing; and sometimes there is no exi formula at all, for instance in the following Anglo-Norman version printed by Hunt, *Popular Medicine in 13th-Century England*, p. 367 (Cambridge, MS St. John's College D.4, fol. 100rb; first half 14th-century):
A femme ki travail de enfant:
Liez a sun flanc ceste escrit:
Maria peperit Christum†
Anna Mariam†
Elizabeth Johannem.
Sator arepo tenet opera rotas.
Absence of the exi-formula does not mean that the exi-formula was not known or used. On the contrary, the formula was probably so well-known that it was tacitly implied. Almost all of the versions without an exi-formula are supposed to be written down.

[25] Cf. Franz, *Die kirchlichen Benediktionen im Mittelalter*, vol. 2, p. 200, note 1: "exeas

There is more variation in the wording of the 'exi' command. The length of the phrase, however, is usually quite short, and its meaning does not change either. A few of the variants we found: *exi foras, ut exeas et recedas, sic veni foras, ut exeas foras, quod cita exeas, eius exijt foras mater, exinanite*.[26] Sometimes, another historiola, the story of Lazarus[27] (Luke 16:20 ff. and John 11:1 ff.), is referred to, probably because Lazarus, like the infant, is commanded by Christ to 'come forth' (John 11:43) alive out of a dark compartment (the tomb—the womb).[28] In an eleventh-century version from the Continent the Lazarus story is added as an extra charm to be used if the first one does not have the desired effect: *quod si hoc tam cito non proderit, tunc in alio membranulo scribas*, 'If after this she shall not have given birth promptly, then write on another paper'.[29] Because both charms are included in this early version, one is tempted to wonder if these two charm texts were integrated at some stage.[30]

---

et recedas aus der Exorzismusformel". This does not mean that these words are used in a negative sense here. Cf. Claude Lecouteux, *Charmes, conjurations et bénédictions; lexique et formules*. Essais sur le moyen âge, 17 (Paris: Champion, 1996), p. 57: "... le verbe *exorcizo* est synonyme d'*adiuro, convenio, alloquor* et *benedico*; une bénédiction n'est donc ni plus ni moins qu'une forme d'exorcisme".

[26] Sometimes wrongly read as *exinamte*, cf. W. Crecelius, "Alte Segensformeln", *Zeitschrift für deutsche Mythologie und Sittenkunde* 2 (1855), pp. 77–78 at p. 77 or *exmamte*, cf. A. Birlinger, "Bairische Besegnungen. Aus einer Papierhandschrift 15. Jhd. Pflanzenbuch, ehemals Hasslers Bibl. in Ulm," *Germania* 24 (1879), pp. 73–76 at p. 74.

[27] See, for instance: Franz, *Die kirchlichen Benediktionen im Mittelalter*, vol. 2, pp. 199–200 nr. 4 (München, Staatsbibliothek, Clm 19411, "auf dem vorderen Deckel"; 12th-century): *Christus quadrinuanum Lazarum uocauit et dixit: Lazare, ueni foras. Et ego adiuro et, infans etc.*

[28] Metaphorically speaking Lazarus is often considered to have been born twice, once at the time of his real birth and once when he was raised from the dead. Finucane, *The Rescue of the Innocents* (draft version), pp. 43–44 observes that *non utero sed tumulo* 'not womb but tomb' was a well-worn phrase, having to do with the mother's fear of giving birth to a dead child.

[29] Translation by Forbes, *The Midwife and the Witch*, p. 81. This version was first published by Heim, "Incantamenta magica graeca latina", p. 550 (Bonn, Codex Bonnensis 218 (66a), formerly at the Maria Laach Monastery near Cologne, fol. 40r; 11th-century):
 (...) Quod si hoc tam cito non proderit, tunc in alio membranulo scribas:
 Lazare, veni foras,
 salvator revocat te.
 et super pectus feminae mitte.

[30] There seems to be corroborative evidence, because there are other versions in which the Lazarus passage was added at the end of the text, after a full stop. In a version from England the 'Lazarus' charm was added after the word *Amen*—clearly an indication of a full stop, cf. Gotfried Storms, *Anglo-Saxon Magic*. (Den

The 'vocat' formula has many variant versions. It is the most unstable part of the 'exi' formula, even though, here too, meaning, length and structure of the line don't change significantly. The order of the words varies, synonyms and synonymous phrases are used, but semantically the 'vocat' formula remains identical to the 'exi' command, i.e. a rewording of the command to the child to be born, e.g.:

te uocat	saluator	ad lucem
salvator	revocat te	
Christus	te uocat	
Christus	te uocat	ut nascaris
ut vuideas	[—]	lumen dei

Most of the versions of the 'peperit' charm contain the 'sive' formula: *sive masculus sive femina*. Occasionally it is expanded with a parallelism: *siue uiuus siue mortuus*.[31] The 'sive' formula is very stable, both in wording and in length, with only minimal variations, none of which alter its meaning, or affect the rhythm of the line. The stability of the formula, obviously due to the short and rigid syntactic, parallelistic construction *sive... sive*, is complemented by the instability of its position in the 'peperit' charm; it is found in almost every part of the prayer.

The variation we found in the 'exi' formula is on the word and the phrase level, not in the length or structure of the lines, nor in the semantic content of the formula, thus not altering the rhythm of the prayer. Although not every version contains each element of the 'exi' formula, the elements present are quite stable. Again, this type of variation combined with syntactic stability points to orality, and therefore to usage of the charm within an oral tradition.

Variation: Expansion or Addition of Other Formulas

Lines from other charms and prayers, bits of liturgy, and other formulas were often added to the 'core' text of the 'peperit' charm. We will mention a few of the most common expansions, because they illustrate the flexibility of oral texts, i.e. the ease with which an

---

Haag: Nijhoff, 1948), p. 283 nr. 45 (Oxford, Bodleian Library, MS Junius 85, fol. 17; 11th-century). The fact that the manuscripts containing these versions were compiled in different parts of Europe: one on the Continent and one in England, makes the 'Lazarus' passage even more intriguing.

[31] Also: *siue uiuus an mortuus* or *siue sis mortua siue uiua*.

oral text can incorporate other texts, thus making each performance of the oral text unique. Before we look at a few of the extra formulas, it must be remembered that the 'peperit' charm was to be used when the parturient woman was in great pain. She is appealing for help, and because she is in great distress, any kind of help is welcome, whether it is medical, miraculous, or magical.

The version of the 'peperit' charm printed below—the longest version we found—has an extremely high proportion of additional formulaic passages.[32]

```
1   For a womon þat travels on child:
    Bind þis writt to hir theghe
    † in † nomine † Patris † et Filii
    † et Spiritus Sancti † amen
5   et per virtutem Dei sint medicina mea.
    Sancta † Maria † peperit † Christum †
    Sancta Anna † peperit † Mariam †
    Sancta † Elizabeth † peperit † Johannem †
    Sancta Cecilia † peperit † Reonigium [corr.
    Remigium] †
10  sator † arepo † tenet † opera † rotas †
    Christus † vincit † Christus † regnat †
    Christus † imperat †
    Christus † te † vocat †
    mundas † te † gaudet †
15  lex † te † desiderat †
    Christus † dixit †
    Lazaro † veni foras †
    deus ulcionum † dominus † deus ulcionum †
    libera famulam tuam † .N. †
20  dextra domini fecit virtutem
    † a † g † l † a † alpha † et o †
    Anna † peperit † Mariam †
    Elizabet † precursorem †
    Maria † dominum † nostrum † Jhesum † Christum †
25  sine dolore et tristicia.
    O infans,
    sive vivus sive mortuus,
    exi foras,
    quia Christus vocat te ad lucem †
30  agios † agios † agios †
    Christus † vincit † Christus † regnat †
```

---

[32] Hunt, *Popular Medicine in 13th-Century England*, p. 98 nr. 89 (London, MS B.L. Sloane 3160, fol. 169r; 15th-century; Anglo-Norman).

```
              Christus † imperat †
              sanctus † sanctus † sanctus †
              dominus † deus † omnipotens †
       35     qui † es et qui eras †
              et qui venturus es, amen.
              Blrurcion † blrurun † blutanno † bluttiono †
              Jhesus † nazarenus † rex †
              judeorum † fili † dei †
       40     miserere † mei † etc.
```

The addition of prayers or formulas taken from church liturgy enhances the verbal power of the woman's plea for a safe delivery. The version above contains a lot of formulas from church liturgy, e.g. lines 3–4 ('the sign of the cross'), lines 35–36, and lines 33–34 (the 'sanctus').[33] Not only do we find versions in which powerful prayers and analogies are added (such as the story of Lazarus), but influential intermediaries such as the three wise men (renowned for their magical powers),[34] the evangelists,[35] the apostles and other saints[36] can also be prevailed upon to intercede on behalf of the woman in labor. The phrase *Christus vincit, Christus regnat, Christus imperat* (above, lines 11–12 & 31–32), a formula commonly included in healing

---

[33] These stock phrases are often abbreviated: *per p. et f. et s.s.* (Crecelius, "Alte Segensformeln," pp. 77–78 & Braekman, "Magische experimenten en toverpraktijken uit een Middelnederlands handschrift," p. 22; 14th-century German manuscript). Not all of the abbreviations are intelligible to us now, e.g. *q. h. n. c. f. a. re.* (Franz, *Die kirchlichen Benediktionen im Mittelalter*, vol. 2, p. 201 nr. 8; Altovadensis, CAltov LXII, Bl. 47).

[34] Braekman, "Magische experimenten en toverpraktijken uit een Middelnederlands handschrift," p. 20, nr. 10 (London, MS Wellcome 517, fol. 67r; 2nd half fifteenth-century).

[35] Franz, *Die kirchlichen Benediktionen im Mittelalter*, vol.2, p. 200 nr. 7 (Göttweig, CGottw 104, fol. 4'–5; 13th-century); Braekman, "Magische experimenten en toverpraktijken uit een Middelnederlands handschrift", p. 20, nr. 10 (London, MS Wellcome 517, fol. 67r; 2nd half fifteenth-century). In the latter version the names of the evangelists were written in a (magic?) square.

[36] Sometimes specific saints are invoked such as St. Agatha, St. Barbara or St. Margaret (cf. Franz, *Die kirchlichen Benediktionen im Mittelalter*, vol. 2, p. 201 nr. 8; Altovadensis, CAltov LXII, fol. 47), and sometimes all the saints together are asked for help: *Sancta Maria, Dei genitrix, & omnes apostoli & omnes martires & omnes sancti confessores & omnes sancte virgines, intercedant pro famula Dei. N. Amen* (Ogden, *The 'Liber de Diversis Medicinis' in the Thornton Manuscript*, p. 57; Lincoln, MS Lincoln Cathedral (Thornton MS) A.5.2., fol. 303v; late 15th-century) or *omnes sancti dei intercedite pro me* (J.H. Gallée, "Segensprüche", *Germania* 32 (1887), pp. 452–460 at p. 458 nr. VI & Agi Lindgren, *Das Utrechter Arzneibuch (Ms. 1355, 16°, Bibliotheek der Rijksuniversiteit Utrecht)*. Acta Universitatis Stockholmiensis, Stockholmer Germanistische Forschungen, 21 (Stockholm: Almqvist & Wiksell, 1977), p. 90; Utrecht, UB MS 1355 (Olim. var. 414), fol. 122b; 2nd half 14th-century).

charms,[37] is often found in the 'peperit' charm. From the 13th-century onwards the prayer frequently opens with the formula: *de viro vir, virgo de virgine, vicit leo de tribu Iuda, radix David*;[38] the last lines, 'behold the lion of the tribe of Jude, the root of David,' are a quote from the Bible (Apoc. 5:5). Again a formula we also find in other healing charms.[39]

Magico-religious formulas which are also found in other healing charms, can be added to the 'core' text, such as *AGLA*, an abbreviation of the Hebrew words *Atlah Gabor Leolam, Adonay*, meaning 'You are mighty in eternity, Lord',[40] the Greek letters '*alpha et omega*', signifying the name of God,[41] or the magic 'sator-arepo' square: *sator arepo tenet opera rotas*.[42] Probably magical in intent are the following unintelligible lines, classified as gibberish by many scholars:[43] *boro berto briore (...) † Tahebal †† ghether ††† guthman etc.*[44] and *Blrurcion †*

---

[37] See, for instance, Franz. *Die kirchlichen Benediktionen im Mittelalter*, vol. 2, p. 496 ff.: a charm or benedictio for the eyes. The formula must be accompanied by the sign of the cross, cf. Willy L. Braekman, "Enkele zegeningen en krachtige gebeden in een Vlaams devotieboek uit de vijftiende eeuw", *Volkskunde* 79 (1978), pp. 285–307 at p. 297.

[38] Franz, *Die kirchlichen Benediktionen im Mittelalter*, vol. 2, p. 200 nr. 7 (Göttweig, CGottw 104; "am unteren Rande von Bl. 4' und 5 von einer Hand des 13. Jahrhunderts"). The length of the formula varies from version to version.

[39] Cf. Braekman, "Enkele zegeningen en krachtige gebeden in een Vlaams devotieboek uit de vijftiende eeuw", p. 306; Willy L. Braekman, "Notes on Old English Charms II", *Neophilologus* 67 (1983), pp. 605–610. Braekman 1983, p. 609; Ohrt, "Gebärsegen", p. 344.

[40] Cf. Braekman, "Magische experimenten en toverpraktijken uit een Middelnederlands handschrift", p. 22, and Lecouteux, *Charmes, conjurations et bénédictions; lexique et formules*, p. 20 with a different Hebrew transcription. We find *AGLA* in Braekman, "Magische experimenten etc.", p. 20, nr. 10 (London, MS Wellcome 517, fol. 67r; 2nd half fifteenth-century).

[41] 'I am the Alpha and the Omega, the beginning and the end' (Apoc. 21:6). See, for instance, Braekman, "Enkele zegeningen en krachtige gebeden in een Vlaams devotieboek uit de vijftiende eeuw", p. 293.

[42] 'Pater noster' according to some, cf. Richard Kieckhefer, *Magic in the Middle Ages*. (Cambridge: Cambridge University Press, 1990; repr. of 1989 ed.), pp. 77–78, or Hunt, *Popular Medicine in 13th-Century England*, p. 358, note 100. In one version the words are to be written in butter or cheese and given to the woman in labor to eat (Ogden, *The 'Liber de Diversis Medicinis' in the Thornton Manuscript*, p. 57; Lincoln, MS Lincoln Cathedral (Thornton MS) A.5.2., fol. 303v; late 15th-century).

[43] Cf. J.H. Grattan & Charles Singer, *Anglo-Saxon Magic and Medicine: illustrated specially from the semi-pagan text 'Lacnunga'*. (London: Oxford University Press, 1952), p. 11 & Felix Grendon, "The Anglo-Saxon Charms", *The Journal of American Folklore* 22 (1909), no. LXXXIV, pp. 105–237, passim.

[44] Felix Holthausen, "Rezepte, Segen und Zaubersprüche aus zwei Stockholmer Handschriften", *Anglia* 19 (1897), pp. 75–88 at p. 85 nr. 26 (MS Stockholm, Kgl. Bibl. Miscellan-Hs. XIV, Bl. 146; second half 14th-century).

blrurun ✝ blutanno ✝ bluttiono (line 37 in the 'peperit' version quoted in full above). Even though the words have no meaning to us, they *sound* magical, because they alliterate (which is characteristic of Germanic poetry), and seem to form a rhythmic group. Could these lines or words be remnants of Germanic magic formulas?

When the 'peperit' charm was written down, it also became part of the literary tradition. This means that, besides being influenced by the oral tradition, the literary tradition could now also leave its mark on the charm text. And it did. In several versions we find lines or fragments from Vergil's *Aeneid*, a text which was widely used for didactic purposes in the Middle Ages; large parts of it were known by heart by many of the literati. The following lines are found in the 'peperit' charm: *Oceanum interea surgens Aurora reliquit* 'Meanwhile Aurora arose and left the ocean' (*Aeneid* IV,129 = *Aeneid* XI,1) and *Panditur interea domus omnipotentis Olympi* 'Meanwhile the gateway to Olympus, the seat of supreme power, was flung open wide' (*Aeneid* X,1).[45]

The textual expansions we find in the 'peperit' charm illustrate the ease with which the text could draw on christian, magical and literary sources; this flexibility is characteristic of orality. The form of some of the textual additions: alliterative lines, liturgical texts (often sung in church) or hexameters from Vergil seems to indicate that these texts were considered to be poetry, i.e. they were felt to be rhythmic, and could therefore easily function as a mnemonic device. The fact that texts from the written tradition could also be added, shows us that the oral and the written traditions were not two completely different worlds as they are now.

---

[45] Cf. Franz, *Die kirchlichen Benediktionen im Mittelalter*, vol. 2, p. 201 nr. 8 (Altovadensis, CAltov LXII, fol. 47) which contains both lines, and Franz, *Die kirchlichen Benediktionen im Mittelalter*, vol. 2, p. 202 nr. 2 (München, Staatsbibliothek, Clm 7021, fol. 188'; 13th–14th-century) containing only the *panditur* line. Sometimes just a single word in a 'peperit' version (e.g. *pandunt* in the version mentioned in note 37) reminds us of Vergil. Heim, "Incantamenta magica graeca latina", p. 502 quotes a fever charm with one of the lines from Vergil quoted above (*Aeneid* IV,129 = *Aeneid* XI,1), and there is a 15th-century childbirth charm consisting of just one line: *A charme. Occeanum age, surge, rumpe & explica moras. Write this charme & bynde it to hir knee righte with-in &, alsone als scho es deyuered, tak it a-waye.* (Ogden, *The 'Liber de Diversis Medicinis*, p. 57 Lincoln, MS Lincoln Cathedral (Thornton MS) A.5.2., fol. A.5.2.; late 15th-century) which is also vaguely reminscent of Vergil, e.g. *Aeneid* IV,129 = XI,1; IV,569; IX,13; *Georgics* 3, 42–43. These lines from Vergil all contain commands which sound quite appropriate in a childbirth charm.

Instructions

Many of the 'peperit' charms we collected contain instructions. The instructions often start off with the indication or "medical condition for which the prescription is a remedy"—in this case childbirth.[46] They usually precede the text of the prayer, sometimes more are included at the end of the prayer, and in one or two versions they are incorporated in the charm text.[47] The fact that a small number of versions lacks instructions does not mean that no instructions were required. On the contrary, the large number of versions we found seems to indicate that this childbirth charm was so well-known that instructions were not necessary at all: women knew exactly what to do and probably passed this knowledge on by word of mouth. This brings us to the *function* of the text. From the instructions it is clear that the charm was meant to be used during childbirth and that active participation of those attending the woman in labor is required. The activities prescribed vary from text to text.

The prayer is often supposed to be *written* down. The substance on (or in) which the charm is to be inscribed can be a piece of bread, butter or cheese, wax,[48] a note, card, letter or parchment.[49]

---

[46] Cf. Hunt, *Popular Medicine in 13th-Century England*, p. 16 ff. on the form of the medical receipt. Hunt distinguishes six parts of the medical receipt: rubric (heading), indication, composition (ingredients), preparation, application, and statement of efficacy. The texts discussed here are not medical receipts in the strict sense of the word, but they do belong to the corpus of medieval medical texts because they are concerned with healing. The 'peperit' texts resemble the medical receipt, especially when instructions were added.

[47] The † symbol which is frequently found in the prayer text indicates that those present are supposed to make the sign of the cross while reciting the prayer.

[48] Storms, *Anglo-Saxon Magic*, p. 283, gives the following explanation for the use of wax: "The magician presumably thought that the wax, a sticky material, attracted and drew out the child, and as OE. *swiþ* means 'strong' the operation was assisted by binding the wax on the right or 'stronger' foot. If the wax had served any other purpose beforehand, it would have lost its sacred and magic character". This rather far fetched explanation is probably the reason Storms classifies the charm as pagan: "This charm against childbirth is made up of Christian elements, and yet its atmosphere is pagan".

[49] In London, Wellcome MS 517, fol. 67r, 12th-century (cf. Braekman, "Magische experimenten en toverpraktijken uit een Middelnederlands handschrift", p. 20 nr. 10) virgin parchment (*scribe ... in percameno virgineo*) is to be used. This may be a reference to the miraculous virgin birth, but then again, there are numerous examples of charms in which 'virgin' substances (i.e. substances which have never been used before) such as 'virgin wax' are to be used. So it could also simply refer to the uncontaminated state of the substance, in the sense that such a 'pure' substance would be more likely to effect a cure.

In some versions the woman is told to eat the edible substance,[50] and occasionally the text adds a promise that the woman will be liberated (*liberabitur*) after eating the words of the prayer, i.e. when the words literally become part of her body.[51] Is this a way to guarantee that the woman will internalize the text of the prayer so she will not forget it when labor pains start, and she is really in need of it? In other versions the prayer has to be attached to part of the woman's body. The written word then functions as an amulet. Prescribing a written text as an amulet or word charm in a society where the majority of the population is illiterate suggests that writing—whatever the language—was considered magical.[52] The amulet was thought to possess such powerful magical properties that sometimes instructions at the end of the text tell the bystanders to quickly take it away as soon as the child is born.[53] Besides having magical properties, the amulet, may also have functioned as a reminder to the woman in labor that she might benefit from using this text— regardless whether she could read or not, i.e. the written text or amulet functioned as the proverbial knot in the handkerchief or string around the finger.

The amulet can also be tied around the belly of the woman like a girdle or belt.[54] Girdles are often referred to in connection with childbirth. Franz[55] gives an example in which the cinxture belonging

---

[50] See, for instance: Franz, *Die kirchlichen Benediktionen im Mittelalter*, vol. 2, pp. 201–202 nr. 1 (Vienna, Hofbibliothek, CVP 2532, fol. 125; 12th-century).

[51] Perhaps this might be called an internal amulet.

[52] Cf. Frankfurter, "Narrating power", passim; Karen Louise Jolly, *Popular Religion in Late Saxon England; Elf Charms in Context.* (Chapel Hill & London: University of North Carolina Press, 1996), pp. 109–110.

Of course the charm must have been written down by one of the litterati. I do not think clerics were present in the birth chamber in order to recite the charm; the women present (midwife, helpers, mother-to-be) probably all knew it by heart. Charms written on scraps of parchment preserved in libraries and museums—the creases showing repeated folding of the parchment—prove that these 'written' charms were used again and again, and probably circulated widely in the community. One can imagine the women in the birth chamber tracing the symbols on the parchment in butter or on the stomach of the parturient woman without really understanding them, this in itself again intensifying the magical impact of these actions.

[53] See, for instance Gustaf E. Klemming (ed.), *Läke och Örte-böcker från Sveriges Medeltid*. (Stockholm: Kongl. Boktryckeriet P.A. Norstedt & Söner, 1883–1886), p. 213 (Linköpings Stifts-bibliothek HS. M.5. (= XCIV); early 15th-century).

[54] E.g. *et cingatur circa uentrem uel ligetur subtus genu circa crus et tunc peperit* (Franz, *Die kirchlichen Benediktionen im Mittelalter*, p. 202 nr. 2: München, Staatsbibliothek, Clm 7021, fol. 188'; 13th–14th-century).

[55] Franz, *Die kirchlichen Benediktionen im Mittelalter*, vol. 2, pp. 206–207.

to a priest who has just said his first mass is to be bound around the woman's body, and quoting Grimm, he tells us of a statue which was measured after which the measuring tape was wrapped around the pregnant woman's stomach.[56] Measuring as a means of healing seems to have been widespread in the Middle Ages.[57] The measurements of the sick person are taken, or alternatively, the measurements of some holy object, e.g. the statue of a patron saint. In the first case the piece of string or thread the sick person was measured with is incorporated in an object (often a candle) into which the illness is to be transferred. The candle or other object is then offered in church.[58] In the second case the reverse takes place: the thread with the measurements of the holy object is fastened to the sick person in the hope that its miraculous powers of healing will be transferred to the sick person. These threads, strings, girdles, belts, ribbons, and knots[59] may be remnants of ancient binding and loosing rituals, or of rituals involving sympathetic magic or magical transference. As early as the first-century A.D. Plinius the Elder mentions binding and loosing with the aid of a girdle in his *Natural History*:[60]

partus accelerat hic mas ex quo quaeque conceperit, si cinctu suo soluto feminam cinxerit, dein solverit adiecta precatione se vinxisse, eundem et soluturum, atque abierit.	. . . to hasten child-birth. . . . If the man by whom a woman has conceived unties his girdle and puts it round her waist, and then unties it with the ritual formula: "I bound, and I too will unloose," then taking his departure, child-birth is made more rapid.

---

[56] Franz, *Die kirchlichen Benediktionen im Mittelalter*, vol. 2, p. 207; Jakob Grimm, *Deutsche Mythologie*. Hrsg. Elard H. Meyer. 4. Aufl. (Berlin: F. Dümmler, 1875–1878; repr. Graz: Akademische Druck- und Verlagsanstalt, 1968), vol. 3, p. 417 nr. 31.

[57] Finucane, *Miracles and Pilgrims*, pp. 95–96 calls it a universal custom which goes back to at least the sixth-century.

[58] Cf. Finucane, *Miracles and Pilgrims*, pp. 95 ff.; Jolly, *Popular Religion in Late Saxon England*, pp. 109–110.

[59] Franz, *Die kirchlichen Benediktionen im Mittelalter*, vol. 2, pp. 188 ff., especially pp. 205 ff.

[60] Gaius Plinius Secundus, *Historia Naturalis*/Pliny. *Natural History*, vol. 8. Libri XXVIII–XXXII, ed. & trans. W.H.S. Jones (Cambridge, Mass.: Harvard University Press, 1963), pp. 32–33; cf. Iona Opie & Moira Tatem, *A Dictionary of Superstitions*. (Oxford: Oxford University Press, 1989), pp. 220–221. In the text quoted by Grimm, *Deutsche Mythologie*, vol. 3, p. 417 nr. 31, it is also the husband's belt which is to be tied around the woman's belly.

Customs involving binding and loosing, amulets, girdles and measuring tapes have been recorded to this day by folklorists and anthropologists, and they illustrate the importance of rituals and their somatic components in oral traditions.[61] These somatic or performative components requiring some form of active involvement of those present at the birth again strengthen our belief that these texts were part of an oral tradition.

Recitation of the charm is referred to in the instructions of a number of texts, e.g.: *dic, dic ad mulierem, per hec uerba, say this charme thris*. The directness and simplicity of the language of the charm text also seems to imply recitation. Although reciting is not explicitly mentioned in most of the texts, it seems reasonable to assume that the 'peperit' prayer was recited out loud. The presence of instructions requiring writing does not preclude recitation, and recitation was probably so obvious to the charm's users that there was no need to mention it. And as we said above, the written text might function as an amulet or just simply as a mnemonic device. The fact that both writing and reciting are mentioned in the instructions—in a few versions both are required—can also indicate that the text functioned in a society which was slowly becoming literate. But one wonders what the function of this text which was handed down in so many versions, would be if it was *not* meant to be recited. The instructions in the 'peperit' charm all prescribe active participation of the 'birth crew' in some form or another, and this points to an oral setting for the prayer text.

Language Variation

In almost all the versions we found the 'peperit' prayer was in Latin.[62] The language of the instructions accompanying the charms, how-

---

[61] See for instance: Heinrich Ploss & Max Bartels, *Das Weib in der Natur- und Völkerkunde: anthropologische Studien*. 10. verm. Aufl. (Leipzig: Grieben, 1913), vol. 2, passim; Jozef van Haver, *Nederlandse incantatieliteratuur; een gecommentarieerd compendium van Nederlandse bezweringsformules*. (Gent: Koninklijke Vlaamse Academie voor taal- en letterkunde, 1964), p. 60; William George Black, *Folk-Medicine: a Chapter in the History of Culture*. (New York: Burt Franklin, 1970; repr. of 1883 ed.), p. 93 & passim.

[62] Just as this paper was being finished Britta-Juliane Kruse's *Verborgene Heilkünste* came to my attention. Here we find a late medieval version of the 'peperit' charm (pp. 54–55; UB Graz, HS. 1609, fol. 211v–212r) in which the prayer was written in the vernacular (Middle High German). The early modern fragments printed by

ever, varies. This language variation is intriguing, because it stresses the difference in style between the two sections we noted before, and, besides, it makes us wonder why the language of the instructions varies, whereas the language of the prayer is Latin in almost every single one of the versions we found. And why was *Latin* used?

Latin was the language of literacy, but also the language of the church: liturgy and prayers were in Latin and this means that Latin must have at least sounded familiar. Biblical characters and stories, christian prayers and rituals had become part of everyday life in the Middle Ages. People must have known a lot of Latin liturgical texts and prayers by heart from singing, reciting and hearing them in church, and this might be one of the reasons that prayers and bits of liturgy were easily inserted into the text. The Latin versions of the Our Father and Hail Mary, for instance, were probably just as well-known as their vernacular counterparts. It is quite possible that the illiterate churchgoer was able to grasp the meaning of certain Latin phrases which were continually repeated in the liturgy, and explained in sermons. The meaning of a short, simple phrase like *Maria peperit Christum* must have been obvious because the stories about Mary and Christ were common knowledge. Whether Latin was fully understood remains debatable, but at least some of it must have been intelligible, and, then again, some of it probably remained wrapped in mystery. Because of its semi-intelligibility Latin was enigmatic and therefore eminently suited for magical and ritual purposes. The liturgical context in which it was used must have reinforced the idea that Latin was a ritualistic language. And the language of ritual is powerful, so powerful that its effectiveness might change if the medium is tampered with. It looks like the language of prayer was considered magical and sacrosanct, and that the use of Latin was functional and therefore mandatory—which explains the almost complete lack of language variation in the variant versions of the 'peperit' prayer.

In the charm's instructions the language varies: in some versions the instructions are in Latin, but usually they are in the vernacular. This is because the function of the instructions is different from that of the 'prayer' text. The instructions were meant to be fully comprehended because correct performance of the ritual depended on cor-

---

Olbrechts, *Een oud Mechelsch bezweringsformulier* (cf. note 7) are a curious mixture of Latin and Flemish.

rect understanding of the directions. This makes it is quite understandable that the instructions were in the vernacular in so many of our versions. If we look at the language variation in the 'peperit' charms, we see that it is quite functional. This functional and at the same time practical language variation seems to strengthen our case in favor of orality.

Rituals

Focal point of the ritualistic language of the prayer and the rituals described in the instructions is the parturient woman. Both the verbal and the performative rituals are centered around the body of the woman in labor. The verbal rituals direct the attention of those present in the delivery room to the body of the mother-to-be by the sheer power of the word. This focussing on the mother while the charm is recited, is accentuated in the versions which contain bits of church ritual, quotes from the liturgy, and other prayers, because these add extra ritualistic power to the words of the prayer, and therefore seem to function as an extra insurance policy. The nonverbal or performative rituals involving touching, inscribing, girding, gesticulating[63] and so on are enacted on or near the pregnant woman's body, again causing the focus of the actions to center around the body of the woman in labor. The touching, binding, tasting (or eating), and reciting, implicitly also including seeing, hearing and smelling, activate the senses of all the participants, preparing them for whatever is about to happen. The sensory awareness of the body of the *parturiens* is further enhanced by the words of the prayer, especially when the pains and dangers of childbirth are referred to.[64] The verbal and nonverbal rituals reinforce each other, together creating a powerful physical focus on the woman in pain. On both the verbal and the performative level the prayer seems to be admonishing the woman's body to be cooperative using magical and ritualistic gestures, actions, objects (amulets) and words to emphasize this.

The physical focussing on the *parturiens* described above is complemented by a focus on another level. The precedents of painless

---

[63] See note 47.
[64] Cf. Franz, *Die kirchlichen Benediktionen im Mittelalter*, vol. 2, p. 201 nr. 8 (Altovadensis, Cistercienserstift Hohenfurt, CAltov LXII, fol. 47): *et ancilla dei non moriatur in partu.*

childbirth which are explicitly mentioned in phrases such as *Maria... absque omni dolore et tribulatione... Elisabeth... non doluit*[65] remind us of biblical healing miracles. Miracle stories in the Bible often mention healing rituals which help evoke an atmosphere of sensory awareness. These biblical healing rituals can include the laying on of hands, anointing or spitting, and they set the scene for the occurrence of the miracle—at the same time drawing attention to the body of the person who is to be cured. The result is a kind of double focus. We find the same double focus in the 'peperit' charms. The rituals focus on the woman about to deliver her child, and at the same time the scene for a miracle is set by the references to other miraculous births. The rituals help create a situation, an atmosphere, that is analogous to the situation in which Mary, the two Annas and Elizabeth gave birth. Not only does the charm text make everyone alert and ready for the birth of a child, but it also makes them ready to experience a miracle. The charm is in fact a strong plea for a miracle, an attempt to invoke a miracle by setting the scene for one using all kinds of powerful rituals. And this tells us why the charm was recited, and why the rituals are so important.

Wyse Bademoder

Historical evidence for female medical practitioners, including midwives, collected and analysed by Monica Green, indeed seems to indicate that childbirth was "women's business" in the Middle Ages.[66] Literary sources also provide evidence for the presence of 'wise' or 'skillful' women at childbirth.[67] In a source contemporary to the 'peperit' charms, the Old Norse *Edda*, we come across wise women

---

[65] Cf. Franz, *Die kirchlichen Benediktionen im Mittelalter*, vol. 2, pp. 199–200 nr. 4 (München, Staatsbibliothek, Clm 19411; 12th-century; "auf dem vorderen Deckel").

[66] Monica Green, "Women's Medical Practice and Health Care in Medieval Europe", *Sisters and Workers in the Middle* Ages, ed. Judith M. Bennett e.a. (Chicago: The Univeriosity of Chicago Press, 1989), pp. 39–78; see also L.M.C. Weston, "Women's Medicine, Women's Magic: the Old English Metrical Childbirth Charms", *Modern Philology* 92 (1995), pp. 279–293 and Finucane, *The rescue of the innocents*, chapter 2, passim.

[67] In the Plinius text quoted above the husband leaves after the 'loosing' ceremony, before the child is born.

assisting at birth. The norns and the dísir,[68] female goddesses who "determine the destiny of an individual and may be present at the birth of a child",[69] can act as midwives, as is illustrated in the following quotations from the *Edda*:[70]

'Segðu mér, Fáfnir, (. . .) hveriar ro þær nornir, er nauðgonglar ro ok kiósa mœðr frá mogom?' *Fáfnismál* 12,1,3–4.	'Say now, Fáfnir, (. . .) which norns are near when need there is to help mothers give birth to their babes?' *Fáfnismál*
Biargrúnar skaltu nema, ef þú biarga vilt ok leysa kind frá konom; á lófa þær skal rísta ok of liðo spenna ok biðia þá dísir duga. (. . .) Á skildi kvað ristnar, (. . .) á lausnar lófa (. . .)[71] *Sigrdrífumál* 9,1–4; 15,1; 16,4.	Learn help runes eke, if help thou wilt, a woman to bring forth her babe: on thy palms wear them and grasp her wrists and ask the dísir's aid. (. . .) on the shield graven (. . .) on the midwife's hand (. . .) *Sigrdrífumál*

In another part of the *Edda*, the *Oddrúnargrátr*, we see a wise and experienced woman in action at childbirth singing loosing charms and incantations to help deliver the child.[72]

---

[68] On the norns, cf. Lee M. Hollander (trans.), *The Poetic Edda*. 2nd ed. (Austin: University of Texas Press, 1962), p. 225, note 11; Hilda Ellis Davidson, *Myths and Symbols in Pagan Europe: Early Scandinavian and Celtic Religions*. (Manchester: Manchester University Press, 1988), pp. 96, 106, 164, 140 ff. On the dísir, cf. Hollander, *The Poetic Edda*, p. 235 note 19; Hilda Ellis Davidson, *The Lost Beliefs of Northern Europe*. (London: Routledge, 1993), pp. 61, 107, 113, 118.

[69] Hilda Ellis Davidson, *The Lost Beliefs of Northern Europe*, p. 118. In Grimm's fairy tales the fairies present at the birth of Sleeping Beauty are vaguely reminiscent of the norns.

[70] The quotations are from: Gustav Neckel (Hrsg.), *Edda; die Lieder des Codex Regius nebst verwandten Denkmälern*, Bd. I. Text (Heidelberg: Carl Winter, 1914), pp. 178, 187–189, and Hollander, *The Poetic Edda*, pp. 225, 235, 237.

[71] Hugo Gering, *Glossar zu den Liedern der Edda. (Saemundar Edda)*. 3. Aufl. (Paderborn: Ferd. Schöningh, 1907) gives the following translation of *á lausnar lófa* on p. 110: "auf der erlösenden hand, d.h. auf der hand der geburtshelferin".

[72] Neckel, *Edda*, pp. 228–229; Hollander, *The Poetic Edda*, p. 279.

Hér liggr Borgný, of borin verkiom,	Here lieth Borgný by labor o'ercome,
(...)	(...)
gekk mild fyr kné meyio at sitia;	nigh her, Oddrún did kneel to help:
ríkt gól Oddrún, ramt gól Oddrún,	stern spells she spake, strong spells she spake,
bitra galdra, at Borgnýio.	for womb-bound woman witchcraft might.[73]
Knátti mær ok mogr moldveg sporna,	Two bonny babes were born to the world,
(...)	(...)
Oddrúnargrátr 4,3; 7,2–4; 8,1.	*Oddrúnargrátr*

These passages from the *Edda* give us a picture of the use of incantations and runes during the birthing process. Oddrún, obviously a midwife, helped Borgný, who was unable to deliver until Oddrún came and helped her by kneeling down before her and coaching her. This passage describes a real-life situation: the midwife is at work in the lying-in chamber, kneeling in front of the laboring woman (who is probably sitting in some kind of birth stool or leaning on something)[74] and holding her wrists. The words *leysa* 'to loosen' and *lausn* 'loosing' or 'loosening' in the *Sigrdrífumál* remind us of the binding and loosing rituals we mentioned before, and the use of runes evokes a sense of mystery and ritual.[75] This picture of singing, chanting or reciting at childbirth with magical or ritualistic connotations— the runes—on the one hand and the practical helping hand of the midwife on the other hand, is almost exactly the same as the picture we have been developing of the performance of the 'peperit' charm. More proof is supplied in four late medieval variants of the 'peperit' charm which actually call for a *wyse bademoder*[76] or midwife in the instructions: *so hebbe sy yo by sik ene wyse bademoder* 'she must certainly have with her a wise midwife'.[77]

---

[73] W.H. Auden & Paul B. Taylor (trans.), *Norse Poems*. (London: The Athlone Press, 1981), p. 115 translates: "loosening charms for luckless Borgny".

[74] Cf. Finucane, *The rescue of the innocents*, (draft version), p. 59.

[75] Carving runes on the midwife's hand (*Sigrdrífumál* 15,1; 16,4) may be tattooing, dyeing or staining of some kind. Evidently the magic words or mantra must be impressed upon her mind, never to be forgotten. This 'impressing' seems comparable to the inscribing (and sometimes even eating) of the charm text mentioned in many of the instructions.

[76] The Dutch word for midwife, *vroedvrouw*, literally means 'wise woman'.

[77] Cf. Sven Norrbom (Hrsg.), *Das Gothaer mittelniederdeutsche Arzneibuch und seine Sippe*.

Literary evidence seems to confirm our suspicion that charms, prayers, and incantations were really used during childbirth, and that they were not only part of a literary tradition, but that they were used by illiterate or semi-literate women within an oral tradition. We saw above that analysis of the charm shows that the 'peperit' charm text undoubtedly belonged to the oral tradition. Literary and formal evidence, therefore, agree and together point to actual usage of the charm at childbirth. The question is: Was the 'peperit' charm only a prayer, or invocation, a ritualistic plea for a miracle? Or did the 'peperit' charm really have some practical function or use which has been lost, and which might explain the immense popularity of this text in medieval Europe? Let's take one more look at the charm text.

Medieval Lamaze?

Oral texts are often used in practical situations. Work songs, for instance, can rhythmically accompany monotonous and boring work such as sowing, reaping, mowing or even assembly line work. Such work songs are repeated over and over and over again to the rhythm of the work at hand.

The 'peperit' prayer consists of two parts which are different in tone and voice: the narrative 'peperit' formula and the imperative 'exi' formula. In the version we discussed above the two sections alternate twice which means that the prayer might have been repeated cyclically. Perhaps, if we envisage women present at childbirth, singing or chanting the charm again and again, the two sections alternating, the 'peperit' charm might be called a kind of work song which accompanies labor. Labor, after all, is work, hard work, and labor is also in essence rhythmic: contractions and periods of relaxation alternate just like the sections in the 'peperit' charm. Not only is birthing rhythmic, but its rhythm is not constant: the tempo changes at every stage. As the birthing process progresses, the speed of the birthing rhythm is gradually accelerated, progressing from initial labor, through advanced labor to active labor, when the contractions are close together and intense, finally culminating in the birth of the child. The rhythm of the 'peperit' charm can easily accommodate itself to

---

Mittelniederdeutsche Arzneibücher, 1 (Hamburg: Hartung, 1921), p. 122. Norrbom edited four manuscripts of the 'Düdesche Arstedie', a Middle Low German 'Arzneibuch'.

the changes in speed which are inherent to the birthing process. It looks like this charm may indeed have functioned as a work song.[78]

Today expectant mothers take Lamaze classes where they are taught how to breathe through labor. They are taught how to pant, puff, moan, groan, grunt and finally push and bear down. If natural childbirth is *chosen* the mother-to-be is advised to have a 'birth crew' handy who know what to do, and who can coach her, telling her how to breathe and when to puff or pant or push.[79] A birth team is necessary, because when labor starts the labor pains will take over and the laboring woman will forget her exercises. Medieval women did not have a choice. Natural childbirth was the only real option. The medieval 'birth crew' must have consisted of female friends, neighbors and *wyse bademoder*, and its function was exactly the same as that of the twentieth-century birth team: to coach the mother through labor! Medieval helpers must have been well-versed in the breathing techniques, and they must have known exactly how to assist the mother with her breathing. Since there were no epidurals to relieve the pain, the right kind of breathing at the right time was very important, because the breathing techniques for the different stages of labor can help relax the mother. With the right breathing the labor pains can 'go with the flow' of the contractions.

Concentration during labor is important, and this is where the 'peperit' charm might have come in handy. The recitation of the alternating sections of the prayer: the slow, narrative sections and the faster and louder imperative sections may have constituted a rhythmic mnemonic device, a reminder of how to breathe. If the 'peperit' charm functioned as a work song and a rhythmic mnemonic device, the narrative 'peperit' sections would correspond to relaxed breathing, and the 'exi' formula would correspond to the panting

---

[78] Cf. Joachim Telle, *Petrus Hispanus in der altdeutschen Medizinliteratur; Untersuchungen und Texte unter besonderer Berücksichtigung des 'Thesaurus pauperum'*. Inaugural-Dissertation Heidelberg (Heidelberg: s.n., 1972), p. 187 on the 'peperit' charm: "Man maß ihm starke wehenfördernde und heraustreibende Kräfte zu"; he goes on to quote Heidelberg manuscript Cpg. 545 fol. 60: "So du einer frawen wilt bej gestenn, so siehe zu der gepurd sol arbeitten, so du gest yn ihr gemach, so spriche, das sie es hore: 'Anna gepar Mariam, Maria gepar Jhesum Cristum' etc."

[79] When discussing the 'peperit' charm, Weston, "Women's Medicine, Women's Magic", p. 292 says: "Far from actively managing the birth, the women around the mother become, like sisters of Lazarus, audience rather than actors". This seems to me to be a too literary interpretation of the function of the story of Lazarus. As I hope to have demonstrated, the women present were engaged in actively managing the birth at hand.

which should accompany the contractions. If the contractions were prolonged, the 'exi' part could be repeated, and during the intervals the soothing narrative sections could be recited to help the laboring woman relax her breathing. When pushing and bearing down were required, the 'exi' formula could be shortened to *exi, exi* or *exinanite, exinanite*, 'push, push'. Such a rhythmic mnemonic function of the prayer might also explain why the instructions often tell the bystanders to write the text of the prayer down and attach it to the expectant mother. The amulet would then function as a tangible reminder of the charm text and the breathing techniques it stood for. If we consider the 'peperit' charm a work song, a verbal accompaniment to and reminder of the different kinds of breathing required when giving birth, the prayer acquires a very practical function. We cannot prove that this is the way the 'peperit' charm was used, but this explanation could account for the popularity of the charm all over medieval Europe.[80]

Conclusion

Formal analysis of the medieval 'peperit' charm and its variant versions from all over Europe shows that the charm must have been part of an oral tradition: there is variation and formulaic repetition on every level (word, line, phrase, etc.), mnemonic devices are used, and instructions requiring active participation in word and deed of all present explain the practical function of the charm. Prayer and instructions make us aware of the somatic component of the charm and its (christianized) magic: the reciting and writing, the amulets, the measuring, and the binding and loosing rituals. The Latin of the prayer stresses its ritualistic power, at the same time, by contrast, explaining why the vernacular was so frequently used for the instructions. These verbal and performative rituals with their focussing on the parturient woman help to set the scene for the miracle the woman in labor so fervently desires. But the charm was also practical; evidence in literary texts corroborates this. In her hour of need the woman

---

[80] It is quite possible that the function of the 'peperit' charm was forgotten when men took over midwifery in the 16th, 17th and 18th centuries. In The Netherlands midwives still teach expectant mothers verses such as *Deze wee komt nooit meer terug* ('This contraction will never come *back*') to help them with their breathing during labor.

about to deliver was provided with every kind of help imaginable: medical, magical and divine assistance in the form of skillful women, magic, and the prayer itself. The prayer could even have offered real practical help to the soon-to-be mother because, as we saw above, the two rhythmically different sections of the prayer may represent a mnemonic device to help the woman with her breathing techniques: medieval Lamaze.

It should be remembered that the medieval expectant mother was at a much greater risk than a twentieth-century expectant mom, so it seems quite understandable that, besides enlisting the practical help of midwives, the mother-to-be would also put her faith in prayers. To us, twentieth-century women, it is strange not to have to choose between one kind of medicine and an other, and it is hard to comprehend that for medieval women human and supernatural medicine went hand in hand. If we look at the advice Trotula and Hildegard of Bingen, two medieval female healers, gave to women in labor, we see that medieval women put their trust in spiritual, magical, and physical powers of healing without really distinguishing between them.

> *Above all things when there is difficulty in child-birth one must have recourse to God.* Trotula of Salerno, *Diseases of Women*.[81]

> *Et si aliqua mulier praegnans cum dolore oppressa non poterit, sardium circa ambas* **lenden** *ejus* **striche** *(...).* 'If a pregnant woman oppressed with pain cannot deliver [her child], rub her loins with [the stone] sardus (...).' Hildegard of Bingen, *Physica*.[82]

Medieval medicine consisted of empirical healing combined with different forms of supernatural healing. All of these forms of healing are represented in the 'peperit' charm, but the prayer with its religious metaphors seems to be the frame within which medical and magical healing function. The prayer with its ritualistic language, analogous miracle stories, and its plea for a miracle is accompanied by magic and practical breathing techniques which are embedded in the rhythm of the prayer. It is the prayer which might actually help the woman in labor through her birth pains, and thus, God willing, effectuate a miraculously safe delivery.

---

[81] Atkinson, *The Oldest Vocation*, p. 53, quoting Elizabeth Mason-Hohl's translation of Trotula of Salerno's *Diseases of women* (Los Angeles: Ward Ritchie Press, 1940).

[82] J.-P. Migne, *Patrologiae Latina*, vol. 197, 1255ab.

Select Secondary References

Ashford, Janet Isaacs, "Doing it myself," *Birth Stories; the Experience Remembered.* ed. Janet Isaacs Ashford. Trumansburg, N.Y.: The Crossing Press, 1984, pp. 68–80.
Cockayne, Th. Oswald, *Leechdoms, Wortcunning and Starcraft of Early England.* 3 vols. London: Longman, 1864–1866.
Finnegan, Ruth, *Oral Poetry, its Nature, Significance and Social Context.* Cambridge: Cambridge University Press, 1977.
Flint, Valerie I.J., *The Rise of Magic in Early Medieval Europe.* Oxford: Clarendon Press, 1993.
Hälsig, Friedrich, *Der Zauberspruch bei den Germanen bis um die Mitte des XVI. Jahrhunderts.* Leipzig: Seele, 1910. (Diss. Leipzig).
Jeitteles, Adalbert, "Zu den 'Bairischen Besegnungen," *Germania* 24 (1879), pp. 311–312.
Lemaire, Ria (ed.), *Ik zing mijn lied voor al die met mij gaat.* Utrecht: Hes, 1986.
London, Jonathan, "Lushness, Magic, Mystery and Work." *Birth Stories; the Experience Remembered.* ed. Janet Isaacs Ashford. Trumansburg, N.Y.: The Crossing Press, 1984, pp. 161–166.
MacKinney, Loren C., *Early Medieval Medicine; with Special Reference to France and Chartres.* New York: Arno Press, 1979. (Repr. of 1937 ed.)
Meaney, Audrey L., *Anglo-Saxon Amulets and Curing Stones.* Oxford: Bar, 1981. (BAR British series, 96).
———, "Women, Witchcraft and Magic in Anglo-Saxon England," *Superstition and Popular Medicine in Anglo-Saxon England,* ed. D.G. Scragg. Manchester: Centre for Anglo-Saxon studies, 1989, pp. 9–40.
Meyer, P., "Recettes médicales en français." *Bulletin de la société des anciens textes français* 32 (1906), pp. 37–52; pp. 78–87.
Ong, Walter J., *Orality and Literacy; the Technologizing of the Word.* London etc.: Methuen, 1982.
Otten, Marcel (transl.), *Edda.* met een inl. van Kees Samplonius. Baarn: Ambo, 1994.
Rowland, Beryl, *Medieval Woman's Guide to Health.* Kent, Ohio: The Kent State University Press, 1981.
Schipperges, Heinrich, *Die Benediktiner in der Medizin des frühen Mittelalters.* Leipzig: St. Benno Verlag, 1964. (Erfurter theologische Schriften, 7).
Smith, Gayle, "Angry and Happy at the same Time," *Birth stories; the Experience Remembered.* ed. Janet Isaacs Ashford. Trumansburg, N.Y.: The Crossing Press, 1984, pp. 101–106.
Tambiah, Stanley J., "The Magical Power of Words," *Man* 3 (1968), pp. 175–208.
Telting, A., "Angel-saksische bezweringsformulieren," *De Vrije Fries* 2 (1842), pp. 1–9.
Thomas, Keith, *Religion and the Decline of Magic; Studies in Popular Beliefs in Sixteenth- and Seventeenth-Century England.* Harmondsworth: Penguin Books, 1988. (Repr. of 1971 ed.)
Zingerle, Oswald von, "Segen und Heilmittel aus einer Wolfsthurner Handschrift des XV. Jahrhunderts," *Zeitschrift des Vereins für Volkskunde* 1 (1891), pp. 172–177.

APPENDIX: Four Versions of the 'Peperit' Charm

Quando mulier parturiendo periclitatur, dicenda sunt hec. Primum tange uentremper umbilicum et dic: *Increatus pater etc.* Et tunc ad dextrum latus: *Inmensus pater etc.* Et tunc ad sinistrum latus: *Eternus pater etc.* Hoc fac ter et dic:	Wiþ wif bearn eacenu (For a woman big with child).
<u>Anna peperit Samuelem,</u> <u>Elisabeth Iohannem,</u> <u>Anna peperit Mariam,</u> <u>Maria peperit Christum.</u>	<u>Maria virgo peperit Christum,</u> <u>Elisabet sterelis peperit Iohannem baptistam.</u>
Infans siue masculus siue femina, siue mortuus siue uiuus, exi foras, te uocat saluator ad lucem.	*Adiuro te infans, si es masculus an femina, per Patrem et Filium et Spiritum sanctum, ut exeas et recedas,* *et ultra ei non noceas neque insipientiam illi facias. Amen.* *Videns dominus flentes sorores Lazari ad monumentum lacrimatus est coram Iudeis et clamabat: Lazare veni foras.* *Et prodiit ligatis manibus et pedibus qui fuerat quatriduanus mortuus.*
Hoc fac ter et lege euangelium 'In principio' super caput eius imposita manu et da ei ad ieiundandum uigiliam sancte Margarete et tolle licnum, unde uenter eiusdem mulieris potest amplecti, et fac, ut uoueat inde candelam et offer eam in honorem sante Margarete uirginis.	Writ ðis on wexe ðe næfre ne com to nanen wyrce, and bind under hire swiðran fot.
München, Staatsbibliothek, CLM 100. HS, fol. 40, 40', 12th-century. Franz, *Die kirchlichen Benediktionen*, vol. 2, pp. 198–199, nr. 1.	Oxford, Bodleian Library, MS Junius 85, fol. 17, 11th century. Storms, *Anglo-Saxon Magic*, p. 283 nr. 45.

Jsta verba debent scribi et poni super ventrem mulieris que grauatur ante partum et statim post partum debet littera remoueri ne intestina simul exeant,	Hefft eyn wyf grote wedaghe vnde kan des kyndes nicht ghenesen, alzo dat dar vare ane sy dat se beyde steruen, so hebbe sy yo by sik ene wyse bademoder, wente id enis neyn kynderspil. So schrif dessen bref vnde make ene so langk dat he er neddene vmme dat lyff gae, vnde schrif dyt darynne:
De viro vir, virgo de virgine, *vicit leo de tribu Juda,*	*De viro virgo.* *Vincet leo de tribu iudia*
Anna peperit mariam, *maria peperit Christum,* *Elizabet sterilis Johannem baptistam,*	*Maria peperit Christum,* *Elizabet sterilis peperit Johannem baptistam.*
Adiuro te infans *per patrem et filium et spiritum sanctum* *vt exeas de wlua ista,* *ex via vita, ex uia uita* *Si masculus sis uel femina, Amen*	*Adiuro te, infans,* *per patrem † et filium † [et] spiritum sanctum,* *si masculus es aut femina,* *ut exias de ista vulua est [= ex] matrice exinanite*
	Wen dat kynt geboren ys, so legghe den bref einwech vnde schaue so vele elpenbens alzo ij suluerpenynghe weghen moghen, vnde gif er dat drinken myt wyne, so wert se gelozet altohant, vnde endo des nicht, du enhebbest de bademoder darby.
Linköpings Stifts-bibliotek, handskrift, M. 5 (= XCIV); first quarter 15th-century. Klemming, *Läke och Öre-böker*, p. 213.	Gotha, Herzogl. Bibliothek. Cod. chart. nr. 980. (= Gothaer Arzneibuch), fol. 46a. early 15th-century. Norrbom, *Das Gothaer mittelniederdeutsche Arzneibuch*, p. 122.

8

A WOMAN ALONE: THE BEATIFICATION OF FRIEDERIKE HAUFFE *NÉE* WANNER (1801–1829)[1]

Wouter J. Hanegraaff

Non enim silice nati sumus, sed est natura in animis tenerum quiddam atque molle, quod aegritudine quasi tempestate quatiatur

Cicero[2]

Introduction

When the popular Victorian novelist Catherine Crowe published her abridged translation of Justinus Kerner's *The Seeress of Prevorst* in 1845, she made it possible for an English-speaking audience to become familiar with a 'miracle story' which had quickly achieved notoriety in Germany after it was first published in 1829.[3] To this day, overviews in the English language of the history of psychiatry, parapsychology, occultism, and related fields duly mention the pioneering importance of Justinus Kerner and 'his' Seeress, but none of them goes beyond a brief presentation based on secondary sources.[4] In

---

[1] This research was supported by the Foundation for Research in the Field of Philosophy and Theology in the Netherlands, which is subsidized by the Netherlands Organization for the Advancement of Research (NWO). A substantially extended version of the present article is available in German ("Versuch über Friederike Hauffe: Zum Verhältnis zwischen Lebensgeschichte und Mythos der 'Seherin von Prevorst'", *Suevica: Beiträge zur Schwäbischen Literatur- und Geistesgeschichte* 9/10 [2000]).

[2] 'For we are not sprung from rock, but our souls have a strain of tenderness and sensitiveness of a kind to be shaken by distress as by a storm' (Cicero, *Tusculan Disputations*, III.vi.12, ed. J.E. King, *The Loeb Classical Library* [Cambridge, Mass. & London, 1971], pp. 238–239).

[3] Alan Gauld, *A History of Hypnotism* (Cambridge, 1992), p. 190. For Crowe, and the significance to her of Kerner's *Seeress*, see the Introduction by Colin Wilson to the modern reedition of Catherine Crowe, *The Night-Side of Nature: Or, Ghosts and Ghost-Seers* [orig. 1848] (Wellingborough, 1986). A long appendix on the Seeress of Prevorst was included in George Bush, *Mesmer and Swedenborg: Or, the Relation of the Development of Mesmerism to the Doctrines and Disclosures of Swedenborg* [2nd ed.] (New York, 1847).

[4] Henri F. Ellenberger, *The Discovery of the Unconscious: The History and Evolution of*

this article I intend, firstly, to provide an English readership with a more complete and accurate picture than is currently available, taking advantage of older as well as recent German research. Secondly, I will address some practical and theoretical problems involved in an attempt to disentangle 'myth' from 'reality', in a story which owes its very fame to its 'miraculous'—and therefore historically problematic—aspects. Thirdly, I will address some problems bearing on the relationship (personal, professional, literary) between the male poet and physician Justinus Kerner, on the one hand, and his female patient Friederike Hauffe, on the other.

The Story

The official story of *The Seeress of Prevorst*, as it impressed itself on Kerner's readership, can be summarized briefly.[5] Friederike Wanner was born on September 23, 1801, in the small Souabian forestry village of Prevorst. When she was 19 years old, her family arranged for her to marry a distantly related merchant, Gottlieb Hauffe; a decision which caused Friederike to sink into a period of depression. The very day of her official engagement happened to coincide with the burial of the Lutheran minister of Oberstenfeld—the family had moved there in 1818—with whom she had used to talk much about spiritual subjects, and to whom she seems to have felt very close. When she visited the grave she saw his spirit hovering over it, and at the same moment felt a profound inner change coming over her. After this spiritual experience her outward symptoms of depression ended, but inwardly she no longer cared about what happened to her in the outside world.

Dynamic Psychiatry (Basic Books, 1970), pp. 78–81; Gauld, *History of Hypnotism*, pp. 149–152; Joscelyn Godwin, *The Theosophical Enlightenment* (Albany, 1994), pp. 161–162. Cf. Heinrich G. Brugsch, "Doctors Afield: Justinus Kerner (a Romantic Physician)", *The New England Journal of Medicine*, 270:14 (1964), pp. 729–730; Uwe Henrik Peters, *Studies in German Romantic Psychiatry: Justinus Kerner as a Psychiatric Practitioner. E.T.A. Hoffmann as a Psychiatric Theorist* (London, 1990).

[5] All further references, unless stated otherwise, refer to the relatively accessible Reclam edition: Justinus Kerner, *Die Seherin von Prevorst: Eröffnungen über das innere Leben des Menschen und über das Hereinragen einer Geisterwelt in die unsere* [orig. 1829] (4th ed. Leipzig, 1846) [referred to in the text as "SP"]. All translations from the German are by the author. The only edition currently in print (with Preface by Joachim Bodamer [Stuttgart, 1958] and later reprints) is heavily abridged and unsuitable for scholarly ends. It must be noticed that there are substantial differences between the contents of the different complete editions since the first one of 1829.

Having married, she moved to her husband's house in Kürnbach. After half a year (february 13, 1822), she had a disturbing dream: she found the corpse of the minister lying in her bed; and in the next room she heard her father and two physicians discussing a heavy illness which had befallen her. She cried to them "Just leave me in quiet with this deceased, he heals me, I will be healed by no doctor [*mich heilt kein Arzt*]" (SP 56), and then felt that people tried to tear her away from the corpse. While she was having this dream, her husband heard her talk in her sleep: 'How well I feel beside this deceased; now I will be completely healed' (SP 56). The next day, Friederike was running a high fever which stayed on for 14 days. It was followed by extremely severe breast cramps which kept returning daily for the next eighteen weeks.

Thus began her illness, which caused her to be in a so-called 'magnetic' or mesmeric trance state (or, rather, various gradations of such states) almost permanently until her death in 1829. Apart from the daily recurring cramps, Friederike was plagued by an extreme sensitivity to even the slightest disturbances, such as iron nails in the wall of her room; and she already displayed many of the unusual abilities, experiences and phenomena which would eventually make her famous. Her husband and family desperately attempted any conceivable type of cure, but with very little success. It became apparent that only magnetic treatment (by making 'passes' over her body) brought her at least temporary relief, and Friederike herself appeared to be able to prescribe procedures for her own treatment. Two nearly fatal pregnancies did not lead to the improvement in her condition which her relatives seem to have expected of them. Her first son died within six month; the second became twelve years old, and displayed similar 'paranormal' abilities as his mother. Friederike's suffering grew worse; she hardly slept anymore, was often crying the whole night, and suffered recurring cramps, epileptic fits and nightsweats. Finally, her relatives decided to bring her to Weinsberg, in the hope that Dr. Justinus Kerner, known for his previous successes with so-called somnambulic patients, might perhaps know how to help Friederike.

Kerner describes her arrival as follows:

> Mrs. H. arrived here on november 25, 1826: an image of death, completely consumed, unable to get herself upright or lie down. Each third or fourth minute one had to give her a spoonful of soup, which she was often unable to swallow, but just took in her mouth and spit out

again. If one did not give it to her, she fell into unconsciousness or cramps.... Cramps and a somnambulic state alternated with nightsweats and a fever combined with bloody diarrhoea. Each evening at seven o'clock she fell into a magnetic sleep. She always began these with silent prayers, in which she had her arms crossed over her breast. Then she spread her arms straight outwards and was on that moment in a visionary state; and only when she had placed them back on the bedcloth did she begin to speak. Her eyes were then closed, her face quiet and transfigured (SP 70–71).

Initially, Kerner adopted the attitude of a stern physician who had no use for Friederike's 'hysterical' behaviour, and tried to put an end to the magnetic treatment. But this had a contrary effect and his patient deteriorated quickly. In her trance states she continued to give prescriptions for herself, and Kerner had to admit that these proved more effective than whatever he had to offer. After several weeks, regular magnetic treatment was resumed, which produced an immediate improvement beyond anything Kerner had been able to accomplish by regular medical procedures. On April 6, 1827, Friederike came to live permanently in Kerner's own house, where she would stay as a patient until briefly before her death in 1829. Under the regime of regular magnetic treatment she eventually seems to have reached a state of relative equilibrium. During these years in Weinsberg, stories about her miraculous abilities spread widely, causing Friederike Hauffe to become known as 'the Seeress'. Kerner paints the following picture of sanctity and transfiguration:

> ... lies of the most nonsensical kind were spread about this woman all over the country, and all sorts of people imposed themselves on her (to my deep worry), coming to her sickbed expecting to see miracles. Many that were not admitted took revenge by spreading lies...
> She, however, approached all people with the same kindness, even though it required sacrifices of her body; and even those who slandered her most, were defended by her. Evil and good people came to her. She did feel the evil in people, but never judged them, and took up no stone against any sinner; but in many sinners whose presence she endured around her, she will have awakened the belief in a spiritual life...
> Already years before Mrs. H. was brought here, the whole earth and its atmosphere, and all that is around and on it, including human beings, were no longer reality for her. She needed more than a magnetizer; she needed more, too, than a loved one; she needed a seriousness, an understanding, of a kind as could hardly have been in the ability of a human being—she needed what no mortal was able to give her: another heaven, another sky, another sustenance, than this

earth can give. She belonged in a world of spirits, being herself already more than half spirit; she belonged in the state after death in which, often, here already, she more than half found herself (SP 79).

Kerner characterized her as a person fixed on the threshold between life and death; and in the spring of 1829 it became increasingly clear that the end was near. On the 5th of May her relatives took her back to Löwenstein, for unclear reasons and against Kerner's medical advice. Her condition deteriorated quickly, and Friederike predicted her own death. A farewell poem written during these days contain these famous lines:

> Wie soll ich euch denn nennen,
> Ihr, die ihr mich betrübt?
> Ich nenn' auch euch nur—*Freunde*;
> Ihr habt mich nur geübt.[6]

Friederike seems to have remained in a magnetic state until her death, on August 5. At 10 o'clock, her sister (who is known to have shared some of Friederike's visionary abilities) saw a 'high, shining figure' enter the room. At the same moment, Friederike is said to have uttered a loud cry of joy, and died. Kerner, who was not present, comments that he dreamt of her that same night—while still not in the least suspecting her death—and saw her walking, completely healed, accompanied by two female figures. Friederike Hauffe was buried in Löwenstein on August 8, 1829.

The Miracles

Friederike's fame is based on the miraculous occurrences reported of her, many of which have subsequently become a matter for interpretation from (para-)psychological perspectives. Although sceptics have tried from the very beginning to dispose of Friederike Hauffe as a fraud, often ridiculing Kerner as a credulous poet who allowed himself to be deluded by a woman,[7] there is actually no good reason

---

[6] SP 626. A rough translation, which unfortunately does not preserve the poetic poignancy of the fragment, would be: 'How then shall I call you; / you, who have brought me grief? / You, too, I just call—*friends*; / you have only trained me'.

[7] See for example A.K.A. Eschenmayer, "Aphorismen über Freiheit und inneres Leben", *Blätter aus Prevorst* I (Karlsruhe, 1831), p. 1, about these reactions: "Bald drücken sie ein Bedauern aus, daß der Dichter und der Philosoph von einem Weib sich haben irre führen lassen, bald brechen sie in Vorwürfe aus...".

to doubt the sincerity of either of them or to dismiss the factual foundation of Kerner's observations. Without for a moment denying the critical and hermeneutical issues involved,[8] we can safely assume that those who were present at Friederike Hauffe's sickbed did indeed witness strange and unusual things happening on a regular basis. Equally important, as we will see, was a special atmosphere which might easily convince the visitor that he was in direct touch with the supernatural even if no tangible miracles occurred. It should be noted that Kerner himself disliked the popular tendency of referring to what happened as 'miracles'. He wanted to present them as normal phenomena (*"nichts Ungewöhnliches, sondern schon oft... Vorgefallenes, in der Natur gegründetes, durchaus Wunderloses"* [SP 73]) belonging to the *Nachtseite der Naturwissenschaft*.[9] Throughout his writings he repeats that these phenomena are normal and natural, and that only those who are deluded by a mechanistic worldview and rationalist prejudice will be forced to see them as 'miracles' (i.e., as supernatural, hence impossible, hence necessarily based on superstition and delusion).

Kerner's detailed account of his observations and his experiments with Friederike are consistent with this perspective. They are clearly not designed as a catalogue of miracles but as a systematic clinical report of observed 'facts' (*Thatsachen*), some of which just happen to be of a quite 'miraculous' kind. Kerner does not strictly separate his empirical observations from his theoretical interpretations, but it is usually possible to distinguish the two.

---

[8] At least three points must be made about these. 1. Accepting Kerner's reports as based on fact does not automatically imply accepting his interpretations; 2. This distinction between observation and interpretation is however not always clearcut, and one has to be alert to many specific instances where Kerner's religious convictions may unconsciously have coloured or distorted his observations and his descriptions of them; 3. At least since the period of the Enlightenment, presenting oneself as a strict empirical observer has been a common strategy for attempting to convince sceptics of the reality of the occult.

[9] According to the terminology of Gotthilf Heinrich Schubert, *Ansichten von der Nachtseite der Naturwissenschaft* (Dresden, 1808). This fundamental work of German Romantic *Naturphilosophie* had provided Kerner with the fundamentals of his own worldview. Note that Schubert himself characterized his book as concerned primarily with the phenomena "die man zu dem Gebiet des sogenannten Wunderglaubens gezählt hat" (*Ansichten*, p. 2), i.e. largely with the "occult" phenomena especially associated with magnetism and somnambulism in Schubert's own time.

Here I will merely give a listing of the types of 'miracles' reported by Kerner, without discussing them in further detail.[10] Firstly, Friederike displayed an extreme sensitivity to the imponderable 'spirit' (*Geist*) of various physical influences (minerals, fluids, lights, sounds, the moon, etc.). Secondly, she displayed the complete standard repertoire of 'paranormal' visionary experience; in a trance state, it was not her eyes but her heart region (*Herzgrube*) which seemed to become the most sensitive organ of perception. Thirdly, she gave various prescriptions for self-healing, which were all based upon the number seven (for example, magnetic passes would not be effective unless 7 of them were given at 7 o'clock; herbal medicines had to be administered in portions of 7, and so on); and a particularly important role was played by the use of amulets, the effectiveness of which was supposed to be based upon the magical power of words written in her 'inner language' (see *infra*). Fourthly, she was extremely sensitive to other people's illnesses, the symptoms of which (and the accompanying emotions) she experienced in her own body; she gave prescriptions for healing, generally based upon the magical power of words and numbers; and she became particularly famous by her succesful treatment of the Countess of Maldeghem, who seems to have suffered from psychotic delusions. Fifthly, mention must be made of the closely interrelated phenomena of Friederike's 'inner circles', 'inner language' and 'inner arithmetic'. She spoke and wrote in a personal 'language of the soul', which appears to have been consistent and could eventually be learned by others; this language was closely linked to a system of 'inner arithmetic' according to which all events in human life had a numerical value, and which caused Friederike to be continuously occupied with calculating the advances and losses in her condition caused by various influences from the outside world; and finally, at a certain moment she began to draw her so-called 'Solar circles' and 'Circles of life'. On one level, these were merely a kind of circular calendars, on the periphery of which Friederike noted down all the events in her life which had a bearing on her physical, mental and spiritual condition; but on another level they represented her 'inner world', in which she could find refuge when the circumstances of the outside

---

[10] An extended discussion is included in Hanegraaff, "Versuch" (see note 1).

world were too trying, and in the very center of which (the *Gnadensonne*: 'sun of grace') she experienced the impenetrable mystery of the divine. Sixthly and finally, Kerner provides detailed descriptions of Friederike's experiences with ghosts, i.e., with the spirits of the deceased which had not as yet attained salvation and which were visible to her on a regular basis.

Given the nature of the abilities and phenomena displayed by Friederike Hauffe, one might ask whether it is correct to describe her as a woman who 'performed miracles'. Strictly speaking, it seems that the answer must be negative. Much that happened could be qualified as 'miraculous', without however automatically qualifying as 'miracles'. For example: that a person can feel a tiny iron nail in the wall is certainly a miraculous feat, but it is not a *miracle* according to any commonly accepted usage. Unquestionably miraculous events were reported about Friederike, and one can understand that people came to her from all over the country 'expecting to see miracles' (see *supra*). Were they, then, disappointed in their expectations, because they witnessed strange phenomena but no 'true' miracles? Hardly. The more information became available, the more famous Friederike became. This might suggest that dogmatic definitions of 'miracle', as involving cases where natural law is overruled by supernatural intervention—the kinds of definition expressly rejected by Kerner—are not very helpful for understanding what is really going on in so-called 'miracle stories'. Having summarized the canonical story of 'The Seeress of Prevorst' and the miraculous events reported of her, I will now proceed to the question of *what*, actually, may have been going on.

The Woman

If a biography achieves fame because of its miraculous aspects, the interpreter is inevitably confronted with the problem of how the official, canonized myth is related to the actual reality of what has historically happened. One is tempted to write, rather, 'the *underlying* reality'—but this very automatism points to a common assumption which needs to be questioned. Intuitively, it may seem natural to imagine the reality 'behind' the myth as a sort of pure 'core', which has been overgrown and partly or completely hidden from sight by subsequent accretions produced by the mythical imagination. The task, then, would be to clean away the accretions so as to recover the original historical core. The implication is that the process of demythologizing a miracle story consists in a reduction from 'more' to 'less': one does away with various phantasies and fabrications, so as to discover that what really happened wasn't such a big deal as the enthusiast would like us to believe.

I suggest that, as a general procedure for interpreting miracle stories, this approach is fundamentally flawed. The original historical reality from which the miracle story emerged is invariably much richer and more complicated than any story (including the historian's story) that might possibly be told about it. The myth is produced by a narrator's perspective which is heavily biased towards emphasizing certain aspects of this complex reality to the exclusion of others: it therefore consists of a reductive version of reality. It follows that the historian's task consists in replacing this reductive presentation by one which restores the original complexity as much as possible, i.e. in *adding* what has been left out. This procedure, too, results in demythologization (possibly even more thorough than the reductionist alternative), for it does away with the narrative bias necessary for any good story. On the positive side, however, it may restore to the actors of the story their original *humanity*. And even more importantly, it may make us aware of a universal phenomenon of extreme importance: that of real people being overtaken—even swallowed—by the myths of their own (and others') making, so that they may end up living their own myth. This, I suggest, is what happened with the woman who was born as Friederike Wanner but died—and achieved immortality—quasi-anonymously, as 'The Seeress of Prevorst'.

By way of introduction, I would like to call attention to fragments from Friederike's personal diaries inserted by Kerner in the second part of his *Seherin* (SP 614–618). On December 26, 1827, she writes:

> I would so gladly share my experiences and the feelings of my soul with a friend each day, with a friend such as to whom I might even express the innermost of my silent thoughts, whose soul would be in harmony with mine, and who might give me comfort and rest in my suffering. Is it my own fault that I do not have such a friend? Am I too shy, or do I not put enough trust in the friends that I have? Ah! I do not find all that in myself, but my feeling always holds me back, because I find that they will never or only rarely know me, and readily

misinterpret all. But I am glad that I know *one*, who sees and knows me, whose possession I am and will remain, and that is you, Father in heaven!

The next day she speaks again about her feelings of utter spiritual loneliness, and her longing for a true soulmate [*Seelenfreund*] who knows her from within. Undoubtedly we may interpret her Solar circle as corroboration of this. Enclosed in her 'dream circle', the artificial magnetic *rapport* with Kerner and his wife seems to have been her closest approximation of a true human bond; other human beings were experienced mainly as harmful external intrusions. The profound need of this evidently very sensitive woman for a true spiritual mate runs through her life like a red thread. To understand how this need was to be frustrated is important for understanding how she developed the condition which made her a 'seeress'.

Prevorst: A Souabian Hamlet

Prevorst was a forestry hamlet of ca. 150 inhabitants, surrounded by woods, located in the middle of Souabia. This country, in the early 19th century, was in several respects a unique part of Germany. Since the first half of the 16th century it had been a Protestant/pietist island surrounded by Catholic lands. Traditions of folk magic, especially for healing purposes, were strong among the peasant population. Dependent in particular on the Paracelsian heritage, this folk healing was connected in various ways with more intellectual types of esoteric speculation hailing back to Renaissance hermeticism. Many of Friederike's medical prescriptions, including herbal cures and amulets, are based immediately upon this heritage.[11] Franz Anton Mesmer (1734-1815), the 'inventor' of animal magnetism, had been a product of this same cultural constellation. The Souabian population was known not only for its magical traditions but also for its unusual 'paranormal' sensitivity. Ghost stories and hauntings belonged to the stock-in-trade of Souabian folklore; and the phenomenon of somnambulic women was to prove particularly common here. Therefore Friederike Wanner was in many respects a typical product of her environment.

---

[11] Otto Ackermann, *Schwabentum und Romantik: Geistesgeschichtliche Untersuchungen über Justinus Kerner und Ludwig Uhland* (Breslau, 1939), pp. 99-101 (see especially his useful table of comparison between Friederike's prescriptions and traditional folk medicine).

Her father, Ernst Wanner (1772–1828), a former soldier, had been earning a tight living as a forester since 1800. He seems to have been of a fierce temperament, and ruled over his household in an authoritarian manner. His wife, Friederike Schmidgall (1778–?) came from a much better social background. She was the youngest of the two daughters of a very well-to-do merchant, Johann Georg Schmidgall (1743–1825) and his wife, born as Christine Gommel (1751–1822); Rudolf Lang describes both sisters as 'sensitive and very self-confident', and quite 'emancipated' for the period.[12] Friederike Schmidgall's marriage to Ernst Wanner, to whom she seems to have been superior both intellectually and in terms of social and financial background, can hardly have been without tensions.

Löwenstein and the Schmidgall Family

From her 5th until her 12th year, Friederike was raised not by her parents but by her grandparents Schmidgall in Löwenstein, close to Prevorst. The reasons for this are not entirely clear. Rudolf Lang suggests that in Löwenstein she could find better playmates and a better education. But financial motives probably played a part as well. Friederike's father did not make much money; but his in-laws were very well-to-do, even rich people, for whom it was no problem to have an extra mouth to feed. Friederike thus suddenly saw herself moved from a humble home in a small forestry village hamlet to an upper middle-class household in a larger town, where she seems to have enjoyed a privileged status as her grandparents' favourite grandchild.

Friederike's grandfather was a strong and unusual personality who, interestingly in view of his granddaughter, displayed pronounced 'paranormal' abilities; quite a lot is known about him, due to the existence of an extensive biography written in 1827 by his youngest son and rediscovered by Rudolf Lang in 1981.[13] It seems that his wife (Friederike's grandmother), a sensitive person who originally

---

[12] Rudolf Lang, *Neues zur Seherin von Prevorst* (Innsbruck, 1983), p. 21.

[13] Chr. Schmidgall, *Lebensbild von Johann Georg Schmidgall* (orig. ms 1827; 183 pp.); and a handwritten copy by Erika Burgdorf (185 pp.). See Rudolf Lang, "Der Löwensteiner Großvater der Seherin von Prevorst: Aus dem Leben des Johann Georg Schmidgall (1743–1825) nach einer 1981 wieder aufgefundenen Handschrift von Christian Schmidgall", in: *700 Jahre Stadt Löwenstein (1287–1987)*, ed. K.-H. Dähn (Weinsberg, 1987). For more details on Schmidgall, see the German version of this article (cf. note 1).

displayed a self-conscious and emancipated attitude unusual for this period and culture, eventually had to resign herself to the role of a subordinated housewife and mother; a position which she is said to have endured 'with Christian patience' while seeking comfort in her faith.

In this household, Friederike's religious education was dominated by a specifically Souabian type of Lutheran pietism, characterized by an interest in esoteric speculation, occult forces and pneumatology. The Schmidgalls possessed a personal library of pietist literature which contained numerous mystical and occult works. Some important names in this context are those of F.C. Oetinger, M. Hahn, J.C. Lavater, and especially J.H. Jung-Stilling—author of *Szenen aus dem Geisterreich* and *Theorie der Geister-Kunde*—who was the favourite author of Friederike's grandmother. Apologists of the Seeress of Prevorst have always claimed that Friederike was a simple, uneducated girl who had read no books other than the bible and the Lutheran hymnbook.[14] There can be no doubt, however, that the close contacts with both her grandparents—they even slept in the same room—had equipped Friederike with a solid 'working knowledge' of mystical and occult speculation, and that exposure to the thinking of Jung-Stilling had predisposed her for visions of spirits. One is not surprised to learn that her first vision of a ghost—a huge, black figure with smouldering eyes—occurred in the home of her grandparents (SP 51).

One reads that grandfather Schmidgall used to take walks with his granddaughter, and we can only guess as to the subjects of their conversation. Although commentators have usually painted an idyllic picture of "the worthy grandfather" [*der würdige Großvater*] Schmidgall wandering around with his beloved grandchild, it is difficult to say how close the two really were. We might, however, perceive the beginning of a pattern that would continue throughout Friederike's

---

[14] SP 76–77: "Mrs. H. had no artificial *Bildung* or training. She had only what Nature had given her. She had learned no strange language, nor anything about history, geography, physics, or those other sciences in which institutes are nowadays training the female sex [*in dem man das weibliche Geschlecht jetzt in Instituten dressiert*] had reached her. Bible and hymnbook had remained her only lecture, especially in the long years of her suffering" (N.B. note that Kerner, characteristically, is highly suggestive but stops short of lying: he must have realized that Friederike had read other lecture *before* her illness). The argument was regularly repeated ever since, for example in *Blätter aus Prevorst*; but possibly the most uncritical apologists among later commentators are Erich Sopp & Karl Spiesberger, *Auf den Spuren der Seherin* (Sersheim, 1953): see esp. pp. 17, 60, 73, 79–80.

life. Her closest personal relationships were invariably with much older men holding a position of unquestionable authority.

An Unsolved Enigma

Now, somewhere during her period in Löwenstein, i.e. between her 5th and her 12th year, something happened to Friederike which must have been of the greatest importance to her later development, but about which the sources remain frustratingly elusive. The first edition of Kerner's *Seherin* contains this mysterious passage, which no longer appears in later editions:

> In this same period [i.e. her years in Löwenstein] something happens in the life of this girl which undoubtedly made the profoundest impression on the whole rest of her life; something which explains so much that would later seem unexplainable, and which would serve to clear away many misunderstandings and silly rumours about her as a woman, but over which a veil must be cast.[15]

Ernst Albert Zeller seems to have known—or at least to have been convinced that he could infer—what stands behind these cryptic allusions, and he makes every impression of finding it hard not to give away the secret. His suggestive formulations tip the veil, but do not lift it:

> In this same period something happens in the life of this unfortunate one, which had to alienate her from all earthly reality all the more strongly, the more pure and tender was her sense and her heart, and the more innocent she appears of what occurred. Her whole sensitive being was bound to be shattered inside, because the core of all true female life—the body and shame—[*der Kern alles ächten weiblichen Lebens, die Leibe und die Scham*] was eaten away by an evil worm, which the more surely gnawed all her earthly happiness, the purer and more ardently she could have loved.[16]

Zeller adds that "her earthly happiness had been poisoned for ever", for "there are pains which, in this life, can never again be forgotten".[17] Friederike "had violently been teared out of her playful,

---

[15] SP (1st ed. 1829), 30 (quoted according to Lee B. Jennings, "Geister und Germanisten: Literarisch-parapsychologische Betrachtungen zum Fall Kerner-Mörike", *Psi Und Psyche: Neue Forschungen zur Parapsychologie. Festschrift für Hans Bender*, ed. Eberhard Bauer (Stuttgart, 1974), p. 108 nt 10).

[16] Ernst Albert Zeller, *Das verschleierte Bild zu Sais, oder die Wunder des Magnetismus [etc.]* (Leipzig, 1830), p. 90.

[17] Zeller, *Verschleierte Bild*, pp. 90 & 92.

happy childhood; she henceforth faced the world as an unhappy young woman [*Jungfrau*][18] in desolate independence and inaccessibility [*in trostloser Selbständigkeit und Verschlossenheit*]".[19] She would never be able to forget "this terrible moment", although the memory would be softened by the passing of time, "which closes the wounds of limbs and of the heart [*die Wunden der Glieder und des Gemüthes*]".[20]

What, for heaven's sake, is Zeller trying both to tell and to hide from us? A contemporary psychiatrist, Friedrich Bird, seems to have been convinced that Friederike had been practicing masturbation.[21] Even taking into account time and context, this really seems too tame to account for Zeller's rhetoric; more importantly, public knowledge of that secret would hardly have put an end to the "silly rumours about her as a woman" (Kerner). Jennings sums up the main points that stand out in Kerner's and Zeller's words: whatever had happened, it "had nothing to do with love, but . . . heavily disturbed [Friederike's] capacity for normal love, and . . . was suffered innocently and passively";[22] he infers that probably another person was involved. The most likely explanation is that Friederike was the victim of sexual abuse, and that the experience was suffiently traumatic to make it possible for a psychiatrist such as Zeller to perceive in this the germ of her subsequent illness. Jennings suggests that the abuse may well have been of an incestuous nature.[23] This

---

[18] The word *Jungfrau* would usually be translated as 'virgin'. Jennings ("Geister und Germanisten", p. 108 nt 10), who (correctly, in my opinion) assumes that what had happened must have been of a sexual nature, concludes that the choice of word might therefore be interpreted as an indication that Friederike's virginity had not been affected—unless, he adds, we are here confronted with a semantic problem. Given the context of the passage, I consider it unlikely that Zeller put in this word as an intentional hint; taking into account that the english word 'virgin' does not have the ambiguity of the German *Jungfrau*, to use that word in the translation would imply a far more definite answer to the problem of what happened than can be supported by the evidence.

[19] Zeller, *Verschleierte Bild*, p. 91.

[20] Zeller, *Verschleierte Bild*, p. 91. Again the translation poses problems which are enhanced by the difficulties of interpretation. Does Zeller actually mean to suggest that Friederike was physically wounded? To translate 'Gemüth' as 'heart' is an extremely inadequate solution, chosen only because the alternative 'mind' is even more dubious.

[21] *Mesmerismus und Belletristik in ihren schädlichen Einflüssen auf die Psychiatrie* (Stuttgart, 1839), p. 4; as quoted in Jennings, "Geister und Germanisten", p. 108 nt 10.

[22] Jennings, "Geister und Germanisten", p. 108 nt 10. Jennings adds that what happened had left her purity (i.e., her virginity) intact; this hinges upon the interpretation of the word *Jungfrau*, about which cf. note 18.

[23] Jennings, "Geister und Germanisten", p. 108 nt 10.

would indeed account even better for the motif of abused trust which sounds strongly in Zeller's words. As for the person responsible, we can only speculate. The most obvious candidates are grandfather Schmidgall himself or, perhaps more likely, one of his sons—Friederike's uncles—, about whose personalities the sources tell us little. We saw that one of them, Christian, wrote his father's biography. Prior to Friederike's move to Weinsberg, another uncle (Friedrich) corresponded about her condition with Kerner. In one letter, he called the patient 'spoiled' [*verwöhnt*], and writes that 'by her exaggerated demands she creates an unusual lot of difficulty, misery and trouble for the whole household'.[24] Whatever may have happened to Friederike in Löwenstein was by then lying years back in the past, but we may reasonably accept Zellers suggestion that it indeed spoiled her life and lay at the basis of her illness.

Love and Death

In 1813, Friederike returned to her parents's home in Prevorst. Whether or not this might have something to do with what had happened in Löwenstein is unknown. Officially, she had to return because long illnesses of her parents made her assistance in the household necessary (SP 51). About the nature of the illnesses we are unfortunately kept in the dark. They must have been serious, for Kerner suggests that, during several years, 'worries and nightwakes at sickbeds' kept her inner life in a state of continuous tension. It is important to note that the return to Prevorst did not mean that Friederike's exposure to pietism and the occult had to come to an end: we know that the minister responsible for Prevorst at that time, Johann Friedrich Faber (1765–1820), was an adherent of the influential pietist theosopher F.C. Oetinger.[25]

In 1818—Friederike was about 17 years old—, the family moved to Oberstenfeld. Here, she became friends with the Lutheran minister T., about Kerner tells us only that he was 'very honourable... a very image of integrity', a little over sixty years old, and that he

---

[24] Letter of 16.11.1826, in Schiller-Nationalmuseum, Marbach a.N., quoted according to Lee B. Jennings, "Probleme um Kerners 'Seherin von Prevorst'", *Antaios* 10 (1968/69), p. 134.

[25] Reinhard Breymayer, "Vom Weinsberger Dekan Friedrich Christoph Oetinger zu Justinus Kerner: Theosophische Traditionen", *Justinus Kerner: Jubiläumsband zum 200 Geburtstag* (Weinsberg, 1990), p. 296.

had great influence on Friederike through his sermons, teachings and personal contact (SP 52). This Johann Jakob Tritschler (1757–1821) was described by his superiors in highly positive terms, as a man whose sermons were edifying and well-suited for his audience (they were *populär erbaulich*), but who also possessed 'much learned knowledge' and whose bible interpretation was in the line of the symbolic theology of the Württemberg churches.[26] Indeed he appears to have been an adherent of the type of theosophical pietism so prominent in Souabian Lutheranism.[27] The evidence leaves it in no doubt that Tritschler became highly important to Friederike, as the only person by whom she felt spiritually understood. It has been speculated—quite plausibly given his role in Friederike's later visions and in the dream of February 13, 1822—that this older man became the secret 'wish-partner' of her phantasies.[28]

This *Seelenfreund*—arguably the only one she ever had—died immediately before her official engagement with the succesful businessman Gottlieb Hauffe (1789–?), 12 years her senior, son of a minister, and a distant relative of the family. Rudolf Lang describes him as a practical man of the world with an instinct for making money. This is how Kerner describes Friederike's reaction:

> In her nineteenth year an engagement took place, following the wish of her parents and relatives, between her and Mr. H., who belongs to her uncle's family—an engagement which, considering the integrity of the man and the perspective of a secure existence, she had to wish.
>
> Whether it was because she forefelt the coming years of suffering through illness, or because of other feelings, which she kept hidden inside (only this is certain, that it was not because of feelings for somebody else)—in this same period she sank in a depression which was unexplainable to her relatives; for days on end she was crying under the roof of her parent's house, where she had hidden away; she did not sleep for five whole weeks, and thus suddenly re-evoked the dominant emotional life of her childhood (SP 52).

Kerner seems determined not to understand the reason for Friederike's depression, and a similar lack of understanding is occasionally evi-

---

[26] Lang, *Neues zur Seherin*, pp. 25–26.
[27] For detailed evidence, see Breymayer, "Vom Weinsberger Dekan...", pp. 295–296.
[28] Helmut Siefert, "Die Seherin von Prevorst: Tiefenpsychologische Aspekte", *Justinus Kerner: Jubiläumsband*, p. 424; cf. Lang, *Neues zur Seherin*, p. 29; id., "Die Seherin von Prevorst (1801–1829): Ihr Leben und ihre Verbindung zur Stadt Löwenstein", *700 Jahre Stadt Löwenstein*, ed. Dähn, p. 237.

dent in contemporary interpretations. Rudolf Lang, too, wonders what was wrong with her: why could she not love a man "who [brought] her in an elegant coach to his house, equipped with expensive furniture, at the marketplace of Kürnbach, and who was regarded as the richest man in town?"[29] However, it is clear that Friederike was hardly the kind of girl who would jump at a marriage because it promised wordly luxury, social status and financial security. She took her religion more seriously than most, and would not settle for a compromise between worldly comfort and the promise of heaven. She was looking for a true *Seelenfreund*, to whom she could be connected with body and soul, not merely for a 'good party'. Friederike must have felt the expectations of social life closing in on her: she was going to play the role of a good, subordinated housewife and mother, and to renounce a life of the spirit. It may be noted in passing that this kind of dilemma might impose itself on women of the time and period more strongly than on men, who might always pursue a career as a minister. Had Friederike been Catholic, she would probably have become a nun. The impossibility for women in a Lutheran country of leading a socially recognized spiritual life may be one of the factors that could help explain the prominence of religious somnambulism in a country such as Souabia. Rudolf Lang also expresses some surprise that Friederike did not fight the proposed marriage more strongly, if she really had such a deep aversion against Gottlieb Hauffe.[30] This seems to me to miss the point. I see no indication that she particularly disliked Gottlieb as a person; there are even some indications to the contrary.[31] The point was that she did not want to marry at all, except 'in the spirit'. But she also knew that a marriage would be inevitable sooner or later. Under these circumstances, Gottlieb Hauffe was probably not the worst of alternatives.

Then came June 5, 1821: the day which must be regarded as the decisive turning-point in Friederike's life. Already well in advance, this date must have fixed itself in her mind as the day on which

---

[29] Lang, *Neues zur Seherin*, p. 27.
[30] Lang, "Seherin von Prevorst", p. 238. My impression, however, is that Friederike protested quite strongly, but she simply may not have been strong enough to stand up to her relatives. The minister of Löwenstein later confirmed that Friederike consented in the marriage only with great reluctance (ms letter to Kerner, 26.4.1839, as summarized in Jennings, "Probleme", p. 138 nt 10).
[31] See her private diary, january 6–8 (SP 617).

she would have to enter a normal social existence 'in the world' and renounce her longing for a 'higher' calling. She can hardly have expected, however, that this would also turn out to be the day on which her soulmate, Tritschler, would be buried. The extraordinary coincidence must have impressed itself on Friederike's mind as providential, and it evidently created an unprecedented emotional turmoil. On the most basic level, she now not merely had to enter a marriage she did not want, but had lost her only spiritual recourse at the same time. On the other hand, she could tell herself that this friend had not truly left her but had become her partner in heaven; and that he was taken away from her at this precise moment could not but carry a deeper message that touched upon her own spiritual destiny. In short: God had chosen the very day when Friederike would formally renounce a life of the spirit, to give her a sign that her prayers would be answered in a miraculous and unexpected way. This message of unhoped-for salvation was characteristically mixed of admonition and grace: Friederike should stop wallowing in self-pity and put her trust in the Lord, who would better know how to take care of her destiny than she could do herself. Again and again in Friederike's later life we encounter the motif of inner loneliness in immediate conjunction with that of *Gelassenheit* [abandonment to God], characteristic of Christian theosophy and pietism. Against this background, the burial ceremony must have functioned for Friederike as a sort of initiation. Kerner describes the experience which accompanied her visit to the grave:

> On the day of his burial she went together with others to the cemetary, to accompany the dear corpse. Although her heart had been so heavy before, all at once she felt quite light and clear on this grave. Suddenly a special life was born inside of her; she became wholly quiet, but could be hardly separated from this grave. Finally she left, and no more tears were coming; she was cheerful but also, from this moment on, indifferent about whatever went on in the world; and this was the beginning of the time, not yet of her illness, but of her actual inner life (SP 52–53).

She seems to have seen Tritschler's spirit hovering over the grave. Later, in her somnambulic state, she wrote a poem which suggests what the experience meant to her (SP 53)

> Was mir einst dunkel war,
> Das seh ich jetzt mit Augen klar.
> Es war in jenen Stunden,

> Als ich mich ehlich hab verbunden,
> Da stund ich ganz in dich versenkt,
> Du Engelsbild auf deinem Grabeshügel.
> Gern hätt' ich mit dir tauschen mögen,
> Gern dir mein irdisch Glück geschenkt,
> Das sie mir priesen als des Himmels Segen.
> Ich aber bat auf deinem Grabe
> Gott um die einz'ge Gabe:
> Daß dieses Engels Flügel
> Mich möcht fortan
> Auf heißer Lebensbahn
> Mit Himmelsruh umwehn.—
> Da stehst du Engel nun, erhöret ist mein Flehn.[32]

Indeed, Friederike's signs of depression seem to have ended abruptly. Interestingly, Rudolf Lang has suggested that her whole pattern of reaction may have been directly modeled on what she could have read in the books of her grandmother's favourite pietist writer. Jung-Stilling, too, describes in his memorials how, after much suffering, he turned inward and felt how "a complete change of his condition" took place, in which "his whole depression and all his pain" had vanished. He later described his new attitude to life in words that are strikingly similar to what we read of Friederike: "The whole world became alien to him ... all ... left him fully indifferent"; and the same was written about his daughter, who "cut off [from the world], ... had her whole being in a higher sphere only".[33] There can be little doubt that, after Tritschler's death, this became Friederike's ideal of a true christian life.

Marriage and Illness

Friederike married Gottlieb Hauffe on August 27, 1821, and moved with him to Kürnbach. This new environment enhanced her feelings

---

[32] SP 53. Transl.: "What once was dark to me, / I can see clearly now. / It happened in those hours, / when I was bound in marriage, / There I stood, entirely lost in you, / you angel-image on your gravetomb. / Gladly I would have taken your place, / Gladly I would have given you my earthly happiness, / that they would praise me as the grace from heaven. / But I prayed on this grave / to God, for only this: / that this angel's wings / would henceforth / during the fiery path of life / surround me with the peace of heaven.—/ Now there you stand, angel, and answered are my prayers".

[33] Lang, "Seherin von Prevorst", nt 29. Quotations from: Johann Heinrich Jung (genannt Stilling), *Lebensgeschichte oder dessen Jugend, Jünglingsjahre, häusliches Leben und Alter: Eine wahrhafte Geschichte von ihm selbst erzählt* [2 vols.] (Berlin, n.d.).

of loneliness and isolation, since it seems she was not accepted by the native inhabitants. She nevertheless seems to have managed for about half a year, until the dream on February 13, 1822, when she saw Tritschler's corpse taking her husband's place in her bed. The conviction during her dream that no doctor but only this corpse could heal her is remarkable, as Kerner notes, because at this moment she was not yet ill.

With respect to the first period of Friederike's illness, Kerner later complained about all sorts of unqualified people who had been trying a hand at curing her, by magnetic and other means. Later commentators seem to have ignored the remarkable and dubious role that was played by a peasant woman from the neighborhood (Kürnbach) (SP 57, 59). This woman came to her uninvited, sat down, told her not to waste her time consulting regular physicians, and proceeded to lay her hand on her forehead. Judging from Kerner's text, this resulted in what actually appears to have been the *very first* beginning of her magnetic state—and it seemed to do her more harm than good. Friederike immediately "got into a cramp of the most terrible kind, and her forehead became as if dead and cold. The whole night through she cried as if out of her senses; that woman had had a demonic influence on her, and as soon as she returned, the most terrible cramps occurred" (SP 57).

Indeed, one can only be puzzled about the situation around Friederike's sickbed, where strangers might apparently walk in uninvited, even if they clearly did more harm than good.[34] In general, the attitude of her relatives strikes one as careless, sometimes incredibly so. Kerner later described his patient as "a fully innocent victim of... fools. For several weeks they wanted to drive the devil out of her and did not give her any food but merely sang and prayed the louder, the more she wasted away. Similar follies were committed even by doctors...".[35]

Finally, she was moved to Weinsberg. Her remarkable abilities

---

[34] The same woman returned later, and had an equally negative influence on Friederike's child, who eventually died (in August) "during convulsions of the most terrible kind" (SP 59). All this would have been more than enough reason for a witch-lynching in earlier periods. To this may be added the strange episode with a "black magician", on which see the long German version of the present article (see nt 1).

[35] Letter to Julie Hartmann, 29.11.1826, as quoted in Jennings, "Probleme", p. 135.

notwithstanding, the woman who arrived at Kerner's house in November 1826 was still not a 'seeress', but merely a very sick patient who had already been given up by her relatives. The process of 'beatification', by which Friederike Hauffe was to be transformed into 'The Seeress of Prevorst' would take place in Weinsberg under the decisive influence of Justinus Kerner. Nevertheless, one might say that, already long before, she had entered a circle, and fallen under a spell, out of which she would no more be able to escape for the remainder of her life. This circle was woven in a complicated pattern, fabricated from various strands of her native culture, and it had begun to be spun from the moment of her birth. It would have had far less power over her if Friederike had been less sensitive by nature, if her urge for a deep spiritual fellowship had been less profound, and if she had been more fortunate in her personal life. As it was, however, the course of her life left her increasingly helpless to withstand the power of myth closing in on her.

The Man

It was not Justinus Kerner who produced the myth of 'The Seeress of Prevorst', although he was responsible for writing down the story. It would be more accurate to say that he and 'his' Seeress are themselves products of myth, or, alternatively, instruments through which an intricate mythical complex produced one of its specific (but characteristic) manifestations. There is nothing special or remarkable about this process, which is just the way in which all human culture normally expresses itself, in our own days as surely as it did in the past. Truly original innovations are very rare, and even these never appear in a cultural vacuum. The myth of the Poet/Physician and the Seeress certainly cannot claim such originality: it is made of the common stuff of their cultural environment, although moulded in a unique shape. In Kerner's perception and presentation of the Seeress we perceive, as if reflected in a mirror, a highly complex cultural constellation which may be strange to us in many respects but was simply 'reality' for them. Our own attempts, as present-day interpreters, to approach the myth historically (i.e., by attempting to 'add' what they left out) has its own in-built limitations, due to the myths on which our own culture is based. Therefore we cannot claim that such a procedure brings us closer to *the* truth; all we can hope for is that it contributes to a somewhat better understanding of those aspects which *we* wish to grasp. Undoubtedly we leave out, often without knowing that we do so, whole parts of the original tissue.

Keeping this in mind, we may observe how Friederike almost literally fell into a net, which Kerner had woven for himself from the stuff of his own culture. This net stood ready to catch her, so to speak, the moment she arrived in Weinsberg. Kerner himself almost certainly did not realize that his new patient was all he could ever have hoped for: a God-given answer to questions and doubts which had obsessed him since his youth.

Friederike's Reception in Weinsberg

We already saw in how miserable a state Friederike was when she arrived. To understand Kerner's initial reaction it is useful to realize that a few years earlier, after his publication of his *Geschichte zweyer Somnambulen* [History of Two Somnambules], Kerner's regular correspondent Therese Huber had sharply critized Kerner's 'soft' empathic attitude towards such 'transparent, talkative' ladies.[36] It seems that Kerner took Huber's reprimand seriously, for he precisely copied her advice when Friederike arrived. Kerner's description of his initial stern attitude is complemented by a letter written to Julie Hartmann on November 20, 1826,[37] which suggests that he was anything but happy to see her and treated her even more severely than one would conclude from his later book:

> I was interrupted here in a most irritating manner, by a maid who called me to a somnambule and cramp-sufferer, who was actually deposited right at my gate ... so that I might cure her. This is a young woman who, all in all, has been living in this misery for 6 years already. By a wrong treatment—i.e., by the fact that they magnetized her endlessly and increased her clairvoyant condition for years—she was ruined to such an extent that she is an outrage now. With this case I now have to play around [*mich herumbalgen*]. And that did happen when, during the very first hour of her presence here, I took off

---

[36] Therese Huber to J.K., February 6, 1824, *Justinus Kerners Briefwechsel mit seinen Freunden*, I, ed. Theobald Kerner (Stuttgart & Leipzig, 1897), pp. 546–548. Cf. Heinz Büttiker, *Justinus Kerner: Ein Beitrag zur Geschichte der Spätromantik* (Zürich, 1952), pp. 181–182.

[37] According to SP 70, Friederike arrived on the 25th. There must be some mistake in the chronology.

her guest-cap and threatened her with punishment and the madhouse, if she would not stop with her crying and her cramps. She is so ruined that her family eagerly expects her death. I will not give her this, but I will, even if this [i.e. death. W.H.] comes of it, bring her out of her belly-enchantment by restoring the life of her brain. However, it will already be too late for that—but she just was not deposited before my house earlier. It is Mrs. Haufe [sic] from Kirnbach [sic], a daughter of the forester Wanner of Oberstenfeld. It is really a dreadful business!![38]

The somewhat callous tone of this letter[39] may have been a defense mechanism rather than a correct reflection of how Kerner used to approach his patients. He is generally regarded as having been an unusually devoted doctor who was often deprived of his night's sleep by worries about his patients, and who was a pioneer in recognizing the therapeutic importance of human empathy. Indeed, Kerner's attitude had already changed a few days later. He no longer blamed Friederike for her condition, but had now come to see her as a fully innocent victim. This may have been partly because he had learned in the meantime about the mysterious *Ereignis* of her youth; this, at least, seems the most plausible explanation for the following passage in a letter to Julie Hartmann: "One has to be very sorry for this woman, for she is a victim, a fully innocent one, of an awful magnetic treatment by fools; and if I could tell you yet another thing about her condition—you would cry".[40] Kerner was evidently moved by pity:

> This woman will soon be at the end of her life. She is only 25 years old and has already been martyred by magnetism for six years. She is now completely consumed, lamed, and has cramps which are *infernal*.... Initially I wanted to bring her out of this condition by great severity, but now that I see that she is of the best will... although I do not stop, to be sure, to approach her seriously and severely, I can no longer be threatening and rude, especially since healing is no longer to be expected in any way.[41]

---

[38] Kerner, letter 20.11.1826 to Julie Hartmann, as quoted in Jennings, "Probleme", p. 134 (from the original in Schiller-Nationalmuseum, Marbach a.N.; not included in the published correspondence).
[39] Cf. also a much later letter from the minister Hegler in Löwenstein, quoted in Jennings, "Probleme", p. 138 nt 10.
[40] Kerner to Julie Hartmann, 29.11.1996, as quoted in Jennings, "Probleme", p. 135.
[41] Letter to Julie Hartmann, 29.11.1996, in: Jennings, "Probleme", p. 135.

Although there is a frustrating contradiction in the official chronology of these first days (see note 38), it seems evident that Kerner very quickly came to change his mind about Friederike's hopes for recovery. The contents of a letter to the lawyer Tafel, written in these same days but without an exact date, suggest that it must reflect Kerner's thoughts in a very early phase of his acquaintance with Friederike. I consider this unpublished letter, fortunately made available in an article by Lee B. Jennings, as of the utmost importance for understanding the 'beatification' of Friederike Hauffe. Tafel seems to have been eager to make use of Friederike as an medium for making contact with the spirit world. Kerner's reply reveals a profound dilemma that existed between his responsibility as a physician, on the one hand, and his spiritual perspective, on the other. It demonstrates how the latter perspective could take over, once Kerner had convinced himself that Friederike could not be cured. This is what he writes:

> Most honoured friend! Your thoughts are very beautiful and if, God willing!, I were not a *physician*—I would follow them. But unfortunately, medical experience shows—and this already since five years in the history of the girl Hauffe—that one has to avoid as much as possible all difficult questions put to her while she sleeps [i.e., while she is in trance. W.H.], since these only increase this somnambulic unnatural state. In this way she would never come out of this state, which just happens not to be the beneficial one for this life. Up to now, my guideline was—and its success proved this to be good—to let her speak in her sleep whatever she wanted, and to lead her back to a lower level only in case she visibly lost herself too much. I have to heal her body, I have to *lead her downwards* to *normal* humanity. I have to do this, difficult though I find it—I must end her somnambulic state as soon as possible, and you will agree yourself—by such speculations it would be prolonged. My job is pathetic [*Mein Geschäft ist erbärmlich*]— but I must fulfil it—to make sure that she can soon devour a calf's leg and dip a liver sausage in her coffee [*daß sie bald einen Kalbsschlegel fressen und eine Leberwurst in den Kaffee tauchen kann*], I must gather the shit around her body so that she may return to the *life of our State*, darn her husband's socks and wipe her child's behind; *after death she can live with the spirits.*[42]

These sentences are utterly revealing. Soon afterwards, Kerner would come to the conclusion that Friederike had no chance of recovery and would never have to return to the stupid and mind-numbing existence society required of her. The spirit world had already become

---

[42] Letter to the lawyer Tafel, n.d., as quoted in: Jennings, "Probleme", p. 135.

her natural environment, and it was just her body which still kept a tenuous connection with the brutal realities of this world. All the arguments which Kerner had given to Tafel therefore lost their force, and he no longer needed to have scruples in following his deeper wish: to seize the opportunity and learn as much as he could about the spirit world.

"Weib zu sein ist Eigentlich Krankheit": Kerner on Women and Nature

Justinus Kerner's personal and intellectual development is not the subject of this article. I will concentrate only on some aspects which I believe to be especially important with respect to his treatment of Friederike Hauffe. In 1808, while Justinus was studying medicine in Tübingen, two books appeared which were to play a central role in his later thinking: Schubert's *Ansichten von der Nachtseite der Naturwissenschaft* and Jung-Stilling's *Theorie der Geister-Kunde*. Kerner had been fascinated by spirits and ghosts of the dead from an early age, and his interest was anything but detached. His friend, the poet Karl August Varnhagen, writes in his diary how he and Kerner were scared out of their wits by reading Jung-Stilling together one evening. In the end, Kerner no longer dared to cross the dark passageway back to his own room, while Varnhagen for his part begged him not to be left alone.[43] In spite of this reaction, it would be a mistake to imagine Jung-Stilling's book as a collection of horror stories. It is in fact a serious attempt, from a pronounced christian pietist perspective, to distinguish between truth and fiction with respect to ghosts, and especially to give advice about how to react to experiences with them. Jung-Stilling's general line is to warn against actively seeking commerce with spirits, out of mere curiosity. Ghosts are deluded in their belief that they need human assistance in order to find rest; if one is plagued by their visits, one should react compassionately, but firmly refer them to Jesus Christ as their sole saviour. Jung-Stilling seeks to demonstrate his argument by giving numerous examples of ghost stories, and one suspects that Varnhagen and Kerner concentrated on these stories while perhaps skipping over the theoretical parts.

---

[43] Karl August Varnhagen von Ense, *Denkwürdigkeiten und vermischte Schriften*, III (Mannheim, 1838), pp. 107 & 110, as quoted in: Heinrich Straumann, *Justinus Kerner und der Okkultismus in der Deutschen Romantik* (Horgen-Zürich/Leipzig, 1928), p. 76.

Friederike Hauffe seems to have absorbed the basic message of her grandmother's favourite writer much more faithfully than Kerner. She was neither afraid of ghosts nor fascinated by them, but merely attempted to help them find their way back to their saviour. Kerner's attitude, in contrast, was a mixture of fear and fascination with the occult; and we will see that his curiosity would actually bring him into conflict with Friederike. Kerner's mature thinking is undoubtedly influenced by Jung-Stilling in many respects,[44] but this dependence does not necessarily imply that Kerner liked or appreciated his basic message. Some years after the evening with Varnhagen, Kerner read *Theorie der Geister-Kunde* again, apparently including the theoretical chapters. He wrote to his friend Uhland: "At the moment I am reading Jung's theory of ghosts. Terrible stupidity mixed with many misunderstood truths".[45] In spite of the pious tones (undoubtedly sincere, as far as they go) in which Kerner later defended the Seeress, there yawns a gulf between Jung-Stilling's pastoral-theological motivation (which is ultimately Friederike Hauffe's motivation as well), on the one hand, and Kerner's primary interest in an empirical 'study of the occult', on the other.[46]

Friederike Hauffe provided Kerner with an ideal opportunity for such a study. The letter to Tafel, quoted above, already indicates a conflict between Kerner the physician and Kerner the investigator of the occult; and behind this conflict lies his profoundly ambivalent attitude towards the phenomenon of illness. In this connection we must look at another crucial letter, written to his friend Uhland on November 26, 1812. Uhland had criticized Kerner's morbid views of death, as expressed in his recent novel *Die Heimatlosen* [The Homeless]. This is the defense of the man who was at that moment a practicing physician in Welzheim:

> Death I call the profoundest union with the Spirit of Nature; illness is striving for that union. Death is the highest glorification attained by

---

[44] As convincingly demonstrated by Sukeyoshi Shimbo, "Kerners Parapsychologie im Lichte der Jung-Stillingschen 'Geisterkunde'", *Justinus Kerner: Jubiläumsband*, pp. 311–320.

[45] Unpublished part of letter to Uhland, 20.9.1811 (ms in Schiller-Nationalmuseum, Marbach a.N.), quoted according to Jennings, "Geister und Germanisten", pp. 107–108 nt 9. This passage does not have to mean that Jung-Stilling's influence on Kerner's thinking has been overestimated, as concluded by Jennings; I would argue, rather, that Kerner accepted only the 'misunderstood truths' while rejecting the 'terrible stupidity'.

[46] Cf. Shimbo, "Kerners Parapsychologie", p. 319.

man in his life. Magnetic sleep, epilepsy . . ., catalepsy, ecstasy, madness (Pythia on the tripod), feeling for metals (siderism), organic destruction in single parts of the body, old scars which predict changes in the atmosphere: all these are conditions through which man comes closer to, and on more friendly terms with the Spirit of Nature, a universal life, the life of the spirits and the stars. Magnetic sleep is like death: a momentary withdrawal of the spirit from the body, an approach towards the spirit world or Nature, however one wants to call it. . . . However, this union, this inner commerce with Nature, this withdrawal, can never occur as long as the body is a bastion, which is dominant, is *healthy*: a bounded mass existing in and for itself. It requires disintegration, in order for the autonomous frozen mass of ice to flow towards the sea as blue and soft flood from the mother's breast, and to predict storm and to follow the movements of the moon, may this disintegration now be called illness, disruption, death etc. . . .

In the profoundest commerce with Nature, one may be brought to feel minerals and water in the depths, look into the future, see spirits etc., in short: to gain knowledge of everything which is concealed from the spirit by the merely autonomous, hard, bounded bastion of the body (by health, the condition which is so fully fit and proper for earthly life).

Woman (to be woman is really illness)[*Weib zu sein ist eigentlich Krankheit*] is already in a closer union with Nature than man, is therefore susceptible to more illnesses, and moves faster towards the complete union with Nature—death—: she dies mostly younger than man. Even while still in the bastion of the body, she is in closer union with the stars, with the moon, and has a stronger talent for premonition [*Ahnungsvermögen*] than man. Pythia, the sybills, the witches.

Before the heavy caterpillar floats up into space as lightly as a spirit, she falls ill, peels, and falls into a magnetic sleep. In this she already feels growing on her the wings that will carry her over flowers; she has premonitions of the next life, breaks through the envelope and floats towards it. (I cannot resist the temptation to add something more. It is striking how this creature, prior to its transfiguration, changes fully into dirt. In the still incomplete pupa there actually lies merely a decayed, melted matter, the caterpillar, from which the spiritual sylph slowly moulds itself).[47]

The image of the caterpillar and the butterfly recurs throughout Kerner's writings as his favourite metaphor for explaining the movement from life via death to afterlife.[48] There can be little doubt that

---

[47] Letter to Ludwig Uhland, 26.11.1812, *Justinus Kerners Briefwechsel*, I, pp. 340–342.
[48] See especially how Kerner applies it to Friederike Hauffe, in the Introduction to his (SP 47–48): "But, my dear reader, given the conditions which happen to prevail in our public life (this mean life!), a human being in this condition [i.e., a

Kerner's speculations about illness have much to with a personal need to make sense of the suffering with which his medical practice confronted him daily. The quoted passage from the letter to Hufeland would require an extensive commentary with reference to similar speculations in the sphere of Romantic *Naturphilosophie*; I will have to restrict myself to the essential. Kerner's initial stern attitude towards Friederike was explained by him as an attempt "to make the brain suppress the dominating activity of her belly system". This reflected an opposition which was common in contemporary medical theory, enhanced further by the concept of 'polarity' which is fundamental to German *Naturphilosophie*.[49] This opposition commonly led to series of associations roughly along the following lines:

belly-system	brain-system
female	male
matter	spirit
nature	transcendence
realm of gravity	principle of Light
[*Reich der Schwere*]	[*das Lichtwesen*]
sleeping state	waking state

Such oppositions could easily be interpreted as legitimating the superiority of man over woman, as demonstrated in extreme fashion by Lorenz Oken's presentation of woman as the 'primal animal' [*das Urtier*].[50] It is important to recognize that Kerner's perspective, summarized in the lapidary statement '*Weib zu sein ist eigentlich Krankheit*' (*supra*), stands in this same tradition but is not intended to carry the misogynic connotations that might seem so evident at first sight. One

---

magnetic one. W.H.] easily becomes a pupa to which falls the unlucky fate of having to unfold into a butterfly among a crowd of schoolboys. Behold, dear reader, one of them blows on it, another hits it, yet another pierces it with a needle; and, interrupted in its unfolding, it slowly dies while still half a pupa. And that, my dear reader, is also the image of an unhappy magnetic life, the phenomena of which are the major subject of these pages".

[49] An adequate discussion is given by Straumann, *Justinus Kerner und der Okkultismus*, pp. 30–37.

[50] Lorenz Oken, as quoted in Ricarda Huch, *Die Romantik: Blütezeit, Ausbreitung und Verfall* (Tübingen, 1951), p. 437: "The primal animal is woman [*Das Urtier ist das Weib*]. Man is a higher development of woman... Man stands a whole animal class higher than woman. Slug, fish, water-animal is woman; bird, mammal is man. Man relates to woman as light to water... Woman, as incomplete [*das Unvollendete*], cannot stop reproducing. It wants to become man and to this end it produces eggs. Pregnancy is the female drive to change itself into male...".

might even argue that Kerner's change of attitude during the first days after Friederike's arrival in Weinsberg reflected his move from a traditional misogynic perspective to one in which woman's abilities are considered superior to man's. The letter to Uhland directly reflects the influence of Schubert's *Ansichten von der Nachtseite der Naturwissenschaft*, which he had read the summer before.[51] Schubert's third chapter contains the same Romantic philosophy of illness, death and transfiguration, culminating in the statement that "... precisely the highest striving in us ... leads us to the grave; so that we might be reborn from it towards ever higher striving, ever higher longing".[52] By such transfiguration one may regain—but on a higher level—the original state of grace when humanity was still in a 'magical' *rapport* with Nature. What, however, is meant by this recurring but evasive word 'Nature'? Straumann has called attention to its strange ambivalence in Kerner's thinking. Kerner tends to use 'spirit world', 'spirit of Nature', and 'Nature' itself as synonyms:

> Nature, for him, is ... not simply the whole world of sense experience but the Whole as such, including all spiritual being; or rather, it seems that, for him, Nature means precisely *not* the world of sense experience, but its hidden spiritual forces. For it is out of an intimate commerce with 'Nature' (i.e., the attempt to neutralize the Fall) that human beings gain these occult faculties which amount to power over these hidden forces, and death means the complete union with Nature.[53]

The implications with respect to a traditional linkage between 'woman' and 'nature' were far-reaching. Kerner's position amounted to a revised version of the table of opposites referred to above, in which a positive concept of 'Nature' was opposed to its negative alternative, referred to as 'reality': this latter term referred to the brutal world of daily social existence, the world which had resulted from the Fall, the world of the cold rationalist whose 'glass skull' (*tabula vitrea*) keeps him isolated from intuitions of a higher world. The result may be summarized as follows:

Nature		*Reality*
heart-system	–	brain-system
female	–	male

---

[51] Walter Hagen, "Justinus Kerner: Arzt und Dichter 1786–1862", *Lebensbilder aus Schwaben und Franken*, eds. Max Miller & Robert Uhland (Stuttgart, 1963), p. 156.
[52] Schubert, *Ansichten*, p. 81; cf. also o.c., pp. 70, 79.
[53] Straumann, *Justinus Kerner und der Okkultismus*, p. 84.

spiritual	–	materialist
sleeping state	–	waking state
(= true awakeness)	–	(= being spiritually asleep)
illness	–	health

Since nature is no longer the inferior but the superior principle, all principles which are associated with it are reinterpreted accordingly. The true battle is not between 'brain' and 'belly', as the rationalist would say, but between mere rationality and the deeper, non-rational knowledge of the heart. Women have a natural tendency towards such 'intuitive' knowledge. Since 'Nature' encompasses the whole of reality, a traditional opposition between a world of material nature and a transcendent spiritual reality cannot be maintained: a dualistic framework is replaced by a panentheistic one, in which 'reality' is the result of ignorance and blindness. Although one might say that a human being's 'principle of light' still has to free itself from the 'realm of gravity' (as the butterfly frees itself from its existence as caterpillar), this process is now more accurately described in terms of 'awakening' from the sleep of spiritual ignorance. One can readily understand that the phenomenon of somnambulic sleep had to strike Kerner as the confirmation *par excellence* of this whole perspective: "Dear reader, do not call this condition sleep: for it is rather a condition of the most perfect awakeness, the rising of an inner, much brighter sun ... a light which is clearer than what you may attain in your waking life by relying on concepts, conclusions, definitions and systems" (SP 43). For women, who already tend to think with the heart rather than the brain, this condition is easier to attain than for men (in contrast with the earlier framework, which connected women with the *Reich der Schwere* which pulls the spirit downward). And if it does, it is typically accompanied by symptoms of physical illness and leads ultimately to death, just as the butterfly cannot become free unless the caterpillar becomes sick and dies. In short: for Kerner, the statement *"Weib zu sein ist eigentlich Krankheit"* meant that women were naturally closer to the spirit world than men.

What are the implications of such convictions for the daily practice of a physician? Straumann recognizes the problem but merely says that Kerner kept silent about it, and faithfully fulfilled his professional duty of fighting against disease and death.[54] The letter to

---

[54] Straumann, *Justinus Kerner und der Okkultismus*, p. 87.

Tafel confirms this, but also reveals Kerner's deeply ambiguous feelings about his 'pathetic' job of having to lead people back to the stupidity of normal life. Once he had become convinced that it was too late for Friederike to be cured, Kerner must have felt himself excused, and free to seize the opportunity of learning from her as much as possible about the spirit world. Friederike's condition eventually permitted him to add yet another element: she was incurable, not because help had come too late, but because she was a natural-born somnambule. On May 1, 1827, he could write to Julie Hartmann: "Do not worry about the health of this woman.—In her youth she already lived with spirits; she was born with it, and it will remain with her until her death".[55] Had he written such a thing about his earlier patient Christiane Käpplinger, for example (who must have been born to be ill, like all women, but who was succesfully cured), the implications might well have cost him his license to practice medicine.

A 'Forschergeist' met by 'Gelassenheit'

Friederike had arrived in Weinsberg in search for a doctor but, instead, was caught in the conceptual net of a Romantic *Naturphilosoph* looking for spirits. This summary of the situation might sound too harsh on Kerner, who was undoubtedly filled with the best of intentions and seems to have been sincere in his (plausible) conviction that her condition was incurable. It is also true that the move to Weinsberg meant a big step forward, compared to what she had come from; and one readily believes Kerner when he claims that Friederike came to consider her period in Weinsberg as the best years of her life.[56] However, although Friederike may well have dreamed of a life of spiritual contemplation, nothing suggests that she was looking for a quasi-public career as a seeress. Nor does she seem to have been interested in parapsychological experiments, not to mention ghosts. Kerner led her, gently but firmly, towards a new and unexpected role which must have been at best a mixed blessing for an extremely sick patient. Of course she knew that her condition

[55] Letter to Julie Hartmann, 1.5.1827 (orig. in Schiller-Nationalmuseum, Marbach a.N.), as quoted in: Jennings, "Probleme", p. 136. Cf. Jennings, "Justinus Kerner und die Geisterwelt", *Neue Wissenschaft* 14 (1966), p. 82.
[56] Kerner, in A.K.A. Eschenmayer, *Mysterien des inneren Lebens* (Tübingen, 1830), pp. 95ff, as quoted in Jennings, "Probleme", p. 137.

imposed a heavy burden on her environment, and that her relatives had more than enough of the situation. That Kerner (and, not to forget, his wife)[57] took over this burden, even taking her into his own house, must have made it psychologically difficult for her to say no when he asked for her collaboration. On the other hand, in spite of her extreme vulnerability to human 'intrusions', one may assume that part of her was proud of her new role. As her fame grew, people from all over the country flocked to her sickbed; learned philosophers and theologians—among them were von Baader, Eschenmayer, Görres, Passavant, Schelling, Schleiermacher, Schubert, and Strauss[58]— listened attentively to her every word.[59] Soon, she had become the center of a cult: daily life in the *Kernerhaus* revolved around her.

I already mentioned the difference in perspective between Friederike's basically religious perspective, inspired by Jung-Stilling, and Kerner's passion for active investigation of the occult. Friederike did not seek the commerce with spirits, but Kerner did. This difference occasionally led to conflicts. Interestingly, Friederike later reproached Kerner, saying that during her early days in Weinsberg she had still possessed the ability to steer clear of spirit visitations; but her environment had kept begging her not to, and she had done what she could to oblige them. Now she could no longer cut the connection.

---

[57] The near-legendary hospitality of Kerner's home came down mainly on the shoulders of Kerner's wife, who once half-jested that 'she would probably have died long ago, but the many guests did not leave her time for it' (Hagen, "Justinus Kerner", p. 166).

[58] Jacques Fabry, *Le théosophe de Francfort Johann Friedrich von Meyer (1772–1849) et l'ésotérisme en Allemagne au XIXe siècle*, I, (Berne etc., 1989), pp. 357 & 594 nt 1752. Most of these names require no further introduction. Adolph Karl August von Eschenmayer (1768–1852), who has played a particularly important role as a passionate defender of the Seeress of Prevorst, would merit a separate discussion. Most of the longer theoretical, rather than descriptive, parts of Kerner's *Seherin* are by Eschenmayer (SP 272, 281, 287–315, 357, 361ff, 389, 407–408). In "Aphorismen über Freiheit und inneres Leben", *Blätter aus Prevorst* I, pp. 1–12. Eschenmayer indicates that his acquaintance with the Seeress was decisive for his philosophical and theological development: 'What I used to propose as theory, has now become not more than a mere introduction . . . for it is only now that everything becomes clearer to me; and, in the end, my whole philosophie slips over into this woman and looks back at me through her seeress-eyes [*am Ende schlüpft meine ganze Philosophie in dieses Weib hinüber und guckt aus ihren Seheraugen wieder hervor*]'. Eventually, even Kerner seems to have become irritated by Eschenmayer's limitless credulity, and he has received a bad press under most later commentators (Hagen, "Justinus Kerner", p. 163; Jennings, "Geister und Germanisten", p. 98; Werner Mohr, "Justinus Kerner als Arzt und Psychotherapeut", in: *Justinus Kerner: Jubiläumsband*, p. 44).

[59] Jennings, "Justinus Kerner und die Geisterwelt", p. 81.

Kerner honestly admits that this was the truth.[60] In the 1846 edition of *Seherin*, he tries to defend himself. He confirms that Friederike never had an interest in convincing others of the existence of spirits; according to her, "*Such* a conviction does not belong to religious conviction, and man does not need it in order to please God, which is why Holy Scripture speaks little about it" (SP 374–375). Nevertheless, Kerner kept begging Friederike to make him hear a ghost; and when that had happened, he was still not convinced and now wanted to *see* one. On this, he received a reprimand in verse:

> Diese Sehnsucht dir zu stillen,
> Lieget nicht in meinem Willen,
> Wär' es gut dir, würd's geschehn;
> Hörtest sie, nun willst sie sehn.
> Sahst du sie, dann willst sie greifen,
> Nicht als zarte Wolkenstreifen,
> Nein, zur Untersuchung stehn
> Sollen dir sie, halten Stich.
> Also ist der Mensch und war auch ich.[61]

Kerner cannot have been too impressed, for he continues to defend himself against those who reproached him for his wish to see ghosts. Against the critics who state that *he* was responsible for Friederike's ghosts (having fed her stories about them until she ended up seeing them) he emphasizes that, far from swallowing all she had to say, he had kept confronting Friederike with arguments against the reality of her phenomena. This indeed seems to have been the case.[62] It is remarkable that Friederike herself, who did not share his interests, felt no strong need to defend the reality of what she saw: "I will readily let them tell me that it is just a vision or an optical

---

[60] See the presentation in Zeller, *Verschleierte Bild*, pp. 142–143, with reference to the first edition of *Seherin*. Cf. Jennings, "Probleme", p. 138 and nt 13, who refers to Part II, pp. 146ff of the first edition, and adds that Kerner qualified the statement in later editions. I have indeed not been able to find the passage in the edition of 1846. Cf. Jennings, "Justinus Kerner und die Geisterwelt", p. 83.

[61] SP 375. Transl.: "To satisfy this desire of you / is not according to my wish. / If it were good for you, it would happen; / You heard them—now you want to see them. / If you saw them, you would want to grab them, / and not just as tender strips of cloud, / No: they have to submit / to your investigation, produce convincing evidence. / Thus is man; thus I, too, once have been".

[62] We know now what Kerner's contemporaries probably did not, i.e., Friederike's long-standing exposure to authors such as Jung-Stilling. She did not need Kerners suggestions.

illusion. But unfortunately *my* life just happens to be of such a nature that I see in the spirit world and it sees me" (SP 375).

Kerner has been heavily criticized for using Friederike as a guinea pig for parapsychological experiments, against her real wishes. His sworn enemy Carové compared her room with a torture chamber,[63] and Ernst Albert Zeller called her a 'martyr for science'.[64] This may have been somewhat exaggerated; but one tends to agree with Zeller when he expresses his hope that Friederike will find eternal rest, having been mistreated all her life by her friends no less than by her enemies.[65]

The Beatification of Friederike Hauffe

It is evident that Kerner was in a position of power and authority, both as a doctor versus his patient and as a middle-aged man versus a young woman. This situation was further enhanced, as I suggested, because Friederike must have felt that she had to repay him for his kindness. Finally, their relationship had a highly special and privileged, even intimate dimension, due to the special condition of magnetic *rapport*. In a clairvoyant trance state, Friederike could hear only Kerner's voice; and she mistakenly assumed that he was the only one who could hear what she said (SP 227). Only Kerner (and, admittedly, his wife) could enter her personal circle—although on its periphery only—; the rest of the world stood on the outside. By now, all her true friends and supporters (both grandparents Schmidgall; Tritschler) had already made the transition to the spirit world. In this world, only Kerner seems to have come anywhere close to their importance in her earlier life. Naturally, Friederike would come to depend on his affection and approval.

Still, it would be onesided to emphasize only Kerner's position of authority and imagine Friederike as the passive victim of events. I already suggested that not Kerner but Friederike became the real center around whom the household revolved; in the end it was *she* who had the power to decide what happened each minute of the

---

[63] F.W. Carové, *Literaturblatt* 6–9 (1830), pp. 21ff, 25ff, 29ff, 33ff. (according to Jennings, "Probleme", p. 136 and nt 11).
[64] Zeller, *Verschleierte Bild*, pp. 105–106.
[65] Zeller, *Verschleierte Bild*, p. 129; and cf. pp. 105–106, where he criticizes Kerner for turning Friederike into a 'martyr for science' while losing sight of his primary responsibilities as a doctor.

day, not in the least by giving precise predictions and exactly-timed prescriptions for her cure. We saw that her 'excessive demands' seem to have gotten on the nerves of her relatives, who interpreted them as 'spoiled' behaviour. There may have been at least a core of truth in this, based on her childhood as her grandparents' favourite granddaughter. It is quite plausible that Friederike had become used to getting what she wanted, and to being treated as somehow 'special'. Obviously this would make it much easier to conform to her role as the 'Seeress'.

Kerner became more and more impressed by Friederike's phenomena, and his persistent attempts at falsification finally convinced him that the evidence was irrefutable. On August 17, 1827, he writes to Julie Hartmann: "It is all true, it is pure fact. In case you do not believe my phantasy, Rickele [his wife. W.H.] must write you about it. We are through [*Wir sind im Reinen*].—Dear Schilli! the spirits exist, and this unfortunate woman is in contact with them".[66] By now, the *Kernerhaus* had come to be pervaded by a new atmosphere of pious awe, which made people feel that they were in touch with the miraculous on a daily basis. Ernst Albert Zeller has described very well how Friederike had become the center of a cult; and in spite of his scepticism, he indicates how natural such a development actually was:

> A mental illness was no longer seriously considered and—it cannot surprise us—in the later development of the story we find so few traces of real mental treatment concentrated on the salvation of her soul, that we have to assume, rather, that her whole environment fell more and more under her spell, and that she now decided, instead of being decided upon [*sie habe bestimmt, anstatt daß sie bestimmt geworden wäre*]. Her opinion was asked about anything that went on around her; she was the center around which revolved all the strange phenomena that now occurred with great frequency.
>
> . . .
>
> Still to consider the possibility of error seemed sinful and silly. Whoever wanted to be a christian had to be silent, admire, and believe. True: just to read about such phenomena on paper is . . . something very different from beholding them in person, in the hair-raising state of being of a spirit-seeress who, her limbs tightly clenched or stretched in contortions, gazes into space with wide and staring eyes, who bursts

---

[66] Letter to Julie Hartmann, August 17, 1827 (in Schiller-Nationalmuseum, Marbach a.N.), as quoted in Straumann, *Justinus Kerner und der Okkultismus*, p. 105.

out in sounds which can shatter mortal ears, and is thus transformed into a phantom herself. If one imagines for oneself such a sight, endlessly repeated for many days and years and accompanied by all sorts of strange noises, the quality of all this is so dazzling for the senses and the heart that the majority of those who now coldly ridicule the chimaeras of spirit phenomena would have been pulled into the ghostly circle quite as magically as her environment.[67]

And not only her environment was pulled into the enchanted circle of the Seeress, but Friederike Hauffe herself as well. During the last years of her life, it becomes less and less possible to distinguish between the myth of the Seeress of Prevorst and the life story of Friederike Hauffe. Even a critical spirit such as David Friedrich Strauss, who observed Friederike for a long time, could not resist the enchantment. He has left us a Romantic description which serves as an interesting complement and counterpoint to Zeller's:

> Her face, full of suffering but of noble and tender built, bathed in heavenly transfiguration; her language the purest German, her diction gentle, slow, solemn, musical, almost like a recitative; its contents of excessive feelings, moving through the soul and melting again like light or dark clouds,—sometimes stronger, sometimes gentler breaths of air through the strings of an aeolsharp—conversations with or about blessed or unhappy spirits, held with such truth that we could not doubt really having before us a Seeress, blessed with the commerce with a higher world.[68]

As a sick patient, Friederike Hauffe had been a frustration to Kerner the physician; as the Seeress of Prevorst, she ended as a blessing for Kerner the Romantic poet. To Kerner's mind, this very transformation must have been seen as symbolic of the salvational journey which must be made by each human soul, *per aspera ad astra*.

A Closing Metaphor

Kerner's *Seherin von Prevorst* ends with a poem by Kerner, glorifying the way of salvation through suffering. But how did the story end

---

[67] Zeller, *Verschleierte Bild*, pp. 110 & 144.
[68] David Friedrich Strauss, *Zwei friedliche Blätter*, p. 18, as quoted in Emil Bock, "Justinus Kerner: Der Okkultismus des Herzens", *Boten des Geistes: Schwäbische Geistesgeschichte und christliche Zukunft* (Stuttgart 3rd. ed., 1955), p. 175 (cf. Fabry, *Théosophe de Francfort*, pp. 358 & 595 nt 1757).

for Friederike Hauffe? The truth is that we do not really know: by the time we have reached the end of Kerner's book, we have lost sight of her. The amount of historicity in our knowledge of Friederike Hauffe's life remains strongest with respect to her earlier years; from her arrival in Weinsberg, it becomes increasingly entangled with myth; and by the end of her life, the myth has taken over almost completely. Instead of a picture of real life, we now have before us a painting. It depicts a woman in a strange and unfamiliar environment; it shows her from a definite perspective, that of the painter; it has an inconspicous but undeniable composition, intended to achieve maximum effect; objects and details are arranged so as to lead the audience's attention into definite directions; the painting is well-executed, and speaks to the emotions—and, like all paintings, we may appreciate it without needing to know the identity of the model.

We have learned something about that identity, however, and what we know suggests that something remarkable happened to the model. The painter's mold must have gained a hold over her because it offered her a better identity: one which would help her cope with the realities of her life. She was not made of stone, and it must have seemed easy enough to her to pay the price: that of sacrificing the tensions, ambiguities and unsolved questions of her worldly existence, in favour of the essential clarity and directedness of a religious icon. We cannot say with certainty whether the model ever, even towards the end of her life, identified with her role as completely as the painter wishes us to believe. Having thrown a look behind the canvas, we are entitled to doubt it.

Finally, in order to do justice to Friederike Hauffe, we should recognize that she herself would hardly have attached much importance to the problem of how myth and reality (painting and model) are related. She would have seen both as of minor significance, compared to a third and all-important dimension: that of heaven. It may be true that a real woman was depicted on the canvas as though enveloped in a halo of light, but even the brightest such light is made only of plain gilded paint. Friederike would have referred us to its real origin, in the unfathomable center of her *Gnadensonne*. But we are standing just outside the periphery of her circle, and cannot follow her there.

9

MĀRIYAMMAN'S ŚAKTI: THE MIRACULOUS POWER OF A SMALLPOX GODDESS

Anne van Voorthuizen

Introduction

Māriyamman is a goddess worshipped primarily in South India. Originally, she was the goddess of smallpox. Until the mid-1970s, smallpox killed large numbers of people in India. Now that smallpox epidemics have been eliminated, Māriyamman is associated with other diseases, often of an equally deadly or contagious nature. The goddess is believed to be able to cure even those who seem beyond all hope. Māriyamman is also thought to possess the power to overcome other kinds of adversity. Believers worship Māriyamman so as to stay on good terms with her and to ensure she does not turn against them. She is credited with many miracles. Thanks to Māriyamman, sick children are cured, jobs secured and lost wallets recovered.

The most important characteristic of Māriyamman and other goddesses is their *śakti*: literally their (supernatural) powers, which allow them to act upon the worldly sphere. Although every god in the pantheon can influence the real world, minor gods and goddesses—like Māriyamman—have greater earthly powers than the higher deities. Her power to cause and cure disease gives Māriyamman the capacity to directly influence people's lives. This ability accounts for the countless miracles she performs. My definition of a miracle is any intervention in the existing world order which cannot be explained within that world order and which is therefore attributed to a higher, divine power.[1]

However, my analysis of Māriyamman's power to work miracles starts 'on the other side', in the divine world rather than the human

---

[1] M. Eliade's definition of miracles includes rare events attributed to supernatural powers of charismatic people. "Miracles", *The Encyclopedia of Religion vol. 9* (New York, 1987), pp. 541–542.

realm. Hinduism has produced countless stories about the world of the gods. Tales about Māriyamma<u>n</u> explain how she became the goddess of smallpox. Interestingly, versions of the story vary widely; some are passed down through the popular and primarily oral tradition of folk Hinduism, others are Sanskrit texts with great authority in the orthodox Brahmin tradition. This article compares different versions of the story for the first time, focusing on how they reflect their social, religious and gender-specific context. A number of important questions are raised: How do the stories differ? What differences are there in gender-specific themes? Is there a link between gender-specific themes and the significance of gender in social reality? Can women's voices be detected beneath or behind the androcentric tale? How much influence did women have on the telling and recording of these stories, and what impact did this have on the narratives? And finally, do women appropriate Māriyamma<u>n</u>'s miraculous powers in a gender-specific manner?

Before dealing with these questions, I will briefly describe the Māriyamma<u>n</u> cult in South India. I will then analyze and interpret a version of the Māriyamma<u>n</u> story orally passed down in Tamil Nadu, another written in Sanskrit, and an interpretation of the story by a Māriyamma<u>n</u> priestess and medium from Madras.

The Māriyamma<u>n</u> Cult

During my travels in South India in 1993 and 1994, I found Māriyamma<u>n</u> temples in villages and towns all over Tamil Nadu. Her popularity is far greater than one might expect from the scarcity of scholarly research into Māriyamma<u>n</u> and other minor goddesses.[2]

---

[2] References to Māriyamma<u>n</u> are found in texts by early twentieth century missionaries and 'colonial collectors'. Henry Whitehead, *The Village Gods of South India* (Calcutta, 1921), pp. 116–117; Edgar Thurston, *Omens and Superstitions of Southern India* (London, 1912), pp. 148–149; Wilber T. Elmore, *Dravidian Gods in Modern Hinduism* (New Delhi, 1984 (1913)). More recently, articles on Māriyamma<u>n</u> have appeared, but no books: Brenda E.F. Beck, "Māriyamma<u>n</u>: The Vacillating Goddess", Unpublished Paper 1971; Brenda E.F. Beck, "The Goddess and the Demon: A Local South Indian Festival and its Wider Context", *Autour de la déesse hindoue. Puruṣārtha: Sciences sociales en Asie du Sud*, ed. Madeleine Biardeau (ed.), (Paris, 1981), pp. 83–136; Michael Moffatt *An Untouchable Community in South India. Structure and Consensus* (Princeton/New Jersey, 1979), pp. 246–270; Hans Manndorff, "Die Dorfgöttin Māramma und andere weibliche Gottheiten in Züdindien", *Archiv für Völkerkunde* 15 (1960), pp. 17–33; Paul Younger, "A Temple Festival of Māriyamma<u>n</u>", *Journal of*

The lack of research is partly due to the fact that minor deities originated in folk Hinduism, which has received far less attention than the more highly respected Sanskrit tradition. In Tamil Nadu, Māriyamma<u>n</u> is primarily known as a village goddess (*grāmadevatā*), a local deity who protects the villagers against disease and other misfortune. In some instances, statues of Māriyamma<u>n</u> guard the village borders against unwelcome outsiders.[3] Typically, Māriyamma<u>n</u> is represented as a black (bodiless) head protected by a cobra. Like other local goddesses, however, she is also worshipped in village temples in non-anthropomorphic forms, such as termite hills, uncarved stones or trees. These village temples usually belong to the lower castes. In a number of places, Māriyamma<u>n</u> has outgrown her role of minor deity over the past few decades. For example, Cāmiyapuram (near Trichy) is home to a very popular Māriyamma<u>n</u> temple which attracts some of the largest crowds in Tamil Nadu. In Tiruvērkāṭu (near Madras), there is a similar place of pilgrimage devoted to Karumāriyamma<u>n</u> (*karu* means black) which attracts people of all different castes from Madras and its surroundings. Both temples have fallen under Brahmin control, so blood sacrifice is no longer allowed: a clear sign of their Sanskritization.[4] Images of Māriyamma<u>n</u> in these temples correspond more closely to those of higher deities. In Cāmiyapuram, she is depicted in a sitting position, with a white face. In Tiruvērkāṭu, a complete statue is erected behind a black head which rests on the ground. At both sites, however, she is depicted with objects indicating her fierceness. In Cāmiyapuram, she has two objects: a cup of blood symbolizing the skull (*kapāla*) and a dagger. In Tiruvērkāṭu, she has four: a *kapāla*, a dagger, a small, hour-glass shaped drum (*ḍamarū*) and a trident (*triśūla*).

As the goddess of smallpox, Māriyamma<u>n</u> shares many characteristics with Sītalā, the famous Northern Indian goddess of small-

---

the American Academy of Religion 48 (1980), 4, pp. 494–517. Studies on similar local goddesses in South India include: Suzanne Hanchett, *Coloured Rice. Symbolic Structure in Hindu Family Festivals* (Delhi, 1988); Alf Hiltebeitel, *The Cult of Draupadī*. vol. 1 *Mythologies from Gingee to Kurukṣetra;* vol. 2 *On Hindu Ritual and the Goddess* (Chicago, 1988/1991); David Kinsley, *Hindu Goddesses. Visions of the Divine Feminine in the Hindu Religious Traditions* (Delhi, 1987), pp. 197–210.

[3] For example, I noted the presence of a statue of Reṇukā's head on the outskirts of the village of Govindavadi Agaram (near Kāñchipuram).

[4] Margaret Trawick Egnor, "The Changed Mother or What the Smallpox Goddess Did When There Was No More Smallpox", *Contributions to Asian Studies* 18 (1984), p. 41 (note 5); Younger, "A Temple Festival of Māriyamma<u>n</u>", p. 495.

pox. It is no coincidence that both deities are women. Women, and particularly pregnant women and infants, used to run a high risk of contracting smallpox.[5] As a goddess of disease, Māriyamma<u>n</u> plays various roles. She is simultaneously the cause of the disease and its cure. This paradox results from the two contradictory explanations of a smallpox occurrence. It can either be seen as an attack by demons, in which case Māriyamma<u>n</u> fights the demons to protect the village or the individual, or it can be interpreted as an act of anger or revenge by Māriyamma<u>n</u> for not receiving proper worship. These interpretations co-exist. It is also believed that Māriyamma<u>n</u> manifests herself in the symptoms of smallpox. In this view, being infected with the disease equals possession by the goddess: the pocks on the skin become a visible sign of her presence and are metaphorically called the eyes of the goddess. Māriyamma<u>n</u> 'of the thousand eyes' is omniscient and her looks can burn her devotees' skin with pox. In some versions of the Māriyamma<u>n</u> story, the goddess herself suffers from smallpox. She is said to walk among the people as an old woman whose face is covered with a thousand pock-like sores.

The best-known story about Māriyamma<u>n</u> is 'the Reṇukā tale', in which Reṇukā is killed by her son. The same saga is also associated with other goddesses. This is a common phenomenon in India, where gods can assume each other's identity through reincarnation. Māriyamma<u>n</u>, for instance, is worshipped in Northern Tamil Nadu—but so is Reṇukā, whose best-known life story is identical to Māriyamma<u>n</u>'s.[6] In Andhra Pradesh and Karnataka, the exact same story is linked to the goddess Yellamma, to whom a large temple was dedicated in Saundatti (Karnataka, Belgaum district). In Maharashtra, the same story is told of a goddess known locally as Reṇukā. There is a temple in her honour in Mahore (Nanded district) and she is one of the four main goddesses of Maharashtra.

---

[5] Egnor, "The Changed Mother or What the Smallpox Did When There Was No More Smallpox", pp. 32–33.

[6] Paḍaīvīḍu (North Arcot, TN) is home to an important Reṇukā temple. Like Karumāriyamma<u>n</u> in Tiruvērkāṭu, the goddess is represented by a head on the ground with a complete statue behind it. The wall of the temple is decorated with a painted version of the Reṇukā tale (personal observation).

Folk Tale

Even though all versions of the Reṇukā tale share the same plot, no two stories are alike. During my travels through India, I was amazed that every version I was told was different.[7] I will begin my comparison by analyzing a version recorded by anthropologist Eveline Meyer. This tale forms part of a series of myths and stories traditionally performed at festivals by two village priests (*pūjāri*). These priests from Mēl Malaiyaṉūr (Southern Arcot, Tamil Nadu) are members of the Cempaṭavar caste (inland fishermen). The Cempaṭavar and Veṭar castes provide singers and drummers for festivals. In this region, the Reṇukā tale associated with Māriyammaṉ is told as follows:[8]

> At that time I was born as Jamadagni and you as Reṇukā... Every day Reṇukā (Irēṉukai) brought water to Jamadagni (Camatakkiṉimuṉivar) for his *pūcai*. One day, the Ammaṉ (Reṇukā) went as usual to the tank to scoop up water. At that moment, a Gandharva by name Kāttavīriyārjuṉaṉ flew by above. As she collected the water and looked at the fish, she saw the Gandharva and thought: "How is it possible that such a beautiful person could have been created." At that moment she lost her chastity (*karpu*). Jamadagni knew by means of the eye on his forehead that Reṇukā had lost her faithfulness, and decided not to let this pass unpunished. He called his sons, Kāttavarāyaṉ, Karuppaṉacāmi and Paraśurāma (Paracurāmar). These were the three sons born to Ammaṉ, Śakti, Reṇukā. When Reṇukā was not able to scoop up the water, she cried: "Oh my god, I have lost my chastity."
>
> Jamadagni asked his two sons, Kāttavarāyaṉ and Karuppaṉacāmi: "What should be done with a woman who has lost her chastity?" They answered: "Her head should be cut off." "It is your mother who has lost her chastity, so go and cut off her head and bring it to me." "Father, how can you ask us to cut off the head of our mother, we cannot do this!" "You say that you cannot cut off your mother's head?

---

[7] I heard different versions of the Reṇukā-tale in many different places. In Tamil Nadu: Tiruvērkāṭu (Karumāriyammaṉ), Paḍaīvīḍu (Reṇukā), Kāñchipuram (Reṇukā), Thiruvarur (Reṇukā) and Cāmiyapuram (Māriyammaṉ). In Andhra Pradesh: Hyderabad (Yellamma), Alampur (Reṇukā), Kanchupadu and in the vicinity of Alampur (Reṇukā/Yellamma). In Karnataka: Bangalore (Reṇukā) and Saundatti (Yellamma), and in Maharashtra: Mahore (Reṇukā). Aside from these oral variants, I know of twenty different versions in literature. See Anne van Voorthuizen, *Reṇukā-Māriyammaṉ, een beeld van een vrouw? Een analyse van de vrouwelijkheid van een Indiase godin* (Utrecht, 1993), p. 33.

[8] Eveline Meyer, *Aṅkāḷaparamēcuvari. A Goddess of Tamilnadu, her Myths and Cult.* Beiträge zur Südasienforschung, Südasien-Institut, Universität Heidelberg, Band 107 (Stuttgart, 1986), pp. 15–19.

So be it, you shall be transformed into jungle men (*kāṭṭumaṉitar*)!" Thus Jamadagni cursed them.

When Paraśurāma came back from his studies at school, his father asked him: "What should be done with a woman who has lost her chastity?" "One should cut off her head," Paraśurāma replied. "It is your mother!" "My mother? Alright then, give me the big knife, I shall go and cut off her head," said Paraśurāma. As he took the knife, he asked his father for three boons, which his father granted.

Paraśurāma went towards his mother. Reṇukā thought: "What—no, he will not let me get off. He will certainly cut off my head. I should not stay here." She ran away, but Paraśurāma ran after her. They ran and ran and finally Reṇukā escaped into the house of a Cakkilicci who had just reached puberty. Paraśurāma also ran inside and, thinking that he was cutting off the head of his mother, he cut off the head of the Cakkilicci woman—it was dark inside the hut. Then his mother ran out of the house, and Paraśurāma ran after her and cut off her head.

Then he picked up his mother's head and brought it to his father. His father said: "You are indeed my son. What are the three boons which you had asked for?" "The first is to bring my brothers back to their original form." "Okay, I will give you this boon." "The second is to bring my mother back to life." Jamadagni gave him this boon as well. "The third is—you had said that my mother had lost her chastity while she looked at the fish—give me the boon that she, in fact, did not lose her faithfulness."

Jamadagni brought the brothers back to their original form. Then he said to Paraśurāma: "Take this water, place your mother's head onto her body and sprinkle this water over it—she will then come back to life." But Paraśurāma put the head of his mother by mistake onto the body of the Cakkilicci woman and sprinkled the water over it. When his mother got up, she saw that she did not have her own body. She lamented: "Appā, my body has changed. From now on I cannot come (to you) anymore. What can I do?" When all the gods saw this, they said: "Ammā, you have been born here, it has happened like this, and so from now on you are Māriyammaṉ, Karumāri, Urumāri, Taṇṭumāri, Kollamāri, you shall be Māriyāttāḷ."

"What will I eat then? she asked. The gods said: 'You will put the pox pearl (*muttu*) on people on earth and when you have given them the pox, they will offer you *pūcai*.' Then what did the Ammaṉ do? 'It is because my body has changed that they call me Māriyāttāḷ, fine, let it be so, but first of all, I will not let Paramaṉ (Śiva) get off free, even though he is a man,' she said and went straightaway to Paramaṉ. She placed ten pox pearls on him. As soon as she had put them on him, Paramaṉ began to suffer. 'Ammā, what is this, why are you doing this?' he asked. 'What can I do, I placed ten pearls on you; you just have to accept them,' she said. Paramaṉ pleaded: 'Tell me a way to take them off.' The Ammaṉ said a mantra and took off the pearls. In return she asked him to give her his milk cow. When she had received the milk cow, she returned.

Māriyamman[9] continues harassing the gods: she also terrorizes Yama and Vishnu with her pox pearls.

Interpretation

Adulterous Thoughts and Punishment

The central plot, also present in other versions, is that Reṇukā's husband orders her killed by her (youngest) son Paraśurāma. By obeying, Paraśurāma transgresses every social norm in India, where the mother-son relationship is the strongest bond in the entire extended family—and even stronger in the case of the youngest son.[10] According to the Dharmaśāstras, killing one's mother is a serious crime: "If a brāhmana killed his own father, mother, full brother, his teacher of the Veda, a brāhmana who has studied the Veda or has consecrated sacred Vedic fires, he had to undergo penance till his last breath."[11] In this light, it is not surprising that the older brothers refuse to kill their mother. Still, they are supposed to obey their father. Paraśurāma is the only one to fulfil this duty, even though he—in so doing—commits the worst possible crime: he destroys the closest mother-son bond.[12] This may have been what Jamadagni had in mind when he

---

[9] According to Tamil Nadu folk etymology, Māriyamman's name is derived from *mārū* (to change): 'she with a changed body', or 'she in her many manifestations'. In fact, it is derived from Sanskrit *mārī* (death). In some regions, a link is made with *maṛe* (rain), making Māriyamman the goddess of rain. Like *ammāḷ* and *tai*, *ammaṉ* means 'mother' in Tamil. However, rather than referring to her supposedly 'maternal nature', *ammaṉ* here expresses the respect people feel for this goddess. See Susan S. Bean, "Referential and Indexical Meanings of Ammā in Kannada: Mother, Woman, Goddess, Pox and Help", *Journal of Anthropological Research* 31 (1975), pp. 313–330; Moffatt, *An Untouchable Community in South India. Structure and Consensus*, p. 250.

[10] Sudhir Kakar, *The Inner World. A Psycho-analytic Study of Childhood and Society in India* (Delhi, 1981), pp. 79–87.

[11] P.V. Kane, *History of Dharmaśāstra: Ancient and Mediaeval Religious and Civil Law*, Government Oriental Series, vol. 4 (Poona, 1953), p. 94.

[12] In the Reṇukāmāhātmya, a Sanskrit text discussed later in this article, the crime of killing Māriyamman is even more serious than simple matricide. In this version, Māriyamman is killed when she is an *ātreyī*: a woman four days into her menstruation (see RM, 21:3–4). This is believed to be a woman's most fertile day. To kill an *ātreyī*, whether or not she is one's mother, is an extra serious crime (*mahāpātaka*) equal to murdering a Brahmin. For texts, see Kane, *History of Dharmaśāstra*:

had his son kill his wife rather than punishing her himself. However, the fact that Paraśurāma commits the horrific crime, even though he is the youngest son, underscores the severity of Reṇukā's offence. Her amazement at the beauty of a Gandharva, a mythical creature, amounts to a breach of the strict sexual norms for women.

Women in India are put under considerable social and moral pressure to devote themselves entirely to their husbands.[13] While male adultery is easily overlooked, female adultery is considered pernicious. There is a saying which compares women to earthen pots: once dirtied, they can never be cleansed entirely, while men are like copper pots, which are easy to rinse clean. Women who transgress this norm are often punished harshly. Although Reṇukā's decapitation is rather extreme, the Reṇukā tale confirms the strict sexual norms imposed on women. The tale reflects and legitimizes these norms in reality.

This raises the question why India has this double standard, why women's marital fidelity is given so much more value than men's. I believe this is due to the principle of (im)purity on which the Indian caste and family systems are founded. As anthropologist Nur Yalman pointed out, in South India, the purity of the caste is primarily maintained by women.[14] There is a Singhalese saying which proclaims that "the honour and respectability of men is protected and preserved through their women." Although caste is passed on by both

---

Ancient and Mediaeval Religious and Civil Law, vol. 3 (Poona, 1946), p. 527; vol. 4 (Poona, 1953), p. 96.

[13] Vanaja Dhruvarajan, *Hindu Women and the Power of Ideology* (New Delhi, 1989), pp. 28–29; Doranne Jacobson, "The Chaste Wife. Cultural Norm and Individual Experience", *American Studies in the Anthropology of India*, ed. Sylvia Vatuk (New Delhi, 1978), pp. 96–135; Doranne Jacobson and Susan S. Wadley, *Women in India. Two Perspectives* (New Delhi, 1986 (1977)); Bruce Elliot Tapper, "Widows and Goddesses: Female Roles in Deity Symbolism in a South India Village", *Contributions to Indian Sociology* (NS) 13 (1979), 4, pp. 7–8; Leela Dube, "Seed and Earth. The Symbolism of Biological Reproduction and Sexual Relations of Production", *Visibility and Power. Essays on Women in Society and Development*, eds. Leela Dube, Eleanor Leacock and Shirley Ardener (Delhi, 1986), p. 49, note 27.

[14] Nur Yalman, "On the Purity of Women in the Castes of Ceylon and Malabar", *Journal of the Royal Anthropological Institute* 93 (1963), p. 33 and 43. See also: Kane, *History of Dharmaśāstra: Ancient and Mediaeval Religious and Civil Law*, vol. 2, part 1 (Poona, 1974), p. 56; Steve Barnett, "Coconuts and Gold. Relational Identity in a South Indian Caste", *Contributions to Indian Sociology* (NS) 10 (1976), 1, pp. 133–156; Lynn Bennet, *Dangerous Wives and Sacred Sisters. Social and Symbolic Roles of High-Caste Women in Nepal* (New York, 1983), pp. 240–241; Jacobson, "The Chaste Wife. Cultural Norm and Individual Experience", pp. 125–129.

father and mother, the woman's caste is dominant. For example, if a man marries a lower caste woman, their children will inherit their mother's caste. This also explains the tradition of hypergamy, in which men can have sexual relations with lower caste women; after all, a mere ritual bath is sufficient to restore their original purity. For women, however, having sexual relations with lower caste men is out of the question because this would defile their entire caste. Therefore, women who violate this rule become outcasts.[15] Aside from the prohibition of hypergamy, South India has other customs aimed at protecting the purity of women, and thereby the caste. These customs include puberty rites,[16] *tāli*-tying marriage in Malabar,[17] pre-puberty marriage for Brahmin women, a ban on pre-marital sex and a ban on remarriage for widows.

Not only do women help maintain the caste's purity; they are also crucial to the protection of patrilineal purity. The father's seed, which springs from the father's blood, gives the son his lineage and clan identity, perpetuating patrilineage. The Laws of Manu (9.8) literally state: "The husband enters the wife, becomes an embryo, and is born here on earth. That is why a wife is called a wife (*jāyā*), because he is born (*jāyate*) again in her."[18] Paradoxically, the identity of a child's father can never be entirely certain. That is why arranged marriages are so highly valued in India. They are the best guarantee for the purity level of the caste and a pure lineage. Preliminary investigations are held to be sure there is no incompatibility in status or ritual purity between the prospective marriage partners. Women must remain virgins until they marry because pre-marital sex, like extra-marital sex, can bring unclean blood into the family tree.

---

[15] For texts from the Dharmaśāstra, see Kane, *History of Dharmaśāstra: Ancient and Mediaeval Religious and Civil Law*, vol. 3 (Poona, 1946), p. 614; vol. 4 (Poona, 1953), p. 105; vol. 2 (Poona, 1974), pp. 572–573.

[16] Gabriella Eichinger Ferro-Luzzi, "Women's Pollution Periods in Tamilnad (India)", *Anthropos* 69 (1974), pp. 121–127; Susan S. Wadley, "The Paradoxical Powers of Tamil Women", *The Powers of Tamil Women*, ed. Susan S. Wadley, Foreign and Comparative Studies / South Asian Series, no. 6 (New York, 1991 (1980)), p. 163; Yalman, "On the Purity of Women in the Castes of Ceylon and Malabar", p. 45.

[17] Malabar's *tāli*-tying marriage is a symbolic marriage in which a pre-pubescent girl marries a ritual groom from a higher caste. Yalman, "On the Purity of Women in the Castes of Ceylon and Malabar", pp. 33–39.

[18] Wendy Doniger and Brian K. Smith (transl.), *The Laws of Manu* (New Delhi, 1991), p. 197. See also Dube, "Seed and Earth: The Symbolism of Biological Reproduction and Sexual Relations of Production", pp. 28–32.

Returning to the Reṇukā tale, we can see that Reṇukā admires the beauty of Gandharva Kāttavīriyārjuṉaṉ, whose reflection she sees in the water.[19] A Gandharva is a celestial musician, a mythical spirit in the sky with a great predilection for women. In the Reṇukā tale, the Gandharva might symbolize romantic love as opposed to arranged marriages.[20] While in this version of the story Reṇukā only admires his beauty, in other versions she is overcome with desire. Still, no other version mentions any more incriminating 'facts'—inasmuch as one can speak of facts in this context. When her husband finds out what has happened, he orders Reṇukā brutally killed, usually by beheading with an axe. The harsh control of female sexuality is linked to caste hierarchy. When Reṇukā momentarily slips free from this control through adulterous thoughts, the imminent danger—desecration of the caste—becomes a reality: Reṇukā receives the body of an *untouchable* woman.[21]

The unclean body could signify the defilement of the caste by a hypogamous relationship, the greatest (fictional) danger whose prevention is achieved by keeping women in check. It is logical that Reṇukā is given an unclean body in most versions. The body and bodily fluids, ranging from urine to saliva, are considered unclean in Brahmin circles and it is the body which causes women's periodic

---

[19] Reṇukā sees a Gandharva in most versions of the story. In the version Meyer recorded, the Gandharva appears as Kārtavīrya, a character who figures in the larger set of Sanskrit stories which includes the Reṇukā tale.

[20] A 'Gandharva marriage' is one of the eight forms of marriage recognized by the Smṛtis. In contrast to other forms, this marriage of love allows for pre-marital sex (sexual contact preceding the marital rites). A.S. Altekar, *The Position of Women in Hindu Civilization. From Prehistoric Times to the Present Day* (Delhi, 1973 (1938)), pp. 42–43.

[21] A close reading of the Reṇukā tale supports this interpretation. Meyer's version does not explicitly state that Jamadagni fulfils the third wish (for Reṇukā not to have lost her marital fidelity), as he had the first two. Meyer believes that the new, pubescent body Reṇukā is given in this version of the story restores her marital fidelity (*kaṟpu*). However, Yalman, Bennet, David and Wadley have all pointed out that a pubescent woman who is still unmarried finds herself in an extremely vulnerable position. Therefore, I believe that being given the body of pubescent woman should be considered a symbol of potential impurity rather than one of purity restored. In my view, therefore, the impurity of Māriyammaṉ's body is due to her infidelity. Meyer, *Aṅkāḷaparamēcuvari. A Goddess of Tamilnadu, her Myths and Cult*, p. 56; Yalman, "On the Purity of Women in the Castes of Ceylon and Malabar", p. 47; Bennet, *Dangerous Wives and Sacred Sisters. Social and Symbolic Roles of High-Caste Women in Nepal*, pp. 240–242; Kenneth David, "Hidden Powers: Cultural and Socio-Economic Accounts of Jaffna Women", *The Powers of Tamil Women*, ed. Susan S. Wadley, Foreign and Comparative Studies / South Asian Series, no. 6 (New York, 1991 (1980)), pp. 95–96; Wadley, "The Paradoxical Powers of Tamil Women", p. 165.

impurity, during menstruation and childbirth. The impurity of Reṇukā's body is evident in the images of Māriyamman or Reṇukā throughout Tamil Nadu; only her head is worshipped, while her body is sometimes either kept outside the temple or buried in the ground.[22]

Reṇukā's bodily impurity coincides with her transformation into a goddess. Her deification is not unlike the outcast status of a woman who has committed hypogamy. As Hart, professor of Indian Studies, wrote: "It is a universal human theme that an approach to a divine state is often preceded by some transgression which breaks the normal rules for human behaviour."[23] By turning her into a goddess, Reṇukā is rendered harmless and the patriarchal social norms can stay in place. Those who threaten the patriarchal order are either cast out or deified.

Revenge through Śakti

This interpretation is not complete, however, because the Reṇukā legend has a sting in its tail. Once a goddess, Māriyamman first bestows the pox pearls upon Siva and Vishnu, the higher, male gods. When they beg her to lift the curse, the tables seem turned. Where at first it was father and son conspiring to bring her down a peg, now Māriyamman is teaching the higher gods a lesson. She even says she will not spare Siva "even though he is a man."

In the meantime, a fundamental change has occurred: Reṇukā has been transformed into a (minor) goddess. This unexpected twist in the plot is not unique, but rather a deeply ingrained tradition in folk Hinduist storytelling. In South India, there are countless local stories of deceased people whose spirits return to earth. If, in time, a cult develops around such a spirit, it can be 'promoted' to minor deity. As Blackburn, who studied local deities in Tamil Nadu and Kerala, wrote, it is particularly the victims of an untimely or very violent death who live on as deified spirits or minor deities.[24] In

---

[22] In Alampur, the local people maintain that Reṇukā's body is kept outside the temple (elsewhere the same statue is known as Lajjagauri). In Thiruvarur (Tamil Nadu) and Mahore (Maharashtra), I was told that Reṇukā rose from the dead, but accidentally got stuck at the neck.

[23] George L. Hart III, "Some Aspects of Kinship in Ancient Tamil Literature", *Kinship and History in South Asia. Four Lectures*, ed. Thomas R. Trautmann, Michigan Papers on South and Southeast Asia, no. 7 (Ann Arbor, 1974), p. 48.

[24] Stuart H. Blackburn, "Death and Deification. Folk Cults in Hinduism", *History of Religions* 24 (1985), 3, pp. 255–274.

these stories, however, death is not always violent. Sometimes the main character dies of natural causes or simply vanishes. And in the case of women's deification, there is another factor at play; as I showed in an earlier publication, undue suffering is also grounds for deification.[25] An explicit example can be found in the story of Nalla Taṅkāl, a Tamil Nadu village goddess (who Blackburn also mentioned). Formerly, Nalla Taṅkāl was a married woman who lived with her husband's family. To escape a famine, she returned to her native home, where one of her sisters-in-law insulted her and cast her out. Nalla Taṅkāl then drowned herself and her seven children. At Blackburn's suggestion that the sister-in-law was not worshipped because she was evil, the village people replied: "No, the sister-in-law is not a goddess not because she is evil (*keṭṭa*) *but because she didn't suffer*; Nalla Taṅkāl might be evil, too, but we worship her because she suffered and died." (my emphasis, AvV)[26] Here, I find it useful to analyze the stories from a gender-specific angle. Often, the female character is made to suffer by her husband, or her suffering stems from her subordinate position in patriarchal society.[27] As a goddess, she sometimes avenges herself directly on those who caused her suffering in her former life.

This occurs not only in the Reṇukā tale, but also in an equally famous Māriyamman̠ story about a marriage between a Brahmin woman and an untouchable man posing as a Brahmin. The deception is revealed when either a child, or the man's mother, does something

---

[25] Van Voorthuizen, *Reṇukā-Māriyamman̠, een beeld van een vrouw? Een analyse van de vrouwelijkheid van een Indiase godin*, pp. 42–47.

[26] Blackburn, "Death and Deification. Folk Cults in Hinduism", p. 260.

[27] Hanchett's interpretation points towards the same conclusion, although she does not elaborate on this: "Tragedy, frustration and anger are the nature of the ghostly spirits known as amma goddesses. If the married woman and her Gauri are successes, these spirits are failures" and: "These ammas emit the angry power of thwarted women." Hanchett, *Coloured Rice. Symbolic structure in Hindu Family Festivals*, p. 157, 186. Examples of such stories include Mastiamma in: Hanchett, *Coloured Rice. Symbolic Structure in Hindu Family Festivals*, pp. 183–184; Kannagi in: Jacob Pandian, "The Goddess Kannagi. A Dominant Symbol of South Indian Tamil Society", *Mother Worship. Themes and Variations*, ed. James J. Preston (Chapel Hill, 1982), pp. 177–191; Pannaṅgālatamme in: M.N. Srinivas, *Religion and Society Among the Coorgs of South India*, (London, 1965 (1952)), pp. 234–6; Mīnākṣi in: Willam P. Harman, *The Sacred Marriage of a Hindu Goddess* (Bloomington and Indianapolis, 1989), pp. 118–120. Tapper shows that in Andhra Pradesh, *āśa* is another important factor determining whether or not women's spirits return to earth. Considered typical of women's character, *āśa* is a combination of passion, emotion, impulsiveness, jealousy and an attachment to life and earthly affairs. Tapper, "Widows and Goddesses. Female Roles in Deity Symbolism in a South Indian Village", pp. 1–31.

unheard of in Brahmin tradition, such as asking for a piece of buffalo meat. Filled with anger or despair at having married an untouchable, she burns herself to death. In several versions of the story, she first curses her husband: "You must be born as a buffalo, and your people must bring you before me, and sacrifice you."[28] In this story, Māriyamman is unwittingly forced to transgress the social norm of hypergamy. Just as in the Renukā tale, the main theme of the story is the purity of the caste, for which women are primarily responsible. However, Māriyamman takes revenge directly on the man who has tricked her. Similarly, Māriyamman avenges herself in a few versions of the Renukā tale by infecting her husband with smallpox.[29] Although this does not happen in the version recorded by Meyer, there is definitely an element of frustration and vengefulness in her pox pearl attacks on Siva and Vishnu, the higher, male gods.

As a mortal, Renukā could do little to defend herself against Paraśurāma and Jamadagni, but once a goddess she has considerably greater powers, in the shape of *śakti*. *Śakti* is a supernatural and spiritual force unlike any other, although villagers also refer to it as a kind of natural energy.[30] *Śakti* is responsible for extraordinary events and miracles. Primarily a dynamic force, *śakti* is seen as the ability to act, to make others act and to make things happen. It is also action itself. Moreover, *śakti* is characteristically female and is ascribed to goddesses and women alike. Unlike Western thought, Hinduism classifies the feminine as active. A husband would collapse without his wife's *śakti*. As a Tamil saying goes: "Siva without *śakti* is a corpse." Male gods need *śakti* in order to effect any deeds on earth.

---

[28] Hanchett, *Coloured Rice. Symbolic Structure in Hindu Family Festivals*, p. 293. The same story, sometimes with a different curse by the husband, is mentioned in: Beck, "The Goddess and the Demon: A Local South Indian Festival and its Wider Context", p. 95; Whitehead, *The Village Gods of South India*, pp. 73, 84–85, 117–119; Elmore, *Dravidian Gods in Modern Hinduism*, pp. 129–130. Kinsley sees the stories of lower, abused goddesses taking revenge as symptomatic of a broader tendency reflected in the cult of lower goddesses. "The theme of the relationship of an epidemic or a disaster to the invasion of the village by hostile demons from outside echoes the mythic theme of the goddess's abuse by males", Kinsley, *Hindu Goddesses. Visions of the Divine Feminine in the Hindu Religious Traditions*, p. 205.

[29] Beck, "The Goddess and the Demon. A Local South Indian Festival and its Wider Context", pp. 126–127.

[30] Sheryl B. Daniel, "Marriage in Tamil Culture: The Problem of Conflicting 'Models'", *The Powers of Tamil Women*, ed. Susan S. Wadley, Foreign and Comparative Studies / South Asian Series, no. 6 (New York, 1991 (1980)), pp. 78–79; Susan S. Wadley, *Shakti: Power in the Conceptual Structure of Karimpur Religion*, Studies in Anthropology: Series in Social, Cultural, and Linguistic Anthropology, no. 2 (Chicago, 1975).

The *śakti* of minor goddesses like Māriyamman commands universal respect; in the Renukā tale, even Siva and Vishnu must bow to it.

Women's Śakti

Humans, especially women, can also possess *śakti*. It is believed that a woman's *śakti* will bring the whole family prosperity and good fortune. It gives her husband health, power and success and can even shield him from death.[31] Because of women's *śakti*, their prayers are more effective and have greater influence on the divine world than men's. Although women possess more *śakti* to begin with, it is also believed that they can increase their portion by being a good *pativratā*.[32] Literally, a *pativratā* is a woman who is totally devoted to her husband or who adores her husband as a personal god. In a broader sense, however, *pativratā* denotes all the female virtues in a patriarchal society: being married, bearing sons, chastity, marital fidelity, obedience, unselfishness, subordination, modesty, shyness, patience, endurance, kindness, etc. In Tamil Nadu, more than elsewhere in India, the emphasis is on *karpu*: chastity and restraint. This applies to spirituality, morality, sexuality (pre-marital chastity and marital fidelity) and all other behaviour.[33]

Basically, a *pativratā*'s *śakti* is a benevolent power. However, such powers can always be abused, even by simply withholding them. Just as a *pativratā* can keep her husband from dying, she can also cause his death. The *pativratā* status is tenuous. Gossip, slurs or adulterous thoughts can be reason enough for a *pativratā* to be made an outcast, because her status depends partly on factors beyond her control, such as being married and bearing sons. In practise, the *pativratā* ideal is quite rare. No more than one in every few hundred thousand women is a *pativratā*, as the Anuśāsana parva states (Mbh.) 19.93.[34] If anything goes wrong and the woman loses her self-control, or escapes her husband's control, she falls a long way. While the

---

[31] In a recurring theme in the purānas, male gods or demons are strengthened in battle by the power of their faithful wife, and get killed at the moment the wife is unfaithful.

[32] Dhruvarajan, *Hindu Women and the Power of Ideology*, pp. 26–34.

[33] Wadley, "The Paradoxical Powers of Tamil Women", p. 154, 166; Hart, "Woman and the Sacred in Ancient Tamilnad", *Journal of Asian Studies* 32 (1973), 2, pp. 236–243.

[34] Kane, *History of Dharmaśāstra: Ancient and Mediaeval Religious and Civil Law*, Government Oriental Series, vol. 2 (Poona, 1974), p. 578.

pativratā's power is benevolent, the power of a 'fallen women' is unbridled, unpredictable and potentially hazardous. Therefore, women who die virgins, unwed, barren, divorced, adulterers or widows stand a good chance of being transformed into minor, fierce goddesses (*amman̲, devatā*) or malevolent spirits (*pēy, pūtam, picācu*).[35]

The notion that women can acquire spiritual powers by being devoted wives or practising self-restraint derives from Hindu ideas about asceticism.[36] Self-sacrifice and renunciation (*tapas*) cause a sort of internal heat (also *tapas*). This heat is a force or energy which can literally work miracles. For example, the curse of ascetics whose meditation is disrupted can cause terrible things. An ascetic's *tapas* can become so great that it even jeopardizes divine power. Just as ascetics develop *tapas* through renunciation, women increase their *śakti* by being good *pativratā*s and—in Tamil Nadu—by leading a *kar̲pu* life. The difference, however, is that the *pativratā* ideal is in perfect line with patriarchal values. The *pativratā* ideal encourages women to resign themselves to their subordinate social position. Women's self-sacrifice and serfdom is idealized. And as anthropologists Egnor and Reynolds have pointed out, people in Tamil Nadu believe *pativratā*s increase their *śakti* through the suffering which results from their second class position in society.[37] As Egnor puts it: "For each woman the possession of extraordinary *śakti* came as a consequence of the suffering that that subordination entailed."

All these ideas about women's *śakti* have a bearing on the Reṇukā tale. Initially, Reṇukā is an ideal *pativratā*. She is the wife of Jamadagni, the great Brahmin sage. She has borne several sons and no daughters. In many versions of the story, her devotion to her husband and her self-restraint (*pātivratya* and *kar̲pu*) have earned her spiritual powers: *śakti*. I have paid little attention to this aspect of the story, because the version recorded by Meyer provides little information on the subject. In other versions, Reṇukā is initially able to carry water without a vessel, to conjure up a jar from loose sand, or to make laundry suspend itself in midair until the wind blows it dry.

---

[35] Holly Baker Reynolds, "The Auspicious Married Woman", *The Powers of Tamil Women*, ed. Susan S. Wadley, Foreign and Comparative Studies / South Asian Series, no. 6 (New York, 1991 (1980)), pp. 36–37.

[36] Egnor, "On the Meaning of Śakti to Women in Tamil Nadu", p. 17; Daniel, "Marriage in Tamil Culture: The Problem of Conflicting 'Models'", p. 90, note 7.

[37] Reynolds, "The Auspicious Married Woman", pp. 35–60; Egnor, "On the Meaning of Śakti to Women in Tamil Nadu", pp. 1–34; quotation, p. 14.

She loses these supernatural powers the moment she loses control (*karpu*) over her mind and becomes fascinated with a man other than her husband. In the version cited in this paper, she is no longer able "to scoop up the water." Reṇukā has fallen into one of the many traps set for *pativratā*s and has lost her *śakti*. As a punishment for her mistake she is beheaded. This punishment is disproportionate to her negligible offence. As a 'fallen woman', her powers are no longer unambiguously positive (as they are for a *pativratā*), but unpredictable and potentially malevolent.

Her deification is connected to the notion that women's *śakti* increases when they suffer from their secondary position. I believe this explains why so many spirits and minor deities are female. Reṇukā's tragic life ensures her much greater *śakti* after death. She was virtually helpless to fend off the violence done to her when she lived, but after her rebirth as a goddess the tables are turned. Then, there is no match for Māriyammaṉ's *śakti*, not even patriarchal structures. As Māriyammaṉ, she is now ready to do battle with the higher male gods Siva and Vishnu. She takes revenge on those who were unjust to her.[38] Her *śakti*, granted to her by the patriarchal system, ultimately defies patriarchy.

Sanskrit Texts

The same story can be found in Sanskrit texts, in the Mahābhārata (III, 116:5–18), the Viṣṇudharmotta-purāṇa (I, 36:1–17), the Bhāgavata-purāṇa (IX, 16:2–8) and in Reṇukāmāhātmya (chapters 21–26). The Mahābhārata is probably the most ancient of these texts, written and compiled around 200 A.D.[39] The Reṇukā tale here differs considerably from the version I dealt with earlier, from the Tamil oral tradition.

---

[38] Similar interpretations come from: Kinsley, *Hindu Goddesses. Visions of the Divine Feminine in the Hindu Religious Traditions*, p. 200; Younger, "A Temple Festival of Māriyammaṉ", p. 509.

[39] There is also the Reṇukā tale from the Kālikā-purāṇa (86), but this version was copied verbatim from the Mahābhārata. In the Sahyādrikhaṇḍa (Uttarakhaṇḍa 6:23–24) an appendix to the Skanda-purāṇa, there are two verses which explicitly refer to Paraśurāma killing his mother. The Brahmāṇḍa-purāṇa (part II, Upodghāta, 23: 67b–68) only alludes to Paraśurāma's matricide. For dating and details on these Sanskrit texts, see: Ludo Rocher, *The Purāṇas* (Wiesbaden, 1986), pp. 147–152; Adelbert Gail, *Paraśurāma Brahmane und Krieger. Untersuchung über Ursprung und Entwicklung eines Avatāra Viṣṇus und Bhakta Śivas in der indische Literatur* (Wiesbaden, 1977), pp. 211, 223.

In the first three Sanskrit texts mentioned above, the Renukā tale is part of a larger story whose main character is Paraśurāma rather than Renukā. The Paraśurāma legends fall outside the scope of this study.[40]

Apart from some minor details, the Mahābhārata plot of the Renukā tale is quite similar to the orally relayed version. Renukā, wife of the great ascetic Jamadagni, is about to take a bath when she sees king Citraratha and his wives bathing in the water and "desires him" (*tasya spṛhayāmāsa*). Trembling, she returns to her husband's ashram, where Jamadagni is immediately aware that Renukā has lost her virtuousness. In his anger, he commands his four oldest sons to kill their mother. When they refuse to do so, he curses them. However, his fifth and youngest son Rāma does obey him and beheads his mother with an axe. Jamadagni is satisfied and grants Rāma as many wishes as he likes. Then it says:

> He [Rāma] asked for his mother to come back to life without remembering her death, and for his brothers' return to their original state, unaffected by the crime (17). The great ascetic Jamadagni granted him invincibility in battle, a long life and all his wishes. Bhārata (18).[41]

This is how the story ends. Sanskritist Van Buitenen translates verse 17 as follows: "He chose that his mother would rise alive, that *he* forget the murder and be untouched by the crime, and that his brothers return to normality." (my italics, AvV).[42] In this translation,

---

[40] See: Gail, *Paraśurāma Brahmane und Krieger. Untersuchung über Ursprung und Entwicklung eines Avatara Visnus und Bhakta Sivas in der indische Literatur*; Kumar S.S. Janaki, "Paraśurāma", *Purana* 8 (1966), 1, pp. 52–82; Madeleine Biardeau, "La décapitation de Renukā dans le mythe de Paraśurāma", *Pratidānam. Idian, Iranian and Indo-European Studies Presented to Franciscus Bernardus Jacobus Kuiper on his Sixtieth Birthday*, eds. J.C. Heesterman, G.H. Schokker and V.I. Subramoniam (The Hague/Paris, 1968), pp. 563–572; David Dean Shulman, *The King and the Clown in South Indian Myth and Poetry* (Princeton, 1985), pp. 110–129; Robert Goldman, "Some Observations on the Paraśu of Paraśurāma", *Journal of the Oriental Institute (M.S. University of Baroda)* 21 (1972), 3, pp. 153–165; R. Champakalakshmi, *Vaisnava Iconography in the Tamil Country* (New Delhi, 1981), pp. 112–116. Summaries of Paraśurāma stories can be found in: Cornelia Dimmit and J.A.B. Van Buitenen (eds. and transl.), *Classical Hindu Mythology. A Reader in the Sanskrit Purāṇas* (Philadelphia, 1978), pp. 82–85; John Dowson, *A Classical Dictionary of Hindu Mythology and Religion. Geography, History and Literature* (Calcutta, 1991 (1982)), pp. 130–131.

[41] Sanskrit-Dutch trans. AvV; Dutch-English trans. MH. In Sanskrit: *17. sa vavre māturutthānamasmṛtim ca vadhasya vai / pāpena tena cāsparśam bhrātṛṇām prakṛtim tathā / 18. apratidvandvatām yuddhe dīrghamāyuśca bhārata / dadau ca sarvānkāmāmstāñjamadagnirmahātapāḥ* (Mbh. III.116:17–18).

[42] J.A.B. van Buitenen (translated and edited by), *The Mahābhārata, Book 2: The*

Paraśurāma wishes himself to forget his mother's death. However, my translation is more plausible grammatically.

Other Sanskrit texts also mention Paraśurāma's wish for his mother not to remember her death. In Viṣṇudharmottara-purāṇa, Paraśurāma asks for his mother's resurrection, "but without recollection in her" (VdhP, 36:15).[43] This wish is granted: Reṇukā rises "smiling sweetly" (cāruhāsinī; VdhP, 36:17) and does not bear a grudge towards Jamadagni. In Bhāgavata-purāṇa, too, Paraśurāma requests "the resurrection of those who were killed without any recollection of their deaths," and this wish is also fulfilled: "they rose immediately, as if waking up from a sound sleep" (BhP, IX,16:7b–8a).[44]

The Reṇukāmāhātmya version (chapters 21–26) is the most detailed of the four Sanskrit versions of the Reṇukā tale. In this text, Reṇukā is the main character and she is identified with Pārvatī. In this version, Paraśurāma is offered two boons by his father after having killed his mother. His first wish is for his brothers to be brought back to life. His second wish is the following:

> May this mother and goddess, the infallible Reṇukā, quickly revive of her own accord, without any recollection of her death, father. She, who worships you, the mother of the world on whose lotus feet the sages and yogins always meditate, she was killed by me. Ensure that this mother does not remember that it was I who killed her, so that this gruesome matricide will not be mine, my lord. (RM, 25:22–24)[45]

Jamadagni then admits he is guilty and brings Reṇukā back to life. Reṇukā is sprinkled with nectar and then comes to her feet in apparently good health. The sons' question to their mother, "Mother, tell us who was responsible for your long sleep on the ground...?" (RM, 25:29) seems intended to test whether Reṇukā has indeed no recollection of her killer, as Paraśurāma wished. However, the question goes unanswered.

The Reṇukā tales in the Sanskrit texts show a remarkable similarity.

Book of the Assembly Hall and Book 3: The Book of the Forest (Chicago and London, 1975), pp. 445–446.

[43] *rāma uvāca / guru śreṣṭha samutthānaṃ jananyāḥ kathayāmyaham / asmṛtiñca tathā tasyāṃ bhrātṛṇāñca tathā 'smṛtim* (Vdh, 36:15).

[44] *vavre hatānāṃ rāmo 'pi jīvitaṃ cāsmṛtiṃ vadhe / uttasthus te kuśalino nidrāpāya ivāñjasā* (BhP, IX,16:7b–8a).

[45] *22. rāmaḥ / iyaṃ me jananī devī reṇukā 'vyabhicāriṇī / ajñātvā svavadhaṃ tāta kṣipramuttiṣṭhatu svayam / 23. yasyāḥ pādābjayugalaṃ dhyāyaṃti munayaḥ sadā / yogīnaśca jaganmātustvadbhaktyā sā hatā mayā / 24. tathā mātṛvadho ghoro na bhaviṣyati me prabho / mayā hateti māteyaṃ na jānāti tathā kuru* (RM, 25:22–24).

In all four texts, Paraśurāma wishes for the resurrection of his mother (and, in VdhP and BhP, his brothers too), *without her remembering her death*. Nowhere outside the Sanskrit tradition have I been able to find this remarkable 'embellishment'. Because we are familiar with another version of the story from folk Hinduism, we know what would happen if Reṇukā recollected her violent death.[46] In the Sanskrit texts, Paraśurāma prevents his mother from using her increased *śakti* to express her dissatisfaction with the course of events. This allows the narrative about the male heroes Jamadagni and Paraśurāma to continue unimpeded. The men are not held accountable for their actions, and they need not fear revenge. In the Sanskrit texts, Reṇukā is not transformed into a (minor) goddess either. Thus, Māriyamman's feared *śakti* has been rendered harmless in advance.

The difference between the Sanskrit versions and the oral version that Meyer recorded can be explained by the greater influence of women in folk Hinduism.[47] Until the mid-nineteenth century, women were not allowed to study the classical Sanskrit texts. As German sociologist Maria Mies wrote: "If literary education is considered as a criterion for belonging to the 'great tradition', and that is obvious, then the women of *all* castes are excluded from this 'great tradition.'"[48] Mies's distinction between 'great tradition' and 'little tradition' is akin to the opposition between Sanskrit tradition and folk Hinduism. The exclusion of women from the Sanskrit tradition is reflected in proverbs and passages from Sanskrit texts which equate women with *śūdras*, the fourth and lowest class (*varṇa*). By contrast, folk Hinduism is made up of several autonomous religious traditions which have no central decision-making authority (such as Brahmins) which assesses the orthodoxy or heterodoxy of certain elements. Folk Hinduism is a collective term for the religious traditions which fall outside the scope of the Sanskrit tradition. Usually these traditions are more local; they are often practised by the lower castes and usu-

---

[46] This holds true no matter which version is older. To determine which is the older version, much more research would be needed. Richard Brubaker has also compared written and oral versions of the Reṇukā tale. Richard L. Brubaker, "Lustful Woman, Chaste Wife, Ambivalent Goddess. A South India Myth", *Anima* 3 (1977), pp. 59–62.

[47] For the differences between the oral and written traditions in this respect, see: A.K. Ramanujan, "Who Needs Folklore? The Relevance of Oral Traditions to South Asian Studies", *Manushi. A Journal about Women and Society* 69 (1992), pp. 2–16.

[48] Maria Mies, *Indian Women and Patriarchy. Conflicts and Dilemmas of Students and Working Women* (New Delhi, 1980), p. 39.

ally shunned by Brahmins. Within folk Hinduism, there are male-dominated cults, but there are also exclusively female traditions, and festivals and cults dominated by women. In general, I believe folk Hinduism is more accessible to women than the Sanskrit tradition, because its traditions are mainly passed down orally or in the written vernacular.

In the folk version of the Māriyamma<u>n</u> story, which Meyer was told by low caste singers, Māriyamma<u>n</u>'s *śakti* outgrows the patriarchal structure of society. Māriyamma<u>n</u> knows full well what injustices have been done to her. Her unclean body is sufficient reminder of what has transpired. Armed with her boundless *śakti*, she directs her anger at the higher, male gods. This is clearly different from the Sanskrit texts in which Re<u>n</u>ukā is rigorously robbed of any opportunity for resistance and even her memory is erased. This illustrates how, in the words of anthropologist Ardener, women are 'muted' in the male-dominated Sanskrit tradition.[49]

Māriyamma<u>n</u> Priestess

To conclude, I will present an alternative to my interpretation of the Re<u>n</u>ukā tale: an analysis of the tale from the folk Hindu tradition. This is the interpretation by Sarasvati, a Māriyamma<u>n</u> priestess and medium from Madras who belongs to an untouchable caste.[50] Māriyamma<u>n</u> first appeared to her at a time of great adversity. Separated from her husband, she had just married off her eldest daughter and was left with eight children to raise on her own. Poverty drove her to despair. One night, she contemplated killing herself and her children. Then Māriyamma<u>n</u> appeared in a dream and promised to protect her. Later, the goddess tightened her grip on Sarasvati by striking her with tuberculosis, because Sarasvati had temporarily neglected her. However, when Sarasvati was deathly ill and no medical treatment had any effect, Māriyamma<u>n</u> saw to it that she was cured. From then on, Sarasvati devoted herself to Māriyamma<u>n</u> as a priestess and a medium. Sarasvati did good business as a medium,

---

[49] E. Ardener, "Belief and the Problem of Woman / The 'Problem' Revisited", *Perceiving Women*, ed. Shirley Ardener (London, 1975), pp. 21–25.
[50] Egnor, "On the Meaning of Śakti to Women in Tamil Nadu", pp. 11–15; Egnor, "The Changed Mother or What the Smallpox Did when there was no more Smallpox", pp. 24–45.

earning enough to support her entire family. During her sessions, Sarasvati became possessed: the goddess spoke through her to others. Once, Māriyamma<u>n</u> told her life story through Sarasvati's mouth:

> She said that she had been a good married woman, but because of a trivial slip was unjustly accused of unchastity by her husband. Her husband sent her son to kill her, and she fled through the jungle until an untouchable woman offered her refuge. Her son caught and beheaded them both, then realizing his crime, put the heads back on the bodies, but the head of the 'good' woman was put on the untouchable woman's body, and vice versa. Thus the two women were inseparably united, and united also in their suffering. This united pair—the head of one woman, the body of another—became the goddess, *śakti*.[51]

It is for this reason that the goddess identifies with and is most helpful towards suffering women, said Sarasvati. "For Tamil women only I am one who will do much good," she said. Sarasvati stresses the joint suffering of the two women. After the head exchange, the women together become the goddess, also called *śakti*. This is what brings the Māriyamma<u>n</u> priestess to show solidarity with other women and convinces her to help women only.[52] According to Egnor, this interpretation reflects both the notion that suffering increases *śakti* and an awareness of solidarity among Tamil women, based on a shared fate. Although these women perpetuate the tradition of female subordination, they also support each other and share the suffering they experience in their subordinate position. Earlier, in the Meyer version, we saw that *śakti* denotes women's anger and resistance. Now we see *śakti* representing the power of solidarity. According to Egnor, *śakti* refers to the strength of female bonding: "This I believe is the central significance of the doctrine that the goddess *śakti* has many names and many forms and lives in many places, and yet is still *the* goddess: one goddess, one power, one *śakti*. Her power consists in this union of many."[53]

Sarasvati's interpretation exemplifies how women in a patriarchal structure use *śakti* for their own purposes. The idea that self-sacrifice

---

[51] Egnor, "On the Meaning of Śakti to Women in Tamil Nadu", p. 13.
[52] Sarasvati believed that one had to be poor and lower caste in order to become possessed by Māriyamma<u>n</u>. In this respect, she showed solidarity not only with Tamil women, but also with the poor and the untouchables. Egnor, "The Changed Mother or What the Smallpox Goddess Did When There Was No More Smallpox", p. 29.
[53] Egnor, "On the Meaning of Śakti to Women in Tamil Nadu", pp. 27–28.

and suffering increase women's *śakti* is in line with patriarchal ideology. But Sarasvati's spin on this idea shows that women within the patriarchal system also have some influence and power. Based on her personal interpretation of the story, she channels her abilities very selectively: she uses her supernatural powers only to help women. Māriyamma<u>n</u> and Sarasvati seem to form a good pair. They need each other to construct a women's culture within the patriarchal culture. The *śakti* of Māriyamma<u>n</u> and Sarasvati ensures that wonders will never cease.

Double-voiced

We have seen three versions of the same story about Māriyamma<u>n</u>. In the Meyer version, Re<u>n</u>ukā's *śakti* grew so much after she was killed that she was deified and became Māriyamma<u>n</u>, the goddess. This allowed her to right the wrongs done to her. Her *śakti* overcame the patriarchal structure to which it owed its existence. In the Sanskrit texts, this empowerment was prevented by Paraśurāma's wish that his mother be brought back to life "without any recollection of her death". In this way, her *śakti* was defused in advance. In other words, women are muted in the male-dominated Sanskrit tradition. The consequences of this silencing process, which was brought to light by comparing different versions of the narrative, are explained by literary theorist Elaine Showalter. She believes that, within their 'subculture', women redefine reality from their own perspective. But because women are simultaneously part of the dominant culture which marginalizes them, the language they speak is often "*double-voiced*, containing a dominant and a muted story."[54] I believe this is also true of the Māriyamma<u>n</u> stories passed down in folk Hinduism. The heavy punishment Re<u>n</u>ukā receives for her adulterous thoughts is in accordance with dominant patriarchal social norms and the male-dominated Sanskrit tradition. But the oral story also contains a hidden form of resistance: after death, Re<u>n</u>ukā returns to earth as a feared goddess. This second voice reflects the greater influence women have in folk Hinduism than in the Sanskrit tradition.

---

[54] Elaine Showalter, "Feminist Criticism in the Wilderness", *The New Feminist Criticism: Essays on Women, Literature and Theory*, ed. Elaine Showalter (London, 1986), p. 266.

The idiosyncratic interpretation of the story offered by Sarasvati, the priestess, is also double-voiced. She assigns her own meaning to the Māriyamma<u>n</u> story and, as a woman, appropriates Māriyamma<u>n</u>'s *śakti*. She believes *śakti* symbolizes the shared suffering of women and therefore, as a Māriyamma<u>n</u> priestess, she decides to stand by other women and to devote her miraculous powers to the service of women only. This is a revolutionary act in a patriarchy, where men receive preferential treatment all the time. To Sarasvati, Māriyamma<u>n</u> is an exponent of a specific women's culture. Hence, her interpretation gives voice to the muted, female, discourse.

Another striking aspect of this comparison of various versions is the evident ambivalence of Māriyamma<u>n</u>'s *śakti*. Her lethal and her curative powers are inextricably linked. This sets her, like other minor gods in the pantheon, apart from the higher gods, who are ascribed a purely benevolent power. This aspect also distinguishes their powers from the Christian tradition, in which miracles are beneficial by definition. I have put Māriyamma<u>n</u>'s ambivalent nature in the context of her life story, which has much in common with other South Indian stories of people deified after death. The notion that suffering increases *śakti*, which in turn causes deification, plays a crucial role in these myths. Women's subordinate position makes them much more prone to suffering then men. In my opinion, these ideas about *śakti* explain why so many of the minor, ambivalent deities are feminine. By connecting Māriyamma<u>n</u>'s ambivalent nature with her life story and women's everyday lives, I have shown that this ambivalence is not 'inherently feminine', but is a consequence of women's socio-cultural position in the real world.[55] The ambiguous power of minor goddesses, seen in light of their suffering and anger, is yet another double voice reflecting women's marginalized position.

Translation: Mischa F. Hoyinck

---

[55] At a metaphysical level, the ambivalence of goddesses is often described as 'inherently feminine', for instance in the outdated study by Erich Neumann, *The Great Goddess. An Analysis of the Archetype* (Princeton, 1963). I disagree with both his interpretation and that of Lawrence A. Babb in "Marriage and Malevolence. The Uses of Sexual Opposition in a Hindu Pantheon", *Ethnology* 9 (1970), 2, pp. 215–229. My view is in line with Hanchett, *Coloured Rice. Symbolic Structure in Hindu Family Festivals*, pp. 187–188.

10

WOMEN AND MIRACLES IN THE STORIES OF INGEBORG BACHMANN

Ilse N. Bulhof

Introduction

Modern culture frowns upon belief in miracles: miracles do not happen in the real world. Because of the discovery of the laws of nature, modernity was—until recently—confident that in the near future the course of events in this one and only real world could be predicted. The corollary of this confidence was/is the (implicit or explicit) belief that nothing outside this world, no transcendent power or Other could make itself felt in the world as it is. The world was/is one-dimensional. Yet some events in the real world—such as a birth or a full recovery from a sickness—are still experienced as truly wonderful, even as miraculous. In the context of modernity, however, it is self-evident that these are mere feelings and should be taken with a grain of salt: purely private emotional reactions, unreal psychological occurrences. Texts expressing feelings of wonder and thankfulness vis-à-vis the world belong to the non-serious domain of poetry. Poetry speaks metaphorically or figuratively; it speaks the language of somewhat marginalized people like artists, children and women.

As the Austrian philosopher turned novelist Ingeborg Bachmann shows, even the sense of the miraculous in the modern poetic sense of the word is threatened by the modern one-dimensional worldview that excludes the truly Other, Transcendence. Moreover, she discovered painfully that the marginalization of the miraculous and of the others that are women are intimately connected. Bachmann herself does not use the words 'miracle' and 'miraculous' in her texts. Nevertheless, I feel that her fiction can be read as a woman's struggle to rescue a sense of the miraculous from a darkening world by bringing into focus various shapes of 'figurative' miracles: the romantic miracle of a love that works wonders, the democratic miracle of an 'impossible' solidarity between such extremes as men and women and the miracle of simple enjoyment of the elemental—an experience of a sacred dimension in this world.

In the first part of this contribution I will introduce Ingeborg Bachmann and make some remarks on the cultural context in which she wrote.[1] In the second part I will analyze the development of her thinking on women and miracles. I will do this by discussing four of her texts: first, the short story 'The Thirtieth Year,' in which the literally and figuratively closed world of modernity (closed because one cannot escape its one-dimensionality) excludes miracles—and, implicitly, women; second, the short story 'Everything,' in which a (poetically speaking) miracle occurs—the type that is allowed in the context of modernity: democratic solidarity between a woman and a man; third, the novel *Malina* in which the expectation raised by the possibility of miracles in the figurative sense is denied; and fourth, *The Case of Franza* in which both literal and metaphorical miracles are left behind in a new and hopeful experience of what is most common and most ordinary: the elemental.

Auschwitz and the Threat of 'Gnosticism'

Miracles have no place in modern culture. In the modern period the dualistic worldview of God and world[2] slowly gave way to an one-dimensional world from which miracles in the literal sense and Transcendence as the origin of the miraculous were excluded. Even though in the twentieth century nature may no longer be seen by the scientists themselves as ruled by strict laws of cause and effect, the world is still viewed by our culture in general as an autonomously functioning whole that has no 'outside' to it.[3] It was held then and now that the more knowledge we have of the workings of this autonomous domain, the less need we have to explain events as the

---

[1] For an English introduction to the oeuvre of Ingeborg Bachmann see a.o. *Thunder Rumbling at my Heels: Tracing Ingeborg Bachmann*, ed. and introd. by Gudrun Brokoph-Mauch (Riverside, 1997); Karen R. Achberger, *Understanding Ingeborg Bachmann* (Columbia, 1995).

[2] This dualism had been reinforced since the later Middle Ages by nominalism, which did away with the Platonic notion of participation.

[3] It should be added that so-called postmodern philosophy is in the process of reintroducing the notion of an 'outside'—an outside located in our world. See: Henk Oosterling, *Door schijn bewogen: Naar een hypercritiek van de xenofobe rede* (Kampen, 1996).

results of supernatural intervention. In spite of its predictability, however, the modern worldview was not reassuring. Darwin exposed the cruelty of the laws of nature and Nietzsche suggested that the so-called laws of nature and of human history were and are human inventions, ploys made up by humans in their struggle to survive in a chaotic world.[4] It made people wonder whether what was acknowledged as good and evil in our culture might not be impositions by those in power, a matter of force and egoism rather than truth and justice. From there it was only one step further to ask whether brute force was perhaps the supreme ruler of life. Auschwitz intensified the old spectre of 'gnosticism:'[5] the idea that this world cannot be the work of a good God, that it is the devil who made and rules this world, that the good God is somewhere else.

The loss of belief in the good God had alarming consequences. In a culture that had been based on such a belief it suggests that everything is now permitted: 'Gnosticism' threatens ethics. Since World War II the intellectual elite in the Western world—philosophers, artists, columnists—have attempted to avert such a 'gnosticism' without, however, minimalizing evil—the Holocaust—by means of the usual Christian, Hegelian, or 'metaphysical' subterfuges that explain it away. Ingeborg Bachmann has been one of them. For her, too, the good God of traditional Christian faith was 'dead,' leaving an empty space that demonic powers could occupy only too easily. How, she wondered, could this tendency toward evil be checked? Do signs of hope exist? In this dark world are miracles—in the sense of healing events that are above and by now almost outside human expectation—still possible?

Ingeborg Bachmann: A Short Biography

Ingeborg Bachmann (1926–1973) was born thirteen years before the *Anschluss* between Austria and Hitler's Germany in the small town of Klagenfurt, a charming place close to the Austrian border with Italy and the former Yugoslavia. Her parents were Protestants, but

---

[4] Marx had already made this point, but he still believed that this was a passing phenomenon and that the world could become a place of justice. Nietzsche no longer shared this optimism.

[5] See: Hans Blumenberg, *The Legitimacy of the Modern Age* (Cambridge/London, 1983).

she went to Roman Catholic schools. Although highly gifted in the field of music, she decided to study philosophy after the war. During her student years in Vienna she was as much fascinated by her compatriot the philosopher Ludwig Wittgenstein (1889–1951), author of the lucid text *Tractatus logico-philosophicus* (1921) as she was repulsed by the German philosopher Martin Heidegger (1889–1976), author of important but hermetic texts and tainted by his association with the Nazis prior to the war. Although Bachmann appreciated his attempt to bring emotions (anxiety) back within the orbit of philosophy, she deemed the philosophical language in which he did this obscure and unaesthetic. After defending her doctoral thesis,[6] she decided that her future lay in literature rather than philosophy and its pitiful jargon. At first she had to accept minor jobs, such as in radio,[7] but after a few years she could survive on her writing. She wrote poetry, short stories, and a novel. She died from injuries caused by a fire at her home in Rome.

The Move to Literature

In the move from philosophy to literature the influence of Wittgenstein was crucial.[8] Ingeborg Bachmann was deeply impressed by Wittgenstein's "desperate struggle with the unsayable [*das Unaussprechliche*]" or "the mystical [*das Mystische*],"[9] that is to say, by his shipwreck on the rock of 'the positive destination of philosophy.' His struggle and

---

[6] Ingeborg Bachmann, *Die kritische Aufnahme der Existentialphilosophie Martin Heideggers* [Dissertation, Vienna 1949] (Munich, 1985).

[7] Ingeborg Bachmann, *Der gute Gott von Manhattan; Die Zikade; Zwei Hörspiele* (Munich, 1972).

[8] She wrote an important essay on Wittgenstein: "Ludwig Wittgenstein: Zu einem Kapitel der jüngsten Philosophiegeschichte", (1953) in: Ingeborg Bachmann, *Die Wahrheit ist dem Menschen zumutbar: Essays, Reden, Kleinere Schriften* (Munich/Zurich, 1985), pp. 7–18.

[9] Wittgenstein mentions the unsayable in his *Tractatus logico-philosophicus* (1921), trans. D.F. Pears and B.F. Franklin (London/New York, 1974), p. 73: "6.522 There are indeed things that cannot be put into words. They *make themselves manifest*. They are what is mystical". Wittgenstein summarizes the content of this text in his preface as follows: "What can be said at all can be said clearly, and what we cannot talk about we must pass over in silence. Thus the aim of the book is to draw a limit to thought, or rather—not to thought, but to the expression of thoughts: for in order to be able to draw a limit to thought, we should have to find both sides of the limit thinkable (i.e. we should have to be able to think what cannot be thought)".

his repeated failure deserve, she adds, "our thinking participation": they urge us to reflect "time and time again" on what makes it impossible to say what philosophy is all about.[10] This is exactly what Bachmann does in her literary work.

What is this "unsayable?" It is, she explains, quoting Wittgenstein, "what is on the other side" of what can be said and thought. It is that which falls outside of the parameters of the discourses of the natural sciences and scientific philosophy. The sciences can only describe what exists or is, and what is can be stated in exact, univocal language. Philosophy, however scientific it attempts to be, cannot express what it is all about using the language of natural science.[11]

Wittgenstein drew the conclusion—according to Bachmann, quite unexpectedly—that philosophy's focus is 'the unsayable.' He was tormented by the limitations of human reason and language. As Bachmann points out, his torment resulted from a personal "mystical experience," an "archi-experience" of "a presence of the real in a few moments of grace."[12] Although the unsayable is not an existent, it is nevertheless real. But it is not a reality *beyond* or *in* this world. Wittgenstein stated that it makes itself *manifest* [*zeigt sich*]; it makes its presence felt in an indirect manner. Unfortunately, we humans exist, think and speak on this side of the limit of the world, of what is; we cannot get out of the world. But as humans (being metaphysical subjects) we are aware of this limit, and that awareness is the cause of our torment. Positive logical, scientific, ethical or philosophical statements cannot say anything that makes sense on the meaning of being,[13] life, the good or whatever it is that is of existential importance. Wittgenstein saw the only exit was to make philosophy real in silence. He radically withdrew from philosophy and took up a simple life far from the world and from fame.

---

[10] Bachmann, "Ludwig Wittgenstein", p. 8.

[11] One conclusion might be that the object of philosophical reflection does not exist in the way that the objects of natural science exist. Another might be that philosophy is not yet mature enough to speak in the required way. Yet a third might be that philosophy is not a science because its objects of reflection do not exist at all and that to talk about them thus would make no sense. Wittgenstein's neo-positivist colleagues of the 'Vienna circle' happily gave up the fuzzy and sterile metaphysical speculations of traditional philosophy. Wittgenstein reacted to this latter conclusion.

[12] Bachmann, "Ludwig Wittgenstein", p. 10.

[13] This is what Heidegger attempted in *Sein und Zeit*: he advocated renewed attention to "the question of Being".

Bachmann also left the field of philosophy, but she did not think that, given the way the world is, silence was an adequate response. She was driven by a deep sense of responsibility for what was going on in the world. Instead of interpreting Wittgenstein's position vis-à-vis the unsayable as implying that we are not able to state the unsayable in clear language, she understood it to mean that "we are not allowed" to represent the unsayable "because we have no word in our language that is truly important."[14] Language as it is now is too corrupted to be able to say what is truly good and meaningful. Thus she concluded from her study of Wittgenstein that for us the point was now to find a more adequate language—for example, a language that does not directly name and reveal the way the sciences do but points indirectly to (or hints at) what is absent and what used to be called God, the Absolute or the Good. In other words, she wanted to search for a new literary language. The themes taken by such a search would run parallel to those of traditional philosophy: God, the soul, conscience—Kant's unsayable and unthinkable noumena, i.e. the, in his view, "postulates of practical reason." Thus Bachmann the philosopher who wanted to think and speak about what is truly important in life—the good in a world without God—abdicated and gave way to Bachmann the writer.

Miracles in the Dual Context of Wittgenstein and Auschwitz

That "God does not reveal himself in the world" is, according to Ingeborg Bachmann, "one of the most bitter sentences" of the *Tractatus*.[15] On this issue she has not commented directly. As readers we may, however, attempt to clarify her position.

That God does not reveal himself in the world seems to mean to Bachmann that he does not act in the world, that he—or holy persons acting in his name—do not perform miracles in the traditional literal sense of the word. This realization becomes bitter when we think about the profound suffering of the world—the Holocaust being the epitome of suffering. It seems that for Bachmann, God's inactivity implies that God and the Good may make themselves felt in a different, indirect way instead of through miraculous direct action.

---

[14] Bachmann, "Ludwig Wittgenstein", p. 18.
[15] Bachmann, "Ludwig Wittgenstein", p. 17.

As she shows in her literary work, a God who cannot be directly present—who does not work miracles—and who cannot be positively named (for example, by the name of 'God,' or 'heavenly Father' or 'highest Being') can be easily ignored. An inexperienced young person, for example, who simply longs to know God or the Absolute, who would love to feel close and to act in his or its name, is, given this 'absence,' very vulnerable to self-doubt and ridicule and rejection. For indeed, given God's absence she or he has no clear reason to maintain the Good or to believe that the way the world is is, in principle (at bottom, qua essence), good. The best we have is a democratic consensus on what we consider good. The call of conscience to do the Good—the call to justice, love of neighbour, selflessness—is precarious when the traditional caller, God, is 'dead.'

In her essay on Wittgenstein Bachmann mentions in passing Pascal, who had come to realize that he was living in the modern world with its infinite time and space instead of the finite world of pre-modernity. Under these circumstances, Pascal, a deeply religious man, no longer wanted to write about leaving the world in his quest for God but of leaving in this very same world the 'order' of this world, that is to say, the profane orders of power and of knowledge, in order to enter the 'order of love' or charity—that is to say, the holy order of Christ ("My kingdom is not of this world . . ."). For Pascal, the order of Christ was still real in the literal sense: the kind of miracles that had happened at the time of Jesus could still happen in the world of today. Because of his recognition of three qualitatively different but no less real orders inside this (modern) world, Pascal could continue to believe in miracles, such as miraculous healings. He had witnessed one in his family.[16]

Bachmann did not only live under modern but also under post-Holocaust conditions. Auschwitz demonstrated not only that the hope for miracles was vain but also showed what Wittgenstein had not (fore)seen: the growing force of the powers of evil that had become unleashed by the awareness of a God who does not reveal himself in this world. In a desperate attempt to check the powers of evil she held on to an 'irrational' belief in the possibility of goodness on

---

[16] Cf. Colin Brown, *Miracles and the Critical Mind* (Grand Rapids, 1984), pp. 37–40. On Pascal see: Arjan Plaisier, *De mens in het geding: Een kritische vergelijking tussen Pascal en Nietzsche* (Utrecht, 1996).

earth—in a 'once upon a time,' a utopia, an eschatological future—
without belief in a God that would bring this future, this miracle,
about. Hers was an impressive but desperate kind of 'messianism
without a Messiah'—akin to that of Theodor Adorno.[17] But in *The
Case of Franza* she seems to be on the verge of moving out of the
Christian/post-Christian dualism by envisioning a post-post-Christian
way to live in a utopia now.

Women and Miracles

In the premodern and predemocratic period people were oppressed
by ecclesiastical and worldly powers. Under these circumstances
women had suffered even more than men: for the hierarchy that
placed the church above the state was paralleled on earth by the
hierarchy between men and women. In modern democracies the
churches and kings were divested of their power and people were
equal. But that equality did not end oppression. In their struggle for
life—a struggle of all against all in the one-dimensional world—people now oppress one another. Therefore, Bachmann seems to say,
the transition from premodernity to modernity was not progress. On
the contrary: the situation became worse than that which had preceded it. If anything, the transition was regress. And again women
suffered most from this development: for in democracies men continued to consider themselves superior to women. (Bachmann also
indicates some other misplaced feelings of superiority of the same
nature: whites considering themselves superior to non-whites, the
Germans to the Jews, etcetera.) The hierarchical dualism of God
and world was bad, but no dualism at all was even worse: the appeal
to a Transcendence that judged the affairs of the world and the trust
that justice would prevail[18] were now no longer an option.

---

[17] "Die Literatur... die sich nur zu erkennen gibt als ein tausendfacher und mehrtausendjähriger Verstoss gegen die schlechte Sprache—denn das Leben hat nur eine schlechte Sprache—und die ihm darum ein Utopia der Sprache gegenüber-setzt, diese Literatur also, wie eng sie sich auch an die Zeit und ihre schlechte Sprache halten mag, ist zu rühmen wegen ihres verzweiflungsvollen Unterwegsseins zu dieser Sprache und nur darum ein Ruhm und eine Hoffnung der Menschen", Theodor Adorno, *Frankfurter Vorlesungen: Probleme zeitgenössischer Dichtung (1959–1960)* (Zurich/Munich, 1982), p. 92. On Adorno see: Gerrit Steunebrink, "Is Adorno's Philosophy a Negative Theology?" in: Ilse N. Bulhof and Laurens ten Cate (eds.), *Flight of the Gods: Philosophical Perspectives on Negative Theology* (New York, forthcoming).

[18] One should recall here the position of Kant and his "postulates of practical

Bachmann's works speak to us of God (the Absolute) and the Good indirectly, namely 'in the negative:' how dark the world is becoming now that God is 'dead,' now that the rules for good and evil are no longer so easily known and may even be the work of evil rulers, and conscience has no support in clearly stated philosophy or doctrine. Her writings speak of how pure egocentrism seems to be the only viable attitude in such a world, how this situation kills moral sense in sensitive people and how women seem to suffer doubly in this situation: they are the first to become victims, and they seem to be more aware of the injustice that is going on. At first, the heroes of Bachmann's short stories who struggle to resist evil and to behave humanely—the persons the author asks her readers to identify with—are young men, for example, in "The Thirtieth Year" and "Everything." Only gradually did she come to realize that modernity hurts women even more than men. Although officially ('before the law') the equals of men, women are not able to function in the modern world like men—unless they sacrifice their 'femininity.' In the unfinished and posthumously published *The Case of Franza* a new perspective is offered. The Absolute is not the God of the Christian faith and miracles as literal events resulting from divine intervention are indeed impossible. The Absolute is now depicted as the empty sun-filled desert that burns away everything that is not authentic. By the same token the desert frees a person for a new experience—a truly new 'miracle': the experience of the elemental after sunset, at night.

"The Thirtieth Year": No Miracles, No Women

In her story "The Thirtieth Year" Bachmann depicts a young man who gradually becomes an adult in a world in which God does not reveal himself and how this causes him to lose his moral sense.[19] He turns thirty and suddenly realizes that he should stop thinking that the future is open to him, that he can go any direction he wants. He must realize one of all the possibilities before him. He has to

---

reason", which are, according to Adorno, an impressive expression of the human "Unausdenkbarkeit der Verzweiflung". See: Steunebrink, "Is Adorno's Philosophy a Negative Theology?"

[19] Ingeborg Bachmann, "The Thirtieth Year", in: Ingeborg Bachmann, *The Thirtieth Year* (New York, 1987), pp. 18–61. The numbers in the text refer to this edition.

find a place for himself. "Now he knows he too is in the trap" (14). He gets his things together, but it is not easy to enter the 'real world.' That world is no fun: "He becomes aware that malice is possible and that it can reach him; indeed that it has frequently come close to him before . . . this malice . . . will grow and will pervade his life" (17).

In the year he gives himself to make up his mind about what to do he remembers at one point an episode that had occurred in the library ten years earlier. He was thinking about a problem of knowledge. "And as he *thought* and *thought* and flew higher and higher as though on a swing, without feeling dizzy, and as he gave himself the most magnificent push, he felt himself fly against a ceiling through which he had to push his way up" (25). He felt great, "on the point of understanding something relating to everything and the ultimate" (idem). One more push and then he would know. Then it happened. A blow struck and shook him, inside his head; a pain arose that caused him to slacken, he slowed down his thinking, became confused and jumped down from the swing. He had exceeded his capacity for thinking or perhaps no one could go on thinking where he had been. Up above, in his head, against the roof of his skull, something was going click-click-click. It was quite frightening and he almost fainted. "He had come to the end" (26). Something was broken, destroyed: namely a creature that had risen too high, a winged being that had striven to pass through corridors filled with blue dusk to a source of light, to be exact a man, no longer as a counterpart, but as the potential accessory to Creation. He was destroyed as a potential accessory, and from now on he would never be able to rise so high and touch the logic upon which the world is suspended. This young man is like Icharus, the great philosophers or like Lucifer himself, we might say, all of whom had hoped that they could solve the riddle of the world and know the way God knows. What had happened to them? They fell back to the earth; they were banished into hell. And so is this young man.

From that moment on, knowledge became a torment to him, because he had committed a crime there . . . and had been destroyed in the process. Henceforth he could only learn odds and ends, become a hack and keep his intelligence supple, but that did not interest him. He would have liked to set himself up outside, to have looked over the frontier and from there back upon himself and the world and language and every proviso. He would have liked to have come back with another language that would have been capable of expressing the secret he had discovered.

In other words, the dream of total, Godlike knowledge was destroyed. Viewed from that perspective, a down-to-earth life did not seem worth much to him. Now that he could not be the saviour of the world, his role in it could not be impressive in any way. According to the dualist model of thought it was either the old ideal or nothing: either be like God or be lost, abandoned—and become angry, malevolent; either live in heaven or in hell. "He knew now that he was living in a prison, that he had to make the best of it in there and would soon rage and would have to speak this thieves' cant, the only language at his disposal, in order not to be so abandoned" (29). Echoing Wittgenstein, he muses that he could not meet God here and that God had not admitted him there. For if He had anything to do with this world here, with this language, He would not be God. God cannot be in this madness, cannot be in it, can only have to do with the fact that this madness is, that this madness is there and that there is no end to the madness [*Wahn*].

Clearly, in the experience of this young man a world without God is madness. God's absence causes him to complain, to sulk. His pride has been hurt. "The mystical" of which Wittgenstein spoke does not reveal itself to this young man. In the course of the year he experiences "unbelievable love." But it was "unbearable". It expected nothing, demanded nothing and gave nothing. It did not allow itself to be fenced in, cultivated and planted with feelings, but it "stepped over all boundaries and smashed down all feelings". It was "too much" and he sought "refuge in departure (33–34)." Absolute love (God is love!), the love St Paul preached, cannot exist in this world.

On his way back home where his father had arranged a job for him, the young man hitches a ride. He is picked up by a man whose presence makes him feel calmer and comfortable. He wants to speak to him about what really bothers him, "what was to be done and what one was to think of it all" (52). Then they have an accident, in which the driver was killed on the spot. The young man, however, survives and is taken to a hospital. "He sometimes thinks of him, staring at the ceiling. He thinks of him as of someone who has died in his place, and he sees him in front of him with that bright tension in his face, the young, firm hands on the wheel, sees him racing at the centre of the darkness in the world and there going up in flames" (53). For the first time, he begins to wish for life. He is able to formulate sentences "in which the world as a whole appeared" (54). He was beginning to believe—not in God or some such entity but in himself; he was gaining self-confidence. All in all, it had been an awful year—a year that had broken his bones. But he would be healed. He is now interested in the job that he will get and wishes to leave the hospital, "away from the victims of accidents, the infirm and moribund. I say unto thee: Rise up and walk! None of your bones is broken" (55). He will be able to take his place in the world as an adult.

But his reaching adulthood is a fall into the sins of the world. His unhappiness, profound and earnest as it has been, has not taught him solidarity with other suffering humans like him. He is no longer familiar with the Christian story and the values for which it stands and the promises it makes. He has no vision of the possibility of a better world. Making the best of his life in the prison of 'this world' means the worst in the case of this young man. He, like most people, will embrace the sordid life of the world, speak its corrupted language. His sense of the Absolute as a young man does not enable him to do any better than the rest as an adult. Abandoned by God the Father in heaven he now abandons others in his turn.

"Everything": A Modern Democratic Miracle: Solidarity Between a Man and a Woman

"Everything" is a moving story.[20] It depicts the Wittgensteinian thought that the limits of language are the limits of the world. From an irresponsible, somewhat helpless and alienated young man, thirty years old, the hero of the story gradually develops into a responsible person who accepts his position in the world. This young man learns from his suffering. He experiences little by little a conversion—not to the Absolute, God or the Good, but to his wife. At the end of the story the prospect opens to them of sharing their common suffering, the death of their son. "Everything" is the story of a modern democratic miracle of solidarity. Solidarity may be called a miracle only in figurative poetic language—but it is nevertheless a real miracle: it is an event above but not beyond expectation and has

---

[20] Ingeborg Bachmann, "Everything", in: Bachmann, *The Thirtieth Year*, pp. 62–82. The numbers in the text refer to this edition.

the quality of healing. It is the kind of miracle that is possible in an infinite homogeneous world in which the Absolute cannot reveal itself. It is a story of how to live decently after the 'death' of God and the miscarriage of the Enlightenment in bringing about the reign of truth on earth. The Absolute cannot be made present in this world or be represented, as Walter Benjamin, much admired by Bachmann, realized long before postmodern thinkers like Lyotard.[21]

Paradoxically, the story's hero falls step by step into evil by attempting to counteract the fall of mankind into the sordid world of everyday existence. He comes to think that a pure life is possible and decides to help to bring this world about by raising his infant son outside of the sins of the world so that the child can invent a new language to save the world, to "introduce a new era" (62). "He [the baby] was the first man. With him everything started, and it was impossible to say whether everything might not become quite different through him. Should I not leave the world to him, blank and without meaning?" For "here, where we are standing, the world is the worst of all worlds, and no one has understood it up to now, but where he was standing nothing had been decided. Not yet. How much longer?" (61).

Actually, the young father thinks, all existing languages are equally bad, having all originated "in Babel to confuse the world." What is so bad about these languages? What makes them so confused? It is because under existing ordinary language "smoulders another language," which is even worse because it is much less logical or rather totally illogical because it is rooted in the body—a language "that extends to gestures and looks, the unwinding of thoughts and the passage of feelings, and in it is all our misfortune" (62).

The father does not teach the child to speak the corrupted language that he himself had inherited, that is to say, he does not teach him to speak at all. To use Lacan's terms, the child is not introduced into the symbolic order, into the order of culture. But the child learns the language of adults anyway from the boys on the street who have, in turn, learned it from their fathers. His fall into the 'trap' cannot be prevented. Interestingly, the father hates that

---

[21] On Lyotard and the impossibility of making the good present on earth see Ilse N. Bulhof, *Het postmodernisme als uitdaging* (Baarn, 1990), pp. 11–50, in particular pp. 29–34.

language which he characterizes as a language of engineers, of planning and executing projects, a language full of "male tension" (64). Apparently, he is a man who refuses the male-dominated culture of his time. His own fall is not total, for traces of true humanity are preserved in him.

But the world of women repulses him too. The mother of the child, Hanna, who is also thirty, is a marginal character. Nevertheless it is clear that the man loves his wife very much, although it troubles him that the child is everything to her. She is the child's mother and only a mother. If that is so, what is his position as far as she is concerned? The more distantly the father behaves, the closer the child grows to the mother, and the more lovingly Hanna behaves—to compensate for the absence of the father. The father does not like Hanna's way of dealing with the child at all—the way she talks baby-talk to the child, the way she treats him, prays with and for him. As it turns out, the gap between the father and Hanna is the real cause of the problem, for in the final analysis that gap is what causes him to remove himself even farther from the child and from the world as it is. The gap is expressed in the very first sentence of the story:

> When we sit down to a meal like two people who have been turned to stone, or meet in the evening at the door of the apartment because we have both thought of bolting it at the same time, I feel our mourning like a bow stretching from one end of the world to the other—that is to say, from Hanna to me (56).

It is a bow of sadness, as large as a rainbow connecting two continents. In this case, however, the bow does not bridge the gap. Each side mourns in his and her own way and in his or her own place in life. Could the heavens in which the bow is stretched out feel compassion with their suffering? No; the heavens are indifferent: "to the bent bow is fitted an arrow that must strike the impassive sky in the heart" (56). Now that God is 'dead,' we might say, the arrow is aimed in the wrong direction. It should not aim at piercing the heart of God but that of another human being. This should, in the first place, be his own heart: he is the one who should be moved by feelings of guilt over what had happened, by compassion for the child and for Hanna whom he dearly loves and whom he had lost by the child's birth—a loss intensified by its death.

In remembering all that has happened the father slowly begins to learn the mother language buried under all the others, an ancient and timeless language but one new to him, the language that had been marginalized by the modern male-dominated discourse and that he as a man raised in modern culture could 'not consider good.' The language he now learns is the body language that the baby had spoken before he could speak verbally. It is rooted in the body and in the modern period had found a last refuge in women—excluded as they were from public life and public existence in the job market (the story was written in the fifties!). It is, as it turns out, also the language of the heart. Thus we see the father move out of his prison—a kind of emancipation by going backward, going down. It is a kind of inverted exodus. "My wild one. My heart. I am ready to carry him on my back and I promise him a blue balloon, a boat trip on the old Danube and postage stamps. I blow on his knee when he has bumped himself and help him with his sums" (75).

Under modern circumstances salvation, Bachmann seems to be saying, is no longer to be sought in bridging the gap between heaven and earth, between God and man. Nor is it to be sought in being resentful that God does not reveal himself in this world. The vertical metaphysical gap has been replaced by the horizontal gap between the sexes and the longing for the other person. The point is now that—for all practical purposes God is dead—men and women have to find each other: ". . . first one has to be able to tear to pieces the bow of sorrow that leads from a man to a woman" (76). In the modern period that is the real gap now and the question is: "This distance between man and woman that is measurable with silence, how can it ever decrease?' Man and women are strangers to each other. 'For time without end, where for me there is a minefield, there will be a garden for Hanna" (76). The gender gap cannot be bridged by the head but only by the heart and by the body—in other words, by love: not only by longing for the other but by actually going to the other, crossing the gap. This is a purely human miracle—if it succeeds. "I am no longer thinking. The flesh is strong and dark that buries a true feeling under the great laughter of night" (79).[22] Everything images the return of the kind of miracle that still

---

[22] This reminds me of the short story "A Wildermuth" in: Bachmann, *The Thirtieth Year*, pp. 139–176: at the end of this story the hero also experiences the elemental in a very similar way. As we will see below, it is also reminiscent of the end of *The Fall of Franza*.

may occur under modern circumstances—as love in the democratic form of solidarity,[23] i.e. love as day to day mutual support.

Malina: *The Love that Works Miracles—and Its Failure*

Malina was planned by Bachmann as the first volume of a trilogy called "Ways of Dying" [*Todesarten*].[24] In this novel the author locates suffering and the vision of utopia in a woman. The novel is another way of imaging what it means to leave behind the existing language and discourse, but now the author's awareness of what this means under modern conditions, especially for women, has deepened. One either has to die or to become a man—not something to which one can look forward. Moreover, for a person who happens to be a woman to leave the existing discourse means that she has to leave her sex behind; she has to change sex. In order to survive in the modern world she has to become an adult, that is to say, a 'man.' In this novel there is no bridging of the gap between the sexes, no miracle. Malina sketches the replacement of the one extreme, a romantically loving female I, by the other, a rational modern man. This replacement makes the process very violent.[25] By locating suffering in a woman Bachmann suggests that it is especially the task of women to make people really see the evil that is going on everywhere and make them experience the hidden dimension of the heart.[26]

First, let us look at the storyline. In looking back upon her life,

---

[23] Solidarity can occur without healing, without the touching of extremes: namely when it consists merely of sitting life out together, sitting next to one another, struggling side by side, waiting together side by side. In this type of solidarity the otherness of the other remains obscured. On the history of the notion of solidarity see Frans Jespers, "Solidariteit als modern idee", in: Wil Derkse et al. (eds.), *Subliem niemandsland: Intersubjectiviteit, metafysica en transcendentie* (Best, 1996), pp. 215–222.

[24] Ingeborg Bachmann, *Malina*, translated by Philip Boehm with an afterword by Mark Anderson (New York/London, 1990). The numbers in the text refer to this edition.

[25] Horst Richter, "Die Krankheit nicht leiden zu können", in: Horst Richter, *Der Gotteskomplex: Die Geburt und die Krise des Glaubens an die Allmacht des Menschen*, Part II (Hamburg, 1988), pp. 127–188, explains how feelings in general and love and suffering in particular become the 'work' of women.

[26] Cf. the role of the proletariat in Marxism: salvation would come from those who suffered the most, those who knew from their own experience what is going on. Seeing what cannot be seen, seeing what is hidden, can also be a seeing of very concrete, subtle ('unclear') signs that are overlooked by, for example, language expressed in bodily signs such as the baby's facial expressions that the young father in "Everything" does not understand, or the language of animals.

a female 'I' writes the story of her own life, she writes herself. She articulates the meaning of her life, especially of her great and all-encompassing love for Ivan. It is a love that is not of this world; it cannot be stated in words. It displays a fanaticism and exclusivity with which no ordinary human being can live and which an ordinary human partner cannot requite. The I, without words, reason and self, is not a modern subject in her own right. In that sense her words are empty: she is not present in her own words. Only when she is alone, during the night, is she herself—with all her confusion, anxieties and insecurities. Her roommate, Malina, by contrast, speaks self-confidently, calmly, rationally and from a distance. He behaves with an air of superiority toward the I. While the gap between the I and her lover Ivan grows, Malina comes to occupy the centre more and more. When I's wordless surrender turns out to be hopeless, the boundaries between I and Malina dissolve. At the novel's end, I is 'nowhere' (she has disappeared in a crack in the wall), and only Malina is left. In the meantime, it has gradually become clear to the reader that I and Malina are actually two aspects of one person. The male Malina is the typical modern adult. His female side has been murdered by modern culture ('ways of dying'). In a way, the Malina/I personality is the same figure as the young man of "The Thirtieth Year" and the young father of "Everything." The female I exemplifies the Typical Woman for whom the meaning of life is total loving surrender to a man—a type of person modern culture (including women like Bachmann herself who is highly ambivalent toward these romantics) despises.

In the first part *Malina* depicts the love that works miracles—it miraculously transforms I's world into a paradise. She now discovers "the most important thing in the world: that everything within my reach, the telephone, receiver and cord, the bread and the butter and the kippers I save for Monday evening because they're Ivan's favorite, or the special sausage I like best, everything bears Ivan's brand, from the House of Ivan. This benevolent and powerful company must have also acquired and softened the typewriter and the vacuum cleaner which used to make such an unbearable racket; the car doors underneath my windows no longer slam shut with such a bang, and even nature must have fallen under Ivan's protection unintentionally, since the birds sing more quietly in the morning, allowing a second brief sleep" (13–14).

Love, she discovers, is the great healing force in the world. It heals the wound caused by a culture in which technology and science are mistaken as the panacea for all forms of bodily and psychic suffering; a culture in which only the body is taken seriously and the workings of the heart have become invisible. "[I]t seems strange to me that medicine, which considers itself a science and a very rapidly progressing one, knows nothing about the following phenomenon: the incidence of pain in my neighborhood is decreasing, between Ungargasse 6 and 9 [the homes of Ivan and the I], fewer misfortunes occur; cancer and tumors, asthma and heart attacks, fevers, infections and breakdowns, even headaches and discomforts due to weather are in the decline, and I ask myself if it isn't my duty to inform scientists of this simple remedy, so that Research, which claims to be able to combat all disease using more and more sophisticated medications and treatments, could make a great leap forward" (14). Love is the true answer to the real problem of modern life—in this novel the gap between heart and body that is widening every day: "The tremendous anxiety, the high tension hovering over this city and presumably everywhere has almost completely abated here, and schizothymia, the world's schizoid soul, its crazy, gaping split, is healing itself imperceptibly" (14).

In the radio play *Der gute Gott von Manhattan* Bachmann portrays the same type of ecstatic love.[27] She comments that the woman in that play represents a 'borderline case' of love—'border' understood as limit. Women like her, like the female I in *Malina* and, as we will see, like Franza in *The Case of Franza* transgress that limit. These women go too far: the world is no place to receive their love. They are the victims of the slowness of the evolution of the emotions that lags behind the evolution of culture. It is not realized that the transformation from the metaphysical gap between God and men to the gap between men and women requires new attitudes and actions from the two sides. The ecstatic moment that women, the totally others (as formerly God was the totally other), attempt to make present, the miracle that is their speciality, cannot be inserted into the modern world. Consequently, this world destroys it.[28]

As Bachmann herself, however, remarks in one of her interviews, this type of love is passé. The attitude of a modern emancipated

[27] Ingeborg Bachmann, *Der gute Gott von Manhatten* (Munich/Zurich, 1983), pp. 98–155.
[28] Cf. St. John's prologue to his Gospel.

woman cannot be combined with the traditional role of unconditional surrender to an other outside of oneself—under modern circumstances this other is not the Absolute, God, but a human being, thus total surrender would be a form of idolatry, and belief in its power superstition.[29] Nevertheless, Bachmann admires this love and wants to describe it. She speaks of it as a 'work of art,' adding that in her view not many people are capable of that kind of love: "I do not know whether I have succeeded in showing [*zeigen*] the genius of love."[30]

Malina is simultaneously a celebration of the miracle of ecstatic love and a cultural critique, a woman's protest against patriarchy.[31] It is a protest against the 'terror' of which Lyotard speaks in his *The Postmodern Condition of Knowledge*. It is another depiction of Bachmann's theme of the indirect presence of the Absolute in this world, a presence that cannot be noticed by those who acknowledge only reason, who ignore and despise the heart and who remain locked up in the iron cage of modern discourse. *Malina* is therefore also an indirect celebration of the Absolute. The novel is an equally indirect celebration of women, the last refuge of perhaps ridiculous but nevertheless truly human feelings. It shows that women such as I break out of the prison of modernity but pay for it with their lives.

The Case of Franza: *The Miracle of the Elemental*

The Case of Franza is one of the three novels that together with *Malina* and *Fanny Goldmann* were to constitute the trilogy "Ways of Dying",[32]

---

[29] "Die Ehe ist unmöglich für eine Frau, die arbeitet und die denkt und selber etwas will". Ingeborg Bachmann, *Wir müssen wahre Sätze finden: Gespräche und Interviews* (Munich/Zurich, 1983), p. 144.

[30] Bachmann, "Ware Sätze sind dem Menschen zumutbar", p. 109.

[31] Other interpretations are possible. Cf. Joke Hermsen, who in *Nomadisch narcisme: Sekse, liefde en kunst in het werk van Lou Andreas-Salome, Belle van Zuylen, Ingeborg Bachmann* (Kampen, 1993), p. 330 writes: "[The novel *Malina*] attempts to go a step further towards a world in which—thanks to the destruction of the old forms—an open space emerges in which something new can occur". Hermsen assesses the character of Malina/I at the end of the novel much more positively than I do.

[32] Ingeborg Bachmann, "Der Fall Franza", in: Ingeborg Bachmann, *Der Fall Franza: Requiem für Fanny Goldmann* (Munich/Zurich, 1989), pp. 7–150. The numbers in the text refer to this edition. The posthumously edited German edition includes in an appendix (143–150) fragments that are of special interest for the topic of this contribution but were not worked into the main body of the text as it was found after Bachmann's death.

but remained unfinished. The text, according to a planned preface by Bachmann, consists of three parts. The first two deal with the crimes that had been perpetrated against the heroine, Franza, while she was living in Austria. Some are officially recognized as crimes, but the majority are refined crimes condoned by the prevailing culture and consequently not recognized as crimes. The third part, "Egyptian darkness" (83–142), tells of Franza's travel from Austria to Egypt. She accompanies her younger brother Martin who received a stipend to do historical research there. Clearly, the duo Franza/Martin is yet another version of the personage Malina/I, the young man of "The Thirtieth Year" and the young father of "Everything." This third part depicts the crimes that whites perpetrate against the Arabs. It ends with Franza's death.

This, in a nutshell, is the content of the story. But it is "a content which is not the content," as Bachmann herself commented. What is the real, the unsaid, the unsayable content? Let us take a look at the text. "Egyptian Darkness" opens with the words: "They have gone into the desert. The light, thrown out of the heaven, accompanied by a hot clean fragrance, broke [*erbrach sich*] over them. The great healing institution, the great inescapable [*unverlassbar*] purgatorium, although open to all sides: inescapable, Arab, Libyan in its subdivisions, . . . Sahara. The institution had taken them in" (83).

In Martin's guidebook to Egypt they read that even a stranger retains "till his death a nostalgia for her [the desert]" (83). In the desert, "[a]ll is empty and more present than what pretends to be present. Not the nothing—no, the desert has nothing to do with the nothing artificially thought up by professors.[33] She eludes articulation, determination, definition. Is something exclusive [*Ausschliessliches*] and does not tolerate [*dulden*] that which is half" (83). In the desert, Franza realizes, it is either I or I, that is to say, either I or the desert, and the desert is also I. A conflict rages inside of her: I or I; I and the desert. Or I and that other. And exclusively and nothing half tolerated, I and I started to go against each other. The desert is an escape from everything and thus also from evil. Franza can feel free of the fear of being strangled. But to be in the desert is also freedom for something new that could now begin. She is ready for it. Whatever was going to happen, she would freely take it upon herself, however difficult it might be. Meeting the desert,

---

[33] A hint at Heidegger's *Sein und Zeit*.

becoming like it, becoming it, Franza has an intuition that she is going to arrive [*ankommen*] somewhere: "Sire, I will arrive" (84), she thinks. "The eyes and the desert find each other, the desert spreads itself over the retina, walks off, rolls back, lies again in the eye, hours, days in a row. The eyes become ever more empty, ever more attentive, larger, in the one landscape for which eyes are made" (93). What is she doing here, she wonders? "What does she seek in the desert, the voice said in the desert in which nothing is to be heard" (93)? For one thing, the reader may presume, she wants to know why and whence there is evil, why the world is so full of monsters. Even in the midst of the desert, in the Red Sea, are sharks. But the desert does not answer any questions: it is deep silence. In spite of all hardships, Franza's health is miraculously improving.

In visiting the tourist attractions of Egypt she is horrified and ashamed by the way Westerners have defaced the tombs and do not seem to mind: "the whole shame contracts in me, for no one else notices it" (104). The face of Queen Hatchepsut has been removed by her own compatriots and contemporaries—a later king. But the hollow place where the face has been is a reminder, a trace that is a special kind of absent presence: the queen "still can be read—because there is nothing where she should have been" (104).

Franza keeps asking herself: "[w]hat do you seek in this desert, in this city of the dead, east bank, west bank, it does not matter which bank, only the desert is there, here and beyond.... What, in this furnace-like landscape that does not say anything, that does not express itself, about which nothing can be said. What do you want here? Purity before the eyes, and fleeing for what, every day deeper and deeper into the desert in order to penetrate even more desert with the eyes" (106). Whatever it may be, one thing she realizes clearly: "Here I will be recognized for what I am" (106).

In a dramatic episode a miracle seems to be on the verge of happening—truth will be revealed. But it turns out to be a hallucination. The negation of the expectation of a miraculous event underscores the theme of loosing everything that might give support and of the breaking of supportive and encouraging images, representations, forms. She walks along the shores of the Red Sea. "On the most lonely beach of the world she went up [*fuhr in die Höh*]" (110). At one point she stops with the sun right above her.[34] "Then she saw the

---

[34] Cf. Friedrich Nietzsche, "Mittags", in: *Also sprach Zarathustra*, Werke in drei Bände, vol. II. ed. Karl Schlechta (Munich, s.a.), p. 513.

image in red Arabia.... She looked without understanding [*fassungslos*]. I see. And now again. I see what no one has ever seen, an image. She went some steps, too slowly, and the image went backward. Her skin started to burn. I must run, it is already clearer: it is he. I must run to him, but it was not Martin who went backward, but it is he, indeed, he in the white coat. He climbs out of the image; he has arrived from Vienna, in the coat of consolation, in order to take me home, no, in the coat of terror that he throws off, but it is not he. My father. I have seen my father. He throws off his coat, his many coats. She put her hands on her head, in order to prevent her head from burning away. But it is not him, he is not my father. Who is he? She started to run faster—and black and erected it came on the beach and was above the sand and got back on its feet again. But black and dark and now crawling over the beach, rolling, it came. God comes to me, and I come to God.... I have seen God. From so close that I could touch, between, where am I?" (113–114).

What she had seen turned out to be some kind of fish. She put it back into the sea. "I have seen an image.... [S]he laughed and laughed and laughed—and while laughing, the entrance door for decomposition, who am I, where I am from, what is the matter with me, what do I have to seek in this desert, came, indeed, came not, while nothing can enter, there something stepped on her and with her on the other, on the half death, the half reason, the half animal, the half human being, the half five senses, the one sister, the other woman, the flesh, aimed at by the sun, finding itself rotting, transgressing to something that cannot be known" (114–115).

The episode ends with the words: "The Arab desert is surrounded by broken representations of God [*Gottesvorstellungen*]" (115). A fragment specifies that Franza saw the image "like Peter" did (Fragment, 143). It also says that (as I in *Malina*) she took her murderer to be God, that—being blinded by the desert—she had believed in her murderer as in her father [*geglaubt an meinem Mörder wie an meinem Vater*]—that her father is not her murderer. Also, she did not come to the desert in order to find God: "I did not come here in order to seek God. I have sought nothing here. I have found nothing. God was not there, you were not there" (Fragment, 144). The desert, we could say, stands for the breaking of the images of the Absolute and by the Absolute. The burning, empty desert is the Absolute, not an image of it. The breaking of forms is also the destruction of forms and the matter, *materia*, from which forms are made.

By being in the desert Franza prepares herself for passing a limit, for entering a new state of being. During a few moments she actually seems to transgress that limit. Is she in the process of dying? Or is it her common 'worldly' ego that is dying? Is Franza, having broken through all that suffocated her and that stood between her and the Absolute, during a few wonderful moments of experiencing the Absolute in this world—the shape of a new openness for the elemental? In the desert, everything superfluous is removed and life is reduced to (in the positive sense of returned to, given back to) the bare essentials. "Hunger and thirst discovered anew, danger rediscovered, the ears pricked up, the eyes sharpened, oriented toward the outside world, again an awareness of the goal. A roof above one's head, a place to sleep, shadow, some shadow" (92).

The discovery of the elemental is given more weight in the fragments. At one point Franza is alone and hungry. An old Arab man brings her to the last house of the village. The desert is very close. A young woman brings food. It is quiet, nobody speaks, children sleep silently, seemingly without breathing. Franza does not understand what is going on, but there is no need to understand. "The world is gesture, going, light, darkness, waiting, without reason. The young woman put a plate with beans and a smaller one with a sauce on the table.... Give also bread.... Whence bread in a breadless city? The Arab, seeing the hesitation, gives me a little piece of bread in my hand and shows me how to take beans with bread. It is simple, it works right away, four black hands and one white one in turn are in the plate, then all of a sudden all hands simultaneously, they stop for a moment in order to prevent one from hindering the other, polite hands all, one should let the image become of stone, in this moment. (A moment) in which something is perfect, the hand in the food, eating them with fingers what one takes, it is the most conscious moment, the most natural, the first and the only eating has taken place, takes place, it is the first and the only good meal, will remain perhaps the only meal in a lifetime that is not spoiled by barbarity, indifference, greed, thoughtlessness—really none. We have shared and we did not pray, nothing send back, no beans left over, nothing taken away, nothing anticipated, nothing taken afterwards" (Fragment, 147–148).

Afterward, back in the hotel, Franza experiences a new security, but "the security is of another nature" (Fragment, 148). Actually, it is a security beyond security and insecurity: "There is no security, and no insecurity and danger. Security and danger are projections, figments of the imagination, destructions by imaginations. All of that does not exist" (Fragment, 148). It is a truly miraculous moment, a moment of grace, in which she really understands what the desert teaches. For indeed, the desert with all it involves is a proclamation, a preaching—of something that cannot be known:

> The proclamation is of a different nature. I have come to a sermon that is spoken by nobody and that has never been put underneath a temple roof, to a sermon of the desert and of unarticulated laws, to swallowing, biting, going, ways of sleeping which have waited for their time underneath a thin crust of understandings of a different nature, for the mystical coinciding of breathing in, breathing out, going and resting, for the Hallelujah of surviving in nothingness (Fragment, 149).

But this peak experience also indicates the closeness of death. Does Franza die accidentally because a fall from a rock or because now she knows what is truly essential, so that it is no longer necessary for her to live? Or does she die because life in the Absolute that she had now tasted is impossible and ordinary life does not seem worth living? Or is it because in the desert she had already begun to die, so that her physical death is merely the completion of a process that had already begun? While dying she thinks: "The desert, quite something. The round of the Arab desert. Broken through, broken, the breaking. All representations broken" (137). She wants to be put down on the ground: "it is terrible, put me on the ground ... she said, on the ground, I want to lie on the ground. I believe, I die, I believe, it begins" (119).[35]

After returning to Austria, her alter ego, Martin (not being a poet) is unable to explain the desert to anybody—the desert "that he did after all experience by means of the destruction of another" (141). This reminds one of the young man of "The Thirtieth Year," except that Martin seems to have learned something. He does not reject what was revealed to Franza, even though he does not understand it. It also reminds one of the Malina who remains 'in the world' after the death of the female I—but without having learned from

---

[35] The words "I believe" are a characteristic affirmation in—especially New Testamentical—miracle stories.

his sufferings. Thinking back at the only time he and Franza had a drink together he muses, "The Arab desert has broken through broken. How irresistible, what has it been? ... How irresistible is the desert. But that desert. Love however is irresistible" (141).

In my view, *The Case of Franza*'s real content is the depiction of an intuition of a new chance for a human life, a new possibility, a new orientation revealed in the desert. More particularly, the possibility of a transition from the 'old' Absolute (the God of the Christian faith, radically separated from the world as it is, far beyond this world, crushing in its effects, totally spiritualized) to a 'new' Absolute, described as the purifying desert, the soil or the space for love and sharing. This Absolute does not speak and can only be spoken of indirectly; it can be only hinted at. At this point in time this possibility is still unheard of. It is unsaid, unthinkable, inexpressible, unlivable. The new possibility involves two experiences. On the one hand, the desert sun burns away all images and representations, everything that has form, including all doctrines on the Absolute and all old-style miracles—miracles in the strict sense of the word. Finally, literally nothing is left—except for the empty desert itself. At the end of the novel, Franza "is empty of all ties" [*aller Bindungen ledig*], as the author wrote in her preface. On the other hand, the burning away—the breaking—of the images frees her who has nothing left for the nightly miracle of the elemental—actually a kind of non-miracle because it is so common: a simple roof above one's head, plain food, sharing and eating it attentively—without greed.[36]

I see Franza as a female prophet, someone like Moses who saw the promised land from afar; a person who experienced the Absolute but could not say directly what she had to say. Does Franza require a literary writer like Bachmann the way Moses needed Aaron?[37] As 'Everything' tells the modern miracle of solidarity, *Malina* of its

---

[36] This aspect of Franza's desert experience reminds one of a Zen Buddhist saying: "*samsara* is *nirvana*". It means that for those whose eyes are truly opened ordinary life is paradise. At the same time the experience differs from Zen Buddhism in that ultimately one only seems to get a glimpse of the possibility that the full experience is impossible in this life. Cf. also the ambivalent ending of "A Wildermuth", in: Bachmann, *The Thirtieth Year*, pp. 139–176.

[37] We may also think of Bachmann herself who stated that it is the literary writer's task to open people's eyes so that they can truly see what is and what should be. Bachmann, "Die Wahrheit ist dem Menschen zumutbar", pp. 75–77. This essay is the so-called "The Speech of One Blinded in the War" ("Kriegsblindenrede").

failure, so *Franza* tells the miracle of the elemental.[38] The ecstatic tone of Part Three hints at the same time at a miraculous experience of a life beyond life, beyond good and evil, beyond man and woman, at a timeless mystical experience of the elemental here and now in which thinking and speaking stops—and 'the ego dies,' according to the language of mystics—and the Absolute, in which life can be experienced directly, is.

Epilogue: The Promised Land Here and Now?

Can an exodus, we may ask in conclusion, ever succeed, that is, can it ever end in a true emancipation? Can it become anything else than a fall? No, Bachmann seems to answer from the perspective of modern dualism from which she did not free herself. A true exodus is total, and a total exodus to a country where the human person has no common human support whatsoever means death.

But she also suggests that perhaps we need to die in order to truly live. Plato—and with him the whole (Neo)platonic tradition of Western philosophy—thought it possible that one could ascend to true Being—experience salvation—in this life, be it only for a brief moment. Most Christians, however, believed that the final fulfilment of human longing would occur after death.[39] Pascal thought that one could move in this world from the lower order of life, the orders of power and of knowledge, to that sublime one, the order of love. Modernity, as exemplified by Bachmann, does not have any confidence in the possibility of ascent, in an afterlife nor in the reality of the order of love. It stubbornly maintains the either/or logic: one cannot at the same time be alive and be dead, speak and be silent, be in the world and be in the Absolute, be a man and be a woman.[40] Where the world is, the Absolute is not; where the Absolute is, the world is

---

[38] In *Pure Lust: Elemental Feminist Philosophy* (Boston, 1984) Mary F. Daly expresses her fascination with "the elemental". Cf. Anne-Marie Korte, *Een passie voor transcendentie: Feminisme, theologie en moderniteit in het denken van Mary Daly* (Kampen, 1992), 331–341.

[39] In Western Christianity belief in afterlife has all but disappeared. In New Age circles people are again interested in the possibility of a prelife and an afterlife—and some Christian believers are following suit.

[40] In a fragment for "Der Fall Franza" we read: "I do not have a sex, none any more, it has been torn out of me" (Fragment, 144).

not. How can there be reconciliation, the touching of extremes, miracles under such circumstances?

In spite of her deep immersion in modern culture, Bachmann develops a critical distance to it. Through a painful process she came to realize that the Enlightenment poses questions it could not itself see, let alone answer—questions of gender and of the Absolute. 'Different but equal' is in matters of gender a promising and alluring slogan, but it is difficult to make concrete in a cultural setting that, by identifying equality with sameness, subterraneously works against the differences it pretends to embrace. What touches me in Bachmann is that she does not embrace one of those poles—either sameness or difference—but attempts to leave the opposition behind in the figure of loving reconciliation. For the love that bridges the gender gap simultaneously unites the sexes and guards the difference between them. It is, moreover, a human love: a mutual touching of the heart and the body—it is profoundly sensuous. It is a love that flowers most profusely in the night—when the eyes lose their function and the other senses can come into their own. It is, furthermore, a love whose memory has been kept alive most of all by women.

In the course of her life, the author seems to have lost the confidence that human love can work this miracle. Her awareness of the gap has broadened and deepened: the really frightening problem, she senses, is the gap between the Absolute and the finite—a gap so wide that no human love can bridge it. Does that mean that without hope of divine intervention, now that God is dead, the open wound will never heal? *In profundis*, so to speak, Bachmann lives through a new and for me highly inspiring and moving perspective. She remains with the Enlightenment: the Absolute is not the Christian God out there and of course this implies that, for instance, people can no longer identify with this superior being and that miraculous divine interventions from outside are impossible. But, according to this perspective, this is not the point. The miracle is always already there and it is intensively *inside*, it *is* the inside; it is not our work at all. The absence of the Absolute out there frees one for a new experience of the world: not as an ontologically or historically lower realm (a vale of tears or a not-yet) but as the realm of the elemental, the material, the concrete, the sensuous that simply is what it is— a miracle in its utterly simple glory. But in order to experience the world truly in this way one has to go through dark, very dark nights in which one experiences only the absence of the Absolute. The mystics of old knew about that. Because women have remained familiar with sensuous and concrete love and joy—given their experience with the bearing and raising of children and caring for others—and because they are familiar with suffering—given their fate in modern times to 'do' the suffering for those who are incapable of doing so—women may seem relatively well equipped nowadays to accept this passage, sustain it, explore and share with us what lies beyond.

But in *The Case of Franza* Bachmann leaves open the question of whether women or anyone else for that matter can ever feel at home in this experience of the elemental and can teach others who still hesitating at best whether they should follow. Franza left the old world behind but in the other world she dies (as did Simone Weil); her alter ego Martin (a man!) continues to live in the old world (as did Agathe and Ulrich, the protagonists of Robert Musil's *Mann ohne Eigenschaften*). Instead of one world being experienced from different perspectives or two (or more) experiences seemingly creating two (or more) worlds, two very different worlds remain. Perhaps it was not by accident that this volume of the trilogy *Todesarten* has remained unfinished.

Bachmann may be asking: Has Franza seen the Promised Land? Are, her readers may be asking, others continuing Franza's exodus? Can the Promised Land ever be reached?

11

MIRACLES OF DESIRE: TRANSFIGURATIONS IN RHODA LERMAN'S *THE BOOK OF THE NIGHT*

Inez van der Spek

> *You leap from rock to rock. The moment of transcendence is in the leap, not when you touch the rock. Words are springs to take you from the nature of things to the spark. So, why did you choose cow?*
> Rhoda Lerman, *The Book of the Night*

> *No gasp at a miracle that is truly miraculous because the magic lies in the fact that you knew it was there for you all along.*
> Toni Morrison, *Beloved*

Introduction: Postmodernist Miracles

The cover of its British publication praises *The Book of the Night* by the American writer Rhoda Lerman (*née* Sniderman, 1936) as "science fiction at its most challenging and allusive".[1] To the majority of people, this will hardly count as a serious recommendation because science fiction is not exactly their cup of tea. Therefore I make so bold as to rephrase that Lerman's novel is "literature at its most challenging and allusive". Its imaginative dazzle, stream of associations, its language which is both witty and ornate, as well as the blending of widely divergent spatiotemporal worlds and cultural

---

[1] Rhoda Lerman, *The Book of the Night* (London: The Women's Press, 1986; first ed. New York: Holt, Rinehart & Winston, 1984). One may speculate on whether the title is also a cross-reference to Ursula Le Guin's collection of essays on fantasy and science fiction, *The Language of the Night*, ed. Susan Wood (New York: Berkley, 1979). Subsequent references to Lerman's text will appear parenthetically. Information on Lerman and her work in general were found in *Contemporary Authors*, Vol. 49–52 and *Contemporary Literary Criticism* Vol. 56 (Detroit: Gale Research, 1975 & 1990).

domains, recall the writings of famous non-science fiction, often 'postmodernist' labeled writers like Salman Rushdie, Angela Carter and Julio Cortázar.

Lerman worked for ten years on the book; during that time she published three other novels, while several more followed later. Her writings cannot be pinned down to a particular literary genre but are a patchwork of generic styles. Lerman utilizes satire and the fantastic to examine sexuality and sexual relationships, (sub)urban anxieties, and religion. She frequently combines elements of realism, mythology, and theology to comment upon the position of women in history and contemporary society.[2] In *The Book of the Night*, moreover, all of these elements are mingled idiosyncratically with metaphors from cosmological science, as I shall explain below.

The Book of the Night is the story of the girl Celeste who comes with her father to the Isle of Iona (off the Scottish western coast), where the tenth century coexists with the nineteenth and the twentieth, ancient polytheisms with Jewish and Christian monotheisms, medieval magic and sorcery with modern science. Father and daughter lead a secluded life on the eastern flank of Dun Hi (the Mountain of God) in the neighbourhood of the local monastery. Celeste is brought up as a boy, and, at reaching puberty, is sent to the monastery by her father to become a novice. Everything takes a dramatic *and* miraculous turn when she falls in love with the abbot. . . .

In this essay, I will be reading *The Book of the Night* as a miracle story in the context of a postmodern outlook on life and literature. Zooming in on the miraculous that pervades Lerman's text may have the illuminating effect of an old-fashioned magic lantern. Projected in blow-

---

[2] *Call Me Ishtar* (1973) is a novel about the incarnation of Ishtar, the Babylonian goddess of fertility and war, into a twentieth century Jewish housewife with the aim of subverting the influences of Moses and Jesus Christ. *The Girl that He Marries* (1976) revolves around the romance between an intellectual gentile woman and a superficial Jewish man. *Eleanor* (1979) is a piece of fiction featuring Eleanor Roosevelt narrating about a very difficult period in her life with Franklin R. Later Lerman wrote *God's Ear* (1989), the story of a Jewish insurance salesman called upon by the ghost of his dead father, a Hasidic Rabbi, to found a congregation in Kansas. Her next book, *Animal Acts* (1994), is a thriller about a woman who flees from a complacent husband and a sinister lover in the company of a gorilla, whom she slowly comes to love—which in fact is a journey into the woman's own heart and the exploration of the meaning of love and consciousness. (With thanks to Sarah Lefanu for information on the last book.) In 1996, finally, *In the Company of Newfies: A Shared Life* was published, an account of the profound bond between human and dog.

up on the as yet empty pages of the remainder of the essay what seem diverting drawings of bizarre and exotic scenes turn into imaginative explorations of sexuality and sexual difference, the formation and collapse of language, the limits of will and grace, and the site of the sacred in late twentieth century Western culture. And, indeed, of all these queries interconnected. Meditation on the meaning of miracles, moreover, is well fostered by the fact that the miraculous plays a role on more than one level of the text.

What does it mean to characterize Lerman's book as postmodernist fiction? No less rapidly than the notion of postmodernism came into vogue it has become discredited. However, leaving aside the pros and cons of the notion in other discourses, I want to defend its value with respect to literary texts. I therefore turn to literary theorist Brian McHale's view that postmodernist fiction is driven by an *ontological* imperative.[3] The focusing component of modernist fiction, on the other hand, is *epistemological*. Modernist questions refer to the way in which knowledge is obtained: How can I interpret the world of which I am a part? Who am I in it? What is there to be known, who knows it, with what degree of certainty and reliability can it be known? What are the limits of knowledge? Postmodernist fiction, as McHale sees it, deploys strategies which engage and foreground questions about the world of the literary text itself and/or the world it projects. What takes place is a literalization of the modernist metaphorical understanding of 'world'. Questions that it tackles are, What is the mode of existence of a text, and what of the world (or worlds) it projects? What actually is a world? What kinds of world are there, how are they constituted? Is the text itself a world, is there a world in the text? What happens when different worlds are confronted with each other, or when their boundaries are violated or start to dissolve?

The Book of the Night is surely an example of such an 'ontological poetics', in which the coexistence and mingling of different worlds, or modes of being, offers a fertile climate for the miraculous to thrive in. As postmodernist fiction, rather than raising the question *what* a miracle is, and how we are to know it, it deals with the ontological question of *where and when* a miracle is, of its space and time. Its very title points to it: the *when* of miracles is the dark, the nightside of life. Miracles may occur again after the lustre of the Enlightenment,

---

[3] Brian McHale, *Postmodernist Fiction* (London/New York: Routledge, 1987).

the bright lights of a self-sufficient reason have dimmed long since. As the book mentioned in the title indicates, the *where* of the miracle is the literary text itself. Let us now move deeper into this text to further explore its time and space as the environment for a postmodernist understanding of miracles.

The Collapse of Time/Language

The Book of the Night, "in the best science fictional tradition, tackles such great questions as the nature of the universe and the meaning of reality".[4] In other words, cosmological and ontological questions intersect in this book. To turn to McHale once more, science fiction "obeys the same underlying principles of ontological poetics as postmodernist fiction" but "has evolved *topoi* of its own for working out these principles in practice".[5] In many stories and novels one can discern an interplay between science fiction and canonized postmodernist fiction. I see Lerman's *Book* as a splendid example of such an interplay, and hence a boundary breakdown, between 'popular' science fiction and 'high' postmodernist writing.

The most conspicuous science fiction topos employed by Lerman is that of parallel time levels, although not in the conventional sense of two intertwining linear narratives but rather as a maze with no true entrance nor exit. The effect of the mingling of eras is that life on the Isle seems "somehow, mysteriously, outside of time".[6] Iona's Chronicler, the monk Generous, writes that,

> The sea sifts through its bits of time and tosses up on our shores its wastes of past things and future things, known things and unknown things, tolling, turning, mixing the harvest of articles and particles of time in its great-stemmed groves of seaflesh, of olive tangle and black wrack. Sea shells we find and bomb shells, donkey beads and crusted coins, Pop-sickle sticks from Father Time, puns from the Argonauts, argot from the Punic Wars, cargo from the nets of Naught, Naughts that are not, sea-belched they come. (. . .) [And] always the dead.
> We are only the scavengers of a vast existence beyond time (2).

---

[4] Lisa Tuttle, "Pets and monsters: metamorphoses in recent science fiction", in L. Armitt, *Where No Man Has Gone Before* (London/New York: Routledge, 1991), p. 104.
[5] McHale, *Postmodernist Fiction*, p. 60.
[6] Tuttle, "Pets and monsters", p. 105.

Instead of a state 'beyond time', however, it may even be more adequate to speak about a *collapse* of time in *The Book of the Night*, which coincides with a collapse of language. What happens in Lerman's book is that, as Sarah Lefanu words it, "the forces of disorder and entropy are marshalled against the order of language, progress and rationalism".[7] The linguistic order shows its fragility as "language takes on a logic of its own that is unrelated to the objects to which it was formerly tied".[8] As we shall see, the breakdown of time/language implies that self-evident and fixed categories of 'nature', 'woman', and 'human' are undermined.

The weight of the collapse of language falls most obviously on Manuel, Celeste's father, *an architect, a gentleman, and a madman* (18). Manuel spends his time weaving exquisite holy vestments, which the monks ship to *Carthage, Rome, Sophia, Chicago, Troy, Cleveland, Jerusalem* (44). But more and more he neglects this task for making cloths out of stolen bits, both horrible and beautiful. *I think my father was recreating the world in his madness, a world of stones and sticks and bottle caps from Orange Pip and bullet shells and bits of dirty things, the sheepwool stung with dung, a bird leg* (42). As well as *bits of you, Celeste,* says Manuel while showing threads of her infant cloths in the tapestries. Analogously, Manuel is recreating the world by means of language, weaving *equal marvels into lists* (28) instead of cloths. He is an architect of language, chanting litanies of sacred and profane words and names, chains of puns and associations, among which are quite a few referring to the Jewish tradition. *"Ark, d'ark, argo, cargo, argonaut, argotique, gothic. So. Alevai, Halloween, mistletoe, mazeltov"* (28). Although the little Celeste suspects something is wrong with her father's mental sanity, she is swept along by Manuel's listmaking. *The words burst and transformed themselves. They enticed me into paths and labyrinths. They bloomed from word to word without an if, without a then, without a therefore* (29).

At first, she learns, like every child, to write the alphabet and her name and to draw ice cream cones in her copy book, which carries the name Dark Horse Copy Book. Soon, however, Manuel starts to teach her her own set of lists. Celeste recites, *"Zeus, Deus, juice, Jews, Yid, Druid, druse. Methuselah, Medea, Medua, Medusa, Madonna"*. And Manuel instructs, *"Do you hear... in the roots? Listen. The root is*

---

[7] Sarah Lefanu, *In the Chinks of the World Machine: Feminism & Science Fiction* (London: The Women's Press, 1988), p. 99.
[8] Lefanu, *In the Chinks*, p. 99.

the Hebrew 'why', Medua. Why, a God's name. Why. That is the question. That is the Name. Medua-why" (29). Whereupon Celeste continues obediently, "Gaballa, Kabbalah, *Kadosh, cabosh, caboose*", and Manuel explains that,

> It is all so clear. *Gaballa* is *The Book of Takings; Kabbalah, The Work of Receivings.* Kadosh, holy; cabosh, hat of death; caboose, the last car on the train, the end. Kaput, see? Holy, separated (29).

Besides lists, he teaches her questions, only questions for there are *no answers of any importance in this world* (39). Big ontological questions such as: What is life? What is the cause of change? What is difference? What is disorder? Celeste, on the other hand, has her own, existential questions about her unknown mother, the reason for their stay on Iona and her disguise as a boy, and most of all the question whether her father loves her. For a long time her questions remain unanswered as well.

Manuel's peculiar linguistic games, the streams of enigmatic associations, the excessive sets of lists, the questions that should not be answered, remind one of *écrits bruts*, or distorted texts, that is to say texts which display serious deviations from or transgressions of the current (literary) grammar and usage.[9] Texts, mostly, of people who were diagnosed as suffering from schizofrenia, psychotic delusions or certain kinds of autism. Striking resemblances can be noted between radical textual experiments in contemporary literature and the linguistic utterances of these so-called disturbed people. This is just one place where the fences between the normal and the abnormal prove to have but the solidity of chicken wire. On the other hand it would be a misjudgement to romanticize the distorted texts as 'schizophrenic art' or celebrate 'the genius of madness'. Despite their possible structural and aesthetic correspondances, which might provoke a similar reaction of alienation or resistance with the reader, the genesis and motivation of literary and distorted texts are not the same. An important difference is that authors of distorted texts have no meta-language at their disposal, there is no space outside language. Metaphors are not clearly marked and the author coincides with language in a direct corporeal way. While the schizophrenic is

---

[9] On this topic Michel Tévoz, *Écrits Bruts* [Perspectives Critiques] (Paris: PUF, 1979); Theodor Spoerri, *Sprachphänomene und Psychose* (Basel/New York: Karger, 1964); and J. Vogelaar red., *Gestoorde teksten* [Raster, 24] (Amsterdam: De Bezige Bij, 1982).

likely "to perform primary psychic mechanisms (of displacement and condensation), (...) the literary writer to a greater or lesser extent controls these mechanisms and utilizes them as aesthetic resources, thus facilitating a secundary elaboration which, in principal at least, enables larger intelligibility".[10]

Leaving aside the complicated issue of pathology or madness with respect to distorted texts, surely more often than not they are *mad* texts: explosive with anger. Anger perhaps at the prison of language, or at the failing of communication. But then again, what appear as distorted language and communication "need not oppose communication as such, but might just as well be the modeling of a (repressed) communication which resists the limitations and standards of normal communication".[11] Language in that case is highly ambivalent, because it becomes an object of aggression as well as an instrument by which to create one's own system for appropriating the world.

This very ambivalence qualifies the way Manuel inhabits language, and language inhabits him. Mad in every meaning of the word, he chastens language; sometimes he chastens his daughter with language, with silence at other times. Yet his strange words do make sense—be it always in a veiled, almost obfuscated way—once a hermeneutical key to this linguistic bastion is found. By extension, this also bears on the narrrative intricacies and textual impermeability of *The Book of the Night*.[12] Manuel's litanies and chants, his catechisms without answers, can be read as a *mise en abîme* of the novel's linguistic and imaginative experimentation, which seems always on the verge of explosion yet in fact is carefully contained.

Not God and the Broken God

The hermeneutical key, as I believe, is the search for what is *the most holy and pure part of oneself*. Not only Manuel but Lerman's text itself, with Celeste at its center, are imbued with the desire to realize

---

[10] Vogelaar, *Gestoorde teksten*, p. 12.
[11] Vogelaar, *Gestoorde teksten*, p. 12.
[12] I do not agree, therefore, with Diane Bauerle's criticism that although "Lerman weaves an eccentric and sometimes fascinating tapestry, too many ends are left hanging" (cited in *Contemporary Literary Criticism*, p. 179). A possible flaw of the book would rather be its almost hermetic structure, that is, the *absence* of any left ends, for everything appears to be connected with everything in a highly intricate manner.

what is considered holy, to make the unmanifest manifest, to simultaneously release it from and force it into language. First we need to take Manuel's references to the Jewish tradition in consideration, in particular to the Kabbalah, Jewish mysticism, in which the secret meaning of the numerical value of the Hebrew letters plays such an important role. Manuel (or Emanuel, which means 'God with us') stresses the unfathomability of God, the meaning of which is explained in a 'creation story' told to Celeste:

> "I will place this story in time and yet I want you to know later that all Creation happens at once and we are in it, that everything is simultaneous. It is a great loom. So. Once upon a time . . . once upon a time there was the One. Not God. You understand that. Not God, that is his name. Not. And he was lonely and divided himself and created all that beyond himself although he is still himself—in the way a spider weaves her web. And all that beyond the original unmanifested became Two. It was called the scission; the One splitting into the Two. Numbers weave the Universe into patterns.
>
> Letters weave also. A is the unmanifest, this Not God, the great breath of existence, the One" (32–33).

Perhaps this could best be qualified as a negative theology: this unmanifest, unified, all-encompassing breath of universe is *Not God*. Manuel continues to clarify this in terms of the Hebrew alphabet:

> "B represents the manifest, Two that the One made. So. B is the house, the container. In Hebrew Aleph is the sign of the cow. See the horns." He drew a cow in the notebook. Then he drew an A and turned it upside down. "See. B, Beth is the name for house. See the roof." He drew a broken square (33).

Next he gives this pictography a concrete, anthropological twist, making use again of the ambiguity of language to play with the word 'stable'.

> "The cow is A for breath, the breath and the spirit of the Not God as One. The cow A lives in the stable B. Now we play with the words. That which is stable is solid and still and unchanging." (. . .) "That which is unstable is amorphous, changing." He stuck two fingers on either side of his head through his hair and wiggled them.
>
> "Cow!" I called out. I can remember how happy I was.
>
> "A makes change. Remember this. A is change. A is unstable. A becomes stable within containers. The world is a container. A is a power, an idea, a force. And that which is stable contains, limits, and resists the force of A. But this is very complicated. A cow is an A, a force in the stable of B. But a cow is also a B, a container. Man is

both A and B. Part of him limits the holiest part of him, resists, contains it. It is that part we fight against, our boundaries, our B's" (34).

Let us recall for a moment the commonly accepted Jewish view that the sacred is present only in enclosed, secluded and detached places, that is, in the Temple and in the *male* body, which is not flowing but solid. The 'leaking' *female* body thus represents impurity and defilement. All Jewish laws of purity aim at sustaining this (sexual) difference: do not eat or touch anything polluted, or wash it away thoroughly, in particular what has to do with women's blood. Menstruating women and women who have just given birth, therefore, are not allowed to enter the Temple and participate in divine worship, while men should avoid contamination through sexual intimicy with such women.[13]

Manuel's explanation suggests a different appraisal of holiness, for in his view the container does not accomodate the sacred or Not God but rather *limits* and *resists* its force. That which is stable and solid locks change. Manuel's view proposes, instead, an understanding of holiness and purity which are not warranted by enclosure and separation. Holiness might come into existence by opening oneself up for what is amorphous, changing, and disorderly, including that which points to the (blood-)flowing female body. In my perception, the very search for female corporality and sexuality as a possible site of the manifestation of holiness is the motive force of Lerman's text.

Although revisions of the Jewish tradition and its understandings of God and holiness reverberate in *The Book of the Night*, they should not be isolated from the novel's re-creation of ancient goddess mythology. The opening scene of the book is densely revealing in this matter. Generous writes of the vast woman washing ashore, *her length nine score and twelve feet. The length of her hair fifteen feet* (3). She has wings and *the ears those of a cow, twisted, tipped with fair down silk* (4). She is dying, Generous calls her *the broken God*. The scrivener is the only one who sees how a beast-like, crippled child was born out of the loins of the dying goddess, and next sent off to *the darkness* (5)

---

[13] Grietje Dresen, "Het betere bloed: Over het ritueel van de kerkgang en het offer in de katholieke traditie," in: Idem, *Is dit mijn lichaam? Visioenen van het volmaakte lichaam in katholieke moraal en mystiek* (Nijmegen, Valkhof Pers, 1998), pp. 41–60; pp. 151–154; Anne-Marie Korte, "Reclaiming Ritual: A Gendered Approach to (Im)Purity," in: Marcel Poorthuis and Joshua Schwartz (eds.), *Purity and Holiness* [Jewish and Christian Perspectives, 2] (Leiden: Brill, 1999), pp. 313–327.

by its mother. To me, this crippled child remains a mysterious thing. I suggest to understand it as a symbol of disorder and change: *between dark and shape, not yet dense, between manifest and unmanifest* (8).

The Abbot Isaac, sent for by the vast woman, performs a variety of rituals of death on the huge body.

> With a scarlet alter cloth the monks fashioned the great woman a hat of death. Isaac held it above her head and chanted, "Cabosh, Kadosh" (5).

> She stroked Isaac gently. He closed her eye. Isaac drew out his flint knife and cut on her stone-smooth belly the circle of Heaven within the square of earth and then lay himself down in the circle and spread his limbs to touch the edges, so large she was, so brave he was. She whispered instructions to him. He obeyed (6).

After breathing her last, the primitive crofters of the island, apparently according to local cannibalist customs, immediately show up to cut her vast body to pieces.

> [A]nd the beach that night was blood and fiery stars flashing above her holy carcass where metal met bone, and flesh roasted in fires and the Splitnoses carving and carrying baskets of bones away. Sizzling the flesh. The people greedy with fleshforks, the monks praying. Her silken thighs gave up slices the size of grown pigs. Her paps fed families. Sawing, hacking, tearing, until the next sun (7).

In this way the vast woman was *sacrificed* (8), Generous concludes his report. Although at this place there is no explicit mention of the Egyptian goddess Isis, I think there is enough reason to interpret the vast woman as an Isis figure. As the goddess of the heavens, Isis had wings, like the 'broken God' in *The Book of the Night*. The heavenly connection becomes clear in the figure of Celeste herself. When her noviciate in the monastery begins—which in a sense is a movement into normality because her task is to learn copying from Generous—the name of CuRoi is bestowed on Celeste by the old Abbot Isaac. Her father, in his oracular idiom, explains to her that,

> "Your new name means Hound of the King, the Canaanite, Canine, Khan, Konig, Cain, Co'in, Conn, Cohen, from the royal race of Sirius, Dog Star, Kion, the star of Osiris and Isis. These are the tribes of priests who watch the Heavens, whose days are the Dog Days. Dog means rach, rach means clock, clock means time. We watch time. Dog is God involuted, manifested" (49).

Whereupon Celeste protests, whining, *"But my name is Celeste"* (49). She obviously wants more than to be the watch-dog of the sacred, she wants to be 'heaven' herself, celest-ial. Celeste does not want to live disguised as a boy in a monastery, she wants to become woman. *Or more* (9).

In my view, the death of the vast woman represents the exile, or repression, of maternity, reproduction, and (female) sexuality from patriarchal religions. Isaac's Hebrew chant *"Cabosh, Kadosh"* (hat of death, holy) will return, as we saw above, in Manuel's list *Kadosh, holy; cabosh, hat of death; caboose, the last car on the train, the end. Kaput, see? Holy, separated* (29). The great goddess is *kaput*, broken. She is holy and consecrated, indeed, yet no longer as an integral experience of religious life but as a chimera haunting—or perhaps, nourishing—the religions that have banned her.[14] As I read it, Lerman's text surely does not propagate a reincarnation of the goddess Isis—a resurrection of 'the broken God' in twentieth century goddess religion—but a present-day rehabilitation of female corporality as a possible site of holiness instead of sacrifice.

Celeste wants to become woman, or more. First, however, she becomes a cow.

Becoming a Cow

The dog days Manuel is speaking of refer to the warmest time of the year on the Northern hemisphere, when Sirius, the Dog star, rises together with the sun. It is a time when, according to popular belief, dogs turn rabid, and people go berserk (remember Al Pacino in *Dog Day Afternoon*). The crucial date of this period is, in *The Book of the Night*'s narrative, August fifteenth. *"Here it is . . . no time, all time. Here it is always August fifteenth"* (21), Manuel says. To Celeste, it is *a day in which terrible and wonderful things may happen* (10); it is the day of her own radical transformation. August fifteenth is the time of the Dark Gods, whom we have forgotten but *they have not forgotten us* (11). August fifteenth is their time.

---

[14] Very interesting in this respect is the remarkable "Queen of Heaven" or "Woman clothed with the sun", the protagonist of Rev. 12., who resonates the goddess Isis as well. Cf. Catherine Keller, *Apocalypse Now and Then. A Feminist Guide to the End of the World* (Boston: Beacon Press, 1996), pp. 64–83.

It is the time when An, the real Article, Lady Luck no less, mother of Lug, Fate, Nem-Isis, Mary, forget the etymology, was assumed. In Jerusalem it is the time of the destruction of the Temple. In Mexico it will be the last day of the Fifth Mayan Sun and the first day of the Sixth Mayan Sun. In Japan it is the day the dead return through a crack in the night sky to punish the living. It is the day of the beheading of John the Baptist (think Lunar), the beginning of the Inquisition, Custer's last stand, the day Rama Krishna died, the day Napoleon was born, the Assumption of the Blessed Virgin (see above), the day World War One began (Watch the W's, forget the logic), the end for the Japanese of World War Two, and the day I became a cow.
A cow. Yes (11).

Which are these "terrible and wonderful things" that happen to Celeste/CuRoi on August fifteenth? When Celeste is fifteen years old, and living now in the monastery (in secret burying her *bloodied rags* (77) each months in the fields!), the Abbot's sister accompanied by a younger woman, only known as Cook, arrives with the *Prince George* tourist boat to stay on Iona. One day Celeste furtively watches her father and Cook make love in a grove. On the day her father sets fire to himself and burns to death, Cook disappears. Six weeks later she returns on the *Prince George*, carrying a bundle of rags in her arms, which she pushes into Celeste's arms, simply stating *"Your brother"* (129). And flees again. The old Abbot happens to see the handing over of the baby and concludes that CuRoi is the father. The shock causes him a fatal heart attack. Celeste is threatened with excommunication. Pending the arrival of the new Abbot, who has to decide her fate, Celeste sleeps with the baby in the monastery's barn in the hay with the cows. The child is fed milk from a cow.

One morning at the beach Celeste witnesses a stranger locked in a terrible fight with a group of intruders. When, ultimately, she sees the man flung sideways from a cliff into the see, she tears her cloths from her and swims to *the spot of brightness* (136) to rescue him. After Celeste has dragged him onto the shore, they make love in a dreamlike state, *and while I didn't understand the licking as if it were a mother cow grooming her new-born calf, surely I understood the pleasure as he lifted me and pulled me onto himself and entered me as if he too were the red hot sun rising within me, two suns suspended within me* (138). Later the man turns out to be the new Abbot, but he does not recognize CuRoi as the girl on the beach. Instead, he reads her punishment: exile, together with the child. At Matins she is brought to the stones that form a bridge to the mainland. At the prospect of the child's furious hunger, Celeste rocks the baby until her breasts fill with milk. Because she is *filled with the miracle of the milk* (143), but of course hiding it, she dares to walk back to the monastery. The Abbot allows her to stay for another three weeks in the barn, yet urges her to give up the child and do penance to obtain admittance to the monastery. She refuses. Nevertheless she is passionately in love with Thomas.

On the morning after the three weeks have passed, Celeste wakes up to find the infant gone, *no gurgling sweetness, no fat arms and legs aswim in the air, no angelic cheek* (147), only the traces of wet blood in the hay beside her. The monks claim that a cow stepped on the baby.

Then the Abbot discovers wet spots of milk on her cassock, and, finally, he allows the scales to fall from his eyes. He understands it was she on the beach and that he owes his life to Celeste. She confesses him her love. Shattered by desire as much as fear himself, Thomas attempts to expel her from his sight. Celeste flees in agony. And then it happens.

> [And] I writhed in pain as my bones and my skin and my spine and my self and my hands and my fingers and my heart hardened in agony and I bit my lips so as not to call out to him or any other and I crawled into the cave of an uprooted tree trunk as if it were an empty skull, its nerves and brain torn, as mine, from the matrix of its life, and I felt my jaws stretching, my eyes rounding, my nostrils spreading, my teeth digging at my gums, my tongue pulling and pulling until I was myself, at last, a cow, and I could stay (151).

Why does a teenager turn into a cow—where and when? Moreover, together with the Abbot Thomas—like everybody else on Iona not aware of the identity of the newly appeared white cow—we may wonder whether *"it [is] not possible in this cow we bear witness to a miracle—not a singular event, but a new form of intelligence that we must breed and nurture?"* (186)

Leaving this question of whether we are dealing with a miracle still aside for the moment, we observe that Celeste's metamorphosis in the first place represents a practical solution to an imminent danger. By changing from young woman into *wee white cow*, Celeste is able to stay on the island, near the monastery, near Thomas. Odd and disquieting though such a metamorphosis may seem, it also attests to the inventive powers of love. Echoes of Zeus' cunning sound in it, such as his transformation of the girl Io, whom he was in love with, into a cow to mislead his spouse Hera. Or we recognize the reversal—a covert parody, perhaps—of the myth of Zeus' shapeshifting into a handsome white bull to abduct King Agenor's daughter, Europa. In *The Book of the Night* the girl-cow metamorphosis starts a highly unusual and ambivalent love-affair, because not only the cow Celeste keeps on loving Thomas, but the latter for his part is tormented by passionate feelings for what he thinks and doubts to be a cow.

> I lust. I desire. Am I wounded in such a way by my passion—a wound that flies deep to my center and reaches out to some sort of metaphysical depravity? Is it the Universe wounded? Well have I fornicated, murdered, decimated clans, stolen cows, holy books, relics... yet this troubles me more. I know it is sin and I know it is not sin (158).

In her essay "Animal Sex: Libido as Desire and Death", philosopher Elisabeth Grosz approaches sexuality in a way pertinent to *The Book of the Night*.[15] The popularity of nature films on television and books of full-colour photographs on the 'secrets of the animal world' testify to a pervasive fascination with animal sex of all kinds. At the same time two species in particular, the black widow spider and the praying mantis, continue to haunt the imaginations and the projections of men. Grosz states that they have come to represent, in scientific theory no less than in mythology and literature, a close and persistent link between sex and death, pleasure and pain, desire and revenge. Moreover, they often serve as a source and model of fantasms about human female sexuality and the female lover as castrating and devouring. Seeing sex as a kind of anticipation of death in this way causes woman to be represented as a living threat of death.

In a more sophisticated mode, Freudian psychoanalysis maintains a similar close linkage between sex and death in various of its assumptions. This is not only the case in the theory of complementarity of pleasure principle and death drive, for instance, but also in what Grosz names the fantasy of a hydraulic sexuality. She refers to Freud's

---

[15] Elisabeth Grosz, "Animal Sex: Libido as Desire and Death", in *Space, Time and Perversion* (London and New York: Routledge, 1995), pp. 187–205. In terms of intellectual genealogy, she relies heavily on Alphonso Lingis's materialist theory of sexual desire—in his turn building on Merleau-Ponty, Lyotard, and Deleuze and Guattari.

model of the eroticism of orgasm, utterly based on the male orgasm, of tumescence, accumulation of energies and fluids, release, and, finally, detumescence and death-like state of contentment and quiescence. Grosz, on the other hand, seeks a mode of speaking and imagining sexuality that severs the intrinsic link between sex and death—although connections between pleasure and horror need not be denied—and thinks libido in other than 'hydraulic' terms.

She advocates a view of sexuality and desire as a dynamic of undirected libidinal intensities. "Not simply a rise and fall, a waxing and waning, but movement, processes, transmutations."[16] This view rests on an understanding of corporality, of carnality, not in terms of interiority—in terms of concepts, motives, causes, intentions, fantasies—but in terms of the body's 'outside', its surface. Each part of the body can momentarily become a site or zone of intensity, the body becomes a site of intensive disruptions.

> The subject ceases to be *a* subject, giving way to pulsations, gyrations, flux, secretions, swellings, processes over which it can exert no control and to which it only wants to succumb. Its borders blur, seep, so that, for a while at least, it is no longer clear where one organ, body, or subject stops and another begins.[17]

At this point we hear Celeste again, *Oh, Thomas, the word for moon is Sin and Sin means All-Embracing and Lamentation and One, the Other of the sun. Sin is the name of the moon. Our shadows fused on the sand in a new corpus* (157).

Desire as corporeal intensification means that a subject is flung into a force field of intensities, thus stripped of its coherence and opened up to an interaction with an other whose surface intersects one's own. I think this is a proper perspective to direct our understanding of the cow/Celeste's and human/Thomas's carnal interchange. Their desire does not represent animal sex as an emblem of the intrinsic link between sex and death, with its projection of woman as aggressive and murderous. No more does it simply repeat the classical myths of seduction and rape of innocent femininity. In Lerman's tale, desire, coupled with however much reluctance and shame, in particular from the Abbot's part, is pictured as a nonteleological transformative dynamic. In Grosz's words one more time,

---

[16] Grosz, "Animal sex", p. 204.
[17] Grosz, "Animal sex", p. 198.

The point is that both a world and a body are opened up for redistribution, dis-organization, transformation; each is metamorphosed in the encounter, both becoming something other, something incapable of being determined in advance, and perhaps even in retrospect, but which nonetheless have perceptibly shifted and realigned.[18]

Order Out of Chaos

For Celeste, however, being a cow surely is not an ideal state but rather a temporary solution in an awkward situation tending towards tragedy. She desperately longs to continue her transfiguration towards womanhood, as is well expressed in the following key extract at the beginning of *The Book of the Night*. It densely shows the intermingling of the languages of scientific cosmological speculation, sexual desire and revision of what counts as holy distinctive of the novel:

> There are many endings and many beginnings and there is always between ending and beginning the very briefest of moments and in those moments change, deep volatile change, is possible. To find that moment, to grasp it, embrace it, to change within it, that is the thrust of evolution. That is the moment of chaos, of a higher order, the disorder of the Gods, but order nevertheless. And to change within that moment takes the most terrible of wills. But it is possible. And then change becomes not evolution but exaltation. Once I was in that moment, that crack between ending and beginning, but I was without will. I became somehow a cow. Now I am searching for that moment again so that I may become woman. Or more (9).

These words already indicate that Celeste's transformation is imagined in connection to Ilya Prigogine's theory of non-equilibrium (or un-stable!) thermodynamic self-organization. Lerman refers to this theory in a sort of epigraph, at various sites in the text of the novel itself, and in the acknowledgements.[19] The ideas about change, chaos

---

[18] Grosz, "Animal sex", p. 200.
[19] The Russian-Belgium scientist Prigogine received the Nobel Prize for Chemistry in 1977. *Order Out of Chaos*, the book which made him known to a larger public, and which was an English revision of *La Nouvelle Alliance* from 1979, was co-authored by Isabelle Stengers, who, however, remains unmentioned by Lerman. In the acknowledgements added to her novel, Lerman expresses her gratitude to Prigogine for allowing her to read his unpublished manuscript of *Order Out of Chaos*. The manuscript was published in 1984, the same year Lerman's book appeared. Prigogine's theory has been a source of inspiration for other science fiction authors as well. See on this topic David Porush, "Prigogine, Chaos, and Contemporary Science Fiction", *Science Fiction Studies* 18 (1991), pp. 367–386.

and order, about being and becoming, which pervade the novel's text, should be understood largely through this frame.

Prigogine and Stengers present a radical modification of the so-called Second Law of Thermodynamics, or, the principle of entropy. Entropy is a functional measure to determine the amount of heat in any system that is lost for useful purposes. The second law states that in a closed system entropy always tends to increase to a maximum whereas the available energy tends to a minimum. If the implications of the second law are fully considered, the running down of the most closed system, the universe, comes inevitably into sight. Lerman herself notes in the epigraph that, *[a]ccording to the Second Law of Thermodynamics, the world will eventually die, decay, fall into drift, come to a hopeless end, burn out, slide into disorder*. Prigogine's and Stengers's main point is that the second law only applies to conditions which are in equilibrium. According to them, the universe has a pluralistic, temporal and complex character, its processes being marked by nonlinearity, instability and fluctuations. Taking this as their point of departure, they focus on the study of the appearance and evolution of new structures that originate spontaneously in far-from-equilibrium conditions, so-called dissipative structures. Here, unlike in systems governed by equilibrium, a local entropy *decrease* may occur.

> [W]e may have transformation from disorder, from thermal chaos, into order. New dynamic states of matter may originate, states that reflect the interaction of a given system with its surroundings.[20]

The new states of matter survive in an open exchange of energy with the generally entropic universe in order to dissipate the products of their instabilities and evolve to higher complexities. This approach implies that the mechanistic idea of matter as passive substance is abandoned for a view of matter as capable of spontaneous activity. It is above all this aspect that Lerman has made operative in her book, as indicated in the epigraph:

> Energy increases. An organism is able to reorganize itself into a higher level of order, to *transcend itself*. What it is that conducts this self-organization, implicit in evolution, seems to be an inherent property of matter itself, as if, indeed, matter had *mind*. As if, indeed, the thrust of evolution is *will* (Emphasis added).

---

[20] Ilya Prigogine and Isabelle Stengers, *Order Out of Chaos: Man's New Dialogue with Nature* (London: William Heinemann, 1984), p. 12.

The suggestion that matter might possess consciousness marks Lerman's own application of the theory's gist. She largely anthropomorphizes it by making the girl Celeste conceived of/conceive herself as an organism under conditions far-from-equilibrium.

> According to the good Dr. Prigogine's text, which must still lie on the shelf in my childhood room, at the point farthest from equilibrium, self-organization to a more complex form is possible. And at that terrible moment when I became a cow, I had been far from stable. I had been in the very crack of change (238).

The awakening of powerful sexual desire when she reaches puberty pushes her into an un-stability and chaos which, paradoxically, entails a new order as well.

A Miracle by Her Own Doing

The model of change inspired by thermodynamics also feeds the particular understanding of miracle in *The Book of the Night*. First we need to consider the various levels of the miraculous in the novel. The novel is pervaded by miraculous things and events, to be sure, but it is in the first place the reader in whom they arouse wonder and marvel. The characters, on the other hand, accept the extraordinary as part of the ordinary—not only all kinds of acts of magic, charms and incantations, apparitions and shapeshifting, and *disorderly things* (183) like a woman birthing a dog and a child born with the head of a donkey, but also the ontological hotchpotch which is the result of the juxtaposition of several ages on one island. The chronicler Generous, like a bookkeeper, records odd events and phenomena in long lists.[21] Yet there is another kind of miracle too. The

---

[21] Compare this to what historian Caroline Walker Bynum notes about which kinds of event referred to in medieval accounts or artistic representations tended to trigger wonder (understood in its full range of awe and dread). "Miracles, for example—though routinely referred to as 'marvelous'—are seldom represented as evoking or intended to evoke wonder. Indeed, the didactic purposes to which miracle collections were directed and the hair-splitting distinctions about ontological status indulged in by theologians seem to have reduced miracle accounts to rather dull enumerations of events. (. . .) Although chronicles and annals sometimes couch their descriptions of unusual natural events such as eclipses, earthquakes, and famines in terms of dread and a kind of hovering significance, these events are also sometimes listed in clipped, matter-of-fact prose. Thus miracles, portens, and oddities are sites and stagings of wonder less often than we might suppose." Caroline Walker Bynum, "Wonder", *The American Historical Review* 102 (1997), p. 17.

pivotal event of the narrative, the girl who transforms into a cow, is conceived of as a wonder and debate-evoking miracle indeed.

The idea that in this cow *we bear witness to a miracle—not a singular event, but a new form of intelligence that we must breed and nurture* (186) is brought forward by the *Pelagian* (275) Abbot Thomas in a wrangle with Nicholas, Iona's representative of Rome and the doctrine of the Church. Pelagius was a fifth century British monk, who was engaged in a polemic with Augustine about the doctrine of divine grace. He repudiated original sin and conceived of grace as the freedom to choose between doing good and evil. Pelagianism was denounced at the Council of Ephese in 431. In Lerman's novel, its spirit is revitalized in the figure of Thomas. However, his ideas should not be read as a defense of a kind of twentieth century neo-Pelagianism. The controversy between Thomas and Nicholas, in my view, is a point of reflection for a contemporary approach to miracles. It may result in an understanding of a miracle as, in Thomas's words, "a new form of intelligence" instead of some singular deviation of the natural order. That is to say, a miracle becomes a *sign of a change of order* (185).

Nicholas aptly frames the issue of his debate with Thomas, *"This is not about a cow. It is about will and grace"* (186). Thomas defends the possibility that the white cow is not an ordinary creature and might even be a woman who somehow transformed herself, *"with some inner force"* (185). As the chronicler Generous echoes with amazement, *"A wonder by her own doing!"*. Nicholas vehemently rejects this idea, *"You also, Generous? Know you that man has fallen and cannot find grace except through God through the offices of the Mother Church, not by one's own doing"*. Thomas for his part regards this as *"fatalism under the cover of grace"* (186), defending the soundness of human nature and free will. *"The Creation itself is grace. Grace comes from in here. From my will to be pure"* (187).

To a certain extent the tension between will and grace, and hence, between an understanding of a miracle as gift of grace and extraordinary self-willed act, also is what Lerman's book is about. Yet I do not think that the overall view of the book simply coincides with Thomas's fierce defense of the human will as such. In a conversation with Celeste-cow much later, Thomas gets carried away when considering Celeste's transformations.

> This means that ... this is the single ever-deepening note of evolution, Celeste, that man's consciousness will be free, that one can change, that one can choose ... the creature becomes the Creator (261).

Celeste's response, however, puts a stop to phantasies with universal and abstract claims. *"Don't make me an example, Thomas"*. What is explored in the novel, I would say, is a redefinition of grace as the gift of the power to fulfill one's will to become who one is. For Celeste, however, this is no philosophical maxim but a matter of life and death: if she wants to survive, she has to become a woman, or: to fulfill herself as a woman. When Celeste-cow asks herself in desperation if she is her *own màker, autopoetic, self-organizing, Creator, not creature?* (160), it does not reflect a wish to be a God-like autonomous person. Rather, it displays a longing to take part in the difficult and intricate processes of the creation of a female sexual self. To be able *to find that moment, to grasp it, embrace it, to change within it* (9) could be called grace. The will, however, is not opposed to it but forms its indispensable condition. To complete the transformation from girl to woman requires even *the most terrible of wills* (9). For Celeste, the appearance of the wee white cow is not so much a miracle but rather the result of a lack of will! After all, she got stuck half-way the process, which Thomas is not to know. *I who thought I was a miracle, am not* (153).

From her viewpoint, the miracle would be the realization of the process of becoming a woman. The miraculous transformation was already in bud when Celeste was filled with the 'miracle of the milk' to keep her baby-stepbrother alive. Turning into a cow, then, was only a half-way transformation, yet one of great significance. Lisa Tuttle reminds us with respect to *The Book of the Night* that "in world mythology the cow—white, horned, milk-giving—is one of the most common manifestations of the Great Mother and the creator of the world".[22] It was no coincidence that the vast woman from the opening scene had *ears those of a cow*. Moreover, we have seen how Manuel associated the Hebrew letter Aleph with cow's horns: *The cow is A for breath, the breath and the spirit of the Not God as One* (34), as well as a B, a container of one's holiest part.

Celeste's burning question is whether she will be capable of finding her most holy part, that is, of fulfilling the miracle of *auto-poesis*, of self-creation. In her own words, will she have the courage and the power to go *There?* "There" is a place with no certainty, *with no law, no universal principle, no unified field theory, nothing, no connectives, no metaphor,*

---

[22] Tuttle, "Pets and monsters", p. 105.

no perspective, no causes, effects, no visions, no verse. The unmanifest (215). Becoming woman for Celeste, to put it differently, is not complying with a prescribed female way of being but a lonely and risky adventure beyond or outside cultural inscription. *It is safe in my stall. To strip oneself of all the B, the containers, the stable, the resistances is too terrifying. To move to the edge of great non-linear dissipate instability, far from equilibrium where shadows are cockhorses and fireflies are stars, is to face death* (240). And yet, Celeste knows, *that is the place I must find if I'm to become a woman* (215).

Celeste's "there" recalls, on the one hand, what philosopher and psychoanalyst Luce Irigaray has called a horizon, an image of the realization of womanhood.[23] In reference to Ludwig Feuerbach's *Das Wesen des Christentums*, Irigaray states that human beings create or project a God as a safeguard and a horizon of infinity. But infinity, as she sees it, means infinite becoming within the finiteness of one's sex. The history of Christian faith and theology, however, has largely denied this finiteness by attributing universal validity to the projected male God. Images of the infinite becoming of the female sex have thus been entirely precluded. Yet to be able to realize their female subjectivity in all its possiblities women need images of female divinity, that is, in Irigaray's understanding, mirrors of the perfection of the female sex.

It is possible, then, to interpret in this perspective the miraculous vision Celeste has one night during her ambiguous existence as a cow. Standing in her stall in the barn, she watches the moon drawing near the window of the abbey.

> The finger of the moon touched the face of the rose window and suddenly, as if in answer, a thin film of flesh covered the bones of the abbey and the bones of the abbey became rounded and soft, and the towers became... what is it... knees. And the crack of doors, a human, fleshly ass, and the rose window—the great seat of birth—burst open with the light of birth as a living eye. A cathedral of flesh, the abbey became, her belly the roof of it all. I raced from the barn but stopped at the Tree of Life and hid, somehow, in its shadow (. . .). There I saw her navel, the nave, her arms outstreched into the apse, and her head as altar. Her woman part opened in the red-gold of light. I saw her and knew I looked upon a woman with her knees in

---

[23] Luce Irigaray, "Divine Women", in: *Sexes and Genealogies*. Translated by Gillian C. Gill (New York: Columbia University Press, 1993).

the air, giving birth to living light. What had been the soft gold reflection on the glass, now became her own fire. I watched. Stars rested on her fingers and glinted on her kneecaps.

And then she stood and shook stiffness from her limbs and the transparacency of flesh became solid and she walked along the Street of the Dead down toward the sea, past me, knelt, dropped her long hair into the pool of the sea, and washed herself. And then she stood and spun over the fields, her robes of moonlight twisting about her, twisting until she became a triangle of light, five parts four, four parts three, shimmering, and the moisture from her hair dropped as dew on the fields. She lay down again where the abbey had been, lifted her knees to the sky, stretched out her arms across the fields, opened herself, her woman part, and was stone again. Doors, towers, window, stone (240/41).

Celeste's vision of the abbey's transfiguration into a gigantic and divine-like woman indeed embodies a horizon, a promise even of realizing her own sex, of "being born as a woman".[24] For a woman, being born means the power "to emerge from the hells, the gulfs and the abysses, the oceans and the ice/mirrors . . .".[25] To emerge, that is, from her existence as man's 'other', which is non-existence *as a woman*.

The Darkness of the Night

In Celeste's vision, the apparently solid building of patriarchal religion has turned dynamic and flowing so as to be radically transformed by/into female presence. The abbey-woman appears as a momentary return of the vast woman, the 'broken God'. *I had seen the abbey dance. I had seen the meaning of the abbey, dancing, deconstructed, alive. Thomas says there are things which perdure. Surely not order, not construction* (241/42).

At this point, however, Lerman's text not just tallies with Irigaray's perspective but disrupts it too. The latter's project of deconstruction of the Western stock of ideas—from Plato to Freud—aims at creating space for the construction of a female symbolic. She wishes for women the strength 'to accede to the light—for herself and for

---

[24] Luce Irigaray, "A Natal Lacuna". Translated by Margaret Whitford. *Women's Art*, May/June 1994, pp. 11–13.
[25] Irigaray, "A Natal Lacuna", p. 13.

the other—within a finite and in-finite horizon, a place of breath and gestation which is not the void'.[26] Celeste's experience of deconstruction, on the other hand, seems more radical. More abysmal, we might say. Changing into womanhood appears as something much more frightening, chaotic and ambiguous than the process of growth and 'entering the light' that Irigaray envisions. Celeste says, *I saw the miracle, that night, only once, but I knew then that the true light came from the darkness and it was to the darkness I must go. I could not hide* (241).

Thus we find the question of the where and the when of the miracle explicitly addressed: metamorphoses and transfigurations take place in the darkness of the night. Entering the light means at the same time going to the dark, for one enters the land of desire and sexuality, whose prominent features are not brightness and coherence but corporeal confusion and opacity of the mind. The miracle of transfiguration from liminal condition (*neither cow nor woman* 261) into womanhood occurs at the moment of ultimate cosmic and subjective chaos. In keeping with Prigogine and Stengers, Lerman has Celeste saying that from this chaos a higher order emerges. Very unlike Prigogine's and Stengers's scientific-philosophical mindset, however, is the idiosyncratic sexuo-religious idiom attached to the idea of chaos and change in Lerman's textual universe. Celeste refers to the moment of transformative chaos as *the disorder of the Gods* (9), that is, a moment in which linear logic breaks down and the divine manifests itself as many-faced.

Most important are the faces of the Dark Gods (or the Night Gods or the Gods of Death), the ones denied by doctrinal Christianity, as Thomas helds against Nicholas.

> "What will become of them [the Gods of Death] in your City of God? Isis, Nem-Isis, Nepthys, Osiris, Seth?" (224)

> "You cannot deny death or darkness. Before many years, Nicholas, I see in the waves and in the wind, you will forget this and think of Christ as the only God. Cows will wander in these holy halls and the nut gardens will turn to mast for profane pigs" (225).

The most prominent divinity of the night is Seth. Lerman's text alludes to several connotations of this name. In the first place to

---

[26] Irigaray, "A Natal Lacuna", p. 13.

Seth, the ancient Egyptian god of the desert, storm and foreign countries, who killed his brother Osiris, Isis' spouse. But also to the biblical figure Seth (= 'buttocks'), Adam and Eve's third son (Gn 4:25). The Abbot Thomas defends Seth over against Nicholas's Christ who professes to have *"destroyed the underworld for all time, cleaned the Augean stables of the shit of death, harrowed Hell"* (224). Lerman's Seth stands for a both pre- and post-Christian understanding of the divine as encompassing multiple forces and fragments, including the dark powers of sexuality and violence. But he is not an almighty Creator; he guides you to self-creation—which is a terrifying process of negativity, of entering the unknown behind the ostensible balance of life. *The Other Side is the crack from which novelty emerges. Seth leads the way to the Naught* (253).

In a series of overwhelmingly kaleidoscopic and hallucinatory scenes at the end of the novel, featuring the battle between the troops of the Church of Rome and the 'old powers' on the shores of Iona, as well as Celeste's own quest for transformation through the nightworld, Celeste—still a cow—meets Seth. In her eyes, he embodies sexuality and spirituality at the same time.

> Seth. Ham. Pig. His semen is in his head and he burst forth with the seed of wisdom and enlightenment. This then is the true snake in the Garden, the enlightenend man whose sex has become his consciousness, kundalini (278).

Celeste begs Seth to change her. Seth, however, mocks her. *"Would you rather be a pig? (. . .) Pig, pork, Phorcus, Orcus, Orkneys, Hocus, Pocus?"* (282). And when Celeste insists, *"What do you wish now? Wheels? Three breasts? Weak-kneed Thomas? Spotted buttocks?"* (283). Instead, he incites her to draw on her own powers. *"The future is not given, Celeste! It is taken, taken, taken. Take it!"* (285).

Whereas in Irigaray's view the underworld is the place of patriarchal repression of the feminine from which women must free themselves, Lerman's underworld is a place where Celeste must go *in order to* become a woman on her own terms. On the one hand, indeed, Lerman's choice of a masculine and virile god as a guidance to womanhood is pretty odd. It certainly opposes Irigaray's emphasis on the necessity of imagining a divine of the feminine, of creating a divine for women. I want to put forward, however, that Seth obviously does not represent an ideal, neither for women nor for men. According to himself, he leads the way to the "Naught": in my view, he is the deconstructive factor which undermines any 'natural' cultural order. Thus he embodies the condition of change, of the 'deep volatile change' Celeste speaks about, and which also involves the transcendence of the disciplinary force of language. She expresses this transcendence as the desire to

> fly out of the orbits and orders and predestinies, out of the stories others write about me, out of interpretation and into eternity where every thing, every word, is spirit and new and without metaphor and I should wrestle with the Motley Crew of Naught, the Angels of Death, the Dark Pig Gods of Disorder... (12).

The break down of the disciplinary language of culture seems to imply a transcendence of corporeal existence altogether: *Naming I should go, creating anew and living forever after in the Milky Way of wisdom, unincarnated, unincarcerated in the prison of flesh word meaning* (12).

Yet it turns out to be not a breaking away from the flesh but a transfiguration of the flesh that shapes Celeste's miracle of self-creation into womanhood. In one of the scenes describing her Dantesque tour with Seth through the night- or underworld, the embodiment of womanhood is announced in a grotesque image of drifting uteruses.

> At my feet in the next room are moving gardens of violet creatures, flowerlike, soft and fleshy, faceless with long fallopian arms. On each arm, eight elegant fingers clasp ovaries to soft shoulders. They dance toward me. They reach to my knees. One rubs against my leg as a cat, begging, promising (281).

Celeste, with all her powers of will, strives to act upon Seth's incitement to 'take the future'. It means a vehement struggle to overcome the fragmentation of body and mind in order to give birth to herself and become woman.

> Flesh leaves bone. I pull my patterns into my head. There is not a part of me that is not now in my head. A leg leaves my consciousness. I draw it back in. My head is filled with radiances. The violet creature clinging to my leg tucks herself into me, mewing. I close around her. (...) I hold desperately to the idea of me. I am all pattern now, all dark (285).

Ultimately, we read Celeste's cry of death-and-birth, which echoes the paradoxical passion and of the great mystics, *My body burns with great fevers and dark lights. Still, I am. This is not evolution. This is exaltation* (285). A beautiful yet muted girl-cow transfigures into a woman.

Or more (9). She has experienced a miracle realized by her own intense desire to become a female sexual subject, which means to her: to incarnate yet to be *unincarcerated in the prison of flesh word meaning* (12). This desire is not opposed to grace but means a redefinition of grace as the gift of transformation of religious and cultural order.

12

A DIFFERENT GRACE: EPILOGUE

Anne-Marie Korte

Introduction

It is with great precision that the articles in this book show how women are involved in miracles. Referring to a variety of writings from different historical contexts, the essays describe women who have undergone or initiated miracles, performed them, or possessed supernatural, miraculous powers—and they reveal the price some women have had to pay for this.

In an analysis of miracle stories it is unproductive to presume that women resort to miracles mainly because they lack autonomy, power and rationality. Miracles perform a unique function in religious expression and communication—and women's involvement in miracles should be explored from this angle. It is true that miracles, and stories about them, can evoke and confirm every conceivable stereotype of woman as 'the other'—and some miracle stories do just that. Yet, the realm of miracles also shows us how women appropriate common religious discourses and practices and leave their own marks on them. Women do derive religious influence and authority from miracles, but that is not all. They also acquire the ability to recognize and fight personal and communal suffering. Moreover, miracles help women to confront and to overcome the stigmas of corporeality which most religious traditions have assigned to women's bodies in particular. By focusing on miracles, we can trace how women contribute to the continual reshaping of religious tradition at the conceptual, ritual and institutional levels. These conclusions can be brought to the fore through a number of examples and insights from the studies in this book.

The Modelling of Miraculous Women

Most of the texts studied in this book express explicit surprise at the fact—or the thought—that *women* perform miracles. Many Western miracle stories are based on biblical 'blueprints', such as omens, miracles and miraculous healing episodes from the Old and New Testaments and from (apocalyptic) literature associated with these bodies of texts. Since these prototype miracle stories hardly ever overtly refer to miracle-working women, it seems only logical that this unexpected phenomenon met with amazement and wonder—sentiments that, incidentally, lasted well into the modern era.[1]

According to Elena Giannarelli, the absence of biblical miracle-working women explains why early Western Christianity acknowledged so few female saints, that is, female miracle performers. In her examination of the fourth century saint cult, Giannarelli argues that especially Mary, mother of God, functioned as a role model for women. As we know, the Virgin Mary does not personally perform miracles in biblical texts; she is a vehicle and mediator of God's actions. She serves as an example to women in quite a different area, namely in her virginity and maternity.[2] The first section of this anthology, which deals with formative Christianity and the early Middle Ages, sheds a different light on this thesis.

In considering role models for miracle-performing women, should we limit ourselves exclusively to female and feminine biblical examples? Apparently, this would oversimplify matters. In a far more subtle analysis, Giselle de Nie writes about the miracles ascribed to Radegund (in sixth-century Gaul). Radegund performs unique miracles; her gestures are reminiscent of 'maternal' acts: giving birth, feeding and providing care. These gestures, however, are modelled on the death and resurrection of Christ—not on the Virgin Mary's role as mother.[3] A second series of Radegund's miracles, which are also unparalleled by male miracle workers in the same period, does

---

[1] This ancient tone of surprise at the fact that *women* are able to perform miracles is emphatically present in Rhoda Lerman's *The Book of the Night* (London: The Women's Press, 1986). See Inez van der Spek's article in this book.

[2] Elena Giannarelli, "Women and Miracles in Christian biography (IVth–Vth centuries)", *Studia Patristica* 25 (1991), pp. 376–380.

[3] These findings are confirmed by Lynda L. Coon, *Sacred Fictions: Holy Women and Hagiography in Late Antiquity* (Philadelphia: University of Pennsylvania Press, 1997), pp. 126–135.

refer to a female image from the Bible. Radegund's crushing of worms refers to the Virgin Mary, but not in her role as the mother of God. Instead, it is Mary as the new Eve, the woman from John's Revelations who tramples evil—in the shape of a snake.

According to Jacqueline Borsje, even the female figures who are little more than 'extras' in St. Columba's miracle stories from sixth- and seventh-century Ireland display much more than virginal or maternal virtue. Others may argue that the author of *Vita Sancti Columbae* sees women only in their procreative or maternal role, but Borsje shows that the circle of women surrounding St. Columba are given a much more differentiated depiction. The women reflect the saint's average audience. They are not St. Columba's opposites, magical or otherwise, and their religious views do not contrast sharply with his. On the contrary, some of the women in the story even set a positive religious example. The one woman who is motivated purely by her role as a mother is in fact an adversary of St. Columba's, while those women with no direct connection to motherhood appear to have acquired religious insight and judiciousness. The latter group also includes the female figures that are actively involved in miracles. In this case, it seems that the Martha-Mary distinction[4] functions as a biblical role model and enables women to be involved in miracles.

Depictions of women involved in miracles have alluded to a broad spectrum of biblical figures and stories, as we see from later texts studied in this research project.[5] Marianne Elsakkers's study of the *peperit* charm—which was probably often used during childbirth in medieval Europe—seems to make the strongest case for the Virgin Mary's position as a great biblical example and role model for women. The *peperit* charms focus on the image of the Madonna who bore Christ. On closer inspection, however, one sees that they are not intended to uphold the mother of God as a paragon of feminine virtue and maternal self-sacrifice. The incantations refer to the Virgin Mary in connection with other biblical women such as her mother

---

[4] See Lk 10, 38–42; Jn 11–12,11.

[5] Aside from biblical and other early Christian writings, philosophical and literary texts from Antiquity also served as models for medieval descriptions of miracle-working women. See Kathleen Ashley and Pamela Sheingorn, *Writing Faith: Text, Sign and History in the Miracles of Sainte Foy* (Chicago/London: University of Chicago Press, 1999), pp. 49–53.

Anna and her niece Elizabeth: women of flesh and blood who withstood the pain and fear of delivery and successfully bore children, a delivery moreover which brought salvation to all of humankind (*Elisabet peperit Iohannem, Anna peperit Mariam, Maria peperit Christum*).[6] It is precisely the *non* self-evident, miraculous nature of this successful delivery—for both mother and baby—which is emphasized in these prayers. One example of this is a reference to the raising of Lazarus from the dead which has been found in some versions of the *peperit* incantation.

The Contrariant Powers of Miracles

Magda Misset–van de Weg's study of the *Acta Theclae* provides further reasons why research into the depiction of women who perform miracles should not limit itself to female examples and role models. She shows that Thecla's 'miraculous' deeds in the *Acta Theclae* are modelled on those of the apostles and are a reflection of Paul's actions in particular. This is partly due to the fact that some early Christian women in Asia Minor expressed their faith through a new code of celibacy and asceticism for which there were no female biblical examples or role models. The article's main point, however, is that any discussion of miracle-performing women is related to issues of religious power (influence) and authority (sanctioned exercising of power) and is directly linked to the question whether women (can) possess religious authority and what kind of authority they may lay claim to.[7]

Miracles are crucial to supporting the religious authority and credibility of religious leaders and traditions. This is why there are miracle stories about nearly every founder of a new religion or religious reformation. Within religious establishments, miracles moreover are

---

[6] Compare this with the subtle shift Chava Weissler detects in prayer books belonging to Eastern European Jewish women: some prayers invoke Eve not as the bearer of guilt (the well-known normative image), but as one who knows suffering. Chava Weissler, "*Mizvot* Built into the Body: *Tzikines* for *Niddah*, Pregnancy and Childbirth", Howard Eilberg-Schwartz (ed.), *People of the Body: Jews and Judaism from an Embodied Perspective* (Albany: State University of New York Press, 1992), pp. 101–116.

[7] For an explanation of the distinction between power and authority related to women's religious activities, see Margaret Y. MacDonald, *Early Christian Women and Pagan Opinion: The Power of Hysterical Women* (Cambridge: University Press, 1996), pp. 41–47.

regarded as important pillars of religious truth and authority. But miracles also function to call existing religious authorities into doubt and to establish new ones.[8] As we see in Misset-van de Weg's study of the *Acta Theclae*, Paul's religious authority is assumed to be established and endorsed. His example, particularly his apostolic power to preach and to baptize, creates a clear framework in which Thecla's remarkable and miraculous acts can be appreciated. At the same time, Paul's religious authority is subtly criticized and put into perspective to make room for Thecla's own, unprecedented expression of her religious mission as a woman. Ultimately it is Thecla who preaches, converts and baptizes—and the miraculous events in this story serve to support her personal, God-given mandate to do so.

Scholars of religion have long held the view that religious discourse about miracles and miracle-workers largely refers to (religious) power struggles. In the same vein women are assumed to resort to miracles as a means of exercising power. In this view, women use miracles—as well as possession and other charismatic or ecstatic religious expressions—as an instrument of power, because they are denied influence in so many other ways.[9] Miracles, therefore, are seen as a unique 'source of empowerment'. It is the unique and entirely out of the ordinary nature of miracles which lends their makers a kind of social and religious authority independent of their education and social or religious status.

As the number of women miracle-performers in Christian Europe continually increased until the Reformation, it would seem that women used this unique source of empowerment to claim religious autonomy and authority in a religious climate increasingly domi-

---

[8] See Peter Brown, *Authority and the Sacred: Aspects of the Christianisation of the Roman World* (Cambridge: Cambridge University Press, 1995); Torsten Fremer, "Wunder und Magie: Zur Funktion der Heiligen im frühmittelalterlichen Christianisierungsprozess", *Hagiographica* 3 (1996), pp. 15–88; Mart Bax, *Medjugorje: Religion, Politics and Violence in Rural Bosnia* (Amsterdam: VU Uitgeverij, 1995); Richard H. Davis (ed.), *Images, Miracles, and Authority in Asian Religious Traditions* (Boulder/Oxford: Westview Press, 1998).

[9] Rosemary Ruether and Eleanor McLaughlin, "Introduction: Women's Leadership in the Jewish and Christian Traditions: Continuity and Change", Rosemary Ruether and Eleanor McLaughlin (eds.), *Women of Spirit: Female Leadership in the Jewish and Christian Traditions* (New York: Simon and Schuster, 1979), pp. 16–28; Alex Owen, *The Darkened Room: Women Power and Spirituality in late Victorian England* (Philadelphia: The University of Pennsylvania Press, 1990); Sandra L. Zimdars-Swartz, *Encountering Mary: From La Salette to Medjugorje* (Princeton: Princeton University Press, 1991); Bax, *Medjugorje*.

nated by an exclusively male hierarchy. A number of women employed the unique power of miracles to forge their own brand of faith, to devote their lives to God against the social conventions of marriage and motherhood. In general, however, women's religious independence rarely appeared in conjunction with religious authority. Far more often, their 'extraordinary act' was associated with magic, witchcraft and heresy, particularly in the late medieval and early modern periods.[10]

However, most studies in this anthology show that, for women, the relationship between miracle-performing and religious power or authority is less straightforward—as is the link between charismatic or other extraordinary acts and magic and witchcraft. Miracles performed by women which legitimize established religious authority are by definition extremely rare and controversial, *because* they refer to religious authority. Yet, since miracles also play a role in the establishment of a new or alternative religious authority, the appearance of miracle-working women need neither be exceptional nor disputatious. Giselle de Nie shows that miraculous powers akin to those of Saint Martin of Tours were ascribed to early medieval women with religious authority, such as the abbesses Radegund and Monegunde. This abbott was one of the first Western saints who was beatified not on grounds of martyrdom, but because of his asceticism, his missionary works and miracles. Since these remarkable abbesses were accorded religious authority after St. Martin's mould, they were also ascribed similar miraculous powers.

Charismatic or miraculous power is in itself not sufficient to guarantee religious influence and power. A prime example of this can be found in Marcel Poorthuis and Chana Safrai's article about the miracles that befall a Jewish woman as described in the 'Messianic document' from the *Genizah of Cairo*. What makes this woman excep-

---

[10] See Gottfried Koch, *Frauenfrage und Ketzertum im Mittelalter: Die Frauenbewegung im Rahmen des Katharismus und des Waldensertums und ihre sozialen Wurzeln (12.–14. Jahrhundert)* (Berlin: Akademie-Verlag, 1962); Ruether and McLaughlin, "Introduction: Women's Leadership"; Carol Frances Karlsen, *The Devil in the Shape of a Woman: The Witch in Seventeenth Century New England*, PhD Yale University (Ann Arbor: University Microfilms, 1982); Lène Dresen-Coenders, *Het verbond van heks en duivel: Een waandenkbeeld aan het begin van de moderne tijd als symptoom van een veranderende situatie van de vrouw en als middel tot hervorming van de zeden* (Baarn: Ambo, 1983); Brian P. Levack (ed.), *Witchcraft, Women and Society: Articles on Witchcraft, Magic & Demonology* (New York: Garland Publishing, 1992); Dorothée van Paassen en Anke Passenier (red.), *Op zoek naar vrouwen in ketterij en sekte: Een bronnenonderzoek* (Kampen: Kok, 1993).

tional and memorable are not just the miracles in the strictest sense (the letters, signs, images, blood and oil which appear on her body and clothes), but also the fact that she wears a prayer shawl and makes priestly gestures, deeds which are the religious prerogative of priests and other men. The miracles she experiences are reinforced by these unmistakable signs of established religious authority—a remarkable and rather crude example of how charismatic or prophetic women ward off associations with magic or heresy.

Anke Passenier's article about the *Vita* of Christina Mirabilis shows us that in medieval times, ascribing miraculous power to women could be a means of controlling and manipulating them in matters of faith. Christina Mirabilis' hagiographer stressed the entirely strange nature of her acts and characterized her trials and tribulations as an exception not to be repeated. According to Passenier, the miraculous framework of the *Vita*, depicting Christina as super-human, a wanderer between worlds, seems to function as a diversion, distracting the reader's attention from a religious woman who practised a *vita apostolica*—comprising mendicancy, vagrancy and preaching in a way that was largely deemed unfit for women. The authority of the 'real' woman living an 'extra-regular' religious life is camouflaged by the authority of an extraordinary saint who remains aloof from human society. Passenier suspects that behind the hagiographer's depiction stands a woman who developed a public ministry in her own right, without being supervised by the clergy or a spiritual director from regular orders. By describing Christina as an exceptional human being, the hagiographer was probably trying to prevent the church establishment from being angered by the liberties she took. Depicting miracle-working women in this way marginalizes them and keeps them from acquiring any real religious authority, which thus remains the prerogative of ordinated men.

Women's Bodies as a 'Site of Miracles'

The idea that miracle-working equals influence or power and establishes or confirms religious authority is at odds with the fundamental meaning of miracles in most religious traditions. In Judaism and Christianity, God is the performer of miracles. God's miraculous power is manifest in the saints and prophets. Worldly miracle-workers are instruments, signs or intermediaries which serve this power.

Their role is one of 'receptiveness' and 'passivity', stereotypically 'feminine' characteristics. Seen in this light, it is imaginable that women can also perform miracles; it is God, after all, who takes the initiative.

The idea that women are the 'vehicle' par excellence for Divine acts—and in the most literal, corporeal sense—is already present in prototypical form in the series of Old Testament stories about barren women whose wombs are opened by God. The notion takes wing in the early Middle Ages, as people begin to worship Mary as *theotokos*, Mother of God (fifth century). It is not until the high Middle Ages, however, that the idea is linked to the performance of miracles. As God is depicted as an increasingly transcendental divinity and Christ becomes more powerful and exalted, there seems to be more room for women to act as intermediaries. They mediate both at the heavenly level, in the church—where the Virgin Mary is described as a *mediatrix* (ninth century) and *redemptrix* or *mater redemptoris* (eleventh century)—and on earth, as becomes manifest in the growing number of female saints and miracle workers.

That women are depicted as vehicles for divine acts in a particular way is clear from the type and number of miracles ascribed to them. The relics of female saints are associated with fewer miracles than those of male saints. Miracles ascribed to women are different from the wonders performed by their male counterparts. A woman's miracle is often more physical in nature, involving a change either in her body or brought about by her body, and serves less often to establish religious authority. Women are more likely to be God's vehicle than God's personal representative, due to their obligation to conform to feminine norms.[11] As the medieval God was depicted as more powerful, exalted and transcendental, women's miracle-

---

[11] Giannarelli, "Women and Miracles in Christian biography"; Benedicta Ward, "Apophtegmata Matrum", Benedicta Ward, *Signs and Wonders: Saints, Miracles and Prayers from the 4th Century to the 14th* (Aldershot: Variorum, 1992), I, pp. 63–66; H.-W. Goetz, "Heiligenkult und Geslecht: Geschlechtspezifisches Wunderwirken in frühmittelalterlichen Mirakelberichten?", *Das Mittelalter* 1 (1996), pp. 89–111; Elizabeth Alvida Petroff, *Medieval Women's Visionary Literature* (New York/Oxford: Oxford University Press, 1986), esp. Part III, "Women Mystics and the Acquisition of Power", pp. 137–224; Caroline Walker Bynum, *Fragmentation and Redemption: Essays on Gender and the Human Body in Medieval Religion* (New York: Zone Books, 1991), esp. Chapter V, "'And Woman His Humanity': Female Imagery in the Religious Writing of the Later Middle Ages," pp. 151–179.

working power became more literally attached to their bodily condition and functions.

In modern times, the expectation that God acts through miracles has dwindled. Still, the mediation of women based on extraordinary and non-rational religious receptiveness has survived. It has taken on new forms and has in some cases expanded, for instance in women's leading roles in pietism, quietism and spiritism. Apparitions of the Virgin Mary in nineteenth and twentieth century Europe have hinged on women's mediation. These apparitions are cases of multi-level mediation—the Virgin being an actively mediating divine being, whose apparition is mediated by women and children.[12]

The idea that women are literally, physically, a 'vehicle' of God confirms the traditional socio-anthropological view that women have a passive and 'merely bodily' role and a derivative or secondary social status. However, a number of studies in this book show how women have turned this association with 'passive' and 'physical' mediation to their own advantage. They have co-opted this association, renamed it to suit their own purposes or given it its own (ritual) form in order to gain a more independent, authoritative voice and hand in matters of faith. This process is traced meticulously in the analyses of texts about Thecla (Magda Misset-van de Weg), Radegund (Giselle de Nie), the Sicilian rabbi's wife (Marcel Poorthuis and Chana Safrai) and Friederike Hauffe (Wouter Hanegraaff).

Why do women's (own) bodies play a pivotal role in their involvement with miracles? Could the image of woman as God's literal and bodily 'sign' or 'vehicle' be the basis of this remarkable phenomenon?[13] Most of the studies in this book question and analyze the meaning of this physical link. The miracles women are involved in

---

[12] Hilda Graef, *Mary: A History of Doctrine and Devotion* (Westminster: Christian Classics, 1985; 1st ed. 1963;1965); Marina Warner, *Alone of All her Sex: The Myth and Cult of the Virgin Mary* (London: Quartet Books, 1978); Barbara Corrado Pope, "Immaculate and Powerful: The Marian Revival in the Nineteenth Century", Clarissa W. Atkinson et al. (eds.), *Immaculate and Powerful: The Female in Sacred Image and Social Reality* (Boston: Beacon Press, 1985), pp. 173–200; Jaroslav Pelikan, *Mary Through the Centuries: Her Place in the History of Culture* (New Haven: Yale University Press, 1996).

[13] Others who deal with this question are Walker Bynum, *Fragmentation and Redemption*, esp. Chapter VI "The Female Body and Religious Practices in the Later Middle Ages", pp. 181–238; Amy Hollywood, *The Soul as Virgin Wife: Mechthild of Magdeburg, Marguerite Porete, and Meister Eckhart* (Notre Dame/London: University of Notre Dame Press, 1995), esp. Chapter 7, "The Transformation of Suffering in Mechthild of Magdeburg, Marguerite Porete, and Meister Eckhart", pp. 173–206.

are nearly always related to the use of their own body to save, heal or change either their own or someone else's body. This pattern is present in the stories about Thecla, Radegund, and the Sicilian rabbi's wife. It also appears in Marianne Elsakkers's research into the *peperit* charm. Anke Passenier argues that Christina Mirabilis' hagiographer created an unmistakable ideological construct of woman's body as a 'site of wonder', a place where all physical limitations and suffering can be overcome. However, the female body as a 'site of wonder' is equally central to the miracles in Rhoda Lerman's *The Book of the Night*, which, as Inez van der Spek shows, is a postmodern rereading of classical Western miracle stories from a woman's perspective. Of course, the key position of the female body in miracles is related to Western religion and philosophy's persistent association of women with their bodily functions and non-rational powers. It is also connected with the image of woman as a literal, physical mediator. However, this book also asks a more interesting question: given these associations with women's bodies, what do miracles mean to women?

Anne van Voorthuizen's study of the South Indian smallpox goddess Māriyamman̲ shows how women's physical involvement in miracles is crucial to the process of identifying and fighting personal and shared suffering. Their involvement also helps them overcome the negative connotations of corporeality. Comparing written and oral miracle legends about this Indian goddess, Van Voorthuizen concludes that the versions of the story passed down orally by women leave more room for an acknowledgement of women's subordinate position and the suffering this position entails. The notion that suffering increases *śakti*, and that this in turn causes deification, plays a crucial role in Hindu mythology. This explains why so many of the minor, ambivalent deities are feminine and are thought to have ambiguous power. The ambivalence of Māriyamman̲'s *śakti* stems from her lethal and curative powers, which are inextricably linked. This sets her—and other minor gods in the Hindu pantheon—apart from the higher gods, who are ascribed a purely benevolent power. It also distinguishes them from the Christian tradition, in which miracles are beneficial by definition. Van Voorthuizen shows that this ambivalence is not 'inherently feminine', but a reflection of women's socio-cultural position in Indian society; they are expected to keep their caste 'pure' by means of their own bodies—and if they fail to do so, the punishment is severe. Māriyamman̲'s *śakti* combines fury and revenge with great compassion and a solidarity which transcends caste.

What we see here is that miracles can help establish—or undermine—women's religious autonomy and authority; they can help women achieve autonomy or prevent them from doing so and they can be used to stereotype or discipline them. Yet, miracles can also function in a very different way. To some women, they are an empowering force that allows them to physically or spiritually heal themselves or others—a key notion in the significance of miracles as studied in this book. To these women, the meaning of miracles lies in empathy and compassion with others' suffering, in 'feeling for' another with one's own body, expressed in terms of personally experienced physical suffering.

Reframing Suffering

Anke Passenier's study of the *Vita* of Christina Mirabilis brings to light a remarkable difference between the corporeal spirituality or asceticism attributed to medieval women saints and the manner in which the women themselves experienced suffering. The *Vita* of Christina Mirabilis is regarded by many as an example of the extreme bodiliness of medieval women's sanctity and religiosity. From other *Vitae* too, it appears that women were considered particularly apt to embody the divine, to incarnate the Word and to represent the message. Christina is portrayed as living purgatory on earth, vicariously suffering the torments of the souls imprisoned there. Other aspects of her ministry, such as her preaching and teaching, are overshadowed by the miraculous purgatorial sufferings that set the scene for the *Vita*.

According to Passenier, in the general rise of purgatorial piety which began in the late twelfth century we see religious women take on the role of visionary medium between the living and the dead and of intercessor, offering prayers and suffering to ease the pain of agonizing souls in purgatory. To some extent, the particular emphasis hagiographers placed on physical pain in women's apostolate to the dead may well have derived from the wish to establish specific models of female religious ministry. This seems to be confirmed by a certain discrepancy between the representations of female apostolate to the dead in hagiographic texts and in the writings of the women saints themselves. Although some of these women's writings concur with hagiographic representation, most of them show women's concern with the indigent dead to be based not so much on physical suffering as on psychological torment, the pain of love and compassion. In the writings of female mystics tormented souls are generally not released from purgatory by physical suffering through self-mortification and illness. It is rather the mystic's love and the pain that love causes her which make God's mercy prevail.

Wouter Hanegraaff's article brings to the fore a similar disparity between the suffering ascribed to 'holy women' and the way in which they experienced suffering. Hanegraaff studied the story of Friederike Hauffe, the 'Seeress of Prevorst' (1801–1829), as recorded by medical doctor Julius Kerner. Kerner originally intended to heal Hauffe, who was seriously ill, and to wake her from her somnambulistic state. Their frequent consultations led him to recognize her unique spiritual gifts and convinced him that she needed no earthly or medical cure because she already belonged to a world of spirits, a state beyond suffering and death. Once he was convinced that Hauffe could no longer be cured, Kerner must have felt absolved and free to learn as much as possible from her about the spirit world. He justified his examination of the occult via Hauffe as a more or less cultivated 'case', using an argument borrowed from Romantic natural philosophy—that women are naturally closer to the world of spirits than men because of their bodily suffering: "*Weib zu sein ist eigentlich Krankheit*". Hauffe herself seems to have had a much more pastoral, theological motive for mingling with spirits. She was neither afraid of ghosts nor fascinated by them. She merely attempted to help them find a way back to their Saviour. In addition, her association with the world of spirits offered her the opportunity to live a 'life of the spirit', a significant opportunity since women in a Lutheran country could not lead a socially recognized spiritual life. A third reason why Hauffe lived among spirits was that this gave her a spiritual recourse she badly needed, considering her personal experiences of deprivation and abuse.

In her extensive study of the nineteenth- and twentieth-century Western apparitions of the Virgin Mary[14], Sandra Zimdars-Swartz concluded that these apparitions enabled the seers—mostly women

---

[14] Zimdars-Swartz, *Encountering Mary*, passim.

and children—to make a transition from senseless to significant suffering, trading in a strictly personal history of pain and helplessness for public recognition of the relevance of their suffering in bringing God's sacred and just order nearer to fruition. The Friederike Hauffe case seems to fit this picture; she too had an impressive history of personal suffering and shared her desire 'to make sense of suffering' with doctor Kerner. Branding hysteria and other deviant female behaviour a disease—a practice which became very popular from the mid-nineteenth century onwards—effectively robbed women of the opportunity to express pain and suffering in religious terms and the chance of overcoming them.[15] As pain and suffering came to be regarded as strictly individual bio-medical processes which had nothing to do with transgressions of God's sacred order, women were severed from the religious framework in which individual human suffering can be experienced as a shared burden.

Friederike Hauffe's case is illustrative of the emergence of this dichotomy between the religious or supernatural, and bio-medical approaches to physical suffering. The doctor and Romantic philosopher Julius Kerner was torn between a medical therapy and a Romantic approach to Hauffe's suffering. He felt it necessary to make a *choice* between the two. He opted for the latter, which offered both doctor and patient more ways of finding a religious or 'supernatural' explanation for human pain, and elevated Hauffe to the status of 'Seeress of Prevorst'. However, the lack of medical treatment rapidly proved fatal.

Order out of Chaos: The Co-ordinates of Miracles

Many of the studies in this book show that when we focus on women's subjectivity and agency in miracle stories, we end up asking *where* and *when* miracles happened, rather than how and why. First of all, the questions *where* and *when* arise because in Judeo-Christian tradition, miracles performed by women violate normal expectations of the phenomenon of 'miracle'. The *where* of miracles becomes apparent most directly in the way the Judeo-Christian tradition depicts

---

[15] Doris Brelie-Lewien, "'Die Erlösung des Mensengeschlechts': Prophetinnen, Bessesene, Hysterikerinnen (1690–1890)", Karsten Rudolph and Christl Wickert (Hrsg.), *Geschichte als Möglichkeit: Über die Chancen der Demokratie. Festschrift für Helga Grebing* (Essen: Klartext Verlag, 1995), pp. 478–506.

women as vehicles of divine or supernatural power. Women's bodies seem to have a key role both in performing and undergoing miracles. In this sense, women's bodies are an arena, as we have already seen.

If we focus on the social site of women's miracle-working, we find that none of the studies in this book support the idea that women operate only on the periphery of established religious institutions. Even when the actual miracles performed by women only occur at home or in private, as is the case with the Sicilian rabbi's wife and Friederike Hauffe, the miracle acquires significance from its public accessibility and the telling of its story. Similarly, this book does not confirm the notion that miracle-performing women can only be found in the context of folk religion. To begin with, the women who actively perform miracles and become the subject of miracle stories are usually from, or associated with, the social or church elite. Secondly, the followers of these women are not solely or even primarily from lower class or illiterate backgrounds—in spite of the explicit links Western theology and philosophy have drawn between women, miracles, illiteracy and ignorance.[16]

Using the example of Saint Augustine of Hippo, historian Peter Brown shows that an interest in miracles may have its *own* religious motives and may be part of an intellectual point of view. What is more, miracles themselves may in turn provide or invoke knowledge and insight.[17] In his study into the origin of the early Christian cult of the saints, Brown opposes the view that miracles are merely a manifestation of 'popular religion'. He points out that the very learned Augustine gave up his sceptical, rational views on miracles and became deeply fascinated by them. According to Brown, this was not a belated concession to the mindless weight of 'popular belief', but an intellectual breakthrough of the first order. Augustine originally adhered to a strict neo-Platonic immaterialism which held that matters of this world had no intrinsic value. His later thinking was that spirit and flesh were ultimately tied in the deepest way, just as is professed in the Christian testimony of God's incarnation and of Christ's resurrection. "Miracles that had once struck Augustine, the contemplative, as of little significance, as so many lights dimmed by the sun of God's harmonious order, now take on a warmth and a

---

[16] See my *Introduction* to this book.
[17] See also Caroline Walker Bynum, "Wonder", *American Historical Review* 102 (1997), p. 24.

glow of their own, as Augustine pays more heed to the instinctive fears and yearnings of the once-neglected body. (...) The recorded miracles of healing at the shrines show God's power and his abiding concern for the flesh."[18]

An important factor in women's involvement in miracles is the experience or conviction that God's miraculous power is directly related to God's 'abiding concern for the flesh'. This is a religious theme deeply rooted in Judaism and Christianity. This book shows how women typically have this theme attributed to or even foisted upon them, but also how women have appropriated this motif in different ways for their own purposes and visions.

The questions where and when miracles occur take an even more prominent place in Ilse Bulhof's article and Inez van der Spek's contribution, dealing with twentieth century women authors Ingeborg Bachman (Austria) and Rhoda Lerman (North America) respectively. In late modern Western society with its emphasis on technology and science there is no longer a place for God's miraculous power. God's abiding concern for the flesh seems to have no bearing on the horrors of wholesale war and genocide. Yet even in this context, women's bodies—which are still seen as the 'other' in need of suppression and control—can sometimes be turned into a 'site of miracles' and a 'body of grace'. Miracles here are not brought about by an outside intervention, but by recognizing and sanctioning the chaos belying modern Western 'control' of the preconditions of existence, which colonizes women's bodies. Miracles are those moments when people personally experience the creation of 'order out of chaos' and 'grace as the gift of transformation of religious and cultural order' (Inez van der Spek).

In the miracle stories treated in this book, women's bodies play a key role in performing and experiencing miracles. This seemingly simple fact actually reflects a wide range of religious interests and insights, some of them mutually exclusive. What such miracles mean to women appears to be equally multi-faceted. Their significance definitely goes beyond a simple refutation or confirmation of the Judeo-Christian view of women and their bodies as instruments or

---

[18] Peter Brown, *The Cult of the Saints: Its Rise and Function in Latin Christianity* (Chicago: The University of Chicago Press, 1981), pp. 77–78; Peter Brown, "Learning and Imagination", Peter Brown, *Society and the Holy in Late Antiquity* (London: Faber and Faber, 1982), pp. 17–18.

vehicles of divine or supernatural power. Miracles involving women's bodies make personal suffering publicly meaningful, they engender a deep compassion for those who suffer, they claim 'a different justice' and may offer 'a different grace'.[19]

Translation: Mischa F. Hoyinck

---

[19] See also Michael E. Goodich, *Violence and Miracle in the Fourteenth Century: Private Grief and Public Salvation* (Chicago: University of Chicago Press, 1995), esp. Chapter 8 "Conclusion", pp. 147–155.

INDEX OF AUTHORS

Abel, E.A.   11
Abel, E.K.   11
Achberger, K.   272
Achtemeier, P.J.   29, 41, 45, 48
Ackermann, O.   220
Adler, M.   125
Adorno, T.   278
Aescoly, A.   123, 126, 129
Altekar, A.   257
Anderson, M.   89–90, 92, 94–100, 103–113, 115–116, 118–119, 286
Angenendt, A.   60, 75
Arator Subdiaconus   86
Ardener, E.   14, 255, 267
Ardener, S.   14, 255
Aristotle   9
Armitt, L.   300
Ashley, K.   2, 327
Atkinson, C.   179, 206, 333
Auden, W.   202
Auerbach, E.   56
Augustine, Aurelius   8, 60
Aune, D.   29, 37

Baal, J. van   88
Babb, L.   270
Bachmann, I.   271–279, 282–283, 285–290, 295–298
Backus, I.   13
Bal, M.   14
Barnett, S.   255
Bartels, E.   11
Bartels, M.   197
Baudonivia   67, 74, 84–86
Bauer, D.   172
Bauer, E.   223
Bax, M.   2, 11, 239
Bean, S.   254
Beauvoir, S. de   3
Becher, U.   12
Beck, B.   249, 260
Becking, B.   139
Bell, D.R.   83
Bell, R.   146
Ben Sasson, M.   138
Bennet, L.   255, 257
Berger, D.   126

Betz, H.D.   29
Biardeau, M.   249, 264
Bieler, L.   73
Birlinger, A.   188
Bitel, L.   93, 97–98
Black, W.   197
Blackbourn, D.   11
Blackburn, S.   258, 259
Blumenberg, H.   273
Blumenkranz, B.   141
Bock, F.   246
Bodamer, J.   212
Boehm, Ph.   286
Bolton, B.   145, 151, 157
Borsje, J.   13, 17–18, 27, 87–89, 103, 106, 114, 117
Bovon, F.   29
Bowman, S.   131
Braekman, W.   181, 191–192, 194
Bray, D.   101
Brelie-Lewien, D.   337
Bremmer, J.   32, 35, 39, 40
Brennan, B.   53–54
Brenon, A.   176
Breymayerm, R.   225–226
Brokoph-Mauch, G.   272
Brown, C.   5, 277
Brown, P.   2–3, 16, 82, 329, 339
Brubaker, R.   266
Brugsch, H.   211
Brüning, G.   89
Bugge, J.   58
Buitenen, J. van   264
Bulhof, I.   271, 278, 283
Burgdorf, E.   221
Burkert, W.   35
Burrus, V.   33
Bush, G.   211
Büttiker, H.   232
Bynum, C.   145, 160, 163, 166, 173, 176

Cangh, J.-M. van   30
Cantimpré, Thomas of   145–146, 149, 156, 168, 177
Carové, F.   244
Cartusianus, Dionysius   152
Cate, L. ten   278

Champakalakshmi, R. 264
Charles-Edwards, T. 97
Christian Jr, W. 2, 10, 11
Cicero 211
Cohen, J. 128
Cohn, N. 123, 126–127
Corrado Pope, B. 333
Crecelius, W. 188, 191
Crowe, C. 211

Dähn, K.-H. 221, 226
Daly, M. 296
Daniel, S. 260, 262
Daston, L. 2
David, K. 249, 257, 264
Davidson, H. 201
Davies, S. 32–33
Davis, R. 2, 329
Dawkins, R. 5
Dean Shulman, D. 264
Deboutte, A. 145
Degler-Spengler, B. 151
Derkse, W. 286
Derouet, J.-L. 13
Devisch, R. 77–78
Dhruvarajan, V. 255, 261
Dijk-Hemmes, F. 14
Dijkstra, M. 139
Dimmit, C. 264
Dinzelbacher, P. 10, 80, 154, 172
Dodds, E. 37
Doniger, W. 256
Douglas, M. 29
Dowson, J. 264
Dresen, G. 307
Dresen-Coenders, L. 330
Drewermann, E. 13
Dube, L. 255–256
Duchesne, L. 58
Dunn, P. 33

Egnor, M. 250–251, 262, 267–268
Eichinger Ferro-Luzzi, G. 256
Eilberg-Schwartz, H. 328
Eliade, M. 248
Ellenberger, H. 211
Elliott, J. 32
Elmore, W. 249, 260
Epstein, J. 123, 126
Eschenmayer, H. 215, 242

Fabry, J. 242, 246
Fahraeus, R. 63

Faraone, Ch. 29, 37–38, 48
Feiss, H. 146
Fell, C. 179
Festugière, A.-J. 52
Finucane, R. 2, 179–180, 188, 196, 200, 202
Folz, R. 54
Forbes, T. 181, 185, 188
Ford, C. 4
Fortunatus, Venantius 53, 55–56, 58–59
Frankfurter, D. 184–185, 195
Franklin, B. 274
Franz, A. 182, 184–188, 191–193, 195–196, 199–200, 208
Fremer, T. 2, 329
Frevert, U. 12

Gäbe, S. 54
Gail, A. 263–264
Gallée, J. 191
Gamer, H. 180
Gauld, A. 211
George, J. 53
Gering, H. 201
Giannarelli, E. 10, 54, 326, 332
Godwin, J. 211
Goetz, H.-W. 10, 54–55, 332
Goff, J. Le 154, 162, 165
Goitein, S. 125, 133, 137
Goldin, J. 29, 41
Goldman, R. 264
Goodich, M. 2, 153, 340
Goodman, F. 77
Götz von Olenhusen, I. 2, 10, 11
Graef, H. 333
Graf, F. 29, 35
Grattan, J. 192
Green, M. 181, 200
Gregory of Tours *see* Turonensis, Gregorius
Grendon, F. 192
Grimm, J. 196, 201
Grosz, E. 312–314
Grundmann, H. 151

Habermas, R. 10
Hadewijch 167–169
Hagen, W. 239, 242
Hanchett, S. 249, 259–260, 270
Hanegraaff, W. 211, 217
Harman, W. 259
Harris, R. 2
Hart III, G. 258, 261

INDEX OF AUTHORS

Haver, J. van 197
Heesterman, J. 264
Heim, R. 181, 188, 193
Herbert, M. 89, 112
Hermsen, J. 289
Hieronymus 76
Hilhorst, A. 32
Hiltebeitel, A. 249
Hollander, L. 201
Hollywood, A. 145, 156, 163, 165–166, 168, 333
Holthausen, F. 192
Houston, J. 5
Huber, T. 232
Huch, R. 238
Hughes, K. 96
Huizinga, J. 4
Hume, David 8
Hunt, T. 185, 187, 190, 192, 194

Idel, M. 126, 127
Irigaray, L. 319–322

Jacobson, D. 255
Janaki, K. 264
Jennings, L. 223–225, 227, 230, 233–234, 236, 241–244
Jensen, A. 30, 40
Jespers, F. 286
Johnson, S. 12
Jolly, K. 195–196
Jong, A. de 29
Jung-Stilling, J. 222, 229, 235–236, 242–243

Kaestli, J.-D. 33
Kakar, S. 254
Kane, P.V. 254–256, 261
Karlsen, C. 330
Kehl, A. 75
Keller, C. 309
Kenney, J. 89
Kerner, J. 211–220, 222–228, 230–247
Kieckhefer, R. 192
King, J. 211
King, M. 145–147, 150, 152, 170, 172
Kinsley, D. 249, 260, 263
Kippenberg, H. 29, 35
Klemming, G. 195, 208
Koch, G. 330
Korte, A.-M. 1–2, 5, 307
Kraemer, R. 33

Krauss, S. 123, 126
Kruse, B.-J. 181, 184, 197

Ladner, G. 60
Lalleman, P. 39
Lampe, G. 30
Lamphere, L. 142
Lang, R. 221, 226–227, 229
Laurentin, R. 5
Leacock, E. 255
Leclercq, J. 54
Lefanu, S. 300, 303
Lerman, R. 299–303, 305, 307, 309, 313–317, 320–322, 326, 334, 339
Lerner, R. 156
Levack, B. 330
Leyser, H. 179
Lindgren, A. 191

MacDonald, D. 33, 40
MacDonald, M. 328
Magdeburg, Mechthild of 45, 165, 167
Maimonides, Moses 125, 137, 140
Mann, J. 123, 125–126, 129–130, 138
Manndorff, H. 249
Manson-Bahr, P. 83
Marx, T. 140
McCone, K. 88, 94
McDonnell, E. 151
McHale, B. 301–302
McLaughlin, E. 329–330
McLeod, H. 12
McNamara, J. 166
McNeill, J. 180
Mediolanensis, A. 57
Meinhof, U. 12
Meyer, E. 252, 257, 260, 262, 266–269
Michaud, F. 11
Mies, M. 266
Miller, M. 239
Miller, P. 40, 57
Mills, S. 12
Misset-van de Weg, M. 29, 33, 47
Moffatt, M. 249, 254
Mohr, W. 242
Morrison, T. 299
Mullin, R. 2
Murnaghan, S. 49

Nauerth, C. 33
Neckel, G. 201

Neuman, E. 270
Newman, B. 150, 164–165, 167, 169
Ní Dhonnchadha, M. 90–91, 94, 110
Nickell, J. 5
Nie, G. de 13, 53, 58, 60, 63, 71, 83, 85
Nietzsche, F. 273, 277, 291
Norrbom, S. 202, 208

Obbink, D. 29, 37–38, 48
Ogden, M. 185, 191–193
Ohrt, F. 184, 192
Oken, L. 238
Olbrechts, F. 180, 198
O'Loughlin, T. 98
Oosterling, H. 272
Opie, I. 196
Ortner, S. 142
Owen, A. 11, 329

Paassen, D. van 330
Pandian, J. 259
Papa, C. 54
Pardes, I. 14
Park, K. 2
Passenier, A. 145, 155, 160
Patch, H. 154
Pater, W. de 13
Paxton, F. 180
Pears, D. 274
Pelikan, J. 333
Pelletier, A. 10
Peters, U. 211
Philips III, C. 29, 37–38, 48
Picard, J.-M. 89, 92, 94–95
Pihlajamaa, H. 95
Plaisier, A. 277
Plinius Secundus, Gaius 196, 200
Ploss, H. 197
Poorthuis, M. 307
Porush, O. 314
Poupon, G. 29, 35, 37
Preston, J. 259
Prigogine, I. 314–316, 321
Proust, M. 79

Ramanujan, A. 266
Reeves, W. 118
Reitzenstein, R. 30, 45
Reynolds, B. 262
Richter, H. 286
Rocher, L. 263
Roisin, S. 146, 151
Romilly, J. de 35

Rordorf, W. 32
Rosaldo, M. Zimbalist 142
Rosenblatt, S. 137
Roth, C. 128
Rouche, A. 83
Rousselle, A. 10, 54, 61, 65, 74, 82
Rudolph, K. 337
Ruether, R. Radford 329–330
Rüsen, J. 12

Schäfer, P. 29, 35
Scheibelreiter, G. 70
Schlechta, K. 291
Schmidgall, Chr. 221–222, 225, 244
Schokker, G. 264
Scholem, G. 127
Schoon, A. 179
Schubert, C. 216, 235, 239, 242
Schüssler Fiorenza, E. 14, 29, 30
Schutter, W. 47
Schwartz, R. 14, 307
Segal, A. 29
Sharpe, R. 89–90, 92–93, 95–96, 98, 103, 109–110, 112, 114, 120
Sheingorn, P. 2
Shimbo, S. 236
Showalter, E. 269
Siefert, H. 226
Siegel, B. 79
Sijmons, R. 5
Simons, W. 160
Simonsohn, S. 138
Singer, C. 192
Slater, C. 13
Smith, B. 256
Sopp, E. 222
Spiesberger, K. 222
Spoerri, T. 304
Srinivas, M. 259
Steinberg, N. 48
Stengers, I. 314–315, 321
Stern, S. 128
Steunebrink, G. 278, 279
Stillman, Y. 138
Storms, G. 188, 194, 208
Straumann, H. 235, 238–240, 245
Strauss, D. 242, 246
Subramoniam, V. 264
Sulpicius Severus 67, 81
Sweetman, R. 145–146, 150, 158–161, 163, 171

Tapper, E. 255
Tatem, M. 196

Taylor, P.   202
Telle, J.   204
Tévoz, M.   304
Thomas, Y.   48
Thorndike, L.   60
Thurston, E.   249
Tilley, M.   40
Trautmann, T.   258
Tupet, A.-M.   37
Turonensis, Gregorius   53, 54
Tuttle, L.   302, 318

Uhland, R.   220, 236–237, 239

Valantasis, R.   40
Vandenbroeck, P.   161
Varnhagen von Ense, K.   235
Vatuk, S.   255
Verhoeven, G.   10
Versnel, H.S.   29, 48
Vervaet, E.   5
Vitry, Jacob of   145–146, 152, 154, 156, 161, 163, 172
Vogelaar, J.   304–305
Voorthuizen, A. van   248, 252, 259
Vouaux, L.   47
Vranckx, J.   2

Wacker, M.-T.   139
Wadley, S.   255–257, 260–262
Walker Bynum, C.   1, 2, 8, 9, 10, 12, 316
Ward, B.   8–10, 332
Warner, M.   333
Warns, R.   33
Weinmann, U.   151
Weinreich, O.   73
Weinstein, D.   146
Weissler, C.   328
Wemple, S.   84
Weston, L.   200, 204
Whitehead, H.   249, 260
Wickert, C.   337
Williams, T.   5
Wilson, C.   211
Wood, S.   299

Yalman, N.   255–257
Younger, P.   249–250, 263

Zeldes, N.   123, 125–126, 128–129, 143
Zeller, E.   223–225, 243–246
Ziegler, J.   160
Zimdars-Swartz, S.   11, 329, 336

INDEX OF SUBJECTS

Absolute, the 271–298
Abulafia, Abraham 126–128, 142
Adomnán 87–122
Adorno, Theodor 277–278
angel(s) 80, 89, 100, 115–117, 168, 172, 229, 323
animal(s) 44, 44n, 46, 49, 60, 73, 80–83, 85, 106, 120, 292, 300n, 308–314
apocryphal texts 29–52
Ardener, Shirley 14, 267
Aristotle 9
Augustine, St 8, 60, 336–337
asceticism 33–34, 36, 40, 40n, 42, 50–51, 90, 137, 161n, 163n, 164, 164n, 165n, 176, 262
authority *see* women, authority of
autonomy *see* women, autonomy of

Bachmann, Ingeborg 271–298
baptism 32, 43, 45–46, 57–58, 75, 79, 148, 154, 175
  auto- 46
  magical protective power of **43**, 45
  right of women 32
Baudonivia 54, 74, 85
birth
  birth (pangs), metaphor of 76–77, 79, **136–137**
  childbirth 106, 136–137, 139, **179–206**
  self-birth 323
body, female 46, 70–79, 136–137, 145–178, 179–210, 237, 268, 307–308, **331–335**
Brown, Peter 16, 336

celibacy 39, 93n, 96, 98, 109–110, 137, 137n, 326
chaos **315–316**, 321
charms 179–206
childbirth *see* birth
curing *see* healing
Christ 56, **60–61**, 82, 277, 330
  Christi, women's (bodily) *imitatio* 40, 160, 166

Christina Mirabilis 145–178
Columba, St 87–122

deification **259**, 263, 270
demon(s) (devil(s), forces of evil) 88, 93, 95, 115, 117, 119, 120–122, 273
desert 170–172, 279, **290–298**
double-voiced **14–15**, 136, **269–270**
doulē tou theou
  position of authority 51
  status of 44, **47**
Dominicans 127
dream consciousness 57–58, **78–79**, 84–85
dream-vision 44–45
druids(s) (magicians(s), sorcerer(s)) 88, 95, **100–101**, 122
dualism 272

Early Christianity 29–122
ecstasy 161, 173, 177, 288–289, 296
  ecstatic rapture 148–149, 158, 172
Edda, the Old Norse 200–202, 207
Eithne, daughter of Mac Naue (Columba's mother) 105n, 106, 115–116, 121
elemental, the 272, 279, 285n, 289–298, 296n
Eucharist(ical) 56, 56n, 63, 65, 173–174
Eve 105–106, 120–121
  the New 80–86, 327

fatherhood
  father and child relationship 70–71
  father and daughter relationship 300, 303–305
'figural' view of reality 56–57, **60–61**, 69
folk Hinduism **250**, 266, 269
Fortunatus, Venantius 53–86
Franciscans 127

gender *passim*, **1–6, 10–15**
Geniza 123, 125, 138, 143

Germanus, St 55, 62–72, 85
ghosts *see* spirit visions
Gnosticism 272–273
God, the Good **273**
Goddess 309
    see also Indian goddesses
grace 317, **318**, 324
Gregory of Tours 54–55, 58, 60, 69, 75, 81, 83, 85
Grosz, Elizabeth 312–313

hagiography 53–122, 145–178, 211–247
Hauffe, Friederike 211–247
healing
    female healers 71–86, 206
    folk healing 220
    healing charms 191–192
    healing love 286–289
    healing rituals 200
    late antique views of healing 59–61
    magnetic healing 213–214, 217, 220, 230, 233
    miraculous healing 2–3, 7, 10, 55–86, 101–102, 105–106, 170, 174n, 180, 180n, 194n, 196, 334–335, 339
    self-healing 217
Hildegard of Bingen 206
Hinduism 248–270
holiness 4, **307**, 309
Holocaust, the 273, 277–278
Huizinga, Johan 4
Hume, David 3, 8

illness 60, 63n, 75, 77, 81, 85, 166–167, 196, 217, 235–241
Indian goddesses 248–270
Irigaray, Luce 319, 320, 322

Jacob of Vitry 145–146, 152, 154, 156, 161, 163, 172
Jesus 30, 30n, 39n, 39–41, 80, 106, 109, 116, 171, 173–174, 186, 300n
Judaism 87–122
Jung-Stilling, J.H. 222, 229, 235–236, 236n, 242, 243n

Kanagi 259
Kant, Immanuel 276, 278n
Kerner, Justinus 211–247

Lacan, Jacques 283
language 11–12, 79, 81–82, 87, 136n, 138, 197–199, 217, 246, 271, 273, 276–278, **282–288**, 288n, 298, **299–306**, 314, 323
Late Antiquity 29–86
Lerman, Rhoda 299–324
Lutgard of Aywières 145, 146, 159, 165
Lyotard, Jean-François 283, 283n

magic 3, 12, 29–31, 35–37, 50–51, 88, 94–95, 122, 179–206, 217, 220, 230n, 239, 246, 299–300, 316, 330–331
magician *see magos*
magos 29, **35–39**
Maimonides, Moses 125, 137, 140
mammary wonders 148, 170, 173
Mann, Jacob 123, 123n, 126n, 129n, 130n
Margaret of Ypres 145–146, 156
Māriyamma<u>n</u> 248–270
Martha (sister of Mary) 59, 73, 151, 325
Martin, St 54–55, 66–67, 73–74
Mary of Oignies 145–146, 152, 156, 159, 161, 168–169, 172
Mary (mother of Jesus) 2, 86, 106, 116, 121, 173–174, 183, 185–186, 198, 200, 310, 326–328, 332–333, 336
Mary (sister of Martha) 59, 151, 325
materia (matter) 296
medicine 61n, 65, 68, 180, 206
Mesmerism 211, 224
Messianism 123–144
metamorphosis 39–40, 309–314
Middle Ages 123–210
midwives 74, 77, 180–206
Mies, Maria 266
Minaksi 259
miracle
    authority of 29–32, 51, 144, 146, 150, 159, 161, 177, 325, 328–330, 332
    authorization of 330
    definition of 6–10, 59–61, 87–88, 99–89, 124, 141, 180, 216, 218, 248, 248n, 260, 270, 271–273, 301–302

function of 29–31, 41–42, 50–52
(as) gender related 1–28, 49–50, 57–59, 260, 262
hermeneutical approach of 5–6, 13
invocation of 200
(and) medical science 61–62, 65–66, 68, 72, 79, 82, 180, 206, 234–244, 336–337
(and) (post)modernity 276–279, 299–302, 339
multidisciplinary study of 5–10
narrativity of 13–15, 29–30, 124
(by) physical contact 62–70, 71–84, 200
proof of 141–142
(as) related to magic 29–32, 50, 88, 180
rhetoric of 30–31, 141–142
site of 301–302, 331–335, 337–340
(as) source of empowerment 11, 51–52, 134–135, 143–144, 177–178, 329, 335
(as) symbolic enactment 75–80
(and) women's corporeality 28, 29–52, 71–84, 145–178, 331–340
mysterium **55–60**, 67–70, 84–85
mystic(al) 56, 146n, 147n, 151, 159–160, 163n, 167–169, 172–173, 222, 274, 274n, 275, 281, 294, 296, 298, 306, 323
myth vs reality 218–219, 231–232, 246–247
Modernity 271–272, 277–278, 289, 296
Mogain, daughter of Daiméne 104–105, 121
Monegund, St 54–55, 71
Moses 70, 130, 134, 137n, 295, 300n
motherhood 327, 330
   ideal of spiritual **71–80**, 85–86
   mother and child relationship 71–72
   mother and daughter relationship 35, 38, 38n, 39, 44–45
Musil, Robert 298

Naturphilosophie 216, 235–241
Neumann, Erich 270
Ní Dhonnchadha, M. 90–91
nun(s) (virgin(s), ecclesiastical woman) 29–52, 71–86, 90–91, 104–105, 107–110, 121, 145–178

orality, oral traditions 6, **77–78**, 85, 89, 181–205, **249**, 252, 263–269, 266n

Pascal, Blaise 173, 275, 296
patriarchal ideal **70–71**, 85
Paul, St 29–52
Pelagius 317
peperit charm/prayer 179–206
Petroff, Elizabeth Alvilda 3, 4
Pietism 220–222, 241–244
pilgrimage (*peregrinatio*) 96–97, 101, 107–110, 112, 121
Plato 296, 320, 336
Pliny 196
postmodern(ity) 272n, 283, 289, **299–302**
power vs authority 48n, 49, 328
prayer 37n, 41, **45**, 63–64, 66–68, 73, 77, 80, 82, 129–130, **138–140**, 150–151, **179–210**, 214, 228, 261
pregnancy 75, 123–144, 179–206, 238n, 251
priestess 139, 249, 267–270
priestly blessing **139**
Prigogine, Ilya 314–316, 321
private vs public 15, 135, 337–338
prophesy 85, 93–98, 100–101, 105–106, 111–115, 118, 123, 133–135, 140–143, 149, 164
prophet(ess) 63, 100, 106, 115, 135, 137, 141–143, 295, 331
prostitute(s) 92–94, 122
purgatory 147–154, 150n, 160–170, 165n, 170n, 177–178
purity 224, 255, 256, 258, 307

Radegund, St 53–55, 71–86
rationality 1, 3, 12, 28, 216, 239–240, 303, 325
religion, feminization of **4**
resurrection 34, 60, 64, 75, 79, 85, 147–149, 152, 153n, 154, 163, 170, 175, 265–266, 309, 338

miracles of resurrection 149, 163, 265–266
ritual 56–60, 67–69, 75–80, 82–83, 85, 180–182, 196–200, 202
role models, female biblical 59, 73, 151, 200, 325–328
Romanticism 12, 216, 238–239, 241, 246

sacramental signs 170–176
śakti 248–270
Sanskrit texts 262–267
Schubert, Gotthilf Heinrich von 216, 235, 239–240, 242
secularization 1
servant of God *see doulē tou theou*
serpent 80–85, 87, 120
sex(uality) 34, 92–94, 96–98, 107–110, 176, 224, 255–257, 300–301, 307–309, **312–314**, 316, 321–322, 324
shamanism 161
Showalter, Elaine 269
Sicily 123–129, 131, 138
slave(ry) 100–101, 112–114, 119–121
solidarity, female 51, 268, 268n
somatic phenomena 149
somnambulism 211–247
spirit visions 217–218, 222, 228–229
spiritual power **260**, 262
Strabo 2, 3
suffering 11, 28, 51, 132, 134, 137, 162–170, 238, 246, 259, 262, 268–270, 278, 284, 288, 290, 298, 304, 325, 331, 335–337
symbols, enactment of 56–59, **75–80**, 85

Talit 123, 127, 129, 138–139, 141
Tertullianus 37n
Thecla 29–52
Thomas of Cantimpré 145–146, 149, 156, 168, 177
Transcendence 271–272, 278, 299, 323
transfiguration 320, **321**, 323
transformation 56–59, 79, 172, 246, 258, 309–324
transgression 3
Trotula of Salerno 206
Tryphaena 34–35, 44–50
Tudela, Benjamin of 125

underworld **322**

veil(ing) 58, 58n, 60, **138–139**
Virgil 162, 193
virgin(ity) *see also* nun(s) 36, 42, 57, 58n, 72, 86, 90, 104–105, 110, 121, 183–184, 192, 194n, 256, 262

Walker Bynum, Caroline 1, 8–10, 173, 316
Ward, Benedicta 8–10
will 317, **318**
wit **49**, 52
Wittgenstein, Ludwig 274–277, 281
witch(craft) 4, 95, 202, 237, 328
  witch-persecutions 330
womb (*uterus*) 56, 75–76, 85, 183–184, 188, 188n, 202, 332
women
  as visionaries 44–45, 45n, 134–135, 137–141, 143, 159, 165, 165n, 167n, 214–215, 217, 222, 226, 243, 319–320, 335–337
  as intermediaries (*medium*) 3, 165, 234, 334, 332–333, 335
  as miracle workers/performers 1–32
    agency of 3, 32, 36, 44, 46–52, 71–86, 325, 333, 334–335, 337
    as God's vehicle 332–333, 338, 339–340
    authority of 51, 144, 150, 159, 161, 177, 325, 328–330, 332
    corporeality of 28, 29–52, 71–84, 145–178, 331–340
    exceptionality of 13, 326, 330
    historical increase (in Europe) of 10–11, 329
    marginalization of 145–178, 331
    stereotyping of 13, 28
  as religious role models 200, 326–328
  authority of 28, 32, 40, 48–49, 51, 123–124, 135–136, 144, 149–150, 158, 161, 173, 177, 325, 328–331

autonomy of 28, 33, 51, 325, 329
position/status of 31, 33, 47, 48, 49, 51
presumed as superstitious 2, 12
rights of 32, 51

women's culture 14, **269**, 270

Zeldes, N. 125n, 126n, 128n, 129n, 143

Zeller, Ernst Albert 223–225, 244–246

STUDIES IN THE HISTORY OF RELIGIONS
NUMEN BOOK SERIES

8 K.W. Bolle. *The Persistence of Religion*. An Essay on Tantrism and Sri Aurobindo's Philosophy. Repr. 1971. ISBN 90 04 03307 6

17 *Liber Amicorum*. Studies in honour of Professor Dr. C.J. Bleeker. Published on the occasion of his retirement from the Chair of the History of Religions and the Phenomenology of Religion at the University of Amsterdam. 1969. ISBN 90 04 03092 1

19 U. Bianchi, C.J. Bleeker & A. Bausani (eds.). *Problems and Methods of the History of Religions*. Proceedings of the Study Conference organized by the Italian Society for the History of Religions on the Occasion of the Tenth Anniversary of the Death of Raffaele Pettazzoni, Rome 6th to 8th December 1969. Papers and discussions. 1972. ISBN 90 04 02640 1

31 C.J. Bleeker, G. Widengren & E.J. Sharpe (eds.). *Proceedings of the 12th International Congress, Stockholm 1970*. 1975. ISBN 90 04 04318 7

34 V.L. Oliver, *Caodai Spiritism*. A Study of Religion in Vietnamese Society. With a preface by P. Rondot. 1976. ISBN 90 04 04547 3

41 B. Layton (ed.). *The Rediscovery of Gnosticism*. Proceedings of the International Conference on Gnosticism at Yale, New Haven, Conn., March 28-31, 1978. Two vols.
   1. *The School of Valentinus*. 1980. ISBN 90 04 06177 0   *Out of print*
   2. *Sethian Gnosticism*. 1981. ISBN 90 04 06178 9

43 M. Heerma van Voss, D.J. Hoens, G. Mussies, D. van der Plas & H. te Velde (eds.). *Studies in Egyptian Religion, dedicated to Professor Jan Zandee. 1982.* ISBN 90 04 06728 0

44 P.J. Awn. *Satan's Tragedy and Redemption*. Iblīs in Sufi Psychology. With a foreword by A. Schimmel. 1983. ISBN 90 04 06906 2

45 R. Kloppenborg (ed.). *Selected Studies on Ritual in the Indian Religions*. Essays to D.J. Hoens. 1983. ISBN 90 04 07129 6

50 S. Shaked, D. Shulman & G.G. Stroumsa (eds.). *Gilgul*. Essays on Transformation, Revolution and Permanence in the History of Religions, dedicated to R.J. Zwi Werblowsky. 1987. ISBN 90 04 08509 2

52 J.G. Griffiths. *The Divine Verdict*. A Study of Divine Judgement in the Ancient Religions. 1991. ISBN 90 04 09231 5

53 K. Rudolph. *Geschichte und Probleme der Religionswissenschaft*. 1992. ISBN 90 04 09503 9

54 A.N. Balslev & J.N. Mohanty (eds.). Religion and Time. 1993. ISBN 90 04 09583 7

55 E. Jacobson. *The Deer Goddess of Ancient Siberia*. A Study in the Ecology of Belief. 1993. ISBN 90 04 09628 0

56 B. Saler. *Conceptualizing Religion*. Immanent Anthropologists, Transcendent Natives, and Unbounded Categories. 1993. ISBN 90 04 09585 3

57 C. Knox. *Changing Christian Paradigms*. And their Implications for Modern Thought. 1993. ISBN 90 04 09670 1

58 J. Cohen. *The Origins and Evolution of the Moses Nativity Story*. 1993. ISBN 90 04 09652 3

59 S. Benko. *The Virgin Goddess*. Studies in the Pagan and Christian Roots of Mariology. 1993. ISBN 90 04 09747 3
60 Z.P. Thundy. *Buddha and Christ*. Nativity Stories and Indian Traditions. 1993. ISBN 90 04 09741 4
61 S. Hjelde. *Die Religionswissenschaft und das Christentum*. Eine historische Untersuchung über das Verhältnis von Religionswissenschaft und Theologie. 1994. ISBN 90 04 09922 0
62 Th.A. Idinopulos & E.A. Yonan (eds.). *Religion and Reductionism*. Essays on Eliade, Segal, and the Challenge of the Social Sciences for the Study of Religion. 1994. ISBN 90 04 09870 4
63 S. Khalil Samir & J.S. Nielsen (eds.). *Christian Arabic Apologetics during the Abbasid Period (750-1258)*. 1994. ISBN 90 04 09568 3
64 S.N. Balagangadhara. *'The Heathen in His Blindness...'* Asia, the West and the Dynamic of Religion. 1994. ISBN 90 04 09943 3
65 H.G. Kippenberg & G.G. Stroumsa (eds.). *Secrecy and Concealment*. Studies in the History of Mediterranean and Near Eastern Religions. 1995. ISBN 90 04 10235 3
66 R. Kloppenborg & W.J. Hanegraaff (eds.). *Female Stereotypes in Religious Traditions*. 1995. ISBN 90 04 10290 6
67 J. Platvoet & K. van der Toorn (eds.). *Pluralism and Identity*. Studies on Ritual Behaviour. 1995. ISBN 90 04 10373 2
68 G. Jonker. *The Topography of Remembrance*. The Dead, Tradition and Collective Memory in Mesopotamia. 1995. ISBN 90 04 10162 4
69 S. Biderman. *Scripture and Knowledge*. An Essay on Religious Epistemology. 1995. ISBN 90 04 10154 3
70 G.G. Stroumsa. *Hidden Wisdom*. Esoteric Traditions and the Roots of Christian Mysticism. 1996. ISBN 90 04 10504 2
71 J.G. Katz. *Dreams, Sufism and Sainthood*. The Visionary Career of Muhammad al-Zawâwî. 1996. ISBN 90 04 10599 9
72 W.J. Hanegraaff. *New Age Religion and Western Culture*. Esotericism in the Mirror of Secular Thought. 1996. ISBN 90 04 10695 2
73 T.A. Idinopulos & E.A. Yonan (eds.). *The Sacred and its Scholars*. Comparative Methodologies for the Study of Primary Religious Data. 1996. ISBN 90 04 10623 5
74 K. Evans. *Epic Narratives in the Hoysaḷa Temples*. The Rāmāyaṇa, Mahābhārata and Bhāgavata Purāṇa in Haḷebīd, Belūr and Amṛtapura. 1997. ISBN 90 04 10575 1
75 P. Schäfer & H.G. Kippenberg (eds.). *Envisioning Magic*. A Princeton Seminar and Symposium. 1997. ISBN 90 04 10777 0
77 P. Schäfer & M.R. Cohen (eds.). *Toward the Millennium*. Messianic Expectations from the Bible to Waco. 1998. ISBN 90 04 11037 2
78 A.I. Baumgarten, with J. Assmann & G.G. Stroumsa (eds.). *Self, Soul and Body in Religious Experience*. 1998. ISBN 90 04 10943 9
79 M. Houseman & C. Severi. *Naven or the Other Self*. A Relational Approach to Ritual Action. 1998. ISBN 90 04 11220 0
80 A.L. Molendijk & P. Pels (eds.). *Religion in the Making*. The Emergence of the Sciences of Religion. 1998. ISBN 90 04 11239 1

81 Th.A. Idinopulos & B.C. Wilson (eds.). *What is Religion?* Origins, Definitions, & Explanations. 1998. ISBN 90 04 11022 4
82 A. van der Kooij & K. van der Toorn (eds.). *Canonization & Decanonization.* Papers presented to the International Conference of the Leiden Institute for the Study of Religions (LISOR) held at Leiden 9-10 January 1997. 1999. ISBN 90 04 11246 4
83 J. Assmann & G.G. Stroumsa (eds.). *Transformations of the Inner Self in Ancient Religions.* 1999. ISBN 90 04 11356 8
84 J.G. Platvoet & A.L. Molendijk (eds.). *The Pragmatics of Defining Religion.* Contexts, Concepts & Contests. 1999. ISBN 90 04 11544 7
85 B.J. Malkovsky (ed.). *New Perspectives on Advaita Vedānta.* Essays in Commemoration of Professor Richard De Smet, sj. 2000.
ISBN 90 04 11666 4
86 A.I. Baumgarten (ed.). *Apocalyptic Time.* 2000. ISBN 90 04 11879 9
87 S. Hjelde (ed.). *Man, Meaning, and Mystery.* Hundred Years of History of Religions in Norway. The Heritage of W. Brede Kristensen. 2000. ISBN 90 04 11497 1
88 A. Korte (ed.). *Women and Miracle Stories.* A Multidisciplinary Exploration. ISBN 90 04 11681 8 (2000, hardcover), 90 04 13636 3 (2004, paperback)
89 J. Assmann & A.I. Baumgarten (eds.). *Representation in Religion.* Studies in Honor of Moshe Barasch. 2001. ISBN 90 04 11939 6
90 O. Hammer. *Claiming Knowledge.* Strategies of Epistemology from Theosophy to the New Age. ISBN 90 04 12016 5 (2001, hardcover),
90 04 13638 X (2004, paperback)
91 B.J. Malkovsky. *The Role of Divine Grace in the Soteriology of Śaṃkarācārya.* 2001. ISBN 90 04 12044 0
92 T.A. Idinopulos & B.C. Wilson (eds.). *Reappraising Durkheim for the Study and Teaching of Religion Today.* 2002. ISBN 90 04 12339 3.
93 A.I. Baumgarten (eds.). *Sacrifice in Religious Experience.* 2002.
ISBN 90 04 12483 7
94 L.P. van den Bosch. *F.M. Müller. A Life Devoted to the Humanities.* 2002.
ISBN 90 04 12505 1
95 G. Wiegers. *Modern Societies & the Science of Religions.* Studies in Honour of Lammert Leertouwer. 2002. ISBN 90 04 11665 6
96 D. Zeidan. *The Resurgence of Religion.* A Comparative Study of Selected Themes in Christian and Islamic Fundamentalist Discourses. 2003.
ISBN 90 04 12877 8
97 S. Meyer (ed.). *Egypt — Temple of the Whole World / Ägypten — Tempel der Gesamten Welt.* Studies in Honour of Jan Assmann. 2003.
ISBN 90 04 13240 6
98 I. Strenski. *Theology and the First Theory of Sacrifice.* 2003.
ISBN 90 04 13559 6
99 T. Light & B.C. Wilson (eds.). *Religion as a Human Capacity.* A Festschrift in Honor of E. Thomas Lawson. 2003. ISBN 90 04 12676 7
100 A.E. Buss. *The Russian-Orthodox Tradition and Modernity.* 2003.
ISBN 90 04 13324 0
101 K.A. Jacobsen & P.P. Kumar (eds.). *South Asians in the Diaspora.* Histories and Religious Traditions. 2004. ISBN 90 04 12488 8
102 M. Stausberg. *Zoroastrian Rituals in Context.* 2004. ISBN 90 04 13131 0

ISSN 0169-8834